NEGOTIABLE INSTRUMENTS AND OTHER PAYMENT SYSTEMS: PROBLEMS AND MATERIALS

by

WAYNE K. LEWIS
Professor
DePaul University College of Law

STEVEN H. RESNICOFF
Professor
DePaul University College of Law

LexisNexis™

Library of Congress Cataloging-in-Publication Data

Lewis, Wayne K.
    Negotiable instruments : problems and materials / by Wayne K. Lewis, Steven H. Resnicoff p. cm.
    Includes index.
    ISBN 1-58360-790-0 (alk. paper)
    1. Negotiable instruments—United States—Problems, exercises, etc. I. Resnicoff, Steven H.
        II. Title.
    KF957.Z9L49 2004
    346.73'096—dc22   2004048956

Editorial Offices
744 Broad Street, Newark, NJ 07102 (973) 820-2000
201 Mission St., San Francisco, CA 94105-1831 (415) 908-3200
701 East Water Street, Charlottesville, VA 22902-7587 (804) 972-7600
www.lexis.com

(Pub.3634)

DEDICATION

Professor Lewis dedicates this book to:
RACHEL BAYLA GREGG
The new light in his life
and, of course,
her parents, LIZ and BEN, her uncle DANNY
her great-grandmother, ANNE LEWIS, her great-grandfather,
EARL MELTZER
and, most importantly,
her Grandma, my loving and supportive wife,
JUDY

Professor Resnicoff dedicates this book to:
his terrific children,
MENACHEM, BAILA, GOLDIE, ETTIE, TZIPPY & YITZY,
his wonderful and special parents,
JACK IRWIN (ob"m) and BLANCHE FLORENCE RESNICOFF,
his very dear in-laws,
SHMUEL YEHUDA (ob"m) and CHANA GERTNER,
and his loving wife,
GITA

TABLE OF CONTENTS

PREFACE
INTRODUCTION TO PAYMENT SYSTEMS

The first questions that ought to be asked — and answered — in a course on payment systems are what are payments systems and why do we need them. We will answer these questions and, as we do so, we will briefly discuss the principal modern payment systems that we will cover in this book.

By a "payment system" we mean both a set of processes by which one can transfer value from one place to another or from one person to another and the body of law that applies to such processes.

Initially, payment was exclusively made by giving someone something of intrinsic value — either services or goods. Thus, if someone, Able, wanted apples, he would either work for a person, Betty, who had extra apples or give Betty something else of intrinsic value, such as pears. This system had many drawbacks. For example, assume Betty wants cucumbers, but has no need for Able's services or pears. Without the adoption of some generally accepted medium of exchange, it would be difficult for Able to get her apples. Similarly, suppose it takes a while for Betty to find someone who both has cucumbers and wants apples. By the time she finds him, the apples may have spoiled. Accordingly, there is a need to find a way to store value indefinitely.

In response to these problems, and others, a payment system involving "money" or "cash" was developed. In the United States, Congress has the constitutional authority to coin money and regulate its value, and the individual States are constitutionally forbidden from issuing competing forms of money. See Article I, Sections 8 and 10. Because, unlike apples, federally issued money does not generally spoil and because federal law specifies that such money can be used to satisfy all types of debts in the United States, 31 U.S.C. §5103, people are prepared to take this money in exchange for their goods or services.

But the money payment system is imperfect. In order to have enough money available for unanticipated purchases, people would have to carry relatively large sums of cash. But doing so may often be inconvenient. In addition, doing so could also be costly. While a person keeps his money in a bank, for instance, he can earn interest on it. While the cash is in a person's pocket, it earns nothing. Moreover, carrying cash — or sending it through the mail — is risky because it can be lost or stolen. In fact, if everyone carried relatively large amounts of cash, and prospective criminals knew this, the incidence of robberies might increase.

To address these concerns, people started using various forms of writings that they could fill out, sign and give instead of cash. The principal payment system governing such writings is "negotiable instruments law," which we will begin to examine in detail in Chapter 2. You are undoubtedly familiar with the most common type of negotiable instrument, the check. By carrying a few blank checks, a person enjoys the ability to be able to transfer large amounts of money while exposing himself to very little risk of loss.

If a merchant is not prepared to rely on the creditworthiness of a prospective buyer, the negotiable instruments payment system breaks down. Similarly, sometimes there is a need to transfer value to someone who is far away. If there is sufficient lead time, one could mail a negotiable instrument. But if the transfer must be made quickly, the mail is too slow. Alternative payment systems, such as the electronic transfer of funds, discussed in Chapters 18 and 19, and the use of credit cards, discussed in Chapter 20, help resolve these problems. Electronic transfers can be effectuated speedily, sometimes almost instantaneously, thereby minimizing a merchant's risk. Credit card information can be given over the phone to a merchant who is far away, and it enables the merchant to rely on the creditworthiness of the credit card issuer, and not just that of the customer who is the credit card holder.

Chapter 1

AN INTRODUCTION TO NEGOTIABLE INSTRUMENTS LAW

A negotiable instrument is a signed writing (usually a promissory note or an ordinary check) and constitutes an undertaking by the person signing it to pay a sum of money. As mentioned in the Preface, the negotiable instruments payment system is designed to allow a person to transfer value to someone else without the inconvenience, cost and risk associated with the use of cash. For this system to work, of course, it is necessary that the person to whom a negotiable instrument is offered be willing to part with goods and services in exchange for the instrument just as she would be willing to do so for cash. For example, assume Able wants to buy apples from Betty by giving her his check. He can only do so if Betty is willing to take the check. Will she be willing to do so?

The answer depends, in part, on whether Betty will be able to use the check to purchase goods or services from someone else, such as Carl. But will Carl, who was not part of the original transaction between Able and Betty, be willing to give Betty goods and services in exchange for Able's negotiable instrument?

The answer to this question depends, in turn, on the rights that Carl will have on the check. Let's assume that Able signed the check and gave it to Betty to buy apples, and Betty gave it to Carl in exchange for oranges. If the check were simply treated as a contract, and Betty's rights against Able were subject to contract law, then Betty's transfer of the check to Carl would be no more than an assignment to him of Betty's contract rights against Able. If Carl would ever try to enforce these rights against Able, Able could assert all sorts of contract defenses based on the circumstances surrounding the underlying transaction between Able and Betty. For example, if Able had given Betty the check in advance, and Betty had never delivered the apples, Able would argue that he received no consideration for his check, and he would not have to pay Carl. Similarly, if Betty had lied to Able about the quality of the apples, or the apples were defective, Able would not have to pay the full amount of the check and, depending on the extent of the defect, might not have to pay anything at all. Consequently, taking an assignment of rights from Betty would be a risky proposition, and Carl might well be unwilling to take that risk. After all, he was not part of the transaction between Able and Betty and does not know exactly what happened.

This is where negotiable instruments law comes into play. Negotiable instruments law provides that the transfer of an instrument can give the transferee (in our case, Carl) greater rights than he would obtain through the assignment of a contract. If (1) a writing is a negotiable instrument, and (2) it is transferred to Carl in a certain way (i.e., by a process known as "negotiation"), and (3) Carl takes the instrument for value in good faith and without notice of any defenses

1

or other problems with the instrument or the underlying transaction, then Carl becomes a "super-plaintiff" (i.e., Carl is a "holder in due course") who is able to enforce the instrument against Able even if Able could legitimately assert defenses that would be effective under simple contract law. Carl's ability to obtain this right is what makes Carl willing to take the instrument in exchange for his oranges and what makes the negotiable instruments payment system work. For this system to come into play, the writing must be a "negotiable instrument" as defined in Article 3 of the Uniform Commercial Code. The requirements of negotiability are discussed in **Chapter 2**. Once it is determined that the writing is a negotiable instrument, a suit to enforce the instrument — i.e., to force the obligated parties to pay the amount specified — follows a consistent pattern that involves answering these questions in this order:

1. *Is the person seeking to enforce the instrument a proper party plaintiff?*

It must first be determined that the person seeking to enforce the obligation is in fact entitled to do so. Usually this means that the plaintiff in our cases must be in possession of the instrument for which it seeks payment. **Chapter 3** deals with the process by which instruments come into being and are transferred from one party to another. **Chapter 4** considers the criteria for determining whether a person is a person entitled to enforce the instrument (i.e., a proper party plaintiff).

2. *What is the plaintiff's theory for asserting that the defendant is liable?*

Chapters 5, 6 and 7 deal with the defendants in our cases. They identify those parties who are liable on an instrument and the nature of that liability. If the plaintiff is a person entitled to enforce and the defendant is liable on the instrument, the plaintiff wins — unless the defendant can successfully assert a defense to payment.

3. *Can the defendant successfully assert a defense to payment?*

Chapter 8 discusses defenses, grounds for discharge and claims in recoupment that will either allow the defendant to escape having to pay the amount specified on the instrument or limit his/her liability. If the defendant can establish a defense, a discharge or a claim in recoupment, the focus returns to the plaintiff.

4. *Is the plaintiff a holder in due course?*

If the plaintiff is a holder in due course, the "super-plaintiff" referred to above, he/she is not subject to the defenses of the defendant, with specific exceptions. Which parties are holders in due course or are able to assert the rights of a holder in due course and the specific defenses to which even a holder in due course is subject are discussed in **Chapter 9.**

Negotiable instruments law, however, does much more than offer the possibility of a person's becoming a super-plaintiff. It also provides rules for dealing with many contingencies involving such instruments, such as forgeries, robberies, and the like. These situations typically involve the following scenarios:

1. A sues B for breach of a warranty B made about a particular instrument.

2. A sues B for converting a particular instrument.

3. A sues his bank, B, for violating one of the rules set forth in UCC Article 4 that regulate the relationship between a bank and its customer.

Chapters 10 through 17 explore these and other aspects of negotiable instruments law. The remainder of the present chapter, however, will discuss the statutory framework governing negotiable instruments law.

Historical Evolution of the Uniform Commercial Code

The laws governing negotiable instruments have their roots in the mercantile courts of England (where the juries were comprised of merchants) and, later, the common law. In the United States, negotiable instruments are largely governed by state law, and early commercial laws differed from state to state. This introduced undesirable uncertainty into matters affecting more than one state. In 1889, the American Bar Association voted to promote the uniformity of state laws. Shortly thereafter, the New York State legislature authorized the Governor to appoint three commissioners to examine how such uniformity could be best accomplished. This led to the first meeting of the Conference of State Boards of Commissioners on Promoting Uniformity of Law in the United States. This Conference is now known as the National Conference of Commissioners on Uniform State Laws (the "NCCUSL").[1]

The NCCUSL have proposed over 200 uniform laws on a wide variety of topics. In 1896, the NCCUSL promulgated the Negotiable Instruments Law (the "NIL"), which was ultimately enacted by every state.

As time passed, however, it became clear that there was a growing need for a comprehensive statute to deal in a uniform manner with all areas of commerce in an increasingly mobile, complex and expanding business environment. In 1940, the NCCUSL and the American Law Institute (the "ALI"),[2] which had been organized in 1923, joined on a project to create a uniform commercial code.

The first Official Text (known as the 1952 version although actually published in September of 1951) of the Uniform Commercial Code (the "UCC") was not widely accepted. In 1957, a revised version was promulgated, with additional texts (with relatively minor changes) being released in 1958 and 1962. The movement for adoption of the Code was accelerated during the 1960's, and by 1968 the Code was effective in forty-nine states, the District of Columbia and the

---

[1] Its web site is at http://www.nccusl.org/nccusl/default.asp.

[2] Its web site is at http://www.ali.org/

Virgin Islands. Louisiana, the final state to enact the UCC, did so by adopting most, but not all, of the Articles in 1974. Additional Official Texts were promulgated in 1972, 1978, 1987 and 1990.

Structure of the UCC

The UCC comprises eleven "Articles." Each Article is divided into "Parts," and each Part contains various provisions. Each UCC section is designated by the following formula, "X-YZZ," with "X" being the number of the Article in which the provision is found, "Y" being the number of the Part of that Article in which the provision is found, and "ZZ" being the 2-digit number assigned to the particular provision. The first provision in a particular part is assigned the 2-digit number "01." To illustrate this system, suppose we need to find UCC § 3-108. The "3" tells us to look in Article 3. The "1" directs us to Part 1 of Article 3. The "08" tells us to find the eighth provision in that Part. The provision that follows § 3-108 is § 3-201. Why, instead, isn't § 3-108 followed by a provision designated as § 3-109? The answer is that there are only 8 sections in Part 1 of Article 3. Immediately after Part 1 comes Part 2, and § 3-201 is the first provision in Part 2.

The UCC's Treatment of Negotiable Instruments Law

UCC Article 3, entitled "Uniform Commercial Code — Negotiable Instruments," replaced the old NIL. UCC Article 4, entitled "Uniform Commercial Code — Bank Deposits and Collections," also contains many provisions that pertain to negotiable instruments law. Where there is a conflict between Articles 3 and 4, the provisions of Article 4 govern. See § 3-102(b). Additional relevant provisions, including certain definitions and principles of interpretation, are found in UCC Article 1, entitled "Uniform Commercial Code — General Provisions."

Certain writings that might satisfy the definition of a "negotiable instrument" are expressly excluded from Article 3 and are governed by laws other than "negotiable instruments law." See § 3-102. Thus, "payment orders" are governed by Article 4A, and "securities" are governed by Article 8. Prior to enactment of Article 8, corporate bonds had been governed by the NIL. To the extent they are within the definition of "security," these obligations are now governed exclusively by Article 8. See § 8-102(1)(a)). If there is any conflict between the provisions of Article 4 and Article 8, those of Article 8 prevail. See § 4-102(a).

The Official Text of the UCC promulgated in 1990 included a major revision of Article 3 (with conforming and miscellaneous amendments to Articles 1 and 4) to update its provisions and "provide essential rules for the new technologies and practices in payment systems." At the time this manuscript was submitted to the publisher, 48 states, the District of Columbia and Puerto Rico had already adopted most of the provisions of Revised Articles 3 and 4, although some provisions were adopted in slightly altered form. See Appendix 5 for a chart providing statutory citations and effective dates on a state-by-state basis. Only New York and South Carolina retained the former versions of those Articles. In 2002, the NCCUSL adopted some additional revisions to Articles 3 and 4, but, at the time this manuscript was submitted, only one state, Minnesota, had enacted those revisions. *Consequently, unless otherwise indicated, our references to Articles 3 and 4 are to the Official 1990 version of Articles 3 and 4 of the Code, unless a former version or the Revised 2002 version is specifically mentioned.*

Relevant Provisions From UCC Article 1

UCC Article 1 comprises general provisions relating to the construction, application and subject matter of the UCC in its entirety. It includes definitions and principles of interpretation pertinent to Articles 3 and 4. The NCCUSL revised Article 1 in 2001. *Unless otherwise indicated by a reference to "Former Article 1" or "Former § 1-XXX," our references to Article 1 will be to the 2001 Revised version.* Of special significance are:

1. the admonition in § 1-103 (compare to Former § 1-102) that the UCC is to be liberally construed and that the various provisions may be varied by agreement so long as the obligations of good faith, diligence, reasonableness and care prescribed by the UCC are not disclaimed;

2. § 1-103's specific reference to the applicability of all supplemental bodies of law and equity to the provisions of the UCC unless explicitly displaced;

3. the power, subject to certain limitations, given to the parties by § 1-301 (compare to Former § 1-105) to choose by contract which state or nation's law governs; in the case of transactions that do not involve a consumer, this power is subject to fewer restrictions than under Former § 1-105;

4. the guiding principle of remedies in § 1-305 (Former § 1-106) that the aggrieved party should be put in as good a position as if the other party had fully performed, but that neither consequential nor special nor punitive damages may be had unless specially authorized by law; and

5. the obligation of good faith imposed by § 1-304 (Contrast to Former § 1-203) on every contract or duty within the scope of the UCC. Note that the 2001 Revision adopted generally what used to be the definition of "good faith" for only certain parts of the UCC, such as Article 3. *See* § 1-201(20).

Relevant Non-UCC Law That Supercedes UCC Articles 3 and 4

If the United States is a party to a negotiable instrument, its rights and obligations are governed by "federal common law" unless a specific federal statute applies. *See Clearfield Trust Co. v. United States*, 318 U.S. 363, 87 L.Ed. 838, 63 S.Ct. 573 (1943). A three-part test is applied to determine whether the federal common law should follow state law. *See United States v. Kimbell Foods, Inc.*, 440 U.S. 715, 59 L.Ed.2d 711, 99 S.Ct. 1448 (1979)(federal common law follows applicable UCC Article 9 rule); UCC Comment 4 to § 3-102.

Even where the United States is not a party to a negotiable instrument, if there is any conflict between Article 3, on the one hand, and the regulations of the Board of Governors of the Federal Reserve System or operating circulars of the Federal Reserve Banks,[3] on the other, the latter govern. *See* UCC § 3-102(c). Even if § 3-102(c) were silent on this matter, the doctrine of federal preemption would mandate the same result. *See* UCC Comment 3 to § 3-102(c). *See also Fidelity Federal Savings & Loan Association v. De La Cuesta*, 458 U.S. 141, 73 L.Ed.2d 664, 102 S.Ct. 3014 (1982) ("[f]ederal regulations have no less preemptive effect than federal statutes"). Similarly, if the United States becomes a party to the Convention on International Bills of Exchange and International Promissory Notes, completed by the United Nations Commission on International Trade in 1989, the Convention will supersede Article 3. *See* UCC Comment 5 to § 3-102.

Pitfalls in Analyzing UCC Provisions

There are many pitfalls in analyzing UCC provisions. Although we cannot survey all of them, we can point out a few of the most important ones.

One cluster of problems concerns the difficulty in relying on "Comments" that are printed along with the text of the UCC. The NCCUSL provides an "Official Comment" after each UCC section, and these Official Comments are printed in the statutory supplements that are used in virtually all law schools. Moreover, in many states, legal publishers routinely include these Official Comments in their publications of annotated state statutes. The Official Comments are often cited by courts as a guide to construing UCC provisions.[4] One problem

---

[3] The Federal Reserve System and Federal Reserve Banks are discussed in Chapter 17.

[4] Although commentators disagree as to the extent to which the Comments should be followed, see, e.g., Francis J. Facciolo, "Father Knows Best: Revised Article 8 and the Individual Investory," 27 *Fla.St.U.L.Rev.* 615, 714 at n. 285 (citing different views), most courts seem to find the Comments as instructive. *See* Robert H. Skilton, "Some Comments on the Comments to the Uniform Commercial Code," 1966 *Wis.L.Rev* 597 (1966) (the Comments "express opinions on meaning and purpose of the text . . . written by men who supposedly either participated in the drafting of the section involved or were close to those who did. . . . [The Comments] form a treatise on the Code, and may be consulted as any other treatise, standing on its own merits.").

with relying on these Official Comments is that no state has actually enacted them into law. Consequently, the Official Comments cannot override the meaning of the text.[5]

Not only are the Official Comments not law, but, for a number of reasons, they are not necessarily reliable as a source of "legislative history." In fact, some of the Comments, as they are now published, *did not exist* at the time that particular states enacted the relevant UCC provisions. In 1968, the NCCUSL and the ALI established a "Permanent Editorial Board" ("PEB") for the UCC. In addition to considering possible UCC revisions and issuing various reports, the PEB has promulgated several "Commentaries" on various UCC issues. Some of these Commentaries, which are published as an appendix in many of the statutory supplements used in commercial paper courses, propose changes in the language of the Official Comments. These changes sometimes appear in the Official Comments included in new printings of the UCC without adequate explanation as to exactly what has been changed.

Furthermore, many states adopted versions of the UCC that differ from the Official Text. Consequently, particular Official Comments may simply be inapplicable to the law in such states.

In addition to the Official Comments, some state publishers print an entirely different set of comments in their annotated versions of their state version of the UCC. In some cases, such as in New Jersey, these comments reflect the work of an official commission and may have value in discerning the state legislature's intent. In other cases, however, such as in Illinois, the comments were solicited by a publisher from a lawyer or academic — perhaps after the UCC was adopted in that state — and may not be relevant at all in assessing legislative intent.

Another problem arises when someone uses annotated versions of the UCC, even the annotated version of the UCC that is published for a particular state. From time to time, a specific UCC section is revised, sometimes to "overrule" prospectively the result reached in a prior case. Nevertheless, publishers often continue to include prior annotations — including annotations to the very case that prompted the legislative amendment! When dealing with annotated versions of the UCC — or any other statute — be sure that no shortcuts are taken, and that any annotated decision is read and its relevance carefully evaluated.

---

[5] *See, e.g., Burk v. Emmick,* 637 F.2d 1172, 1175 n.5 (8th Cir. 1980) (the Comments cannot "impose restrictions unwarranted by the statutory language"); Robert H. Skilton, "Some Comments on the Comments to the Uniform Commercial Code," 1966 *Wis.L.Rev.* 597, 604, 614, 628 (citing Professor Honnald).

Chapter 2

NEGOTIABILITY

Negotiable instruments law applies to only two types of writings: notes and drafts.

Notes and Drafts — Introductory Comments

A note contains an express promise to pay money either to the order of a particular person or to anyone who has physical possession of the note. The person who makes the promise is called the "maker."

> **NOTE:** The word "person" includes individuals and legal entities. *See* UCC § 1-201(27).

When payment is promised to the order of a particular person, that person is called a named "payee," and the note is said to be payable "to order." When payment is promised to anyone who has physical possession of the note, the note is payable to "bearer." Notes are often referred to as "two-party paper" because each note must involve someone who promises to pay (the maker) and someone to whom the promise is made (a named payee or bearer). Notes are also often referred to as "promissory notes" because each note must contain a promise to pay.

Thus, suppose Mary pays Paul for his services by giving Paul a note for $1,200.00.

The note might look like this:

> I promise to pay to the order of Paul $1,200.00 on May 5, 2004.
>
> /s/ *Mary*

Example

> **NOTE:** Whenever we depict a signature, we use italics, "/s/" and/or "signed" to indicate handwriting. Consequently, Mary signed the above promissory note.

This note is payable to order. Mary is the maker of the note, and Paul is the named payee.

By contrast to a note, a draft does not contain any explicit *promise* to pay. Instead, a draft is a writing in which one person *orders* another person to make a payment. The person giving the order is called the "drawer." The person to whom the order is given is called the "drawee." A draft is often said to be "drawn on" the drawee.

> NOTE: Why the titles "drawer" and "drawee"? Well, why would the drawee be likely to obey the drawer's order to make a payment? Most likely, the reason is that the drawer has a claim for money from the drawee. Instead of demanding payment to himself, the drawer demands payment to a third party. In making this demand, however, the drawer is using up (or "drawing upon") his claim for money from the drawee.

When a draft calls for the drawee to make payment to the order of a particular person, that person is called a named "payee" and the draft is said to be payable "to order." When payment is to be made to anyone who has physical possession of the note, the draft is payable to bearer. Drafts are often referred to as "three-party" instruments because each draft must contain a drawer, a drawee and some person to whom the payment is to be made (a named payee or bearer). By far the most common type of draft is a "check," which is a draft that is drawn on a bank and is payable on demand, i.e., whenever the payee wants the money, he can ask for it.

Thus, suppose Mary pays Paul for his services by giving Paul a check for $1,200.00, drawn on her checking account at First Insatiable Bank. The check might look like this:

Example

May 5, 2004.

Pay to the order of Paul $1,200.00
Twelve hundred and 00 Dollars

First Insatiable Bank

/s/ *Mary*

This check is payable to order. Mary is the drawer, First Insatiable Bank is the drawee, and Paul is the named payee.

Courts frequently err in the terms they use when discussing negotiable instruments issues. *See, e.g., New Jersey Steel Corp. v. Warburton*, 139 N.J. 536, 655 A.2d 1386 (1995) (incorrectly referring to the "maker" of a check instead of to its "drawer"); see discussion in *Kenerson v. FDIC*, 44 F.3d 19 (1st Cir. 1995). Nevertheless, it is very important that you use the correct terms in order to avoid confusion.

There is a lot more to say about specific types of drafts, but we will defer that to the end of this chapter. First, we will explore the criteria that must be satisfied for a note or draft to be a negotiable instrument.

Criteria of Negotiability

UCC Article 3 applies only to those notes and drafts that are negotiable. Indeed, although the word "instrument" is often used in common commercial parlance to describe any note or draft, § 3-104(b) defines an "instrument" as a "negotiable instrument." To be a negotiable instrument a writing must

[1] contain an unconditional promise or order to pay

[2] a fixed amount of money, with or without interest or other charges described in the promise or order, that is

[3] payable to order or to bearer at the time it is issued or first comes into the possession of the holder and

[4] be payable on demand or at a definite time and,

[5] with specified exceptions, state no other undertaking or instruction by the person promising or ordering payment to do any act in addition to the payment of money. Section 3-104(a).

We will review each of these criteria. Before beginning, however, three preliminary points ought to be made. First, other specific statutory provisions define some of these criteria in ways that introduce new requirements that would not otherwise be apparent. For example, an "order" is specifically defined as "a written instruction to pay money signed by the person giving the instruction." *See* § 3-103(a)(8). The requirements of a writing and of a signature are not self-evident from the term "order." Second, on some occasions, other statutory provisions define these § 3-104 criteria in ways that might appear inconsistent with their plain language. *See, e.g.,* §§ 3-106(c), 3-106(d). Third, the negotiability of an instrument is always determined by what appears on the face of the instrument alone. If the instrument is negotiable according to its stated terms, that negotiability is unaffected by any separate writing that purports to affect the terms of the instrument.

> **NOTE**: Although the negotiability of the instrument is unaffected by such a separate writing, a separate writing may affect the relationship between the original parties to the instrument.

With one exception, each and every one of the requirements for negotiability must be met for Article 3 to be applicable. The exception deals with checks. Section 3-104(c) states that an order that otherwise falls within the definition of a "check," see § 3-104(f), and meets all of the requirements of negotiability except that it is not payable to order or to bearer is nevertheless defined as an instrument and governed by Article 3.

The Code also *specifically* gives the parties the ability to opt out of Article 3 coverage. A promise or order other than a check is not an instrument if, at the time it was issued or first came into the possession of a holder, it contained a conspicuous statement, however expressed, that it was not negotiable or not an instrument governed by Article 3. *See* § 3-104(d). If such a statement is placed on a check, however, it is does not render the check non-negotiable. This is partly because the efficient processing of the massive volume of checks requires the use of automated means which could not efficiently discern the presence of such language. Moreover, virtually everyone involved in the check payment system assumes that checks are negotiable instruments. They might therefore not be sensitive to the ramifications of such language even if they did notice it.

1. An Unconditional Order or Promise To Pay

a. What is an Order?

Section 3-103(a)(8) defines an "order" as a "written instruction to pay money signed by the person giving the instruction." The person who gives the instruction, by signing, either directly or through an agent, is called the drawer. *See* § 3-103(a)(5). An authorization to pay is not an order unless the person authorized to pay is also *instructed* to pay. Usually the order is given simply by using the word "pay." Although words of courtesy, such as "please pay," may be used in an order, a statement like "I wish you would pay" is likely to be considered an authorization but not an instruction to pay. *See* UCC Comment to Former § 3-102.

The person to whom the instruction is addressed is the drawee. *See* § 3-103(a)(4). A drawer can address the order to anyone, including the drawer itself. The most common example of an instruction given by the drawer to itself appears in the form of a cashier's check, which is defined as "a draft with respect to which the drawer and drawee are the same bank or branches of the same bank." *See* § 3-104(g).

The instruction may also be addressed to two or more persons jointly or in the alternative, but not in succession. As we will see in more detail in Chapter 4, certain persons have standing to demand payment on an instrument. Each such person is called a "person entitled to enforce an instrument," whom we will call a "PETE." With respect to a draft, a PETE must initially demand payment from the drawee pursuant to a process called "presentment" and may only take legal action against the drawer upon the drawee's refusal to pay, called a "dishonor." The process of presentment and dishonor are discussed in more detail in Chapter 5. If drawees are listed in the alternative, a dishonor by either drawee allows legal recourse against the drawer, and no undue burden is imposed on the PETE. If, however, successive drawees were allowed, it would be necessary to make successive presentments to the drawees before proceeding against the drawer. The rule against successive drawees avoids this inconvenience.

b. What is a Promise?

A "promise" is defined as a "written undertaking to pay money signed by the person undertaking to pay." *See* § 3-103(a)(12). An acknowledgment of an obligation is not a promise unless the obligor also undertakes to pay the obligation. *Id.* This language was drafted to make it clear that an IOU alone is not a negotiable instrument. *See* UCC Comment 3 to § 3-103.

Orders or Promises Must Be Written and Signed

The definitions of both "order" and "promise" require that each be written. Section § 1-201(43) provides that a "writing" includes "printing, typewriting or any other intentional reduction to tangible form." Although there is no requirement that the writing be done on any particular surface, remember that the underlying purpose of commercial paper is that it be freely transferrable.

PROBLEM 2.1

Bob Jones, who owes Bill Thomas $100, records the following into his tape recorder and then sends the tape to Bill: "I, Bob Jones, promise to pay to the order of Bill Thomas $100."

Has the writing requirement for negotiability been met? See § 1-201(43). Does this situation present any other problems? Read on.

The definition of an "order" provides that it must be signed by the person giving the order, while the definition of a "promise" requires that it must be signed by the person making the promise. The Code provides that there need not be a complete signature, but rather that the term "signed" includes "any symbol executed or adopted by a party with present intention to authenticate a writing." *See* § 1-201(37). As such, authentication may be printed, stamped, or handwritten and may consist merely of initials, a thumbprint (see § 1-201, Comment 37) or any name including a trade or assumed name, a word, or a mark, as long as it is intended to signify the liability of the signer on the instrument. *See* § 3-401(b). When necessary, parol evidence is admissible to identify the signer, and once identified, the signature is effective. *See* UCC Comment 2 to § 3-401.

PROBLEM 2.2

John Doe writes the following in his own handwriting:

"I, John Doe, promise to pay to the order of Mary Smith $50."

a. Is this a signed writing?

b. *Would your answer be any different if these words had been type-written?*

c. *What if these words were typed on a page that had a signature line typed at the bottom that was left blank?*

d. *What if John instead took a piece of his personal stationery that at the top had imprinted, "From the desk of John Doe," and wrote "I promise to pay to the order of Mary Smith $100" but did not sign his name after these words?*

(In answering part d, think about your own checks which have your name pre-printed in the upper left hand corner.)

See § 3-401 and its accompanying comments.

It is not enough that the writing is signed, however. It must be signed by the person giving the instruction (i.e., the drawer) in the case of an order or by the person promising to pay (i.e., the maker) in the case of a promise. Of course, the signature of an authorized agent for the drawer or maker is also sufficient. Although people may sign the instrument in other capacities — for example, an "indorser" may sign to negotiate the instrument to someone else or a "guarantor" may sign to guarantee payment if the principal obligor does not pay — if no one signs as a maker or drawer, the writing does not qualify as a negotiable instrument.

PROBLEM 2.3

Frank Forger, claiming to represent his former employer, Marty Maker, obtains a $2,000 cash loan from the Shark Loan Company and signs Marty's name as maker on a promissory note made payable to Shark's order for $2,000 plus interest. In fact, Frank acted with neither Marty's knowledge nor permission. Is this a negotiable instrument (that is, is it signed by the person making the promise)? See §§ 3-401, 3-403.

It is important to note that even if a writing is not signed, so that there is no liability created by the writing itself, nothing in the Code prevents liability from arising or remaining apart from the writing. That is, there may still be liability on the underlying obligation for which the intended instrument was given, such as when a check is sent to pay for a utility bill or for merchandise purchased on credit.

PROBLEM 2.4

On April 15, Nancy Naive orally agrees to sell her computer to Ima D. Seaver, for $400. Nancy delivers the computer to Ima, who claims to be short of cash and instead offers to give Nancy her promissory note. Ima writes the following on a piece of paper and gives it to Nancy in the presence of several witnesses:

"On May 1, 2004, I promise to pay to the order of Nancy Naive $400." However, Ima neglects to sign it. On May 1, Nancy presents the alleged note to Ima and asks for the $400. Ima refuses and points out that the writing was unsigned. Nancy sues Ima on the alleged note and as part of her case calls the witnesses who were present to attest to the transaction and a handwriting expert who can prove that it was written in Ima's handwriting. Is Ima liable on the alleged note? If not, does Ima get the computer without having to pay for it?

c. What is an "Unconditional" Order or Promise?

For a draft or note to be negotiable, the order or promise must be unconditional. The reason for this requirement is to ensure that there is no risk inherent in the writing that might impede its transfer and thereby defeat the purpose of negotiability.

Section 3-106 provides that any promise or order is unconditional unless it states

[1] an express condition to payment; or

[2] that it is subject to or governed by any other writing; or

[3] that rights or obligations with respect to the promise are stated in another writing.

The fact that the order or promise is subject to implied or constructive conditions does not make an otherwise unconditional promise or order conditional. Consider, for instance, the following promissory note:

The promise to pay could be said to be subject to the implied condition that Modern Painting, Inc., actually paint Marty's house. Nevertheless, this implied condition does not affect negotiability. The promise is treated as an uncondi-

---

I promise to pay $2,500 to the order of Modern Painting, Inc.

I am giving this note to Modern Painting, Inc., in exchange for its promise to paint my house.

/s/ *Marty Maker*

---

tional promise to pay. *See generally* 88 A.L.R.3d 1100 (1978, Supp. 1993); UCC Comments to § 3-106.

Furthermore, parol evidence is not admissible to show that an obligation under a note is conditional and, therefore, not negotiable, when it appears absolute on its face. *Tatum v. Bank of Cumming*, 135 Ga.App. 675, 218 S.E.2d 677 (1975), *Houck v. Martin*, 82 Ill.App.3d 205, 402 N.E.2d 421, 37 Ill.Dec. 531 (4th Dist. 1980) (relying on UCC Comment 1 to pre-1990 § 3-413). Nor would other extrinsic evidence, such as usage of trade be admitted, *Holsonback v. First State Bank of Albertville*, 394 So.2d 381 (Ct.Civ.App. Ala.1980).

> **NOTE:** Section 3-117 allows the court to look beyond the instrument to other written agreements, which may modify, supplement, or nullify the obligation of a party to pay, if the instrument was issued in reliance on the agreement or as part of the same transaction giving rise to the instrument. As long as the instrument does not state that it is subject to or governed by the other agreement, the existence of the other agreement does not destroy the negotiability of the instrument. Rather, the other agreement provides the obligor with a defense to his obligation to pay on the instrument.

PROBLEM 2.5

Does the following language destroy negotiability? See § 3-106 and the accompanying Official Comments.

a. *"I promise to pay to the order of John Doe $10,000 if he agrees to sell his automobile to me."*

b. *"In consideration of his promise to transfer title of his automobile to me, I promise to pay to the order of John Doe $10,000."*

c. *"I promise to pay to the order of John Doe $10,000. The agreement made between John Doe and me on July 29, 2004, is hereby incorporated by reference." NOTE: Assume a review of that document discloses no conditions that would affect the payment on the instrument.*

d. *"I promise to pay to the order of John Doe $10,000 in accordance with our agreement of July 29, 2004."*

e. *"I promise to pay to the order of John Doe $10,000 subject to our agreement of July 29, 2004."*

f. *"Pursuant to our agreement of July 29, 2004, I promise to pay to the order of John Doe $10,000."*

g. *"This note is secured by a security interest in collateral described in a security agreement dated April 1, 2004, between the payee and maker of this note. Rights and obligations with respect to the collateral are governed by the securityagreement."*

h. *"I promise to pay to the order of John Doe $10,000 from the refund , if any, due me from the IRS for overpayment of my 2004 taxes."*

d. Other Exceptions to the Requirement That the Promise Must be Unconditional

Section 3-106(c) allows a traveler's check and any other writing that requires a countersignature to meet the definition of instrument under Article 3 by stating that the countersignature condition does not make the promise or order in the writing conditional for purposes of § 3-104(a). Although the failure to countersign will operate as a defense to the obligation of the issuer, it will not prevent a transferee from becoming a holder.

Section 3-106(d) provides that if a promise or order contains a statement required by statutory or administrative law to the effect that the rights of a holder or transferee are subject to the claims or defenses that the issuer could assert against the original payee (much like the Federal Trade Commission rule preserving consumers' claims and defenses — 16 C.F.R. Part 433, discussed in Chapter 9), the promise or order is not thereby made conditional for purposes of § 3-104(a). However, under such circumstances there can be no holder in due course of the instrument.

Common among agreements that are often assigned or transferred by one party to another are retail installment contracts, insurance policies and guaranty agreements that are in a separate document from the promissory note. Because of this provision that the promise to pay needs to be unconditional, courts have usually held that they are not governed by Article 3.

2. Fixed Amount of Money With or Without Interest or Other Charges

In order to ensure transferability, any prospective purchaser must be able to determine how much money will be paid to him pursuant to the instrument — hence the requirement that there must be a "fixed amount." See § 3-112.

a. Rules Regarding Interest

The predecessor to § 3-112 used the phrase "sum certain" and required that the entire amount due, including interest, be ascertainable in almost all instances by looking at the face of the instrument alone, without reference to outside sources. Thus, language such as "at the current rate" or "at the market rate," or references to a bank's prime rate caused the writing to fail the "sum certain" test. By contrast, § 3-112 makes it clear that only the principal amount need be fixed. Instruments may be negotiable even if they call for variable amounts or rates of interest and even if those amounts or rates are formulated in the instrument by reference to external factors, such as "the prime rate of the First Insatiable Bank as reported in the Chicago Tribune on the 15th of each month during the term of this note."

NOTE: Even some of the jurisdictions that have not generally adopted the 1990 revisions to Article 3 have, either by specific amendment to Article 3 or by separate statute, prevented use of a variable interest rate from rendering an instrument non-negotiable. Be sure to check if the state that governs the transaction has done so.

Section 3- 112 provides various rules with respect to interest on a negotiable instrument. Review it and § 3-104 and answer the following questions.

PROBLEM 2.6

Does the following language destroy negotiability?

a. *"I promise to pay to the order of Paul Payee $5,000 plus interest at 2% over the prime rate offered at the Chase Manhattan Bank in New York on January 27, 2005."*

b. *"I promise to pay to the order of Paul Payee $5,000 plus interest." If not, what is the interest rate and when does the interest begin to run? See § 3-112.*

c. *"I promise to pay to the order of Paul Payee $5,000, plus costs of collection and attorney's fees in case of default." See § 3-104. If this is a negotiable instrument, is it payable with interest? If so, at what rate?*

b. Payable "in Money"

If a written promise or order is to be negotiable it must be payable in money. "Money" is defined in § 1-201(24) as "a medium of exchange authorized or adopted by a domestic or foreign government and includes a monetary unit of account established by an intergovernmental organization or by agreement between 2 or more nations." This definition and § 3-107 make it clear that the term is not limited to United States dollars.

Pursuant to § 3-107, when the amount payable is stated in a foreign currency, unless otherwise specified in the instrument, payment may be made in either the foreign currency or in U.S. dollars. The rate of exchange is determined by the current bank-offered spot rate at the place of payment for the purchase of dollars on the day the instrument is paid. If the instrument requires that the medium of payment is to be foreign currency, payment must be made in that currency. Article 3 seems to assume that the requirement that payment be made in a foreign currency is not a condition that impairs negotiability. The reason seems to be that this condition is not a condition as to whether there is a payment obligation but merely a condition regarding the form of such payment.

3. *Payable to Order or to Bearer*

In order for an instrument other than a check to be negotiable, it must, at the time it is issued or first comes into the possession of a holder, be payable either to the order of an identified person or to bearer.

PROBLEM 2.7

Do the following meet the payable to order or bearer requirement? See § 3-109.

   a. *A note that reads*:

   "*I promise to pay to Paula Payee $5,000 on demand.*

   /s/ Marty Maker"

   b. *A check that reads:*

   "*Pay to Paula Payee $5,000*

   /s/ Dan Drawer"

   c. *A draft that reads:*

   "*To: Donald Drawee*

   Pay to Paula Payee $5,000

   /s/ Dan Drawer"

   d. *A note that reads:*

   "*I promise to pay bearer $5,000 on demand.*

   /s/ Marty Maker"

Section 3-109 provides guidance as to the terms that distinguish whether an instrument is payable to bearer or payable to order.

PROBLEM 2.8

Explain whether the following language would render an instrument payable to bearer, payable to order, or neither. If payable to order, to whom is the instrument initially payable? See § 3-109 and 3-110.

   a. *"Pay to the order of bearer."*

   b. *"Pay to Jane Doe or bearer."*

   c. *"Pay to the order of Jane Doe or bearer."*

   d. *"Pay to the order of (blank)."*

e. *"Pay to the order of cash."*

f. *"Pay to a Happy, Happy Birthday."*

g. *"Pay to the order of the Bobby Jones Trust Fund."*

h. *"Pay to John Doe or his order."*

i. *"Pay to John Doe or his assigns."*

           maybe order

4. Payable on Demand or at a Definite Time

In order for an instrument to be negotiable, the holder must be able to ascertain from the face of the instrument when it comes due. As such, it must be payable on demand or at a definite time. Demand instruments are defined in § 3-108(a), and instruments payable at a definite time are described in § 3-108(b). Section 3-108(c) deals with instruments payable at a fixed date and payable on demand before that date.

PROBLEM 2.9

Are the following payable on demand, at a definite time or non-negotiable? See § 3-108.

a. *"This note is payable at sight."* *demand*

b. *"This note is payable on (blank)."*

c. *A check is issued on January 1, 2005, but is dated February 15, 2005.*

d. *"This note is payable 30 days after sight."* *definite time*

e. *Note is dated June 1, 2005 and states, "This note is due 60 days after date of issue."*

f. *"Payable when the Chicago Cubs win the World Series."*   *non-neg.*

g. *"Payment is due January 21, 2005, but the holder may demand payment at any time before then if he deems himself insecure."*

h. *"This note is payable on February 24, 2005, but the holder, at his option, may extend the time of payment to a later date."*

i. *"This note is payable on January 24, 2005, but at the option of the maker, it may be extended to a later date."*

j. *"This note is payable on January 24, 2005, but if my house is not sold by that date, payment shall be extended until July 31, 2005."*

k. *"This note is payable on January 21, 2005, but demand may be made at any time before that date."* *both*

5. No Other Promise, Order, Obligation, or Power Given by the Maker or Drawer Except as Authorized by Article 3

The essence of a negotiable instrument is that it can be freely transferred in commerce without conditions or terms that might increase the risk that a party who takes it would encounter difficulties in attempting to enforce it. Negotiable instruments were thus desired to be "couriers without luggage." Accordingly, the Code provides that an instrument is to contain an unconditional promise or order to pay and no "other undertaking or instruction by the person promising or ordering payment to do any act in addition to the payment of money." *See* § 3-104(a)(3). One significant consequence of this part of the provision is that conditional sales contracts or retail installment contracts, which under the Negotiable Instruments Law were negotiable, are not negotiable instruments for purposes of Article 3. *See, e.g., Massey Ferguson Credit Corp. v. Bice*, 450 N.W.2d 435 (S.D. 1990).

The drafters of the UCC nevertheless recognized that certain terms on the instrument might be desirable to strengthen the obligation to pay, thereby increasing the security of creditors and the likelihood that they would accept an instrument in return for an obligation. They therefore created a list of permissible terms that may appear on an instrument without destroying its negotiability. These terms are provided primarily in § 3-104. *{Exceptions*

PROBLEM 2.10

Do the following terms destroy the negotiability of what would otherwise be a negotiable instrument? *Cognovit?*

a. *"Maker agrees that at any time the holder may authorize his attorney to confess judgment against the maker in an appropriate court."*

b. *"Maker (Purchaser) agrees that this note shall constitute maker's agreement to rent the property, for which this note is given, to payee's son for a period of no less than 3 years."*

c. *"Maker agrees to tender additional collateral in the event that holder deems himself insecure."*

a. *Terms Waiving Statutory Protections*

In addition to the exceptions illustrated by the problem above, § 3-104(a)(3)(iii) provides that a term purporting to waive the benefit of any law intended for the advantage or protection of any obligor does not affect the negotiability of an instrument. Benefits that may be waived include not only those provided under Article 3, such as presentment, dishonor, and notice of dishonor, but those provided by *any* state (and, presumably, federal) statute. However, it is important to realize that this provision, as well as the one described above dealing with confessions of judgment, deals only with the negotiability of the instrument as affected by the clause included on the instrument. The validity of the specific terms must still be determined by reference to any applicable consumer and debtor relief laws since all such terms are subject to any limitations existing therein. The pre-1990 version of § 3-112, on which the exceptions stated in § 3-104(a)(3) are based, specifically provided that "[n]othing in this Section shall validate any term which is otherwise illegal." Pre-1990 § 3-112. Although this admonition does not appear in the current version of the UCC, it seems inconceivable that it would not still hold true.

b. *Permissible Terms Provided by Other Sections*

In addition to the permissible terms specified in § 3-104(a)(3) discussed above, other sections of Article 3 state terms that may be included on the instrument without destroying its negotiability. These include terms that do not render the promise or order conditional as set forth in § 3-106, terms that specify payment in a foreign currency as provided in § 3-107, terms that allow for acceleration or extension in accordance with § 3-108, and terms that determine interest pursuant to § 3-112. Similarly, § 3-117 provides that a party's obligation to pay may be modified by a separate agreement subject to any legal rules that may exclude proof of contemporaneous or prior agreements. The existence of such a separate agreement does not necessarily affect the negotiability of the instrument. Instead, the separate agreement may be asserted by the obligor as a defense. Such a defense, however, would be ineffective against a holder in due course who took the instrument without notice of the separate agreement. *See* UCC Comment 1 to § 3-117.

Drafts and Notes: A More Detailed Look

As mentioned at the outset of this Chapter, negotiable instruments fall into two categories: drafts and notes. We will now survey the various specific types of drafts discussed in UCC Articles 3 and 4.

1. Documentary Drafts

Section 4-104(a)(6) defines "documentary draft" as

> a draft to be presented for acceptance or payment if specified documents, certificated securities (Section 8-102) or instructions for uncertificated securities (Section 8-308), or other certificates, statements, or the like are to be received by the drawee or other payor before acceptance or payment of the draft.

Documentary drafts are commonly used when a seller of goods is unsure of his buyer's creditworthiness or when the seller desires quick payment from the buyer. When a seller delivers goods to a carrier, he obtains a negotiable bill of lading. The seller then draws a demand draft with his bank as the payee and the buyer as the drawee. The draft is sent through the bank collection channels to the buyer's bank. When the buyer pays the demand draft, his bank delivers the bill of lading enabling the buyer to obtain possession of the goods. The proceeds are then transferred back to the seller's bank, which credits the seller's account.

2. Checks

A "check" is a draft, other than a documentary draft, in which the party ordered to pay is a bank and the instrument is payable on demand. This includes a share draft drawn on a credit union because the definition of "bank" (see § 4-105(1) and § 1-201(4)) includes credit unions as well as savings and loan associations and trust companies. The definition of "check" also includes a cashier's check or teller's check. *See* § 3-104(f).

> **NOTE:** The order need not take the ordinary pre-printed form to be a check. In *United Milk Products Co. v. Lawndale National Bank*, 392 F.2d 876 (7th Cir. 1968), under the former version of the Code, the court held that both a letter and a telegram, each directing a bank to pay money out of the account of a depositor corporation to a third party and each signed by an authorized corporate officer, satisfied the requirements of a check under the Code. The court held that the bank was not at fault for failing to insist on a "regular" check in either instance.

Under § 3-104, an instrument may be a check even if it is described on its face by another term, such as "money order." Money orders are sold both by banks and nonbanks. A personal money order sold by a bank is most commonly in the same form as a personal check. The form states that a certain amount is to be paid to the order of some person, leaving a blank for the name of the person to be filled in. The bank fills in the amount to be paid, usually by having the amount impressed by machine. No agent signs the money order for the bank; instead, the form leaves a blank for the signature of the purchaser. The bank will pay the money order only after the purchaser signs it. Thus, by signing the personal money order, the purchaser acts as its drawer. Such a money order is treated as a check under Article 3 because it is an order to pay, it is drawn on a bank, and it is payable on demand.

> **NOTE:** The term "remitter" is commonly used to refer to the purchaser of a money order and may even be typed beneath the blank for the purchaser's signature. Technically, however, "remitter," as defined in § 3-103(a)(15), does not apply to the purchaser of the personal money order described above. Section 3-103(a)(15) defines "remitter" as "a person that purchases an instrument from its issuer if the instrument is payable to an identified person other than the purchaser." Section 3-105 states that the drawer is the issuer of a draft. As explained above, the purchaser is the drawer of a personal money order. Because the purchaser of the personal money order does not buy it from himself, he cannot be said to have purchased it from "its issuer." Therefore, he does not fall within the § 3-103(a)(15) definition of a remitter.

A money order may also be in the form of a teller's check or cashier's check (described below). These money orders are typically signed by an agent for the issuing bank and essentially are checks drawn by the bank on itself. Money orders sold by nonbanks, such as postal money orders, are not defined as checks since they are not drawn on a bank. Even though money orders sold by nonbanks may be payable through a bank, the bank operates only as a collecting bank and has no responsibility to anyone to pay them.

3. Certified Checks

A certified check is a check "accepted" by the bank on which it is drawn. (The liability of an "acceptor" is discussed in Chapter 5.) A bank may accept the check merely by signing it (usually the signature is written, printed, or stamped vertically across the face of the instrument, although it may appear elsewhere or in another form) or by otherwise indicating that it is certified. The drawee of a check has no obligation to certify the check. *See* § 3-409(d).

By certifying the check, the drawee promises to pay the check in accordance with its terms. At the time of certification, the drawer and any party who had indorsed the check before the certification are discharged. *See* §§ 3-414(c), 3-415(d).

4. Cashier's Checks

Section 3-104(g) defines a cashier's check as "a draft with respect to which the drawer and drawee are the same bank or branches of the same bank."

EXAMPLE:

> Pay to the order of Paula Payee $100
> One hundred dollars and 00 cents
>
> First National Bank
>
> > First National Bank
> > by / s / *Peter President*
> > Peter President, authorized
> > agent for First National Bank

Although a bank may use a cashier's check to pay its own obligations, often a cashier's check is purchased by a customer to satisfy an obligation to a creditor who wants assurance that funds will be available when he seeks payment. Nevertheless, the sole liability on a cashier's check is that of the issuing bank as defined in § 3-412. The issuer is obliged to pay the instrument according to its terms at the time it was issued, or if not issued, at the time it first came into the possession of a holder. This obligation is owed to the person entitled to enforce the instrument or to an indorser who paid the instrument under § 3-415.

5. *Tellers' Checks*

A "teller's check" is defined as a "draft drawn by a bank (i) on another bank, or (ii) payable at or through a bank." *See* § 3-104(h).

EXAMPLE:

> Pay to the order of Paula Payee $100
> One hundred dollars and 00 cents
>
> Second National Bank
>
> > First National Bank
> > by / s / *Peter President*
> > Peter President, authorized
> > agent for First National Bank

A teller's check is always drawn by a bank and is usually drawn on a bank. In the case in which it is drawn on a nonbank, it will be made payable at or through a bank. Article 3 treats both kinds of tellers' checks the same, and both are included in the definition of "check." When the instrument is drawn on a nonbank, the place of payment will usually be stated on the instrument. When an instrument is payable at a bank in the United States, presentment of the instrument must be made at the bank specified. *See* § 3-501(b)(1).

6. Traveler's Checks

A "traveler's check" is an instrument that

   (i)   is payable on demand,

   (ii) is drawn on or payable at or through a bank,

   (iii) is designated by the term "traveler's check" or by a substantially similar term, and

   (iv) requires, as a condition to payment, a countersignature by a person whose specimen signature appears on the instrument. Section 3-104(i).

Traveler's checks are issued by both banks and nonbanks and may be in the form of a note or draft. They are often purchased and used by people who wish to have the equivalent of cash wherever they might travel throughout the world. The fact that the drawer of these checks is typically a very large financial organization provides significant security for parties to whom the checks are transferred and makes it likely that the instruments will be taken in exchange for goods and services.

Section 3-106(c) specifically provides that even though a countersignature appears to be a condition to payment, the promise or order is still "unconditional" for purposes of § 3-104(a).

REMEMBER: An instrument that contains an order or promise that is conditional cannot be a negotiable instrument.

The UCC Comments to § 3-104 acknowledge that traveler's checks are treated in the commercial world as money substitutes and therefore should be governed by Article 3.

7. Certificates of Deposit

A "certificate of deposit" (CD) is an acknowledgment *by a bank* that a sum of money has been received by it, and a promise by that bank to repay it (usually after a specified period of time and at a rate of interest). *See* § 3-104(j).

8. Negotiable Orders of Withdrawal

A negotiable order of withdrawal ("NOW") is an instrument by which a depositor may make a transfer of funds to a third party from a savings account. The instrument is much like a check in that it is a draft which orders the bank to pay a specified sum to a designated payee, but the account from which the money is withdrawn and transfers are made is usually an interest bearing account. As such, NOW accounts are either said to be interest bearing checking accounts or savings accounts from which checks may be written.

NOW accounts arose in the early 1970's in the northeastern United States in response to inflationary pressures, consumer demands for access to their deposits and competition from money market funds. Traditionally, there were two types of accounts: checking and savings. Checking accounts did not pay interest, allowed payments to be made to third parties by check and gave the depositor the right to withdraw funds on demand. Savings accounts paid interest, did not allow for checks to be drawn and had the right to require advance notice before funds could be withdrawn. In 1972, however, Massachusetts and New Hampshire authorized their state-chartered savings banks to offer negotiable order of withdrawal accounts, which effectively give consumers access to their savings deposit on demand by allowing them to transfer funds to third parties by way of a written instrument. In 1973, Congress responded by enacting legislation validating the NOW account in only Massachusetts and New Hampshire on an experimental basis and prohibiting it everywhere else — whether it was issued by a state or federal institution. Permission to offer NOW accounts was expanded gradually and was ultimately extended throughout the United States in the Depository Institutions Deregulation and Monetary Control Act of 1980.

Consequences of Non-negotiability

Any writing that does not meet the negotiability requirements set forth in Section 3-104 is not a negotiable instrument and thus not subject to UCC Article 3. Courts generally have taken four approaches to determining liability on these documents. They may, for instance:

1. Apply Article 3 provisions anyway;

2. Apply other UCC Articles;

3. Apply the common law of negotiable instruments; or

4. Apply general contract law principles.

Chapter 3

THE LIFE OF AN INSTRUMENT

There are three basic stages in the life of an instrument, whether a note or a draft, and a fourth possible stage in the life of a draft. Both notes and drafts may be the subject of issue, transfer or presentment for payment. An instrument is "issued" when its maker or drawer first voluntarily gives it to someone with the intention that either that person or someone else will be entitled to enforce the instrument. *See* § 3-105. An instrument is "presented" for payment when someone entitled to enforce it makes a demand for payment upon a party that is obligated or ordered to pay the instrument. *See* § 3-501. When an instrument presented for payment is paid, the instrument's "life" typically ends.

The other two stages — transfer and presentment for acceptance — usually (but not always) occur after issuance and before presentment for payment. The Code defines a "transfer" as when a person *other than its maker or drawer* voluntarily gives the instrument to someone else in order to enable that party to enforce the instrument. *See* § 3-203. Because an instrument is issued when it is voluntarily given to someone *by its maker or drawer,* issuance is not a "transfer of the instrument." Similarly, because the life of an instrument usually ends when it is paid, a presentment for payment is not made to enable the presentee to enforce the instrument. Therefore, a presentment is not a "transfer of the instrument."

In some instances, an instrument may come into the possession of a different person without a voluntary delivery. Suppose, for example, A issues an instrument to B, and B loses the instrument. If C finds the instrument, there has been a "transfer of possession" of the instrument from B to C, even though there has not been a voluntary "transfer of the instrument" from B to C. When this "transfer of possession" occurs, if the new possessor is a "holder," the transfer of possession is a "negotiation." *See* § 3-201(a).

Finally, the fourth stage, presentment for acceptance, only applies to drafts. It occurs when, before the draft is presented for payment, someone who is entitled to enforce it demands that the drawee sign the draft, thereby agreeing that it will pay the draft as ordered by the drawer. The signing of the draft is called an "acceptance."

Almost all cases other than those in which a signed check or note is lost or stolen from its drawer or maker involve instruments that have been issued. Similarly, all cases in which someone entitled to enforce an instrument is demanding payment involves a presentment for payment. Sometimes, the life of an instrument consists of only these two steps. For example, suppose Mike borrows $100 from his good friend Bob and gives Bob the following promissory note:

> I promise to pay to the order of Bob the sum of
> $100 on 7/02/04.
>
> /s/ *Mike*

When Mike gives Bob this note, the note is issued. Suppose that on July 2,
2004, Bob shows the note to Mike and demands payment of the $100. This con-
stitutes presentment for payment. If Mike then pays the instrument, the instrument is defunct; it's "life" is over, even though the note has never been
transferred by Bob to anyone else. Neither issue nor presentment of the note (or
of a draft) is a "transfer."

On the other hand, suppose that between the time Bob lent the $100 to Mike
and July 2, 2004, Bob wanted to borrow $100 from Sandra, another of Mike's
good friends. Suppose, also, that Bob planned on going away for the entire summer while Mike and Sandra were staying at home. Consequently, instead of
signing a new promissory note and giving it to Sandra, Bob gives the note Mike
signed to Sandra with the intention that she enforce it against Mike. When Bob
gives the note to Sandra, he has transferred the note.

Transfer of a draft is even more common than transfer of a note. It occurs, for
instance, whenever the recipient of a check either cashes it at a Currency
Exchange or at a store or deposits it in his or her bank account. Presentment of
a draft for acceptance, such as where someone presents a check to the drawee
bank for certification, is, by contrast, a relatively uncommon event.

After providing some additional details regarding issuance of an instrument,
this chapter will examine how an instrument is transferred and negotiated
and will focus on "indorsement," a step that is essential to the negotiation of
order paper.

A. *Issue of an Instrument*

Article 3 defines "issue" as the "*first* delivery of an instrument by the maker
or drawer, whether to a holder or nonholder, for the purpose of giving rights on
the instrument to any person." [Emphasis added.] *See* § 3-105(a). "Delivery" is
defined in § 1-201(15) as the "voluntary transfer of possession." Thus, ordinarily, if the person drawing the check or making the note retains possession of it
or if the instrument is stolen from him or lost by him, the instrument has not
been issued.

PROBLEM 3.1

Discuss the question of issuance in the following:

a. *Marty Maker signs a promissory note payable to the order of Paul Payee for $500 but then puts the note in his (Marty's) own safe. Marty then writes a letter to Paul telling Paul what he has done and telling him also that he intends to give the note to Paul the very next time he saw him. Has the note been issued?*

b. *Dan Drawer signs a check made payable to "bearer" and leaves it on his desk. Later that day, a thief comes and steals the check. Has the check been issued? If the thief gives the check to a merchant in exchange for some camera equipment, has the check been issued?*

c. *Dan Drawer writes a check to Penny Payee and puts it in an envelope which he addresses to Penny and drops in a mailbox. It is in fact delivered to Penny's home, but is stolen from her mailbox before she arrives home. Has the check been issued?* voluntary constructive delivery

d. *A note signed by Marty Maker made payable to Patty Payee is given to Marty's attorney for delivery the following day to Patty's attorney. Before the two attorney's meet, has the note been issued? Is it issued after Marty's attorney gives it to Patty's attorney, but before the attorney gives it to Patty?*

e. *A note is signed by Marty Maker made payable to Peter Payee and given by Marty to an escrow agent to be held until Peter can satisfy certain conditions. Has the note been issued? Does it matter whether the conditions have already been satisfied?* only if conditions satisfied

Under § 3-105(b), even if an instrument is not technically issued, if it somehow were to come into the hands of a person entitled to enforce it, the instrument would nevertheless be binding on the maker or drawer. The fact that it was not issued could be used as a defense to liability effective against anyone except a holder in due course. Thus, in Problem 3.1a, above, if Paul were somehow able to get possession of the instrument that Marty put in his safe, without Marty's having delivered it to him, and if Paul were to transfer the instrument to Harry Holder, and Harry were to sue Marty on his maker's obligation, Marty could successfully raise a defense of nonissuance unless Harry were a holder in due course. Similarly, in Problem 3.1b, above, Dan's defense of nonissuance would be effective except as against a holder in due course.

B. Transfers

As explained in Chapter 1, the purpose of negotiable instruments law is to permit instruments to be used as substitutes for cash and, in order to do so, negotiable instruments law must enable people who in good faith give value for them to be confident that they can readily enforce them. Negotiable instruments law accomplishes this by allowing people, when certain criteria are satisfied, to become holders in due course whose rights trump most contract law defenses. These criteria will be discussed in detail in Chapter 9. For our immediate purpose, it is sufficient to note that, at a minimum, in order to be a holder in due course, a person must be a "holder." Consequently, our discussion of transfers will focus, first, on what is necessary for the person who winds up with the instrument to be a holder. A transfer of possession in which the transferee becomes a holder is called a "negotiation." *What is required to negotiate an instrument depends upon the character of the instrument — that is, whether it is payable to bearer or payable to order —* **at the time of transfer.**

1. Negotiation of Bearer Paper — Change of Possession Alone

If an instrument is payable to bearer, anyone who is in physical possession of the instrument is defined as its "holder." *See* § 1-201(21). Consequently, a bearer instrument can be negotiated by a voluntary transfer of the instrument from one person to another. Because the person who receives the instrument will be in possession of bearer paper, he will be its holder.

But bearer paper may also be negotiated through an involuntary transfer of possession. Suppose, for instance, that A issued a check payable to "cash" to B. If C obtains the check by illegally picking B's pocket, C will be in possession of bearer paper and, therefore, its "holder."

PROBLEM 3.2

Under which of the following circumstances has the instrument been negotiated?

> a. *Ima Holder is in possession of a check signed and given to her by the drawer, Dan Drawer that says "Pay to the order of bearer $50."*

> b. *Same as "a," but Ima gives the check to her friend Sally to pay for tickets to the theater that Sally has bought for her.*

> c. *Ima Holder is in possession of a check signed and issued by Dan Drawer that says "Pay to the order of cash $50." It drops out of her pocket book and is picked up by Fred Finder.*

> d. *Ima Holder is in possession of a note signed and given to her by Marty Maker that says "I promise to pay bearer $50." The note is stolen from her desk by Tom Thief.*

2. *Negotiation of Order Paper — Indorsement Plus Change of Possession*

If an instrument is payable to the order of an identified person, the instrument is referred to an "order paper." To be a holder of order paper, a person must be in physical possession of the instrument, and must be the person to whom the instrument is payable. If A issues order paper by delivering it to B, the instrument will usually be payable to the order of B. For the instrument to be negotiated to C, two things have to happen: (1) physical possession of the instrument has to be transferred to C; and (2) the instrument must *either* (a) be changed so that it is made payable to C, *or* (b) transformed from order paper to bearer paper. Once these two things happen, C will be a holder because he will be in physical possession of an instrument that is either payable to him or that is bearer paper. Physical possession can be transferred to C voluntarily — i.e., through transfer of the instrument — or involuntarily.

The question that remains is: how can the instrument be changed so that it is payable to C or so that it is bearer paper? The answer is through an "indorsement." An "indorsement" is generally defined by § 3-204(a) as a signature, other than that of a maker, drawer, or acceptor,

that alone or accompanied by other words is made on an instrument

Note: The signature *must be on the instrument itself*, usually on the reverse side, or on a paper affixed to the instrument. See discussion of an *allonge* later in this chapter.

for the purpose of (i) negotiating the instrument, (ii) restricting payment of the instrument, or (iii) incurring indorser's liability on the instrument.

Note: Regardless of the signer's actual intent, a signature and any accompanying words constitute an indorsement unless it is unambiguously clear that the signature was not intended as an indorsement.

Blank and Special Indorsements

Indorsements are categorized as blank or special. If the indorser merely signs his own name on the instrument and does not specify any particular payee, the indorsement is said to be an "indorsement in blank" or a "blank indorsement." An instrument that is payable to the order of a particular person can be transformed into bearer paper if that particular person indorses the instrument in blank. After this blank indorsement, the instrument, as bearer paper, can be negotiated by transfer of possession alone. *See* §§ 3-109(c), 3-205(b). If, however, an instrument is payable to the order of one person, A, then the blank indorsement of some other person, B, does not transform the instrument from order paper to bearer paper. Instead, the instrument remains order paper, payable to the order of A.

If the indorser specifies the person to whom (or to whose order) the instrument is to be payable, the indorsement is said to be a "special indorsement." Suppose A issues an instrument payable to the order of B, and B wants to negotiate this instrument to C. As mentioned above, it would be possible for B to indorse in blank and transfer the instrument to C. In this case, C would be a holder because he would be in possession of bearer paper. Alternatively, B can specially indorse the instrument by writing "Pay to C" and signing it. In this case, the instrument is still order paper, but it is payable to the order of C. After this special indorsement, the instrument can be negotiated to C by transfer of possession alone. This transfer of possession could be accomplished by a voluntary transfer of the instrument from B to C or even by an involuntary transfer of possession (such as if C stole the indorsed check from B).

> **NOTE:** Bearer paper is very risky because anyone in possession of it is a holder and can enforce it in her own name. To address this risk, the Code allows a holder to convert a blank indorsement into a special indorsement simply by writing "Pay to [the holder's name]" above the signature of the indorser in blank. Instead of her own name, the holder may write the name of any person to whom the holder wishes the instrument to run. *See* § 3-205(c).

PROBLEM 3.3

Paula Payee is in possession of a check signed and issued by Dan Drawer that says "Pay to the order of Paula Payee $50" and a note signed and issued by Marty Maker that says "I promise to pay to the order of Paula Payee $50." What must Paula do to negotiate these instruments to her friend Sally and make Sally a holder?

PROBLEM 3.4

Decide whether there has been a negotiation to Iva Gottit in each of the following cases:

> *a. A check is made payable to the order of Paula Payee. Paula signs the check on the back by writing "Pay to the order of Sally Friend /s/ Paula Payee" and delivers it to Sally. Sally simply hands it over to Iva.*

> *b. A check is made payable to the order of Paula Payee. Paula simply signs her name on the back of the check and delivers it to Sally. Sally simply hands it over to Iva.*

c. *A check is made payable to the order of Paula Payee. Paula simply signs her name on the back of the check and delivers it to Sally. Iva steals the check from Sally's pocketbook.*

d. *A check is made payable to the order of Paula Payee. Paula signs the check on the back by writing "Pay to the order of Sally Friend /s/ Paula Payee" and delivers it to Sally. Sally then writes "Pay Iva Gottit /s/ Sally Friend" and gives it to Iva. Note that Sally did not write "Pay to the order of Iva Gottit." Read § 3-205 carefully.*

e. *A check is made payable to the order of Paula Payee and has been signed by Paula on the back in blank and delivered to Sally Friend.* order —*Sally writes the words "Pay to Sally Friend" above Paula Payee's signature. She then accidentally loses the check and Iva finds it.*

f. *A check is made payable to the order of Paula Payee. The check is stolen by Frank Forger, who indorses it "Paula Payee" in an attempt to negotiate it. Frank gives the check to Sally as payment for some items she had sold him. Sally uses the check to pay Iva for theatre tick-* — holder *ets Iva had bought for her. Both Sally and Iva were completely unaware that the check had been stolen.*

C. *Restrictive and Non-Restrictive Indorsements*

Indorsements (whether blank or special) can also be categorized as restrictive or non-restrictive. A restrictive indorsement tries to limit the rights and powers transferred in the instrument by placing restrictions on the way the proceeds of the instrument are to be applied or paid. Section 3-205 describes four types of indorsements that attempt to be restrictive. An instrument purports to be restrictive if it:

a. states that payment is limited to a particular person or that further transfer of the instrument is prohibited;

b. is conditional;

c. includes the words "for collection," "for deposit," or like terms indicating a purpose of having the item collected for the indorser or a particular account; or

d. otherwise states that it is for the benefit or use of the indorser or of another person.

Restrictions on Further Transfer

The Code specifically provides that indorsements purporting to prohibit further transfer are not effective to prevent further transfer or negotiation of the instrument. *See* § 3-205(a). Although such indorsements rarely appear, when they do occur, holders may completely ignore the purported restriction. Thus, an indorsement that reads "Pay *A* only" is treated as if it read "Pay *A*" or "Pay to the order of *A*" and can be further negotiated with *A*'s proper indorsement.

Conditional Indorsements

A conditional indorsement imposes a condition that must be met before the instrument will be paid.

EXAMPLE: An instrument may be indorsed

> Pay Bob Jones upon successful completion of the library project.
>
>   /s/ John Smith

Such an *indorsement* does not affect the negotiability of an instrument since, to be negotiable, the instrument need be an unconditional promise or order to pay only *at the time it is issued or first comes into the possession of a holder. See* § 3-104(a)(1). Furthermore, under § 3-206(b), a conditional indorsement does not affect the right of the indorsee to enforce the instrument. Thus, the indorsee may enforce the instrument against a party other than his indorser even though the indorsee is well aware that the condition has not been fulfilled.

Furthermore, § 3-206(b) states that if a person pays an instrument or takes it for value or collection, that person "may disregard the condition, and the rights and liabilities of that person are not affected by whether the condition has been fulfilled." Although this language is *arguably* ambiguous, it seems *at a minimum* to provide that even if the conditional indorsement is not satisfied, the instrument is properly payable and a person taking the instrument for value or collection (if the other criteria of § 3-302 are satisfied) could qualify as a holder in due course as long as they did not *know* that the condition was not fulfilled.

Under Former § 3-206, conditional indorsements were treated like indorsements for deposit or collection, to be discussed below. Section 3-206(b) rejects that approach and makes the conditional indorsement ineffective.

"For Collection" or "For Deposit" Indorsements

Indorsements that include the words "for collection," "for deposit," or similar terms are by far the most common of the restrictive indorsements. These indorsements restrict the ways in which certain parties to whom the instrument is transferred or presented may give value for or pay the instrument.

A depositary bank, including a payor bank acting as a depositary bank or any other transferee (except an intermediary bank), must pay or apply any value given by it for the instrument consistently with the indorsement. *See* § 4-105 for definitions of "depositary," "intermediary," and "payor banks." Failure to do so will constitute a conversion of the instrument. For a general discussion of conversion liability, see Chapter 11. The same rule applies to a payor bank that takes the instrument for immediate payment over the counter. See § 3-206(c). Compliance with the restrictive indorsement allows the transferee to become a holder in due course, presuming the transferee has complied with all other holder in due course requirements. *See* § 3-206(e).

Intermediary and payor banks, other than those that make immediate payment over the counter, are treated differently with respect to restrictive indorsements because they must handle so many negotiable instruments on a daily basis often using automated systems. The collection process would be greatly impeded if these intermediary and payor banks had to examine each such instrument carefully to ensure that there was no restrictive indorsement or, if there was, to ensure that they complied with its instructions. Section 3-206(c)(4) provides:

> Except as otherwise provided in paragraph (3) [dealing with payor banks that are also the depositary bank or that take an instrument for immediate payment over the counter], a payor bank or intermediary bank may disregard the indorsement and is not liable if the proceeds of the instrument are not received by the indorser or applied consistently with the indorsement.

Thus, the only bank affected by a restrictive indorsement (made by a party other than a collecting bank) is the first bank to deal with the instrument. When a customer deposits a check with a depositary bank, the teller should examine the check for a restrictive indorsement, as should the teller at a drawee bank when someone presents the check directly for payment.

Most commonly, a "for deposit only" restrictive indorsement is effectuated by writing the instruction above the indorser's signature. If done in this way, most courts have held that without additional specification or directives, this instructs the depositary bank to deposit the funds *only* into the payee's (indorser's) account. The payee can direct that the funds be deposited into another person's account by specifying the particular account name or number in the restriction (e.g., "for deposit only into account of John Doe" or "for deposit only into account # 246810").

STATE OF QATAR v. FIRST AMERICAN BANK OF VIRGINIA

885 F.Supp 849 (E.D. Virginia, 1995).

MEMORANDUM OPINION

ELLIS, District Judge.

At issue in this sequel to State of Qatar v. First American Bank of Virginia ("Qatar I ") is the meaning and legal significance of the phrase "for deposit only" following an indorsement on the back of a check. More specifically, the question presented is whether a depositary bank complies with the restrictive indorsement "for deposit only" when it deposits a check bearing that restriction into any person's account, or whether that restriction requires a depositary bank to deposit the check's proceeds only into the account of the named payee. For the reasons that follow, the Court holds that the unqualified language "for deposit only" following an indorsement on the back of a check requires a depositary bank to place the check's proceeds into the payee's account, and the bank violates that restrictive indorsement when it credits the check to any other account.

I.

The facts underlying this case are more fully set forth in Qatar I and are only briefly reiterated here. Plaintiffs are the State of Qatar and certain of its agencies (collectively, "Qatar"). From approximately 1986 to 1992, one of Qatar's employees, Bassam Salous, defrauded his employer by having checks drawn on Qatar's account in purported payment of false or duplicate invoices that he had created. Although all of the unauthorized checks were made payable to individuals and entities other than Salous, he nonetheless successfully deposited the checks into his own personal accounts with Defendant First American Bank of Virginia ("First American") and Central Fidelity Banks, Inc. (collectively, "the depositary banks"). . . .

After Qatar discovered this fraudulent scheme in 1992, it brought suit against the depositary banks for conversion. These banks succeeded on summary judgment in establishing that they were not liable as a matter of law with respect to two categories of checks in dispute,[1] and they prevailed on a factual issue at trial that relieved them from liability for yet another category of checks.

---

[1] [4] The four categories of checks originally in dispute were:

    (1) checks bearing no indorsement at all;

    (2) checks bearing a forged indorsement only;

    (3) checks bearing a forged indorsement, followed by the words "for deposit only";

    (4) checks bearing a forged indorsement, followed by the words "for deposit only", followed by Salous' personal account number.

In Qatar I, the Court ruled that the depositary banks were not liable as a matter of law for the first two categories of checks. 880 F.Supp. at 468.

Only one category of checks remains in dispute. These checks all bear the forged indorsement of the payee named on the face of the check, followed by a stamped "for deposit only" restriction. In Qatar I, the Court denied the depositary banks' motion for summary judgment with respect to these checks on the ground that the depositary banks could be held liable for applying the proceeds of the checks in violation of the restrictive indorsements. Qatar I, 880 F.Supp. at 469, 470-71. Specifically, the Court stated:

[W]hile the forged signature presented no barrier to payment given the effect of [U.C.C.] § 3-405, [*Editor's Note: Section 3-405 makes a forged indorsement by an employee entrusted with responsibility with respect to a negotiable instrument an effective indorsement of the payee's name*] the accompanying restriction ("FOR DEPOSIT ONLY") provided a clear instruction to the depositary banks to deposit the funds only into the account of the last indorser — here, the named payee. The Court did not hold the depositary banks liable as a matter of law with respect to these checks, but decided to await the banks' presentation of defenses, if any, at trial. At trial, the depositary banks raised no defenses, but instead challenged for the first time the Court's assumption in Qatar I that the phrase "for deposit only", without further specification, directs a depositary bank to deposit the funds only into the account of the named payee. An indorsement in this form, they argued, is far less restrictive, as it merely directs that the check's proceeds be deposited in an account, not that they be deposited into a particular account. Thus, the depositary banks urged, they fully complied with the restrictive indorsements on these checks when they deposited the proceeds into Salous' account. Although this issue properly should have been raised at the summary judgment stage, the Court permitted the parties to research the matter and submit post-trial legal memoranda regarding this final, narrow issue. Qatar and First American did so, and the matter is now ripe for disposition.

II.

It is now established that First American may be liable to Qatar for handling a check's proceeds in violation of a restrictive indorsement . . . Under § 3-205(c) of the pre-1993 Uniform Commercial Code,[2] restrictive indorsements are defined to "include the words 'for collection,' 'for deposit,' 'pay any bank,' or like terms signifying a purpose of deposit or collection." Thus, the U.C.C. makes clear that the phrase "for deposit only" is, in fact, a restrictive indorsement. But the Code does not define "for deposit only" or specify what bank conduct would be inconsistent with that restriction.[3] Nor does Virginia decisional law provide any

---

[2] [9] Article three of the U.C.C. governs the law of negotiable instruments and was substantially amended effective January 1, 1993. Because all of the relevant events surrounding this case occurred prior to 1993, the former U.C.C. provisions apply here. All U.C.C. citations are to Va.Code, Title 8.3, amended by Va.Code, Title 8.3A (Supp.1994).

[3] [4] The amended Code provision on restrictive indorsements provides more guidance on the meaning of "for deposit only." § 3A-206. Specifically, in describing particular types of restrictive indorsements, § 3A-206(c)(ii) refers to indorsements "using the words 'for deposit,' 'for collection,' or other words indicating a purpose of having the instrument collected by a bank for the indorser or for a particular account."

guidance on this issue. As a result, reference to decisional law from other jurisdictions is appropriate.

Not surprisingly, most courts confronted with this issue have held that the restriction "for deposit only", without additional specification or directive, instructs depositary banks to deposit the funds only into the payee's account. [citations omitted] In addition, commentators on commercial law uniformly agree that the function of such a restriction is to ensure that the checks' proceeds be deposited into the payee's account. [citations omitted]

This construction of "for deposit only" is commercially sensible and is adopted here. The clear purpose of the restriction is to avoid the hazards of indorsing a check in blank. Pursuant to former § 3-204(2), a check indorsed in blank "becomes payable to bearer." It is, essentially, cash. Thus, a payee who indorses her check in blank runs the risk of having the check stolen and freely negotiated before the check reaches its intended destination. To protect against this vulnerability, the payee can add the restriction "for deposit only" to the indorsement, and the depositary bank is required to handle the check in a manner consistent with that restriction. § 3-206(3). And in so adding the restriction, the payee's intent plainly is to direct that the funds be deposited into her own account, not simply that the funds be deposited into some account . . . Any other construction of the phrase "for deposit only" is illogical and without commercial justification or utility. Indeed, it is virtually impossible to imagine a scenario in which a payee cared that her check be deposited, but was indifferent with respect to the particular account to which the funds would be credited.

First American opposes this result, contending that the unqualified restriction "for deposit only" merely requires a depositary bank to deposit the check into an account, irrespective of which one. In support of this proposition, First American cites only one case, Western Assurance Co. v. Star Financial Bank of Indianapolis, 3 F.3d 1129 (7th Cir. 1993). In Western Assurance, Western Assurance Co. ("Western") and Connors Consulting Group ("CCG") were working together on a contract and decided to open separate accounts at the same bank. Within each account, the companies maintained signature cards that entitled certain officers of either company to endorse checks and perform particular transactions with respect to that account. When their relationship deteriorated, Western sued the bank for permitting an officer of CCG to deposit into CCG's account checks made payable to Western and bearing the restriction "for deposit only." The Seventh Circuit panel in Western Assurance held that the bank behaved in a commercially reasonable manner in depositing the checks into CCG's account because the signature cards vested the CCG official with apparent authority to negotiate the checks. Furthermore, and of particular significance here, the panel held that the bank did not violate the restrictive indorsement "for deposit only" in depositing the Western checks into CCG's account. In so holding, the Seventh Circuit panel noted that "[t]he endorsements . . . did not by their terms require deposit into one of Western's accounts." Rather, the panel determined, the "for deposit only" restriction simply "prevented anyone from negotiating the checks other than for deposit." Similarly, First American argues, the "for deposit only" restrictions on the checks at issue here directed only that the funds be deposited, an instruction with which First American complied by placing the checks' proceeds into Salous' personal account.

Qatar seeks to distinguish Western Assurance's holding regarding the meaning of "for deposit only" based on the fact that the depositor in that case had apparent authority pursuant to the signature cards to deposit the checks into CCG's account. However inviting, this distinction is ultimately unpersuasive. While the factual context in Western Assurance is certainly distinguishable from the case at bar, the Seventh Circuit panel there did not tailor its holding concerning the legal effect of "for deposit only" to the narrow circumstances of that case. The Western Assurance panel held that the bank acted consistently with the "for deposit only" restrictive indorsement not because of the CCG officer's apparent authority, a separate issue in the case, but rather because the bank deposited the funds. Thus, Western Assurance squarely supports First American's position here and must be confronted.

This stated, the portion of Western Assurance dealing with the legal significance of "for deposit only" is nonetheless unconvincing here. The Western Assurance panel cites no authority for its conclusion, nor does it support its ruling with any significant discussion or analysis. While it is true that the literal command of the bare words "for deposit only" is simply that the check be deposited, such rigid reliance on linguistics in disregard of practical considerations and plain common sense is both unwarranted and imprudent. This is especially so given that the individuals writing and relying upon these restrictive indorsements are not apt to be well versed in the subtleties of negotiable instruments law. As evidenced by numerous authorities, and common experience, the unqualified phrase "for deposit only" is almost universally taken to mean "for deposit only into the payee's account." To disregard this common understanding in support of an illogical construction is to elevate form over substance. First American's argument to the contrary is a little like saying that a store sign reading "shirts and shoes required" does not restrict a trouser less man from entering the store.

Finally, it is worth noting that the new revisions to the negotiable instruments provisions of the UCC support the result reached here. Although these revisions are inapplicable to this case, the commentary following § 3A-206 states that the new subdivision dealing with "for deposit only" and like restrictions "continues previous law." § 3A-206 comment 3. Shortly thereafter, the commentary provides an example in which a check bears the words "for deposit only" above the indorsement. In those circumstances, the commentary states, the depositary bank acts inconsistently with the restrictive indorsement where it deposits the check into an account other than that of the payee. Id. Although the restriction in that example precedes the signature, whereas the restrictions on the checks at issue here follow the signature, this distinction is immaterial. The clear meaning of the restriction in both circumstances is that the funds should be placed into the payee's account.

Therefore, First American violated the restrictive indorsements in depositing into Bassam Salous' account checks made payable to others and restrictively indorsed "for deposit only." Pursuant to the holding in Qatar I, then, First American is liable to Qatar for conversion in the amount of the total face values of these checks.

NOTES

1. In *Mid-Atlantic Tennis Cts. v. Citizens Bank & Trust Co.*, 658 F.Supp. 140, 143 (D.Md.1987), the court even held that the words "for deposit only" on the back of a check, *without an accompanying indorsement,* required that the depositary bank credit the account of the payee (depositing a check's proceeds into the payee's account is "the only treatment consistent with a 'for deposit only' restrictive endorsement made by, or (even purportedly) on behalf of, a named payee").

2. The more difficult question arises when the words "for deposit only" follow the indorsement, either on the same line or below the signature. The court addressed this question in *Qatar, supra,* and held that a distinction between the restriction preceding the signature and following the signature is "immaterial." It wrote "[t]he clear meaning of the restriction in both circumstances is that the funds should be placed into the payee's account." *Id.* at 854. The result in *Qatar* makes a great deal of sense, especially since the indorsement of the payee was forged by the person who then added the restriction and had the funds deposited into his own account. But a different situation arose in *La Junta State Bank v. Travis*, 727 P.2d 48 (Colo. 1986) which illustrates the difficulty of such a blanket approach to the problem as suggested in *Qatar*.

In *La Junta,* a certified check was issued to Katherine Warnock, who indorsed the check in blank and gave it to her attorney Jerry Quick. Quick then wrote the words "For deposit only" below Warnock's indorsement without signing his own name and submitted the check to his bank to be deposited into his account. When the depositary bank was sued for conversion by Warnock's estate, the court noted that when the bank received what appeared to be a restrictive indorsement by Ms. Warnock, it perhaps should have at least made an inquiry into whether depositing the check into an account other than the indorser's was proper. However, the court found no liability on the part of the depositary bank, because, in fact, depositing the check in Quick's account was appropriate. The court said that since the check was bearer paper at the time Quick received it, as a holder, "he was free to direct its deposit in any manner he elected." When the words "deposit only" were added by Quick on his own behalf, it was a restrictive indorsement by Quick and the bank "owed a duty to [him] to honor his restrictive indorsement." *Id.* at 55.

Thus, although the back of the checks looked the same in each of these cases — the payee's indorsement followed on a line below by the words "for deposit only" — whether the indorsement was to be treated as a restrictive indorsement, and if so, to whose account must the amount be deposited, was a consequence of the circumstances surrounding the transaction. Neither the case law nor the Code's provisions provide certainty as how to resolve the issue.

3. The *La Junta* decision implies that a restriction can be effective even if it is supplied by a holder who does not also indorse the instrument himself. However, the Code is not so clear as to whether this is true. Although the Code specifies that a holder can change a blank indorsement to a special indorsement pursuant to § 3-205(c), the Code does not say that the same is true with respect to changing an unrestricted indorsement to a restricted one. An argument can therefore be made that a restriction is of no effect unless the person who makes the restriction also adds an indorsement to it.

Trust Indorsements:

"Trust indorsements" are those that indicate that the indorsee holds the instrument for the benefit of a third party.

EXAMPLES:

"Pay Tom Trustee in trust for Billy Beneficiary."

"Pay Tom for the benefit of Billy."

"Pay Tom as agent for Billy."

D. Qualified Indorsements

Indorsements can also be categorized as "qualified" or "unqualified." A party who indorses an instrument will normally incur secondary liability on that instrument, as provided in § 3-415(a). That is, if the instrument has been dishonored and the indorser has received any necessary notice of dishonor, the indorser is obligated to pay an appropriate party according to the tenor of the instrument at the time he indorsed it. The indorser may, however, disclaim such contractual liability by affixing a qualified indorsement to the instrument. *See* § 3-415(b). The way this is almost always done is to include the words "without recourse" before (most commonly) or after the signature. Other words to that effect may be used, but the disclaimer must appear on the instrument itself; it cannot be proven by parol evidence since the disclaimer varies the written contract of indorsement.

Some courts, under Former Article 3, held that an indorser may also use the recourse language to *limit*, as opposed to disclaim, her liability on the instrument. There is no language in Revised Article 3 that would seem to prohibit this interpretation. In *Northern Trust Co. v. E. T. Clancy Export Corp.,* 612 F.Supp.

712, 716 (N.D.Ill. 1985), the indorser signed the instrument and added the following: "90% without recourse, 10% with recourse." The court found the indorser secondarily liable on the instrument but limited that which could be collected from the indorser to ten percent of the total amount payable on the note. 612 F.Supp. at 717. Be sure to understand that the indorser in the above example is transferring the *entire* instrument so as not to contravene § 3-203(d), which provides, "If a transferor purports to transfer less than the entire instrument, negotiation of the instrument does not occur." The indorser here is merely limiting its liability on the instrument. While the holder is still entitled to the face amount of the instrument, the holder can receive no more than ten percent of it from *this* particular indorser pursuant to his § 3-415 obligation.

E. More About Indorsements

1. Location:

Normally the indorsement appears on the reverse side of the instrument, but it can appear anywhere on the instrument. The Code provides that any signature on an instrument is an indorsement if the instrument *itself* does not indicate an unambiguous intent of the signer not to sign as an indorser. *See* § 3-204. To determine intent, one might consider

(1) **the accompanying words**, e.g., "I, John Doe, promise to pay . . ." clearly indicates that John Doe is a maker or "Jane Doe, witness" indicates Jane has signed for a purpose other than to incur liability;

(2) **the nature of the instrument**, e.g., A traveler's check very often requires the countersignature of the owner as a means of verifying the identity of the person negotiating the check;

(3) **the place of the signature**, e.g., according to long-standing custom and usage, a signature in the lower right-hand corner indicates an intent to sign as maker of a note or drawer of a draft. Nonetheless, this indication may, in a particular case, be outweighed by other factors. For example, assume a note reads as follows:

> I, Mary Maker, promise to pay to the order of Paul Payee $500.
>
>   /s/ Mary Maker
>   /s/ Fred Friend

Under these circumstances, despite signing in the lower right corner, Fred would be liable as an indorser and not as a maker. This is because the promissory language of the note indicates that only Mary is undertaking primary liability to pay the instrument. *See Binford v. L. W. Lictenberger Estate*, 62 Or.App.

439, 660 P.2d 1077, 1078 (1983)); or (4) **other circumstances** (e.g., the drawee signs in an unusual place and there is no visible reason to sign at all. The drawee is an acceptor.)

The indorsement must, of course, appear somewhere *on* the instrument itself. It may also appear on a separate piece of paper, which is affixed to the instrument. (This is called an "allonge.") It is not entirely clear, however, to what extent a separate sheet of paper needs to be affixed to the instrument in order to qualify as an allonge. The Negotiable Instruments Law allowed an allonge to be on a paper "attached to the negotiable instrument." Former § 3-202(2) required that an allonge had to be "so firmly attached" as "to become a part thereof." At least one case reasoned that this change in language manifested a "clear intent" to restrict the use of allonges. *Estrada v. River Oaks Bank & Trust Company*, 550 S.W.2d 719 (Tex.Civ.App. 1977). Section 3-204(a), however, represents a return to more general language. It states simply that "a paper affixed to the instrument is a part of the instrument." Consequently, if particular forms of affixation were sufficient under prior law, they should be sufficient under § 3-204(a). Thus, a paper pasted to an instrument should still constitute an allonge. *Crutchfield v. Easton*, 13 Ala. 337 (1848). The Supreme Court of Colorado has held that a paper stapled to an instrument can be an allonge, because it is the modern equivalent of paste and glue. *Lamison v. Commercial Credit Corp.*, 187 Colo. 382, 531 P.2d 966 (1975). *But see Estrada v. River Oaks Bank & Trust Co.*, 550 S.W.2d 719 (Tex.Civ.App.14th Dist. 1977) (even if there were no room for an additional indorsement on the notes, a paper stapled to four notes cannot be an allonge to all four notes; the paper cannot be considered sufficiently affixed to each of the notes). Prior to enactment of § 3-204(a), pins or clips were held to be insufficient. *See, e.g., Tallahassee Bank & Trust Company v. Raines*, 125 Ga.App. 263, 187 S.E.2d 320 (1972) (a separate paper pinned or clipped to an instrument is not an allonge); *See also*, Comment 3 to Former § 3-202. Similarly, separate sheets of paper that are transferred together with an instrument, *Adams v. Madison Realty & Development*, 853 F.2d 163 (3rd Cir. 1988), deposit slips submitted with an instrument, *Society National Bank v. Security Federal Savings & Loan*, 71 Ohio St.3d 321, 643 N.E.2d 1090 (1994), and a separate paper folded together with a promissory note, *National Bank of Columbus v. Leonard*, 91 Ga. 805, 18 S.E. 32 (1893), have been held not to constitute allonges.

Contrary to the majority of holdings under previous case law, UCC Comment 1 to § 3-204 states that an indorsement on an allonge is valid even though there is sufficient space on the instrument for an indorsement.

2. *Deviation of Indorsement from That Called For*

Frequently an instrument may be made payable to a payee whose name is misspelled or whose legal name differs from the name designated on the instrument. The Code allows the payee to indorse in the name as it appears or in his own name or both. If the indorsement is made only as it appears on the instrument, although legally effective, a holder may have some difficulty proving the identity of the indorser since the indorser's proof of identification will not match the name he signed. If the indorsement is made solely in the indorser's true name, this brings into question the veracity of the indorsement (since it may not match the name of the person identified by the order) and, therefore, whether the party in possession of the instrument is a person entitled to enforce it. In order to avoid these problems, the Code provides that any person paying or giving value for the instrument may demand a signature in both names. *See* § 3-204(d).

3. *Multiple Payees*

An instrument may be made payable to the order of more than one person.

PROBLEM 3.5

Under each of the following circumstances, state who must indorse the instrument in order to negotiate it:

a. *"Pay to the order of Jane Doe or John Doe"* either

b. *"Pay to the order of Jane Doe and John Doe"* both

c. *"Pay to the order of Jane Doe and/or John Doe"* either

See § 3-110(d)

4. *Depositary Banks No Longer Need To Supply Missing Indorsements*

Under usual circumstances, a necessary indorsement may be made by only the actual payee of an instrument (or the person to whom it has been specially indorsed) or the authorized representative of any such person. Under Former Article 4, however, when an instrument had been deposited in a bank for collection without having been properly indorsed, the depositary bank could supply any necessary indorsement unless the item contained the words "payee's indorsement required" or the like. *See* Former § 4-205(1). Alternatively, the depositary bank could indicate on the item that it was deposited by a customer or credited to his account and that would suffice as the customer's indorsement. *Id.*

Section 4-205 makes this unnecessary by providing that a depositary bank becomes a holder of an item at the time it receives the item for collection if its customer was a holder of the item, whether or not the customer has indorsed it. The bank need not supply the indorsement. Furthermore, if all other requirements of § 3-302 are met, the bank can be a holder in due course.

Chapter 4

PARTIES ENTITLED TO ENFORCE
AN INSTRUMENT

As will be discussed in Chapter 5, there are a variety of ways in which a person may be liable with respect to a negotiable instrument. This chapter, however, focuses on the "persons entitled to enforce" such obligations, who are usually the plaintiffs in our cases. Section 3-301 states that a

> "Person entitled to enforce" an instrument means (i) the holder of the instrument, (ii) a nonholder in possession of the instrument who has the rights of a holder, or (iii) a person not in possession of the instrument who is entitled to enforce the instrument pursuant to Section 3-309 or 3-418(d). . . .

As a general rule, only a person who fits within this definition can successfully force a party to an instrument to fulfill its obligation on the instrument. The language of § 3-301 makes it clear that one need not be a holder to enforce an instrument. Although § 3-301 defines three categories of persons entitled to enforce, a person's precise rights depend on the category to which he belongs. For example, pursuant to § 3-308, a holder can essentially establish a prima facie case simply by producing the instrument. In addition, a holder has the power to make his transferee a holder.

A Holder — Generally

A "holder" of a negotiable instrument is defined as

> the person in possession of a negotiable instrument that is payable either to bearer or to an identified person that is the person in possession. § 1-201(21)(A).

Thus, depending on the nature of the instrument, there are two different tests to determine if a party is a holder of an instrument. If the instrument is "bearer paper," then the person in possession of the instrument is the holder. If the instrument is payable to a specified person ("order paper"), then only that specified person may be its holder, and he must be in possession of the instrument. As discussed in Chapter 3, a person may become a holder of an instrument when the instrument is **issued**, **negotiated**, or, in some cases, **otherwise transferred** to her.

PROBLEM 4.1

Determine whether Amy A. Holter is a holder in each of the following circumstances. If she is a holder, state whether she became a holder because the instrument was either issued, negotiated or otherwise transferred to her.

a. *A check drawn by Dan Drawer is made payable to Paula Payee. Paula signs her name on the back and gives it to Amy.*

b. *A note, signed by Marty Maker and made payable to the order of Amy A. Holter, is delivered to her by Marty.*

c. *A note, signed by Marty Maker and made payable to the order of Amy A. Holter, is placed in an envelope addressed to Amy and brought by Marty to Amy's office. Amy is not in, so Marty leaves it with Amy's receptionist, Seeyu Later. Seeyu decides to start a new life and takes the envelope and its contents and heads for Mexico. [Review question: Has this instrument been issued?]*

d. *A note is signed by Marty Maker and made payable to the order of Amy A. Holter. Marty leaves it on his desk. The wind blows the note out the window, and Bystander Bob, Amy's friend, finds it. Bob gives the note to Amy. [Review question: Has this instrument been issued?]*

e. *A check, drawn by Dan Drawer is made payable to Paula Payee. Dan leaves it on his desk. The wind blows the check out the window, and Bystander Bill finds it. Unbeknownst to Amy, Bill signs Paula's name on the back and gives the check to Amy in exchange for some flowers that Amy is selling.*

f. *A check, drawn by Dan Drawer is made payable to bearer. Dan puts it in his pocket. While walking down the street, Dan is expertly relieved of his check by a pickpocket named Peter. Peter gives the check to Amy in exchange for some flowers that Amy is selling.*

PROBLEM 4.2

Donald Drawstring writes a check for $50 made payable to Harry Holstein. Donald gives the check to Harry, who then signs his name on the back of the check and gives it to his son Elmo. Elmo puts the check in his jacket pocket and leaves to go to the store. The check falls from his pocket and is found by Lucky Lenny. Lenny gives the check to his buddy Hobo Hal, to settle an old, old debt. Hal brings the check to Sam's Hock Shop, where Sam takes the check from Hal and gives Hal $50 cash. Sam writes the words "Pay to Sam's Hock Shop" over Harry's signature and then gives the check to the stock boy, Sonny, to bring upstairs to the bookkeeper, Mrs. Devitt. Sonny gives the check to Mrs. Devitt. On her lunch break, Mrs. Devitt brings the check to First State Bank, where Sam's Hock Shop has an account and she gives the check to Tom Teller and asks him to deposit it in Sam's Hock Shop's account. The check is so deposited and later presented to

Donald's bank, DD Bank, for payment and paid. For every person whose name appears in this scenario, including business entities and banks, determine whether that person was a holder of this instrument.

Other Parties Entitled to Enforce

A "Nonholder in Possession of the Instrument Who Has the Rights of a Holder"

Section 3-301(ii) states that a nonholder in possession of the instrument who has the rights of a holder is also a person entitled to enforce the instrument. The UCC Comment to § 3-301 includes as a "nonholder in possession of the instrument," a person who acquired the rights of a holder by subrogation or under § 3-203(a).

Although not specifically defined in the Code, "subrogation" is an equitable principle involving "the substitution of one person in place of another with reference to a lawful claim, demand, or right, so that he who is substituted succeeds to the rights of the other in relation to the debt or claim, and its rights, remedies, or securities." *J.J. Schaefer Livestock Hauling, Inc. v. Gretna State Bank* 428 N.W.2d 185, 229 Neb. 580 (1988). Subrogation issues arise most often in negotiable instrument cases where a surety pays off the obligation of the principal to the creditor and then seeks to "stand in the shoes" of the creditor with respect to any rights the creditor had against the debtor or in any collateral held as security for the debt. It differs from an assignment in that it does not arise from contract, but is imposed by equity to increase the probability of the surety's obtaining reimbursement.

Section 3-203(a) concerns instances in which an instrument is delivered by someone other than its issuer for the purpose of giving the person to whom it is delivered (i.e., the transferee) the right to enforce the instrument. Normally, such a transfer is accomplished by negotiation. But if the instrument is payable to a specified person other than the transferee, and that specified person fails to indorse the instrument, the transfer is not a negotiation, and the transferee does not become a holder. Nevertheless, § 3-203(a), otherwise known as the "shelter doctrine," generally provides that, even in such a case, the transferee acquires all of the rights to enforce the instrument that his transferor had. Therefore, if his transferor was a holder, the transferee — although not himself a holder — obtains the *rights* of a holder to enforce the instrument. But, because the transferee is not a holder, his mere production of the instrument does not entitle him to a presumption, under § 3-308, that he is entitled to enforce it. He must offer proof as to how he obtained the instrument and as to how § 3-203(a) applies.

The 2002 Revisions to the Comment to § 3-301 state that the phrase, "a nonholder in possession of the instrument who has the rights of a holder" includes "both a remitter that has received an instrument from the issuer but has not yet transferred or negotiated the instrument to another person and also any other person who under applicable law is a successor to the holder or otherwise acquires the holder's rights."

PROBLEM 4.3

Dan Drawer draws a check payable to Paula Payee for $50, and gives it to her. Paula uses the check to purchase goods from Sam Shopowner, but forgets to indorse it over to him. Is Sam a holder? May he enforce the instrument? Assume that Sam, without either obtaining Paula's indorsement or indorsing the instrument himself, sent the check he received from Paula to the gas company to pay part of his monthly bill. Would the gas company be a holder? Would it be entitled to enforce the instrument?

Section 203(c) provides generally that if an order instrument is transferred for value and the transferee fails to become a holder because of the transferor's failure to indorse, the transferee has a specifically enforceable right to the transferor's unqualified indorsement.

PROBLEM 4.4

Pursuant to § 3-203(c), Sam, in Problem 4.3, has a specifically enforceable right to Paula's indorsement. Does the gas company also have that right? Read § 3-203(c) carefully. Does § 3-203(a) help?

A "Person Not in Possession of the Instrument Who Is Entitled To Enforce the Instrument Pursuant to § 3-309 or § 3-418(d)"

The pre-2002 version of 3-309 allows persons who are no longer in possession of instruments that have been lost, stolen, or destroyed to nevertheless qualify as persons entitled to enforce those instruments as long as certain conditions are met. First, the person seeking to enforce must have been in possession of the instrument and must have qualified as a person entitled to enforce it when the loss of possession occurred. Second, the reason the person is not in possession cannot be that it was lawfully seized from him or transferred by him. Finally, the person must be unable to obtain, through reasonable means, possession of the instrument because it was destroyed, its whereabouts cannot be determined, or it is in the wrongful possession of an unknown person or a person that cannot be found or who is not amenable to service of process.

NOTE: The foregoing paragraph describes the pre-2002 version of § 3-309, which, as this casebook goes to print, is the version effective in almost all jurisdictions. This version does not explicitly address the status of a person who — at the time the instrument was lost, destroyed or stolen — was not himself a person entitled to enforce the instrument, but who had acquired ownership — but not possession — of the instrument from a person who was entitled to enforce it. This scenario was addressed in *Dennis Joslin Company, LLC v. Robinson Broadcasting Corporation*, 977 F.Supp. 491, 33 UCC Rep.Serv.2d 1170 (D.C.Cir. 1997), in which the Federal Insurance Deposit Corporation (the FDIC), which was a person entitled to enforce the instrument, sold the instrument to 4M Corporation(4M) but lost the instrument before delivering it to 4M. The Court of Appeals for the District of Columbia Circuit ruled that the successor to 4M's rights (by way of assignment from 4M) did not qualify under § 3-309 as a person entitled to enforce the instrument because 4M did not have possession of the instrument at the time the instrument was lost.

Several courts have disagreed with the *Robinson Broadcasting Corporation* decision, at least as applied to the assignee of someone who was a person entitled to enforce a lost instrument. *See, e.g., Bobby D. Associates v. DiMarcantonio*, 2000 Pa.Super. 132, 751 A.2d 673, 41 UCC Rep.Serv.2d 878 (2000).

In 2002, the Conference of Commissioners on Uniform State Laws amended § 3-309 to reject the *Robinson Broadcasting Corporation* decision. The Revised 2002 version of § 3-309 specifically states that a person who directly or indirectly acquires ownership of an instrument from a person who was entitled to enforce the instrument when loss of possession occurred is treated the same way that the person entitled to enforce the instrument would have been treated. Thus, in Robinson Broadcasting Corporation, since the FDIC was the person entitled to enforce the instrument when the loss occurred, 4M was a person entitled to enforce the instrument under Revised 2002 § 3-309 and so, too, was 4M's assignee.

A person meeting the conditions of § 3-309 must prove the terms of the instrument and his right to enforce the instrument. If that proof is made, § 3-308 applies as if the person seeking enforcement had produced the instrument. The court may not, however, enter judgment in favor of a person seeking enforcement unless it finds that the obligor is adequately protected against loss that might occur by reason of a claim by another person to enforce the instrument. Adequate protection may be provided by any reasonable means, such as executing a written agreement to indemnify the payor, placing money in an escrow account, etc.

In certain circumstances, § 3-418 allows an acceptor or payor who has accepted or paid an instrument by mistake to revoke the acceptance or recover the payment from the person to whom or for whose benefit the payment was made. Under § 3-418(d), when that occurs, the instrument is deemed to have been dishonored, and the person from whom the payment was recovered has the rights of a person entitled to enforce the instrument.

Owners Without Possession Cannot Enforce

Other than when one of the specific exceptions described above applies, a person who has a claim of ownership in an instrument, but does not possess it, cannot enforce the instrument until possession is obtained. *See* UCC Comment 1 to § 3-203.

PROBLEM 4.5

Harry Holder is the owner and holder of an instrument made payable to him. He sells the instrument to Pam Purchaser but is unable to deliver immediate possession to her. Instead, Harry signs a document transferring all of his rights, title, and interest in the instrument to Pam. Is Pam a holder? Is she a person entitled to enforce the instrument pursuant to § 3-203 (the shelter doctrine)?

Persons in Wrongful Possession May Enforce

Just as a legitimate owner of an instrument may not — under the prevalent, pre-2002 version of § 3-309 — qualify as a person entitled to enforce if he never acquired possession of the instrument, a person with actual possession may be a "person entitled to enforce" even though she is not the rightful owner. A thief who has stolen and is in possession of an instrument payable to bearer is a holder and, thus, a "person entitled to enforce" the instrument even though she is not its rightful owner. This is easier to understand when one realizes that the term "person entitled to enforce" is a defined phrase. The drafters never intended the word "entitled" to connote a "legitimate," as opposed to an illegitimate, entitlement. Instead, they merely used the phrase for their convenience in articulating the applicable rules. Nevertheless, the rules protect against actual enforcement by someone who obtained his "person entitled to enforce" status wrongfully. Such a person, for instance, will not be a holder in due course and will be subject to any valid defense an obligor may raise, including proof that the instrument was stolen. Section 3-305(c). See discussion of defenses at Chapter 8. In addition, the thief will be subject to any claim to the instrument made by the instrument's rightful owner. Section 3-306.

Chapter 5
LIABILITY ON AN INSTRUMENT

In the previous chapter, we spoke about the usual plaintiffs in our cases, persons entitled to enforce the instrument. Now we begin our discussion about our usual defendants, persons with liability with respect to a negotiable instrument. There are three bases on which one may become liable with respect to a negotiable instrument:

a. Liability for having signed the instrument (obligation "on the instrument").

b. Liability for having transferred or presented the instrument (warranty liability); or

c. Liability for having wrongfully taken, retained, or paid the instrument (conversion liability).

Actions for breach of warranty or conversion, which are called actions "off the instrument," will be discussed later in Chapters 10 and 11.

Before discussing the potential liability with respect to a negotiable instrument, however, it is important to understand that liability on the instrument is ordinarily created to satisfy an underlying legal obligation. That obligation for which the instrument is given may take the form of a contract or some other transaction in which goods or services are exchanged for payment. The parties have duties and liabilities based on this transaction. Let's quickly discuss what effect taking a negotiable instrument has on the underlying obligation.

Underlying Obligation — Effect of Taking an Instrument

Pursuant to § 3-310, when one takes a negotiable instrument as payment for an underlying obligation, that obligation, absent any agreement to the contrary, is either discharged or suspended. Whether a discharge or suspension results depends on the nature of the instrument taken. If the instrument taken is a certified check, cashier's check, teller's check, or any other instrument of which a bank is the maker or acceptor, the underlying obligation is discharged unless there is an agreement to the contrary. In the event of a discharge, the only rights the person taking the instrument can enforce are those arising in connection with the instrument. Thus, the party taking the instrument must look to the bank and to any other parties liable on the instrument and not to the original obligor. Unless otherwise agreed, when an instrument other than a certified check, cashier's check, teller's check, or check on which a bank is liable as a maker or acceptor is taken for an underlying obligation, the underlying obligation is merely suspended. During such a suspension, the only rights the person taking the instrument can enforce are those arising in connection with the instrument. The suspension lasts until the instrument is either dishonored or paid. Use § 3-310 to do the following problems.

PROBLEM 5.1

Bernard Bernstein had all of his belongings moved from St. Louis to Chicago using Midway Monsters Movers ("MMM"). Bernard agreed to pay MMM $1,000, and the moving company requested to be paid upon delivery by cashier's check. Bernard went to his bank, First State Bank ("FSB") and obtained the following check.

> *Pay to the order of Midway Monsters Movers the sum of $1,000. One thousand dollars and 00 cents*
>
> *FSB*
>
>   */s/ FSB*
>
> *Remitter: Bernard Bernstein*

Upon delivery of his belongings, Bernard gave the check to MMM. Before MMM could get the check cashed, however, FSB went bust, making it impossible to obtain payment from FSB. Not having been paid, Midway looks to Bernard for compensation for the successful move.

May MMM recover from Bernard based on his contractual agreement to pay $1,000? May MMM sue Bernard on his obligation as a party to the instrument?

PROBLEM 5.2

What if in the above problem, the cashier's check was originally issued to Bernard, who then indorsed it over to MMM? May MMM now recover from Bernard based on his contractual agreement to pay $1,000? Can MMM now sue him on his obligation as a party to the instrument?

PROBLEM 5.3

Sally rents an apartment from Judy pursuant to a written lease. The unpaid rent amounts to $1,000 and is due on April 1. Assume Sally comes to Judy on March 28 and says that she is short of cash and asks Judy to take a promissory note due on May 1. Judy takes the note, but then has second thoughts when she prepares her tax return in early April. On April 12, can she sue Sally under the *lease on the theory that the lease said that the rent was due on April 1 and it was not paid at that time. If not, can she ever sue Sally on the lease? If so, when?*

PROBLEM 5.4

What if, instead of a note, Judy takes Sally's personal check for $1,000 on April 1, but leaves it at her friend's office which is locked and inaccessible to Judy for the next few days. On April 2, Judy, desperately needing the money, demands cash from Sally. If Sally does not give it to her immediately, can Judy have her evicted for non-payment of the rent? What if the check had only been written as a partial payment of $600 of the $1,000 rent?

Section 3-310 makes it clear that parties may themselves determine by agreement how the taking of a negotiable instrument affects the underlying agreement. In practice, parties frequently attempt to settle their disputes in full by giving their creditors checks payable for amounts less than the creditors' claim and asserting that once the instrument has been paid, the liability on the underlyong obligation has been discharged.

In a frequently litigated scenario, one party has issued a check with a legend, below which the payee is expected to indorse. The legend typically declares that by indorsing the check, the payee accepts payment in full settlement of its claims against the drawer and waives any and all other claims. When sued for the balance of the obligation, the defendant would then assert an affirmative defense essentially alleging that he and the plaintiff settled the plaintiff's claim when the claimant indorsed the instrument, having reached an "accord and satisfaction." Section 3-311 was designed to deal with this "informal method of dispute resolution carried out by use of a negotiable instrument." UCC Comment 1 to § 3-311. The rules applying to an accord and satisfaction are discussed in Appendix 2.

Liability on the Instrument Generally

By signing an instrument, a person obligates herself to pay the instrument in accordance with the rules set forth in Article 3. If one does not sign the instrument, either personally or through an agent or personal representative, one generally cannot have any liability "on the instrument." *See* § 3-401. Of course, one can be treated as having signed an instrument, if she subsequently "ratifies" or "adopts" an unauthorized signature as her own. Similarly, in certain circumstances, such as when a person's negligence substantially causes the making of his unauthorized signature, the person may be estopped from denying that the signature is authorized.

If a party does sign the instrument, ultimately whether there is liability to the plaintiff depends on several factors, including the status of the plaintiff and the existence of any defenses to liability. In analyzing whether one party, *P*, can prevail against another party, *D*, on the instrument, it is useful to follow a five-step approach:

1. Determine whether *P* is a proper party plaintiff. To be a proper party plaintiff, *P* must either be a "person entitled to enforce the instrument" (see Chapter 4) or a party to the instrument who has paid the instrument to a person entitled to enforce it. If *P* is not a proper party plaintiff, *P* loses.

2. Determine what *P*'s "theory" is for asserting that *D* is liable. This is accomplished by identifying the status in which *D* signed the instrument. For example, if *D* signed as a drawer, then *P*'s theory is "drawer's obligation." When identifying the theory be sure to note whether any conditions to imposing such liability have been met (e.g., a drawer is entitled to presentment and dishonor). (Liability theories and the applicable conditions are discussed here in Chapter 5.) If *P* does not have a coherent theory, such as when *D* has not signed the instrument, then *P* loses, and you do not have to go to step 3.

3. Determine whether there are any applicable defenses, grounds for discharge, or claims in recoupment. (These are discussed in Chapter 8). If *P* is a proper party plaintiff and has a coherent theory, and *D* does not have any defenses, grounds for discharge or claims in recoupment, then *D* loses, and you do not have to go to step 4.

4. If there are one or more defenses, grounds for discharge, or claims in recoupment, determine whether *P* is a holder in due course or has the rights of a holder in due course. (Who is a "holder in due course" and who has holder in due course rights are discussed in Chapter 9). If *P* is a holder in due course, then you must go to step 5 to determine whether *P* or *D* should prevail.

5. If *P* is a holder in due course, determine whether any applicable defense, ground for discharge, or claim in recoupment succeeds against this holder in due course. (For a discussion of "Rights of a Holder in Due Course," see Chapter 9.)

Parties' Obligations

There are five types of "obligations." They are the obligations of:

1. makers;

2. drawers of cashiers' checks or drafts drawn on the drawer;

3. indorsers;

4. drawers; and

5. acceptors.

Maker's Obligation

Section 3-412 sets forth the obligation of an "issuer" of a note. The issuer of a note is defined in § 3-105(c) as its "maker." The maker ordinarily signs in the lower right-hand corner of the note and thereby promises to pay the instrument according to its terms. The maker is primarily liable. Absent a defense, discharge, or claim in recoupment that is effective against the person seeking payment, the maker must pay the note when it becomes due, even without a demand for payment. The maker's obligation is owed to any person entitled to enforce the instrument or to an indorser who paid the instrument as a result of a dishonor in accordance with § 3-415. See discussion of persons entitled to enforce the instrument in Chapter 4 and of indorsers in Chapter 3.

PROBLEM 5.5

Barb Bailey owes Sally Sanders $100, but does not have the money to pay her at this time. To satisfy her obligation, Barb signs a promissory note for $100 to be due 30 days from today's date, which is on the note, and gives it to her. What are Sally's rights if Barb has not paid her the $100, 30 days from today? What is Sally's theory of liability?

Multiple Makers

Section 3-116 states that, unless otherwise provided in the note, if two or more persons sign a note as comakers, they are jointly and severally liable. This is true even if the note contains words such as "I promise to pay." Thus, the holder can enforce the entire note against any of the comakers, although the holder cannot recover an amount greater than that specified in the note. For example, the holder cannot recover the entire note against one comaker and then recover it again against another comaker. Any comaker who pays more than her pro rata share when the instrument is otherwise silent can recover the excess in an action for contribution from the other comakers. *See* § 3-116(b).

PROBLEM 5.6

Tinker, Evers, and Chance are comakers on a note for $30,000 payable to the order of Paul Payee on January 25, 2005. The $30,000 note was given to purchase supplies for a restaurant the three men intended to open. When the note becomes due and remains unpaid, Paul sues Chance on the theory that first basemen have more money. Can Paul collect all $30,000 from Chance or must he sue all three for $10,000 each? If Chance does have to pay the $30,000, what, if anything can he do?

Different rules apply, when one of two or more comakers is a surety, called in the case of a negotiable instrument, an accommodation party. We will talk about this later in Chapter 7.

The maker is simply obligated to pay in accordance with the terms of the note on the due date, or, if no due date is stated, on the demand of the payee or the holder. It is ordinarily the maker's responsibility to find and tender payment to the payee. If the maker does not do so, the maker's liability on the note continues and interest on the obligation, if any is set forth in the note, continues to accrue. If the maker does make tender to the person entitled to enforce the instrument, however, and the tender is refused, the obligation of the maker to pay interest after the due date on the amount tendered is discharged. Section 3-603(c). This prevents a holder from accumulating interest obligations on the instrument by simply refusing tender of the amount due when the tender is made.

A problem might arise, however, when the maker does not know the identity or location of the person entitled to enforce the instrument. Under these circumstances, the maker would be unable to tender the amount due so as to stop the interest from accruing. Under Former Article 3, the maker could avoid the obligation to pay further interest by specifying a place of payment on the note (provided it was a time note) and by being able and ready to pay the note at the specified location(s) when the note was due. A note that so specified a place of payment was referred to as "domiciled paper." *See* Former § 3-604(3). Section 3-603(c), however, limits the "able and ready to pay" rule to instruments for which presentment is required. Because presentment is not generally required for notes, even domiciled notes, the "able and ready rule" may be frequently unavailable to makers pursuant to § 3-603(c).

Drawer of a Cashier's Check or a Draft Drawn on the Drawer

Section 3-412 states that the obligation of the drawer of a cashier's check and the drawer of any other draft drawn on the drawer is the same as that of a maker of a note.

Indorser's Obligation

An indorser is a party who signs an instrument other than as a maker, drawer, or acceptor, and does so for the purpose of negotiating the instrument, restricting payment, or incurring liability. *See* § 3-204. A signature is an indorsement unless it unambiguously indicates it was intended to be otherwise. Intent may be determined by words accompanying the signature, the place of the signature, or other circumstances.

Should an instrument be presented for payment to the party expected to pay (in the case of a note, the maker, and in the case of a draft, the drawee) and payment is refused, this is called a dishonor. Similarly, if a note that is not payable on demand is not paid on the day it becomes payable, the note has been dishonored. If dishonor occurs, an indorser is generally obligated to pay the amount due on the instrument in accordance with its terms at the time of her indorsement. *See* § 3-415(a). Unlike the maker, whose liability is primary, an indorser is not liable until the instrument, be it a note or a draft, is dishonored and, in most instances, until she receives notice that the instrument has been dishonored. The indorser's obligation is owed to any person "entitled to enforce the instrument or to a subsequent indorser who paid the instrument" under § 3-415.

PROBLEM 5.7

Mary Maker issues a note payable to the order of Paul Payee due on January 27, 2005. Paul subsequently indorses the note and gives it to Harriet Holder. When the note becomes due, Harriet demands payment from Mary, who refuses to pay. May Harriet sue Paul directly for the amount owed? If not, what must she do first? If Paul does have to pay, does he have any recourse? If so, against whom and under what theory?

Multiple Indorsers

Unless otherwise indicated in the instrument, if there is more than one indorser, the general rule is that a prior indorser is liable to a "subsequent indorser" who paid the instrument, and the subsequent indorser has no liability to the prior indorser. *See* § 3-415(a). Presumably, the statutory reference to a "subsequent indorser" refers to an indorser who indorsed the instrument at a later point in time.

When an instrument that has been made payable to two or more joint payees is indorsed by those payees, the indorsers are jointly and severally liable with rights of contribution against each other. *See* §§ 3-116(a), 3-116(b). Similarly, two or more "anomalous indorsers" are jointly and severally liable with rights of contribution. *See* §§ 3-116(a), 3-116(b). An "anomalous indorsement" is one made by a person who was not a holder of the instrument. *See* § 3-205(d). Unless an instrument is payable or indorsed to a specific payee, it may be impossible to tell by merely looking at the face of the instrument whether subsequent indorsers were holders or anomalous indorsers.

PROBLEM 5.8

In the following three scenarios, identify whether the indorsers are (1) prior and subsequent indorsers, (2) indorsers who indorse as joint payees or (3) anom-

alous indorsers. Then explain what rights the indorser who pays the instrument has against the other indorser.

Scenario 1:

A check is made payable to Eric Ebony and Irene Ivory, co-owners of a factory that makes pianos. The check is drawn by Liberace and payable to the order of both of them for $10,000. They indorse the check over to First National Bank by signing their names on the back like this:

> /s/ *Eric Ebony* ⟩ joint · payees
> /s/ *Irene Ivory* ⟩

When the bank presents the check, it is dishonored. The bank provides the appropriate notice and sues Irene for the entire amount ($10,000).

— L J+S liability

Scenario 2

A promissory note is given by Marty Maker to Carl Creditor in exchange for a $10,000 loan to Marty. Carl requests that Marty get two of his more solvent friends to incur liability by indorsing the note, thereby further ensuring that Carl will be paid (these two friends are called "accommodation parties" — see discussion in Chapter 7). They sign the back of the note as follows:

> /s/ *Bill Friendwun* ⟩ J+S anomolous endorsers
> /s/ *Bob Friendtu* ⟩

When the note becomes due, Marty is unable to pay. Carl provides the appropriate notice and sues Bob Friendtu for the entire amount ($10,000).

Scenario 3

Dan Drawer writes a check for $10,000 payable to Paul Payee. Paul uses this check to purchase computer equipment from Computer City so he indorses it on the back with a special indorsement payable to Computer City. Computer City indorses the check in blank over to Bell Computer Company, one of its larger suppliers, in partial payment for supplies. The check looks like this on the back:

> *Pay to Computer City*
> /s/ *Paul Payee*   prior indorser
> /s/ *Computer City*   subseq

Bell presents the check to Dan Drawer's bank, but it is dishonored. Bell provides the appropriate notice and sues Computer City for the entire amount ($10,000). Can Bell instead provide the appropriate notice to Paul Payee and sue him first for the entire amount? If so, what rights, IF ANY, does Paul have against Computer City?

indorser's liab. only runs to subsequent indorser

Avoidance or Discharge of Indorser's Liability

An indorser may avoid making an indorser's obligation by writing the words "without recourse" next to her signature on the instrument or otherwise disclaiming liability. *See* § 3-415(b). One might well ask what purpose is served by an indorsement "without recourse." If the signer does not intend to have any contractual liability, why sign it at all? One reason is that if the instrument is order paper, the payee's indorsement is necessary for the instrument to be negotiated and its transferee to become a holder. One might also ask why an indorsement without recourse is sufficient for this purpose. The answer is that the instrument is payable to order to ensure it is paid to the right person. For this purpose, an indorsement without recourse is just as effective as an indorsement with recourse.

PROBLEM 5.9

Cary Customer issues a note payable to the order of Paul Painter for $1,550 plus interest. The note is due on June 5, 2004. Not wanting to wait until then to collect, Paul sells the note to Friendly Finance Company for $1,000. Paul indorses the instrument by signing his name and adding the words "without recourse" after his signature. When Friendly presents the note to Cary, Cary refuses payment arguing that Paul never showed up to paint his apartment. Once Friendly has given notice to Paul of Cary's dishonor, can it sue Paul on his indorser's obligation and recover the amount of the note? can't sue as indorser

Drawer's Obligation

The drawer is the person who signs a draft or a check to order payment. *See* § 3-103(a)(5). A drawer normally signs in the lower right-hand corner of the draft and names the drawee, the person who is ordered to pay, in the lower left-hand corner. The obligation of the drawer of a cashier's check or of one who draws an instrument on herself is governed by § 3-412 and is discussed above. The obligation of drawers of other instruments is the subject of § 3-414.

A party signing a draft as a drawer is generally obligated to pay the draft, should it be dishonored, in accordance with its terms as of the time it was issued or, if it was not issued, at the time the draft initially came into the possession of a holder. *See* § 3-414(b). Much like an indorser, the drawer is not liable until the instrument is dishonored. However, unlike the indorser, notice of dishonor is ordinarily not necessary to charge the drawer since, as the issuer of the instrument, she expects to be ultimately responsible for payment. The drawer's obligation is owed to any person "entitled to enforce" the draft or to an indorser who paid the draft under Section 3-415.

PROBLEM 5.10

Homer Simpson writes a check out of his account at Springfield State Bank, payable to Moe, the neighborhood tavern owner, to pay off his bar bill for the month of January. Moe indorses the check over to one of his suppliers, Duff Beer. May Duff sue Homer for the amount of the check upon receipt of the check from Moe? If not, what must occur first? On what theory would Homer be liable? [3-414 as drawer] *Assume Duff tries to cash the check at Springfield State Bank, but the bank refuses to pay it because Homer's account is overdrawn. May Duff sue Moe for the amount of the check or must Duff sue Homer? If Duff can sue Moe, what is Duff's theory of liability? If Moe has to pay Duff, what recourse, if any does Moe have?* [upon dishonor] [indorser enforce against earliest indorser] [against drawer]

Acceptor's Obligation

[3-413]

Normally, a drawee has no liability on a draft because, although the drawee's name appears on the instrument, its signature does not. *See* §§ 3-401, 3-408. An acceptor is the drawee of a draft who, by signing the instrument, has entered into an agreement to pay the draft as presented. The agreement to pay must be written on the draft but may consist of the drawee's signature alone. Section 3-409. When a check is accepted by the bank on which it is drawn, the check is said to be "certified."

PROBLEM 5.11

a. Donald Drawer issues a check payable to Penny Payee for $50 on his account at First National Bank of Pennsylvania. Penny takes the check to First National, gives it to a teller and asks the teller to give her $50. The teller gives her $50. Has the Drawee Bank accepted the check? [No, paid]

b. Instead, assume Penny doesn't want the money right away, but she also wants to make sure that sufficient funds are available when she does want to cash the check. What can she do? Can the bank refuse to do what Penny wants? See § 3-409(d). [get it certified]

The acceptor's obligation is governed by § 3-413. An acceptor is obligated to pay the draft according to its terms when accepted (even if the acceptance states that it is payable "as originally drawn") provided that the terms of the acceptance do not vary the terms of the draft. If the acceptance does vary the terms of the draft, the acceptor is obligated to pay according to the terms as varied. The obligation of the acceptor is owed to a person entitled to enforce the draft, to the drawer who paid the draft under § 3-414, or to an indorser who paid the draft under § 3-415.

If the certification of a check or the acceptance of a draft states the amount certified or accepted, the acceptor is obligated only in that amount. If no such amount is stated in the certification or acceptance and the amount of the instrument is thereafter increased and subsequently negotiated to a holder in due course, the acceptor's obligation is in the amount of the draft when it was taken by the holder in due course. *See* § 3-413(b). This protects the holder in due course of a certified check or accepted draft that was altered after certification or acceptance but before negotiation to her. The acceptor can avoid liability for the altered amount simply by stating in the acceptance the amount it agrees to pay.

Technical Rights

Parties who are not primarily liable on an instrument are entitled to certain technical rights before they are obligated to pay on the instrument. These rights are "presentment," "dishonor," and "notice of dishonor."

The subject of technical rights is quite complicated. It is critical, however, to recognize from the outset that the practical significance of technical rights law is minimal in many commercial contexts because a party may waive its entitlement to technical rights. In fact, most standard notes used by financial institutions contain such waivers. As a result, the following discussion of technical rights is applicable only when there was no such waiver or when, for one reason or another, a court might find the waiver unenforceable.

Presentment

Purposes of Presentment: Payment and Acceptance

Presentment is a demand for payment or acceptance of a negotiable instrument. Presentment is typically made to the maker of a promissory note, to the drawee of a draft, or in the case of a note or draft payable at a bank, to the bank. Presentment for payment, however, may also be made to any party obliged to pay the instrument. Thus, if a draft is dishonored by the drawee, the holder may make presentment to the drawer or to an indorser. *See* § 3-501.

"Payment" is defined by § 3-602. Basically, payment is made when a drawee or a party with an obligation on the instrument actually pays in accordance with the terms of the instrument to a person entitled to enforce the instrument. Thus, when one person transfers for consideration an instrument to a person who is *not obligated on the instrument*, the transferee has not made "payment" on the instrument. Instead, the transferee has taken the instrument for consideration.

PROBLEM 5.12

Which of the following is a presentment for payment?

  a. *A check for $50 is drawn by Dawn Drawer on First National Bank and made payable to Paula Payee. Paula indorses the check over to Harry Holder, who brings it in to First National Bank, hands the teller the check and asks for $50.*

  b. *A check for $50 is drawn by Dawn Drawer on First National Bank and made payable to Paula Payee. Paula indorses the check over to Harry Holder, who brings it in to the bank where he has his account, Hisown Bank, hands the teller the check and asks for $50.*

  c. *The teller at Hisown Bank in "b," above, gives Harry the $50 and then Hisown Bank sends the check directly to First National Bank asking for reimbursement of that amount.* presentment

  d. *A check for $50 is drawn by Dawn Drawer on First National Bank and made payable to Paula Payee. Paula indorses the check over to Harry Holder, who brings it in to the Local Currency Exchange and asks for cash in exchange for the check.* not

  e. *A check for $50 is drawn by Dawn Drawer on First National Bank and made payable to Paula Payee. Paula indorses the check over to Harry Holder, who brings it in to First National Bank, hands the teller the check and asks for $50. The bank refuses to give Harry the $50 because Dawn's account is overdrawn. Harry takes the check to Dawn and asks her for the $50. What if, instead, Harry takes the check to Paula and asks her for the $50?*

"Acceptance" is defined by § 3-409 as the drawee's written agreement to honor a draft as presented. An acceptance must be written on the draft itself. *See* § 3-409(a). The drawee's signature alone may constitute an acceptance. Although there is no need for any specific language referring to the acceptance, UCC Comment 2 to § 3-409 points out that the drawee's signature must not be accompanied by any language indicating an intent not to honor the draft.

The most common type of acceptance is a drawee bank's certification of a check. *See* § 3-409(d). A person might typically present an item for acceptance in order to have the instrument "backed" by the financial creditworthiness of the drawee bank. In this way, other parties may be more willing to take the check, once certified, in exchange for their goods or services. Section 3-409(d) makes it clear that the drawee of a check has no obligation to certify a check and that refusal to do so does not constitute a dishonor of the check.

When considering presentment, there are four critical issues:

  1. how to make presentment;

2. when to make presentment;

3. when presentment is excused; and

4. what are the consequences of improper or untimely presentment.

How To Make Presentment

Section 3-501 first states that the manner in which presentment may be made is subject to Article 4, the agreement of the parties, clearing-house rules, "and the like." To the extent that these factors do not come into play, § 3-501 prescribes the following rules:

1. If an instrument is payable at a bank in the United States, presentment *must* be made at that bank. If the instrument is payable elsewhere, presentment *may* be at that place.

Section 3-501 is silent as to where else presentment may be made with respect to such an instrument. Nor does § 3-501 prescribe where presentment may be made when the instrument is silent as to where it is payable.

2. Presentment may be made by any commercially reasonable means, including by oral, written, or electronic communication. Presentment is effective when received, not when sent.

3. Presentment may be made to any one of two or more makers, acceptors, drawees, or other payors.

4. Upon demand of the person to whom presentment is made, the presenter must (a) exhibit the instrument; (b) provide reasonable proof of his own identity and, if presentment is made on behalf of someone else, reasonable proof that he has authority to present on that person's behalf; and (c) either sign a receipt on the instrument for any amount paid or surrender the instrument if full payment is made. *See* § 3-501(b)(3).

When To Make Presentment

Two distinct issues arise with respect to when presentment should be made. The first involves the types of situations in which presentment is or is not required. The second involves the timing of any presentment.

PROBLEM 5.13

Look at § 3-502 to determine whether a formal presentment for payment is **necessary** *in the following situations:*

a. to collect from the drawer or indorser of a draft; yes

b. to collect from the maker of a demand note; *no*

c. to collect from the indorser of a demand note;

d. to collect from the indorser on a note whose terms require presentment;

e. to collect from an indorser on a note due on a future specified date (a time note);

f. to collect from an indorser on a time note that is payable at or through a bank.

Presentment for *acceptance* is necessary to collect from the drawer or indorsers of a draft when the draft so provides or its date of payment depends on such presentment. A draft payable "a specified time (e.g., 30 days) after sight" is one whose date of payment depends on a presentment. The draft must be presented for acceptance in order to start the period running. Otherwise, presentment for *acceptance* of any other draft is optional.

Excuse of Presentment

Section 3-504(a) lists several circumstances in which presentment may be excused. These include (1) when the person entitled to present is unable to make presentment despite exercising reasonable diligence; (2) when the maker or acceptor is dead or in insolvency proceedings or has announced that it will not pay the obligation; (3) when the instrument by its terms states that presentment is unnecessary to enforce the drawer's or indorsers' obligations; (4) when the drawer or indorsers have waived presentment; (5) when the drawer or indorsers have no reason to expect nor any right to require that the instrument will be paid or accepted if presented; (6) when the drawer instructed the drawee not to pay or accept the draft; and (7) when the drawee was not obligated to the drawer to pay the draft.

Consequences of Improper or Untimely Presentment

Failure to make a proper, timely presentment has a dramatic direct effect on the obligation of indorsers, but not so on that of the drawer. Look at Sections 3-414(f) and 3-415(e) to do the following problems.

PROBLEM 5.14

Dan Drawer owes Bob Barnes $1,000. He pays Barnes by giving him a check on January 1, 2004, for $1,000 drawn on Last State Bank. On February 22, 2004, and before Tom made presentment, Last State Bank becomes insolvent. Assume Tom made presentment on February 25, 2004, and Last State Bank dishonored *that check. Assume also that at the time Last State Bank became insolvent, Dan Drawer had over $1,000 in his checking account. What happens when Tom sues Dan on his drawer's obligation?*

PROBLEM 5.15

Victor Principal signs a check payable to the order of Patrica Duffy for $300 dated January 3, 2004. On January 10, Duffy endorses the check over to the North Fork Company. North Fork, due to a clerical error in the bookkeeping department, does not present the check for payment until February 15. When it does so the check is dishonored because of insufficient funds in Victor's account. What result if North Fork sues Victor on his drawer's obligation? What if, instead, North Fork promptly notifies Patricia that the check has been dishonored and seeks to recover from her the amount of the check?

Dishonor and Notice of Dishonor

Dishonor

Unless presentment is excused, dishonor must occur before a holder may collect from a drawer or indorser. Consequently, the following sections examine what a dishonor is and when it occurs.

(1) Promissory notes

A note payable on demand is dishonored if presentment is made to the maker and the maker fails to pay it on the day of presentment. *See* § 3-502(a)(1). Under some circumstances, however, the obligation to make presentment may be excused. A time note payable at or through a bank or a time note explicitly requiring presentment is dishonored if it is not paid on the later of the date presented or the date on which it becomes payable. *See* § 3-502(a)(2). Notes not payable on demand at or through a bank and notes not explicitly requiring presentment are dishonored if they are not paid on the day they become payable. *See* § 3-502(a)(3).

(2) Drafts

Section 3-502(b)(1) addresses the dishonor of checks presented to the drawee (payor bank) through the check-collection system, not checks presented for immediate payment over the counter. The basic rule is that the check is dishonored unless the payor bank "pays" the check by giving the presenter an irreversible credit (settlement) within a specified period of time.

When a payor bank is presented with a check, it customarily makes settlement to the presenter for the amount of the check. Then the payor bank has a certain period of time (until its "midnight deadline") to undo (recover) the settlement by either returning the check or, if the check is unavailable for return, by sending written notice of dishonor or nonpayment. If the payor bank acts before its midnight deadline, the check is dishonored.

If a payor bank does not provide a settlement and neither returns the check nor gives notice of dishonor or nonpayment before its midnight deadline, the bank may be liable for the amount of the check. In such a case the check is also dishonored.

If a draft other than a check is payable on demand or is a check that is presented for immediate payment over the counter, the draft is dishonored if it is not paid on the day of presentment. *See* § 3-502(b)(2). If drafts payable on a specified date are presented for payment, they are dishonored if not paid on the later of the date presented or the date they become payable. *See* § 3-502(b)(3).

PROBLEM 5.16

On November 1, 2004, LienCo. gave Supplier a draft that ordered FortNox, Inc., to pay Supplier $20,000 on December 1, 2004. On November 15, 2004, during FortNox's regular business hours, Supplier presented the draft for payment to FortNox, Inc., which did not pay it on that day. Has the draft been dishonored?

If drafts payable on a specified date are presented for *acceptance* before the day they become payable, the drafts are dishonored if not accepted on the day presented. *See* § 3-502(b)(3). Drafts payable after a certain period of time after sight or acceptance are dishonored if they are presented for acceptance but are not accepted on the day so presented. *See* § 3-502(b)(4).

PROBLEM 5.17

On November 1, 2004, LienCo. gave Supplier a draft that ordered FortNox, Inc., to pay Supplier $20,000 on December 1, 2004. Does this draft have to be presented for acceptance? Assume that on November 15, 2004, during FortNox's regular business hours, Supplier presented the draft for acceptance to FortNox, Inc., which refused to accept it. May Supplier sue FortNox, Inc. for the $20,000? May Supplier sue LienCo? If so, when?

PROBLEM 5.18

On November 1,2004, LienCo. gave Supplier a draft that ordered FortNox, Inc., to pay Supplier 30 days after sight. Does this draft have to be presented for acceptance? Assume that on November 15, 2004, during FortNox's regular business hours, Supplier presented the draft for acceptance to FortNox, Inc., which did not accept it. Is this a dishonor?

PROBLEM 5.19

On December 30, 2004, Lienco gave supplier a check for $50,000 drawn on Lienco's bank, Fourth Second Bank. For tax reasons, Supplier did not want to have the income from the check in 2004, but did want to make sure that the monies were available from Lienco's account. To protect itself, Supplier took the check to Fourth Second Bank, and asked the bank to certify (accept) the check. If the bank refuses to certify the check, is that a dishonor?

If a draft is presented for acceptance and the drawee's acceptance varies in any way from the draft as presented, the holder may refuse the acceptance and treat the draft as dishonored. Variances that may constitute dishonor of the draft include conditional acceptances, acceptances for part of the amount or to pay at a different time from that required by the draft, or an acceptance by less than all the drawees. However, an acceptance to pay at a particular bank or place in the United States is not an acceptance varying the draft unless the acceptance states that the draft is to be paid *only* at such bank or place. *See* § 3-410.

Two rules govern the dishonor of accepted drafts. Accepted demand drafts are dishonored if they are not paid on the day they are presented for payment to the acceptor. Accepted time drafts are dishonored if, after being presented for payment, they are not paid on the later of the day of presentment or the day they become payable.

Notice of Dishonor

If an instrument is dishonored, it is sometimes necessary to provide notice of the dishonor to various parties. There are four important issues regarding notice of dishonor:

1. how to give notice of dishonor;

2. when to give notice of dishonor;

3. when notice of dishonor is excused; and

4. the consequences of improper or untimely notice of dishonor.

(1) How notice of dishonor may be given

Section 3-503(b) provides that notice of dishonor may be given "by any commercially reasonable means, including an oral, written or electronic communication." Despite the broad provisions of § 3-503, a number of authorities have ruled that a collecting bank or payor bank may only give written notice of dishonor. The notice is sufficient if it "reasonably identifies the instrument and indicates that the instrument has been dishonored or has not been paid or accepted." To identify an instrument that has been dishonored, it is sufficient to include the maker or drawer of the instrument, its date, the amount, the payees, and the names of the persons to whom notice of dishonor is given. *See First-Stroudsburg National Bank v. Nixon*, 53 Pa.D.& C.2d 672 (1971) (notice need not name the holder).

(2) When to make notice of dishonor

There are special rules regarding instruments taken for collection by a collecting bank. The bank must give notice of dishonor before midnight of the banking day following the banking day on which the bank receives notice of dishonor. Other persons must give notice of dishonor within 30 days after the day on which they receive notice of dishonor. As to other instruments, notice of dishonor must be given within 30 days following the day the instrument is dishonored. *See* § 3-503(c).

PROBLEM 5.20

Jack Dimedaughter, a famous actor, writes a check payable to his girlfriend, Lauroff Lynn Freeze for $1,000 on his account at Hollywood State Bank. Laura indorses the check and gives it to Donald Juan, who indorses it over to Tommy Two, who deposits it in his bank, Third National Bank. Third National presents the check for payment to Hollywood State and it is dishonored on Tuesday, February 4th. Third is informed of the dishonor on that same day. If Third wants to sue any of the previous indorsers, by what date must it give notice of the dishonor to the potential defendant? What if it wants to sue Jack? Assume Third only gives notice to Tommy and does so on Wednesday, February 5th. If Tommy wants to sue any previous indorser by what date must he give notice of dishonor? Assume Tommy only gives notice of dishonor to Donald and does so on February 13. If Donald wants to sue Laura, by what date must he give her notice of dishonor? What if he wants to sue Jack?

(3) Excuse of Notice of Dishonor

Delay in providing notice of dishonor is excused if caused by circumstances beyond one's control provided that one exercises reasonable diligence to provide notice once those circumstances change. Notice of dishonor is entirely excused if (a) presentment is waived by the person whose obligation is being enforced; (b) notice of dishonor is waived by the person whose obligation is being enforced; or (c) the instrument's terms indicate that notice of dishonor is unnecessary to enforce the instrument. *See* §§ 3-504(b), 3-504(c).

(4) Consequences of failure to give prompt notice of dishonor

When an instrument is dishonored, timely notice of dishonor, unless excused, must be given in order to charge any indorsers. *See* § 3-503(a). Timely notice of dishonor is also required to charge drawers of drafts accepted by a nonbank drawee. *Id.* Failure to give prompt notice of dishonor when required to charge a party will result in that party's discharge from any obligation on the instrument.

Chapter 6

LIABILITY ON AN INSTRUMENT SIGNED BY AN AGENT

Sometimes an instrument is signed by a person, but that person (the "agent") asserts that he or she was acting on behalf of another person (the "principal"). Such situations raise important questions as to the liability of the purported principal as well as that of the agent.

A Principal's Liability on an Instrument Signed by an Agent

A party is only liable on an instrument if it signed the instrument, either personally or, if represented by an agent, through the signature made by the agent. When an authorized agent signs for a principal, the principal is liable whether the agent signed the principal's name or the agent's name or used any other mark to authenticate the instrument (see § 3-401 and the discussion in Chapter 2, above) and whether or not the principal is identified somewhere in the instrument. *See* § 3-402(a).

PROBLEM 6.1

Adam Gent is the authorized representative for Victor Principal. When Adam signs a promissory note "Victor Principal" as payment for a transaction in which he represented Victor, is Victor liable on the instrument? Supposed, instead, that Adam signs the note "Adam Gent." Is Victor liable on the instrument?

On the other hand, if the person who signed the instrument was not authorized to do so on behalf of the purported principal, then the principal is not liable on the instrument. Interestingly, Article 3 does not prescribe any particular procedure for authorizing one person to execute an instrument for another. Authorization may be established by the same criteria applied under non-Article 3 agency law. UCC Comment 1 to § 3-401 specifically states:

> **If under the law of agency, the represented person would be bound by the act of the representative in signing either the name of the represented person or that of the representative, the signature is the authorized signature of the represented person.**

Ordinarily what matters is whether authority exists at the time the purported agent signs the instrument. But even if a purported agent is not authorized at the time he signs, a principal may subsequently ratify the purported agent's forgery by knowingly accepting the benefits of the forgery or deliberately deciding not to object thereto. Similarly, a principal may, under certain circumstances, be precluded from denying that the purported agent was authorized to act on its behalf. Rules regarding such preclusion are discussed in Chapter 17.

An Agent's Personal Liability on the Instrument

Business entities, such as corporations and partnerships, can only execute instruments by having human beings (agents) sign on their behalf. Moreover, even individuals sometimes have agents who are authorized to sign for them. In many cases, the issue arises as to whether an agent who signs an instrument becomes *personally* liable. There are two basic scenarios under Article 3. The first is where the alleged agent was authorized to sign for the other person. The second scenario is where the alleged agent was not authorized. Because the law regarding the latter case is fairly straightforward, we will discuss it first.

When the Agent's Signature Was Unauthorized

When the party who signed the instrument was not authorized to sign for another party, the signer is personally liable on the instrument to anyone who in good faith pays the instrument or takes it for value. § 3-403(a) This is the law even if the person who signed the instrument did not sign his own name but, instead, signed only the name of his purported principal. An unauthorized signature in the name of the purported principal is wholly inoperative as that of the person whose name is signed. Instead, it is treated by Article 3 as the signature of the person who signed it, at least as far as those who in good faith pay or who take it for value are concerned. *See* § 3-403(a). For a definition of "value," see § 3-303(a) or the Glossary.

PROBLEM 6.2

Arnold Able, who recently inherited from his father the majority of stock in FAMILICO, Inc., a close corporation, of which Arnold's father used to be treasurer, mistakenly believed he was <u>authorized</u> *to borrow money and sign promissory notes on behalf of FAMILICO. Acting on this belief, Arnold first borrowed $10,000 and then $15,000 from BigBank, which had long done business with FAMILICO and Arnold's father. For each loan, he issued a promissory note, signing the $10,000 note as "FAMILICO, Inc., by Arnold Able, Agent," and the $15,000 note simply as "FAMILICO." Will Arnold be personally liable on either of these notes? Will FAMILICO be liable? What if the second note was issued in* *exchange for a loan that was used by the company to purchase new equipment in the company's processing plant?*

PROBLEM 6.3

Suppose Arnold Able, from the preceding problem, mistakenly believes he is authorized on behalf of FAMILICO to make gifts to long-term employees upon their retirement. Consequently, he issues a promissory note payable to the order of Elwood Chips for $5,000, due on September 10, 2005. He signs the note "FAMILICO." If Mr. Chips tries to enforce the note against FAMILICO, who will win? What if Mr. Chips tries to enforce the note against Arnold personally?

PROBLEM 6.4

Same facts as Problem 6.3, except that, rather than trying to enforce the note itself, Mr. Chips transfers the instrument to First Insatiable Bank ("FIB") for $4,500 on March 3, 2005. When the note comes due, will FIB be able to enforce the note against FAMILICO? Against Arnold personally?
　　　　　　　　↳ No　　　　　　　　　　　　　　　　　↳ yes

When the Agent's Signature Was Authorized

When the party who signed the instrument was authorized to sign for a principal, then the principal is liable if the agent signed either the principal's name or the agent's name. *See* § 3-402(a) and discussion above. Issues regarding the possible personal liability of the authorized agent are more complicated. They involve the following four basic rules:

Rule One: The agent **is *not*** personally liable if he did not sign his own name to the instrument. *See* § 3-401. The signing of the principal's name does not serve as the agent's own signature when the agent was authorized to sign the principal's name.

Rule Two: The agent **is *not*** personally liable even if he signs his own name without indicating his representative status if (1) the instrument is a check; (2) the check is payable from an account of the principal; and (3) the principal, from whose account the check is payable, is identified on the check. *See* § 3-402(c).

The implicit logic of § 3-402(c) is that when one signs a check on someone else's account, it is clear that the signer is signing in a representative capacity for the account holder. Consequently, both the principal's name and the agency relationship are clear on the face of the instrument. *See* UCC Comment 3 to § 3-402.

Rule Three: The agent **is *not*** personally liable if the form of the signature shows unambiguously that the signature is on behalf of the principal who is identified in the instrument. *See* § 3-402(b)(1).

Rule Four: If the instrument neither (1) names the agent's principal nor (2) shows that the agent signed in a representative capacity, *or* does one of the above but not both, then the agent may or may not be personally liable depending on the following:

1. If the party to whom the agent is allegedly obligated (the "third party") is a holder in due course without notice that the agent was not intended by the original parties to be personally liable, then the agent **is** personally liable.

2. If the third-party holder was not a holder in due course or if the third party had notice that the original parties did not intend for the agent to be personally liable, the agent **is** nonetheless personally liable *unless* the agent proves that the original parties did not intend him to be personally liable. The burden of proof as to the intent of the original parties must be carried by the agent. § 3-402(b)(2).

PROBLEM 6.5

In the following scenarios, discuss whether the authorized agent is personally liable to the person entitled to enforce the instrument

a. *ABC Corporation ("ABC") borrows $10,000 from First Insatiable Bank. Douglas Evergreen, president of ABC, signs on its behalf a promissory note to the Bank's order for the $10,000. The signature lines read:*

doesn't say "By:" or title

> "ABC Corporation
> /s/Douglas Evergreen"— personally liable

The note is then negotiated by First Insatiable Bank to the Second Satiable Bank, a holder in due course without notice of Evergreen's status as a representative of ABC. When ABC declares bankruptcy, Second seeks recovery from Douglass in his personal capacity on a maker's obligation theory.

b. *Assume the same facts as "a," above, except for the fact that Douglas signed the note as follows:*

corp. liab.

> "ABC Corporation
> by: /s/ Douglas Evergreen, President"

c. *Adam Gent, the authorized agent of Victor Principal, was involved in negotiations on a real estate purchase on behalf of Victor with the LandHo Real Estate Company. When the parties had reached an agreement on the terms of the sale, Adam signed both the contract for sale and a separate promissory note payable to LandHo for $200,000 on Victor's behalf by simply writing his own name "Adam Gent." Although the contract for sale of the* *property mentions Principal's name as buyer, Principal's name appears nowhere on the promissory note. LandHo now seeks to recover the $200,000 from Adam. For an interesting historical perspective, see First Bank & Trust v. Post, 10 Ill.App.3d 127, 293 N.E.2d 907 (1973).* authorized agent, principal liable

d. *A check appears as follows:*

Reliable, Inc.	January 21, 2003
123450 Street Name	
Anytown, U.S.A	
	Pay to the order of Simon Bros. $300.00
	Three hundred dollars and no cents
Drawee Bank	
	/s/ Brad Zenner

Simon Bros. indorses the check over to Garfinkel Company, a holder in due course who is unaware that Brad Zenner is the bookkeeper of Reliable, Inc. and is authorized to sign checks for the company. When the Drawee Bank dishonors the check, Garfinkels seeks to enforce the check against Brad as the drawer. principal liab.

e. *After prolonged negotiations on behalf of his client, Rodmont Dennis, an eccentric basketball player, Arliss Michaels, sports agent for the stars, signs a promissory note on behalf of Dennis to purchase an interest in a boutique called "Electric Karma" that sells garish women's clothing. Arliss simply signs the note: "Arliss Michaels, Agent." The note is then negotiated by the present owners of "Electric Karma" to a third party known by the owners to have a great interest in sports personalities. To impress the third party and thereby increase the price they could get for the note, the "Karma" owners bragged about the fact that their new partner in the boutique would be a famous basketball player who was a client of Michaels. The third party pays a premium price for the note and, because all requirements are met, is a holder in due course. When the note becomes due, the third party seeks to enforce the note against Arliss.*

What Constitutes a Showing of Representative Capacity?

Section 3-402(b)(1) provides that an agent signing an instrument will have no personal liability if the signature shows unambiguously that it was made in a representative capacity on behalf of a person identified on the instrument. As an example, UCC Comment 2 to § 3-402, offers "P, by A, Treasurer." The Comment provides further insight by giving examples of situations that do not fall within § 3-402(b)(1). Assume John Doe is the agent and Richard Roe is the principal.

a. If the agent signs only "John Doe," there is no showing of representative capacity.

b. If the agent signs "Richard Roe," and immediately below that "John Doe," there is no showing of representative capacity.

c. If the agent signs only "John Doe, Agent," there is a showing of representative capacity, but the signature does not identify the person represented. As such, the signature does not of itself serve to protect John Doe from personal liability.

In many cases, the issue as to whether an instrument shows that the agent signed in a representative capacity cannot be resolved by resort to these examples alone. Consequently, a number of factors must be considered in determining whether or not the signer is personally liable. Unfortunately, the precise significance of a particular factor is often blurred by the fact that it occurs in combination with other factors. Relevant factors include, without limitation: (1) whether the name of the principal appears on the instrument; (2) whether the word "by" precedes the purported agent's signature — although, § 3-402 (and the UCC Comments thereto) does not specifically describe the legal effect of the use of the word "by" and cases under a very similar provision of the former Code are inconsistent; (3) whether the purported agent's corporate title follows his name; (4) whether the purported agent's name, appearing below a corporate name, is indented; (5) whether any other individual's signature appears on the instrument; (6) whether there are any differences between the way two or more individuals signed the instrument; (7) whether the language of the instrument refers to the obligor in the plural or whether it refers to joint and several liability and; (8) whether any other language in the instrument indicates that only the purported principal is liable. *See, e.g., Williamson v.. Bertino*, 685 So.2d 93 (D.Ct.Fla.1997) (although person's signature was followed by corporate title and, on the line below, corporate name, the corporate title was not preceded by "as" or "for," which would have shown the signature was in a representative capacity).

Extrinsic Evidence

When an agent is allowed to prove the intent of the original parties, the types of evidence and considerations that might be evaluated by the court could include the following (drawn primarily from cases under the pre-1990 version of § 3-402):

1. If the agent signed the instrument in more than one place, any discrepancy between the various signatures may be significant. Thus, if the agent indicated a corporate capacity at one point and not at the other, this could indicate that one of the signatures was meant to be personal. *See, e.g., Mountain America*

Credit Union v. McClellan, 854 P.2d 590 (Utah App. 1993) (where an individual signed a note twice, once as the corporate secretary and once without designation of a corporate title, no evidence could be admitted against holder in due course to disprove the signer's personal liability).

2. If the agent signed both as a maker and as an indorser, this might indicate that one of the signatures was intended to be in a representative capacity and one was not; otherwise, the two signatures might be legally redundant. *See Hunt v. Dental Capital Corp.*, 503 A.2d 205 (D.C.App. 1985) (applying Illinois) (dictum); *First Bank & Trust Co. v. Post*, 10 Ill.App.3d 127, 293 N.E.2d 907 (1st Dist. 1973) considering legal redundancy arising from separate documents construed together). *See also United Savings & Loan Association v. Lake of the Ozarks Water Festival, Inc.*, 805 S.W.2d 350 (Mo.App. 1991) redundant for corporation to guaranty its own debt).

3. Other documents involved in the same transaction, particularly those contemporaneously signed regarding the same subject matter, may be used to construe the manner in which the agent signed. *See, e.g., Inside Scoop, Inc. v. Curry,* 755 F.Supp. 426 (D.D.C. 1989), aff'd. 923 F.2d 201 (D.C. Cir. 1991).

4. Admissions acquired through discovery or made during testimony could evidence the original parties' intentions.

5. A course of conduct between the parties may be established that would show the parties' intentions. *See Mestco Distributors, Inc. v. Stamps*, 824 S.W.2d 678 (Tex.App 14th Dist. 1993); *In re Golden Distributors, Ltd.*, 134 Bankr. Rptr. 770 (S.D.N.Y. 1991); *J. P. Sivertson & Co. v. Lolmaugh*, 63 Ill.App.3d 724, 380 N.E.2d 520, 20 Ill.Dec. 542 (2d Dist. 1978).

6. Correspondence between the parties might be adduced or parol evidence of conversations between the parties might be presented that would shed light on the parties' intentions.

7. Indications on the face of the instrument that may not be independently sufficient either to establish representative capacity or to name the principal may be considered by the court. *See Trenton Trust Co. v. Klausman*, 222 Pa. Super. 400, 296 A.2d 275 (1972) (the position, style and arrangement of the writing are all relevant in determining whether a signature is signed in a representative capacity only). Such indications would include use of the word "by" or designation of a corporate office (see, e.g., *Donald M. Clement Contractor, Inc. v. Demon, Inc.*, 364 So.2d 204 (La.Ap.4th Cir. 1978) (handwritten word "president" next to the signer's name helped preclude personal liability even though the signature was on a line designated for an individual's signature) or use of the singular or plural in the body of the promissory note, see, e.g., *Campion v. Wynn*, 486 N.E.2d 543 (Ind.App. 4th Dist. 1985) (use of joint and several language binds individual signer personally); *Maine Gas & Appliances, Inc. v. Siegel*, 438 A.2d 888 (Me. 1981). *But see Kankakee Concrete Products Corp. v. Mans*, 81 Ill.App.3d 53, 400 N.E.2d 637, 36 Ill.Dec. 217 (3d Dist. 1980) (plural language in body of text irrelevant when Former § 3-403(3) is satisfied); *Uptown*

Federal Savings & Loan Association v. Collins, 105 Ill.App.2d 459, 245 N.E.2d 521 (1st Dist. 1969) (language in body of instrument not controlling in light of other evidence).

8. Evidence that the payee never inquired as to the financial status of the individual agents ordinarily tends to indicate that the agents were not expected to be personally liable. *See Maywood-Proviso State Bank v. Sotos*, 95 Ill.App.3d 155, 419 N.E.2d 668, 50 Ill.Dec. 560 (2d Dist. 1981).

Miscellaneous Considerations

Of course, an agent may be able to assert different common law or Article 3 defenses. Thus, except as to a holder in due course, an agent may assert lack of consideration as a defense. *See, e.g., Fischer v. Rodriguez-Capriles*, 472 So.2d 1315 (Fla.App. 1985); *Annot.*, 97 A.L.R.3d 798 (1980). Similarly, when the action by the plaintiff is not "on the instrument" but, for example, by a bank that paid an overdraft, extrinsic evidence is allowed to disprove personal liability. *See, e.g., Federal Deposit Insurance Corp. v. West*, 244 Ga. 396, 260 S.E.2d 89 (1979) (under Former § 3-403). Fraud might also be effective as a defense. *See Hot Springs Nat. Bank v. Stoops*, 94 N.M. 568, 613 P.2d 710 (1980). *Cf. Federal Deposit Insurance Corp v. Tennessee Wildcat Services, Inc.*, 839 F.2d 251 (6th Cir. 1988) (under Former § 3-403).

On the other hand, even if a § 3-402 defense might otherwise be available, non-Article 3 law could nonetheless affix liability, such as by piercing the corporate veil. *See, e.g., Keels v. Turner*, 45 N.C.App. 213, 262 S.E.2d 845, *review denied* 300 N.C. 197, 269 S.E.2d 624 (1980); *Miller & Miller Auctioneers, Inc. v. Mersch*, 442 F.Supp. 570 (W.D.Okla. 1977) (under Former § 3-403); *Annot.*, 97 A.L.R.3d 798 (1980). In *Grotz v. Jerutis*, 13 Ill.App.3d 543, 301 N.E.2d 60, 61 (1st Dist. 1973) (before § 3-402), the court found personal liability with respect to a transaction in which a promissory note was signed "George V. Jerutis, V. President, Region Invest. Prop. Developers Inc." Although this signature would seem to have satisfied Former § 3-403, the plaintiff argued that the note was not a complete integration of the loan agreement and successfully sued on an alleged parol promise, not on the note. An individual may also be personally liable if a court finds that he issued, or acquiesced in the issue of, a check drawn on insufficient funds — and which she knew would not be made good — if the issue was for the purpose of defrauding creditors, such as by inducing them to provide additional supplies on credit. *See, e.g., Klockner v. Keser*, 29 Colo.App. 476, 488 P.2d 1135 (1971); *Lippman Packing Corp. v. Rose*, 203 Misc. 1041, 120 N.Y.S.2d 461 (Mun.Ct. 1953).

Chapter 7

ACCOMMODATION PARTIES

Typically, a person issues an instrument in exchange for a benefit that the person directly receives. For example, a person borrowing money from a bank signs as maker of a promissory note in exchange for money being borrowed. Similarly, a person buying goods at a store may issue a check in exchange for the goods being purchased. Sometimes, however, a person lacks adequate creditworthiness to induce another to give money or goods in exchange for the person's note or check. In such a case, a third person with better credit — often one of the person's relatives or friends — signs the instrument and becomes liable on it, which convinces the payee to give money or goods for the instrument. This third person, who signs the instrument solely "for the purpose of incurring liability on [it] . . . without being a direct beneficiary of the value given for the instrument," is called an *accommodation party*. *See* § 3-419(a). An accommodation party is the specific name given to a surety on a negotiable instrument. Like any other surety, the accommodation party is essentially "lending his name" to give additional security to the provider of the value given in exchange for the instrument. The party who also signs the instrument and directly receives the value given for the instrument is called the *accommodated party*.

An accommodation party may sign the instrument as maker, drawer, acceptor, or indorser and, in general, is obligated in the capacity in which she signs. That is, if she signs as a maker or acceptor, she is primarily liable. If she signs as a drawer or indorser, liability arises only after there has been presentment and dishonor and, in the case of an indorser, notice of dishonor. These rules are not affected by whether the person entitled to enforce the instrument knows or has notice that the signer is an accommodation party. The accommodation party is entitled to assert any defense or discharge available to someone in the capacity in which she signs and any defense or claim in recoupment that the accommodated party could assert, except the defenses of discharge in insolvency proceedings, infancy, and lack of legal capacity. *See* § 3-305(d). But the fact that an accommodation party did not directly receive consideration from the taker of the instrument or from the party accommodated is not a defense to liability on the instrument. Section 3-419(b). UCC Comment 2 to § 3-419 makes it clear that under this provision "[t]he obligation of the accommodation party is supported by *any* consideration for which the instrument is taken before it is due."

PROBLEM 7.1

Ted Partee goes to the First National Bank to get a loan to buy a new car, which Ted needs to drive to and from work every day. Before he signs a promis-

sory note to evidence his promise to repay, the bank asks him to get his rich
brother Shawn to also sign the note to further ensure that the debt will be satisfied. Shawn agrees to sign the note. The next day Ted and Shawn go together to
the bank where each signs the note on the front in the lower right-hand corner.
Shawn signed first, and Ted signed beneath Shawn's signature. The note is due
on March 1, 2004.

a. Who is the accommodation party? Who is the accommodated party?

b. If the note is not paid on March 1, 2004, **must** the bank seek recovery
   from Ted first? Why? Does it matter whether or not the Bank was
   aware of the accommodation party's status?

c. Is the answer to "b" the same if Shawn instead had signed the reverse
   side of the note, but Ted had signed on the front? Why or why not?

d. Can Shawn successfully raise lack of consideration as a defense to
   payment since he received nothing in exchange for signing the note
   and will not be using the car himself? See § 3-419(b).

e. If the car was bought by Ted but there was a binding agreement
   between Ted and Shawn, that Shawn would have exclusive use of the
   car on the weekends, would your answer to "a" change? To "b"? To "c"?
   To "d"?

f. If the loan was used to buy a car for the purpose of making deliveries
   for Partee Pizza, a company jointly owned by Ted and Shawn, and a
   signature in the company's name appeared on the note rather than
   Ted's, would Shawn's own signature as maker or indorser constitute
   that of an accommodation party? See comment 1 to § 3-419.

Guarantors

Under the former version of the Code, the obligation of a party who signed an
instrument as a guarantor was covered in a section (Former § 3-416) separate
from that dealing with accommodation parties (Former § 3-415). This suggested
that a signature accompanied by words of guaranty created an obligation distinct from that of an accommodation party. Any confusion that might have thus
arisen was eliminated under the current Code, which provides that one who
signs as a guarantor is treated just as any other accommodation party. The
guarantor is obliged to pay the instrument in the capacity in which she signs.

PROBLEM 7.2

Shawn Partee, from Problem 7.1, above, once again signs on the face of the note
made payable to First National Bank due on March 1, 2004, in the lower right-
hand corner, but this time he writes the term "Guarantor" after his signature. If

the note is not paid on March 1, 2004, **must** *the bank seek recovery from Ted first? Why? Does it matter that the Bank was aware of Shawn's status as a guarantor? Is the answer to the same if Shawn instead had signed the reverse side of the note with the term "Guarantor" after his signature? Why?*

Section 3-419(d) does, however, preserve a special rule regarding guarantors who guarantee "collection" as opposed to those who guarantee payment. The former are liable only if (a) execution of judgment against the accommodated party has been returned unsatisfied, (b) the accommodated party is insolvent or involved in an insolvency proceeding, (c) process cannot be served on the accommodated party, or (d) for other reasons it is clear that payment cannot be obtained from the accommodated party. *Nevertheless, it is important to note that a guarantor does not guarantee collection unless words accompanying his signature unambiguously indicate such an intention. Otherwise, it is presumed that the guarantor is guaranteeing payment rather than collection and is to be treated the same as any other accommodation party.*

PROBLEM 7.3

Assume once again that Ted goes to First National Bank for a car loan and that his brother Shawn signs the note as requested in the lower right-hand corner. This time however, above his signature Shawn wrote the following: "I hereby guarantee First National and its assignees against loss from nonpayment of this note." The note is still due March 1, 2004. If the note is not paid on March 1, 2004, would First National be able to proceed against Shawn without asking Ted to pay the note first? Would the bank be able to proceed against Shawn if it did go to Ted first, but he claimed he was unable to pay? Floor v. Melvin, 5 Ill.App.3d 463, 283 N.E.2d 303, (1972).

Rights Against the Accommodated Party

Right of Reimbursement — § 3-419(e)

Under both common law and Article 3, an accommodation party has a right of reimbursement against the party accommodated. Section 3-419(e) provides that "[a]n accommodation party who pays the instrument is entitled to reimbursement from the accommodated party and is entitled to enforce the instrument against the accommodated party." This is so even if the parties sign in capacities that, under ordinary circumstances, would afford no right of recovery for the accommodation party against the party accommodated. On the other hand, an accommodation party is never liable on the instrument to the party accommodated. Section 3-419(e).

PROBLEM 7.4

Donny Debtor signed a promissory note for $3,000 made payable to Cary Creditor as a downpayment on a small boat that he ordered from Cary. Cary asked that Donny get his good friends Greg Guarantor, Harry Helpout and Shirley Surety to sign as co-makers, and Donny did so. The note then looked like this:

```
We promise to pay to the order of Cary Creditor
$3,000

                            /s/ Donny Debtor
                            /s/ Greg Guarantor
                            /s/ Harry Helpout
                            /s/ Shirley Surety
```

Cary subsequently transferred the note to the Benny Fishall Credit Company ("Benny Fishall"), which was unaware that Greg, Harry and Shirley were accommodation parties. When the note became due, Benny Fishall presented the note to Harry alone for payment of the full $3,000. Is Harry liable for the whole amount? If Harry in fact pays the whole $3,000, can he recover any money from Shirley? If so, how much? Can Harry instead recover anything from Donny? If so how much?

If Benny Fishall sued Donny and recovered the $3000 from him, can Donny recover any amount from any of the other signers? If so, from whom and how much?

PROBLEM 7.5

Adam Parker wishes to borrow $20,000 from the Friendly Loan Company to purchase a new Mustang convertible. Because of Adam's shaky financial condition, Friendly Loan Company requires him to get his rich uncle, Sam Surety, to sign a promissory note as the maker. Sam Surety signs the note as maker to accommodate Adam, and Adam, the accommodated party, signs the note as an indorser. When the note came due, Sam paid the note in full to the holder. What rights, if any, does Sam have to seek reimbursement from Adam of the amount paid? Assume instead that the instrument had been presented to Sam, and Sam refused to pay. Friendly sued Adam, after giving him notice of dishonor on his indorser's liability, and wins. May Adam then sue Sam on his maker's liability, to recover the money Adam paid on the instrument?

Common Law and Equitable Rights of Sureties

In addition to the right of reimbursement specified in Article 3, the accommodation party, as a surety, has several rights against the principal debtor (accommodated party) under the common law and the law of equity. The right of reimbursement (now under § 3-419(e)) is not the sole recourse for an accommodation party who pays the instrument. *See, e.g., Warren v. Washington Trust Bank,* 19 Wash.App. 348, 575 P.2d 1077 (1977).

For example, a surety has the right to be subrogated to the rights of the creditor on the principal obligation (here, the instrument). Additionally, under the common law, a surety (including an accommodation party) who pays the obligation is also typically subrogated to the creditor's rights in any collateral that secures the debt. *See, e.g., Murray v. Payne,* 437 So.2d 47 (Miss. 1993); *LeRoy v. Marquette National Bank of Minneapolis,* 277 N.W.2d 351 (Minn. 1979); *Farmers Loan & Trust Co. v. Letsinger,* 635 N.E.2d 194 (Ind.App. 3rd Dist. 1994); *Bank of New Jersey v. Pulini,* 194 N.J.Super. 163, 476 A.2d 797 (1984). Therefore, when the accommodation party pays the instrument, he can recover on his right of reimbursement from any collateral that may have been given for the obligation.

Moreover, under the common law, an accommodation party has a right referred to as "right of exoneration." Pursuant to this right, an accommodation party can, by a suit in equity, require the principal debtor to make payment of the obligation when due, thus preventing the need for a later suit for reimbursement. Nevertheless, not all jurisdictions recognize this right. *See, e.g., Wroten v. Evans,* 21 Ark.App. 134, 729 SW.2d 422 (1987) (Arkansas appellate courts have not recognized the right of exoneration). Moreover, because it is an equitable right, it is not always justified by the equities of particular cases. *See, e.g., In re Gas Reclamation, Inc., Securities Litigation,* 741 F.Supp. 1094 (SDNY 1990). *See, generally, Gardner v. Bean,* 677 P.2d 1116 (Utah 1984); 38 A.L.R.3d 680 (1971). Other jurisdictions, however, may recognize an additional common law remedy, *quia timet,* by which a surety may compel a principal to put up a bond to protect the surety against the principal's nonperformance. *See In re Gas Reclamation, Inc., Securities Litigation, supra.*

In some jurisdictions, sureties have additional statutory or common law remedies. The common law in Illinois, for instance, allows a guarantor to sue a co-guarantor to pay his pro rata share of an obligation even though the first guarantor has not yet made any payment to the holder or creditor. *Keach v. Hamilton,* 84 Ill.App. 413 (3rd Dist. 1899). *See also* 38 A.L.R.3d 680. Similarly, Illinois statutory law allows sureties, in certain circumstances and by service upon the holder of an instrument, to require the holder to act with due diligence in enforcing an obligation against the principal debtor. *See* IL ST CH 740, § 155/1. Such specific state laws, however, may be complicated by numerous, detailed rules.

Proving One's Accommodation Party Status

The accommodation party has the burden of proving his status. However, under § 3-419(c) a party signing an instrument is presumed to be an accommodation party if the "signature is an anomalous indorsement or is accompanied by words indicating that the signer is acting as surety or guarantor with respect to the obligation of another party to the instrument."

The phrase "an anomalous indorsement" is defined as an indorsement "made by a person that is not the holder of the instrument." *See* § 3-205(d). A "holder" is defined, with respect to a negotiable instrument, as "the person in possession of a negotiable instrument that is payable either to bearer or to an identified person that is the person in possession." *See* § 1-201(21)(A). These definitions are not always helpful, because, when looking at an instrument that was payable to bearer or indorsed in blank, it would be impossible to tell whether someone who indorsed was a holder at the time of the indorsement and, therefore, whether such a person was an accommodation party.

The Former Code used a slightly different way of determining an accommodation party — it talked about a signature out of the chain of title. Even though the Code language has changed, the old approach is still viable and, in some ways, easier to use. When an instrument is made payable to order, or includes a special indorsement, the next signature that appears on the instrument should be that of the identified payee or of the identified person to whom the instrument has been specifically transferred. Any signature that appears prior to those persons is out of the chain of title and is presumably an accommodation party.

PROBLEM 7.6

By looking at the following instruments, whom can we identify as accommodation parties?

a.

	[Back of note]
I promise to pay $100 to the order of Bob. */s/ Albert*	*/s/ Alice* *Pay to Carol* */s/ Bob* */s/ Ted* */s/ Carol*

b.

I promise to pay $100 to the order of Ross.   /s/ Carol

[Back of note]
/s/ Ross
Pay to Chandler
/s/ Joey
/s/ Rachel
/s/ Monica
/s/ Chandler

c.

I promise to pay $100 to the order of Mick.   /s/ Keith

[Back of note]
/s/ George
/s/ Paul
/s/ John
/s/ Ringo

d.

I promise to pay $100 to bearer.   /s/ Casey

[Back of note]
/s/ Mickey
/s/ Whitey
/s/ Yogi

Presumably the use of certain words in addition to "surety" or "guarantor" might be sufficient to establish accommodation party status. For example, one who follows his signature with "Accommodation Party" should be treated as such. Extrinsic evidence might also be used to prove accommodation status. Although different cases identified slightly varying lists of factors, the following issues were frequently identified as relevant:

  1. The position of the signature.

  2. The language of the instrument, *See, e.g. First National Bank of Barnesville v. Rafoth (In re Baker & Getty Financial Services,*

Inc.), 974 F.2d 712 (6th Cir. 1992) (the court found it significant that a party signed at a place on a note designated for the "borrower" and not on the back of the note in the place which was designated for accommodation parties).

3. If an instrument was issued in connection with a loan, whether the loan would have been granted had the particular party not signed the instrument. If not, this is some evidence of the fact that the party signed in order to lend her creditworthiness to another.

4. Whether the party benefitted from the *transaction* in connection with which the instrument was issued.

5. If an instrument was issued in connection with a loan, whether the party received the proceeds of the loan.

6. If an instrument was issued in connection with a loan, whether the party participated directly in the negotiations leading to the loan.

If accommodation parties are liable to the person entitled to enforce the instrument in the capacity in which they sign, that is, primarily liable if they sign as makers and secondarily liable if as drawers or indorsers, what does it matter if the holder has notice of their accommodation status? Section 3-605 provides special defenses to accommodation parties when changes are made with respect to the instrument without their consent or when collateral securing the instrument is impaired in some way by the holder. Furthermore, if the accommodation party tenders payment to the holder and it is refused, the accommodated party will be discharged pursuant to § 3-603. These defenses and discharges are specifically discussed in Chapter 8.

Chapter 8

A DEFENDANT'S RESPONSES TO A SUIT TO ENFORCE AN INSTRUMENT

Suppose someone sues your client, alleging that your client is obligated to pay an instrument. Depending on the facts, you might make the following types of arguments:

1. The plaintiff is not someone with standing to enforce the instrument;

2. Your client never signed the instrument and, therefore, is not liable on it;

3. Even if your client signed the instrument, he did not do so in his own capacity, but only as an agent for someone else and, therefore, is not liable on it;

4. Even if your client signed the instrument as a party, he qualified his signature so that he did not become liable on the instrument;

5. Even if your client signed the instrument and, therefore, did become theoretically liable as a party, he did so as an accommodation to the plaintiff and, therefore, he is not liable to the plaintiff;

6. Even if your client signed the instrument and, therefore, did become theoretically liable as a party, your client has a valid defense specified by Article 3, a valid defense under contract law or claim in recoupment that can be successfully asserted against the plaintiff;

7. Even if your client signed the instrument and initially did become liable as a party, your client's liability has been subsequently discharged;

8. Even if your client signed the instrument and did become liable on it — and, indeed, still is liable on it — some third person has a claim to possession of the instrument or a defense that can be validly asserted against the plaintiff, and your client has followed the statutorily prescribed procedure for asserting such claim or defense.

We have already covered material relevant to Arguments 1 through 5. Argument 1 states the truism that if the plaintiff lacks standing to enforce the instrument, the defendant wins. To have standing to enforce an instrument, a person must either be: (1) a PETE, (2) an indorser (and usually only a "subsequent" indorser) who has paid the instrument, or (3) an accommodation party who has paid the instrument and is enforcing it against the accommodated party. Chapter 4 explains how someone qualifies as a PETE. Chapter 5 discusses indorsers, and Chapter 7 discusses accommodation parties and accommodated parties.

Arguments 2 and 3 essentially state that a person is only liable on an instrument if he has signed it. It is important to note that the authenticity of each signature on an instrument, and the authority for the making of each such signature, is admitted unless it is specifically denied in the pleadings. *See* § 3-308. A defendant who wants to contest such authenticity or authority cannot simply file an Answer containing a general denial of all of the allegations in the plaintiff's Complaint. Moreover, with a few exceptions, such signatures are rebuttably presumed to be authentic and authorized despite the defendant's specific denials. The defendant bears the burden of producing proof at trial that the signatures were not authentic or authorized. Ibid. Chapter 6 specifically discusses, in detail, when an agent who signs an instrument may be held personally liable as a party

Argument 4 can be raised by indorsers of notes or drafts, and by drawers of non-checks, who qualified their signatures by writing "without recourse" or other language that disclaims liability as indorsers or drawers. *See* §§ 3-414(e), 3-415(b). *See, generally,* Chapter 5.

Argument 5 states the rule, set forth in § 3-419(e), that an accommodated party cannot enforce an instrument against an accommodation party. As discussed in Chapter 7, the accommodation party does not receive the value given for the instrument he signs and, essentially, signs to benefit the accommodated party. For this reason, although an accommodation party is generally liable to PETEs and to subsequent indorsers who have paid the instrument, the accommodation party is not liable to the accommodated party.

A. *Your Client Has a Specified Article 3 Defense, a Contract Law Defense or a Claim in Recoupment*

1. *Defenses*

Section 3-305(a)(2) broadly provides that a defendant in a suit to enforce an instrument can assert not only those defenses that are expressly provided in Article 3, but also any common law defenses that would be available if the plaintiff were trying to enforce a right to payment under a simple contract. Comment 2 to § 3-305 explains:

> **Article 3 defenses are non-issuance of the instrument, conditional issuance, and issuance for a special purpose (Section 3-105(b)); failure to countersign a traveler's check (Section 3-106(c)); modification of the obligation by a separate agreement (Section 3-117); payment that violates a restrictive indorsement (Section 3-206(f)); instruments issued without consideration or for which promised performance has not been given (Section 3-303(b)), and breach of warranty when a draft is accepted (Section 3-417(b)). The most prevalent common law defenses are**

fraud, misrepresentation, or mistake in the issuance of the instrument.

PROBLEM 8.1

Pursuant to a contract for the painting of 2 rooms in her house, Mary Maker issues a promissory note to Paul Painter for $3,000. After Paul is halfway through painting the first room, he explains to Mary that, due to his deteriorating health, he will only be able to complete the first room; he will not paint the second room. Mary and he agree, in front of two witnesses, that, as a result, her liability to Painter on the note will be for only $1,500. After Painter finishes the first room, but before he is paid, Painter has a heart attack and dies. Painter's estate sues Mary to enforce her obligation to pay $3,000 on the note. Identify any Article 3 defense or defenses, if any, which Mary can assert.

PROBLEM 8.2

Pursuant to a contract for the painting of 2 rooms in her house, Mary Maker issues a promissory note to Paul Painter for $3,000. After Paul is halfway through painting the first room, Mary tells Paul that, although she can manage to pay $2,500, she is unwilling to pay the whole $3,000. She says that if he is unwilling to go down to $2,500, she does not want him to finish painting. In front of two witnesses, Paul says, "Don't worry," but when he completes the job he sues Mary to enforce her obligation to pay $3,000 on the note. Identify any Article 3 defense or defenses, if any, which Mary can assert.

The defense that may be raised however, must be that of the person seeking to assert the defense. The issue is not so much whether the holder is entitled to be paid, but more whether the obligor is obligated to pay. Thus, the general rule is that one may not defend himself against a person entitled to enforce the instrument by asserting a defense, claim in recoupment, or claim to the instrument of another person (called *jus tertii*). There are some exceptions, however, that will be discussed more at the end of this chapter. In the meantime, read § 3-305(c) and apply it to the following problem:

PROBLEM 8.3

Marty Maker issues a note payable to his friend George for $400 in exchange for an 18-speed Italian racing bike. George then indorses the note and gives it to Steve Slick as payment for a "valuable" baseball card that George discovers is a fake. George tells Marty about Steve's fraud, and when Steve presents the note to Marty, Marty refuses to pay. Steve sues Marty on his maker's obligation. Marty argues that Steve is not a holder in due course (which is correct) and asserts

George's claim of fraud against Steve. What result? If you think Marty will be
unsuccessful in this lawsuit, what would you have advised him to do?

The defenses discussed so far are referred to as "personal" defenses, and
they cannot be successfully asserted against a person who has the rights of a
holder in due course. (The holder in due course doctrine is the subject of the next
chapter, Chapter 9.) There are some defenses, however, that work even against
a holder in due course. These defenses are called "real defenses" (they "really"
work) and are enumerated in § 3-305(a)(1):

> **a defense of the obligor based on (i) infancy of the obligor to the**
> **extent it is a defense to a simple contract, (ii) duress, lack of**
> **legal capacity, or illegality of the transaction which, under other**
> **law, nullifies the obligation of the obligor, (iii) fraud that**
> **induced the obligor to sign the instrument with neither knowl-**
> **edge nor reasonable opportunity to learn of its character or its**
> **essential terms, or (iv) discharge of the obligor in insolvency**
> **proceedings**

a. Infancy

Suppose the obligor of an instrument were sued on a simple contractual obligation and raised the defense of infancy. To the extent the defense would succeed
in that lawsuit, it would work to defeat the rights of any PETE, including a
holder in due course. So the easy answer to a case involving a negotiable instrument is to look to local law and see how the case would come out if it was a simple suit in contract. Unfortunately, the applicable local law regarding the infancy
defense is surprisingly complex. *See, generally,* Larry A. DiMatteo, *Decon-*
structing the Myth of the Infancy Law Doctrine: From Incapacity to Account-
ability, 21 OHIO N.U.L.REV. 481 (1994). Although most states immunize minors
from certain types of contractual liability, they often limit the availability and
amount of protection. For example, minors are often at least partially liable to
pay pursuant to contracts which provided them with "necessities" (also referred
to as "necessaries"). *Id.* What constitutes a "necessity" varies from jurisdiction
to jurisdiction. Relevant factors considered include the infant's (1) station in life;
(2) physical or mental needs; and, in more modern cases, (3) occupational needs.
See, e.g., Bancredit, Inc. v. Bethea, 65 N.J.Super. 538, 168 A.2d 250 (1961);
Ehrsam v. Borgen, 185 Kan. 776, 347 P.2d 260 (Sup.Ct.1959); *Sykes v. Dicker-*
son, 216 Ark. 116, 224 S.W.2d 360 (Cup.Ct.1949). Consequently, if an instrument
were given in exchange for necessities, an infancy defense would be at least partially ineffective against a holder in due course. *See, e.g., Bancredit, Inc. v.*
Bethea, supra.

Even as to contracts in which minors acquire non-necessities, minors are in
some jurisdictions at least liable for the "benefit" they received. *See Berglund v.*
American Multigraph Sales Co., 160 N.W. 191 (Minn. 1916); *Porter v. Wilson,*

209 A.2d 730 (N.H. 1965). *See, generally,* SAMUEL WILLISTON & WALTER H.E. JAEGER, A TREATISE ON THE LAW OF CONTRACTS (3d ed. 1959), vol 2 at § 238: "In some states . . . an infant [is] bound by his contracts . . . to the extent of the benefit actually derived." Id. Thus, if an infant was benefitted by the transaction for which he became obligated on an instrument, the person entitled to enforce the instrument may be able to force the infant to pay the amount of such benefit. Various other rules may limit the protection afforded to minors, such as where the minors affirmatively misrepresent their age, see, e.g., Valencia v. White, supra (although contract not for a necessity, minor must repay an amount equal to the benefit it received so as to place both parties back to the status quo ante), or where specific statutes render minority unavailability in particular contexts, see, e.g., *Swindell v. Georgia State Dept. of Education,* 138 Ga.App. 57, 225 S.E.2d 503 (1976) (state statute made minority ineffective in an action to enforce a student loan). *See, generally,* DiMatteo, *supra.*

PROBLEM 8.4

Dickie Clark is a 17 year, 11 month old boy, who is emancipated from his parents and married with a 3 month old son. He is prematurely balding, smokes a pipe and regularly wears cardigan sweaters. Prior to his 18th birthday, he goes to Peter's motorcycle shop to purchase a used Harley Davidson. Before even beginning his salestalk, Peter tells Dickie that, although he is embarrassed to do it, as a matter of formality, he must first ask Dickie his age. When Dickie replies that he is 22, Peter accepts that as a fact and asks for no further identification. Peter and Dickie discuss the fact that because his wife will need the family car, Dickie intends to ride the motorcycle to work, rather than take public transportation, every day it is possible to do so. Peter sells Dickie a motorcycle that Peter claims had been excellently cared for and had only 15,000 miles on it. Dickie pays for the motorcycle with a promissory note for $12,000 payable to the order of Peter 6 months from the date of issue. Peter uses the motorcycle for 5 and 1/2 months and is very happy with it. But as the 6 month mark neared, Peter began to experience troubles with the motorcycle. When he brought it in for repairs at a shop owned by one of his friends, he found out that the bike had been in numerous accidents before he bought it, had reconditioned parts and had certainly been used for significantly more than 15,000 miles prior to his ownership. When the note becomes due, demand for payment is made by Honesty National Bank (HNB), an innocent party to whom the instrument had been sold several months earlier. Assume that HNB is a holder in due course. What result when it sues Dickie and Dickie claims a defense of infancy? What result if the note was never transferred and Peter sued Dickie to enforce the note?

b. *Duress, Lack of Legal Capacity, Illegality*

i. *Duress*

Duress is a condition in which one party, by wrongful acts or threats, forces or induces another to enter a contract under circumstances that deprive the other of the exercise of free will. *See Enslen v. Village of Lombard*, 128 Ill.App.3d 531, 470 N.E.2d 1188, 83 Ill.Dec. 768 (2d Dist. 1984). Sometimes duress only renders a contract voidable by the party subjected to the duress, and sometimes it renders a contract absolutely void. When duress only renders a contract voidable, the defense is effective against everyone other than a person with the rights of a holder in due course. When duress renders a contract absolutely void, the defense works even against a holder in due course.

Whether particular facts give rise to duress and whether such duress renders an obligation void or only voidable depends on the law of each jurisdiction. UCC Comment 1 to § 3-305 nonetheless generalizes by stating that if an instrument is signed at gunpoint, the instrument will always be void, while recognizing that if an instrument is signed under a threat to prosecute the signer's son, the instrument may only be voidable. This Comment seems to follow the Restatement (Second) of Contracts, which distinguishes between duress by physical compulsion and duress by threat. Duress by physical compulsion involves the present use (or the immediate threat) of physical force to make one enter a contract such that the person compelled is a "mere instrument" of the other and did not in any way truly assent. RESTATEMENT (SECOND) OF CONTRACTS § 174 CMT. A (1981). This type of duress voids a contract so entered., and even a holder in due course could not enforce a negotiable instrument signed under such circumstances.

If, on the other hand, a party was induced to sign an instrument by improper threats, such as imprisonment, moral duress, economic duress, or future physical harm, see, e.g., *Herget National Bank v. Theede*, 181 Ill.App.3d 1053, 537 N.E.2d 1109, 130 Ill.Dec.780 (3d Dist. 1989), that leaves that party no reasonable alternative, the party's obligation is merely voidable, cf. RESTATEMENT (SECOND) OF CONTRACTS § 175(1) (1981). Although a person lacking holder in due course rights could not enforce the instrument, someone with such rights could. Nevertheless, when a party consents to an agreement just because of annoyance, vexation, personal embarrassment, hard bargaining position or difficult financial circumstances, there is no duress at all. *See, e.g., Resolution Trust Corp. v. Ruggiero*, 977 F.2d 309 (7th Cir. 1992).

PROBLEM 8.5

As to each of the following cases, explain whether the obligor has a valid defense of duress and, if so, whether the defense would work against a holder in due course:

a. *Danny, of average size, owns a bar. One night, just as Danny is closing up shop, Frankie, a well-known local thug about 6'4" tall and weighing about 240, walks in. No one else is around. Frankie approaches Danny, and, in a menacing voice, says, "Listen, Danny. I need you to do me a little favor." Danny says, "How much?" Al replies, "Oh, I don't know. I suppose about $2,500 will do." "Hey, that's an awful lot of money for a guy like me," Danny protests. "Listen, friend," Frankie replies, raising himself to his full height, "I'm letting you off cheap. Unless, of course, you want to face the consequences right now, with no else being around and all." Terrified, Danny says, "Okay, okay. Don't get sore. But I don't have that kind of cash around. I'll give you a check." "Make it payable to cash," Frankie answers, "And do it fast before the effects of, what I call, inflation." Danny issues a check for $2,500 to Frankie, and Frankie cashes it at Currency Exchange. Meanwhile, Danny, emboldened after talking to the police, stops payment on the check. When Currency Exchange sues Danny on his drawer's obligation, Danny asserts duress as a defense.*

b. *Lana has a business selling stationery supplies. One of her steady customers, Luthor, comes into her store and says, "Listen, Lana, the stuff you sent me last week was defective and I got a lot of complaints from customers. I figure you cost me about $150 in damages." Lana, however, is sure that this is a lie. She had personally inspected the supplies before they were delivered. So she tells Luthor that he must be making a mistake. Nevertheless, Luthor tells her, "I get the feeling that you don't trust me, and I can't do business with someone who doesn't trust me. Unless you give me the $150, you can cancel my standing order with you which, as you know, comes to about $900 a week." Lana doesn't want to lose the customer, so she gives Luthor a check for $150. On the way back to his own store, Luthor cashes the check at Currency Exchange. Nevertheless, when he gets back to his store, he calls Lana up and says, "Thanks for the $150. I appreciate your cooperation. Oh, by the way, cancel my standing order with you anyway." Lana calls her bank and issues a stop payment order on the check. When the check is dishonored, Lana asserts economic duress as a defense.*

ii. Lack of Legal Capacity

Lack of legal capacity covers situations such as mental incompetence, guardianship, ultra vires acts, lack of corporate capacity to do business, or any other incapacity besides infancy. *See* UCC Comment 1 to § 3-305. The existence and effect of this type of defense is determined by state law. If, under state law, the obligation is merely voidable, the defense can be asserted against anyone who does not have holder in due course rights. If the obligation is absolutely void, the defense works even against a holder in due course. *Id.*

Lack of mental capacity may be a defense to the extent that it prevents an obligor from understanding the nature of a transaction and effectively prevents him from truly assenting thereto. *See, e.g., In re Wills*, 126 Bankr.Rptr. 489 (Bankr. E.D. Va. 1991). Most modern authority, however, concludes that a lack of mental capacity only renders a contract voidable, not void, unless, at the time of the transaction, the individual had already been adjudicated incompetent. *See* J. CALAMARI AND J. PERILLO, THE LAW OF CONTRACTS, §§ 8-10, P. 249 (2D ED 1977).

Where a lender has acted ultra vires, a number of interrelated issues may arise. For example, a court may find that the fact the lender acted ultra vires, per se, renders a resulting obligation void. *Contrast, e.g., Matter of Lake Hopaton Water Corp.*, 15 Bankr.Rptr. 411 (D. N.J. 1981), *with Payne v. Mundaca Investment Corporation*, 562 N.E.2d 51 (Ind.App. 1st Dist. 1990) and *Valley Stream Teachers Federal Credit Union v. Commissioner of Banks*, 376 Mass. 845, 384 N.E.2d 200 (1978). More likely, courts may permit an ultra vires defense by finding that the statute, if any, that makes the act ultra vires also renders the action absolutely void. *See, e.g., Worthen Bank & Trust Company v. United Underwriters Sales Corporation of America*, 251 Ark. 454, 474 S.W.2d 899 (1971); *Pacific National Bank v. Hernreich*, 240 Ark. 114, 398 S.W.2d 221 (1996).

iii. Illegality

If the illegality of the transaction out of which the instrument arose renders the obligor's duty to pay void, such illegality is a defense that prevails even against someone with holder in due course rights. Thus, some courts state that they will not enforce a contract that is consciously entered into to accomplish an illegal purpose, such as defrauding the Internal Revenue Service. *See, e.g., Shanahan v. Schindler*, 63 Ill.App.3d 82, 379 N.E.2d 1307 (1st Dist. 1978) (although note enforced because the party asserting the illegality adduced inadequate evidence).

In other cases, although reciting that illegality often renders an obligation void, courts sometimes require some showing of legislative intent that the instrument arising from the illegal transaction be void. *See, e.g., Kedzie and 103rd Currency Exchange, Inc. v. Hodge*, 156 Ill.2d 112 (1993), 619 N.E.2d 732 (while the obligation for work performed by an unlicenced plumber was unenforceable, unless statute states that instrument is itself made void, the illegality defense is not available against a holder in due course.). A cursory survey of state laws reveals a variety of statutes that explicitly declare certain promissory notes to be void. Some involve promissory notes given by students to certain types of unlicensed schools. *See, e.g.,* Arkansas, A.C.A. § 6-51-613; Michigan, M.C.L.A. § 395.124; North Carolina, G.S. §§ 93A-37, 115D-97; South Carolina, Code 1976, § 59-58-100. Other statutes deal with notes given for patents, see Nebraska, Neb. Rev. St. § 62-302, or for invention development services, see North Dakota, NDCC, 9-14-07.

Other courts more liberally rule that the illegality of a transaction voids instruments executed in connection with the transaction. *See, e.g., Columbus Checkcashiers v. Stiles*, 56 Ohio App.3d 159 (1990), 565 N.E.2d 883; *Wilson v. Steele*, 211 Cal.App.3d 1053 (1989), 259 Cal.Rptr. 851; *Georgia Livestock Sales v. Commercial Bank & Trust Company*, 123 Ga.App. 733 (Div.1 1971), 182 S.E.2d 533 (instrument issued in connection with contract to purchase stolen goods is void). Sometimes courts ask whether the particular statute violated is affected by a public interest before declaring contracts effectuated in violation of the statute to be void. *See, e.g., Ben E. Keith Company v. Lisle Todd Leasing, Inc.*, 734 S.W.2d 725 (Tex.App. 1987).

Not infrequently, instruments are issued in connection with transactions which illegally violate applicable usury laws. The consequences vary from state. Sometimes usury is simply not a defense against a holder in due course. *See, e.g., Panteleakis v. Kalams*, 659 F.Supp. 212 (D. R.I. 1987). In other jurisdictions, even though usury may be a defense against a holder in due course, see, e.g., *In re Estate of Fauskee*, 497 N.W.2d 324 (1993), the extent to which it provides an obligor relief varies. In most instances, the obligor is only freed from the offensive interest provision. *See, e.g., Bank of North Carolina, N.A. v. Rock Island Bank*, 630 F.2d 1243 (7th Cir. 1980) (only interest provision void under North Carolina law); *Circle v. Jim Walter Homes, Inc.*, 535 F.2d 583 (10th Cir. 1976) (asserting that usury laws only make the transaction a nullity to the extent of the usury).

Similarly, many jurisdictions have statutes that provide that instruments issued or given for all, or certain types of, gambling debts are void. *See, e.g.*, Florida, West's F.S.A. § 849.26; Illinois, 720 ILCS 5/28-7(a); New Jersey, N.J.S.A. 2A:40-3. On the other hand, some statutes explicitly or effectively provide that instruments evidencing illegal gambling debts can be enforced by holders in due course, see, e.g., Georgia, Code 13-8-3.

c. *Fraud in the Factum*

A misrepresentation that induces the obligor to sign a negotiable instrument with neither knowledge nor reasonable opportunity to learn of its character, i.e., that it was a negotiable instrument, or of its essential terms, is a real defense. This is called "fraud in the factum" or "fraud in the execution" and exists "where the instrument is misread to the party signing it, or where there is a surreptitious substitution of one paper for another, or where by some other trick or device a party is made to sign an instrument which he did not intend to execute." *See Belleville National Bank v. Rose*, 119 Ill.App.3d 56, 456 N.E.2d 281, 283, 74 Ill.Dec. 779 (5th Dist. 1983), quoting *Papke v. G. H. Hammond Co.*, 192 Ill. 631, 61 N.E. 910, 912 (1901). The rationale for the defense is that the party did not intend to sign such an instrument and undertake the obligation. "Fraud in the factum" is distinguishable from "fraud in the inducement," in which a party knows she is signing a negotiable instrument and knows its terms, but would not have signed it had she known the truth surrounding the transaction. "Fraud in the inducement" is a personal defense and is cut off by a holder in due course.

PROBLEM 8.6

Ned Naive is induced by Fraudulent Phil to sign a document he believes to be a receipt for money paid him. The document he signs is conspicuously labeled "Receipt," but unknown to him one of the carbon copies beneath the top sheet is in fact a promissory note. Phil transfers the note to a holder in due course, who sues Ned on his maker's contract. Ned asserts that he has a "real defense" based on Phil's fraud. Is Ned right? Yes

PROBLEM 8.7

Ned Naive is induced by Fraudulent Phil to sign what he knows to be a promissory note in exchange for a share of a gold mine he subsequently learns does not exist. Phil has transferred Ned's note to a holder in due course and absconded with the proceeds. The holder in due course sues Ned on his maker's liability. Ned asserts that he has a "real defense" based on Phil's fraud. Is Ned right?

UCC Comment 1 to § 3-305 explains that the test of the fraud in the factum defense is excusable ignorance of the contents of the writing signed. The signer must not only have been ignorant of the nature of the writing but must also have had no reasonable opportunity to have obtained knowledge of the true nature or terms of the instrument. In determining what is a reasonable opportunity, courts are advised by the Comment to take into account all relevant factors, including the intelligence, education, business experience, and ability to read and understand English of the signer. Also relevant is the nature of the representations made, whether reliance on the person making the representations was reasonable, the presence or absence of any third party who might have read or explained the instrument to the signer, and the apparent necessity or lack of it to act without delay. *See* ANNOT., 78 A.L.R.3d 1020 (1977).

PROBLEM 8.8

Would the result have been different in 8.6 above, if the document, with only one carbon copy, had been mailed to Phil for his signature with a cover letter saying the materials sent him were two copies of the same receipt, but that Phil was to personally sign both copies? Phil had the document for a few days and signed both copies without ever reading them.

d. Insolvency Discharge of Debt

If an obligor on an instrument obtains a discharge of his debt in an insolvency proceeding, he may successfully assert this discharge of debt as a defense even against a holder in due course. Sections 3-305(a)(1)(iv), 3-305(b). Thus, if an obligor obtains a discharge of his obligation on an instrument pursuant to a federal bankruptcy proceeding, that bankruptcy discharge is a real defense. Although "insolvency proceedings" is defined as including "any assignment for the benefit of creditors or other proceedings intended to liquidate or rehabilitate the estate of the person involved," most if not all state laws that would involve a discharge of debt would be preempted by the Bankruptcy Code. *See, generally, Straton v. New*, 283 U.S. 318, 75 L.Ed. 1060, 51 S.Ct. 465 (1931); *Stellwagen v. Clum*, 245 U.S. 605, 62 L.Ed. 507, 38 S.Ct. 215 (1918). Consequently, § 3-305(a)(1)(iv), in practice, will probably apply only when a federal bankruptcy discharge has been granted. Indeed, in such cases, because of the supremacy clause, the bankruptcy discharge would in any event defeat the rights of a holder in due course.

2. Claims in Recoupment

A claim in recoupment arises when two parties to a particular transaction have claims against each other based on that transaction. When one party sues the other, the defendant can assert its own claim — which is a claim in recoupment — against the plaintiff.

> **EXAMPLE 1: Suppose A buys a refrigerator from B for $1,200 which is to be delivered to B later that week. A pays B $100 down and gives B a promissory note for $1,100. If the refrigerator is never delivered, A would have a defense to paying the amount due on the note — lack of consideration or breach of contract. But if the refrigerator is delivered, once A has accepted it, the whole purchase price becomes due according to Article 2 of the UCC. If, however, A subsequently finds that the refrigerator he has accepted is defective and needs repair work done, B may be liable to A for breach of warranty. That subsequent claim for damages arising out of this transaction is a claim in recoupment. Assume the breach of warranty claim is worth $300. If B sues A to enforce the promissory note for $1,100, A can assert his $300 claim in recoupment against B, reducing A's liability to B from $1,100 to $800.**

> **EXAMPLE 2: Same facts as in the last EXAMPLE, except that the breach of warranty claim is worth $1,150. If B sues A to enforce the promissory note for $1,100, A can assert his $1,150 claim against B. This would not only eliminate A's liability to B, but would render B liable to A in the amount of $50.**

Section 3-305(a)(3) states that, when sued on an instrument, a defendant can assert against the plaintiff any right in recoupment it has against the original payee of the instrument. If, however, the plaintiff is only a transferee of the instrument, then the defendant's claim in recoupment can only reduce or eliminate the defendant's liability on the instrument; it cannot be the basis of obtaining a judgment against the plaintiff. Thus, in the last example, if B had transferred the note to C and C had sued A for the $1,100, A could assert its claim in recoupment against C only to eliminate its duty to pay on the instrument. A could not use the claim in recoupment to obtain a $50 judgment against C. Another important restriction is that a claim in recoupment may not be asserted at all against a plaintiff who is a holder in due course, unless the claim in recoupment began as a claim directly against the holder in due course himself.

B. Your Client's Liability Has Been Discharged

Even if your client was at one time liable on the instrument, that liability may have subsequently become discharged. Although Part 6 of Article 3, entitled "Discharge and Payment," addresses many of the grounds for discharge, others appear elsewhere in Article 3. This section of the chapter will identify the various bases for discharge and discuss applicable restrictions. As a general rule, however, a defendant being sued on an instrument cannot avoid liability by asserting that his obligation has been discharged, if the plaintiff is a person who acquired the rights of a holder in due course without notice of the discharge.

1. Payment

The 2002 Revisions to Article 3 substantially amended the relevant provisions regarding discharge of a party who has already paid an instrument. As noted elsewhere, at the time this manuscript went to print, only one state, Minnesota, had adopted those revisions. Consequently, we will examine both approaches.

The pre-2002 Revision approach

The pre-2002 Revision version of § 3-602 reads as follows:

§ 3-602 Payment

(a) Subject to subsection (b), an instrument is paid to the extent that payment is made (i) by or on behalf of a party obliged to pay the instrument, and (ii) to a person entitled to enforce the instrument. To the extent of the payment, the obligation of the party obliged to pay the instrument is discharged even though payment is made with knowledge of a claim to the instrument under Section 3-306 by another person,

(b) The obligation of a party to pay the instrument is not discharged under subsection (a) if:

(1) **a claim to the instrument** under Section 3-306 **is enforceable against the party receiving payment** and **(i)** payment is made with knowledge by the payor that payment is prohibited by injunction or similar process of a court of competent jurisdiction, or **(ii)** in the case of an instrument other than a cashier's check, teller's check, or certified check, the party making payment accepted, from the person having a claim to the instrument, indemnity against loss resulting from refusal to pay the person entitled to enforce the instrument; or

(2) the person making payment knows that the instrument is a stolen instrument and pays a person it knows is in wrongful possession of the instrument.

Apply these provisions to the following problems:

PROBLEM 8.9

When Mary Maker borrowed $10,000 from Fast-Talking Finance, Inc. ("FTF"), she issued to FTF the following note:

> *I promise to pay to the order of Fast-Talking Finance, Inc., the sum of $10,000 plus twelve percent (12%) interest on November 1, 2004.*
>
> */s/ Mary Maker*

On September 1, 2004, FTF negotiated the note to BigBank, Inc. (BigBank), in exchange for $9,000. On October 29, 2004, Mary sent FTF a check for the full amount of the note, and FTF cashed the check and disappeared. When BigBank did not receive payment from Mary on November 1, it filed suit against her. Was Mary's obligation on the note discharged by the fact she paid FTF?

PROBLEM 8.10

Same facts as in Problem 8.9 above, except that prior to September 1, 2004, Mary had already paid FTF $5,000 of the amount on the note. Was any part of Mary's obligation on the note discharged? If so, how much was discharged? Does it matter whether Big Bank knew about Mary's payment?

PROBLEM 8.11

Marty Maker issues a bearer note to Patrick Payee in the amount of $1,000, payable on June 1, 2004. On May 31st, 2004, Patrick tells Marty that he has lost the note. Marty says that he's sorry, but he does not know what to do. On June 1, 2004, Phil Finder comes forward and presents the note to Marty for payment. Marty pays Phil, and Phil vanishes. On June 5, Patrick sues Marty, alleging that he (Patrick) is a PETE and that Marty owes him $1,000 on the note. Marty replies by saying that his obligation on the note was discharged. Who should win?

PROBLEM 8.12

Mary Maker issues a promissory note to her best friend Gwen in exchange for a loan from Gwen of $1,000. The note is due on May 12, 2004. Gwen subsequently transfers the note to Sam Slick in exchange for a "gem" that turns out to be worthless. As soon as Gwen finds out that the gem is worthless, she tells Mary on May 8 of the fraud perpetrated by Sam and asks her not to pay the note when it becomes due. Nevertheless, on May 12, despite her knowledge of Gwen's claim Mary pays the note to Sam. Does Mary have any further liability on this instrument?

The 2002 Revision Approach *(minority)*

The 2002 Revision version of § 3-602 retains § 3-602(a), which it splits into Revised 2002 §§ 3-602(a) and (c), and § 3-602(b), which it renames as § 3-602(e). It adds, however, three additional sub-sections: Revised 2002 §§ 3-602(b), (d), and (f). The basic purpose of the 2002 Revision is to provide some protection to obligors on a note who, without knowing that the note has been transferred, make payment to someone who was formerly a person entitled to enforce (a "PETE") the note. Specifically, Revised 2002 § 3-602(b) states that, subject to the § 3-602(e) exceptions, a note is paid to the extent payment is made by, or on behalf of, an obligor to someone who was formerly a PETE before the obligor has received "adequate notification that the note has been transferred and that payment is to be made to the transferee." Notification is only "adequate" if it is "signed" by either the transferor or the transferee, "reasonably identifies the transferred note," and "provides an address at which [subsequent] payments . . . are to be made." Revised 2002 § 3-602(b). Revised 2002 § 3-602(f) states that if notification is given via a "record" that is not a writing, the word "signed" includes "the attachment to or logical association with the record of an electronic symbol, sound, or process with the present intent to adopt or accept the new record." The word "record" is defined in § 1-201(31).

In addition, if an obligor so requests, a transferee must "reasonably furnish reasonable proof that the note has been transferred," and, unless the transferee does so, payment to the former PETE still counts as payment even after the payor receives what would otherwise be adequate "notification." Revised 2002 § 3-602(b)

Revised 2002 § 3-602(d) states that, again subject to the exceptions in subsection (e), a transferee, or any party that acquires rights in a note directly or indirectly from a transferee — including someone with rights as a holder in due course — is deemed to have notice of any payment made by an obligor before the obligor receives adequate notification of the transfer.

PROBLEM 8.13

Apply Revised 2002 § 3-602 to Problem 8.9, above.

2. *"Payment" with a different instrument*

A party's obligation under an instrument may also be satisfied by "payment" if the obligee takes a new instrument for the old instrument. Use § 3-310(a) to do the following problem.

PROBLEM 8.14

On January 12, 2004, Marty Maker issued a note for $5,000, payable to the order of Harry Holder and due July 12, 2004. On June 1, 2004, Marty gave Harry a cashier's check for the $5,000 due pursuant to the note. Is Marty's obligation on the note discharged? Assume that when Harry presents the cashier's check, the bank on which it is drawn refuses to pay. Can Harry successfully sue Marty on the note?

3. *Cancellation or Renunciation*

A PETE may discharge a person obligated to pay the instrument either by an intentional voluntary act, by agreeing not to sue or by otherwise renouncing rights against that person. Voluntary acts that will discharge a party include:

a.   surrendering the instrument to the party;

b.   destroying, mutilating, or canceling the instrument;

c.   canceling or striking out the party's signature; or

d.   adding words to the instrument indicating the discharge.

The act that discharges the party must be voluntary. Cases have found that where the act was a result of a clerical error by a bank employee, was induced by fraud, or was a result of an erroneous belief by the holder that the instrument had been paid, a discharge did not occur. *See, generally,* 59 A.L.R.4th 617. Similarly, if an item is accidently destroyed or mutilated, persons obligated on the instrument will not be discharged. (Section 3-309 provides for how lost, stolen, or destroyed instruments may be enforced.) However, if an item is intentionally destroyed but the party doing so does not understand or appreciate the legal consequences of that act, the discharge may nevertheless be effective.

PROBLEM 8.15

Marty Maker borrows $1,000 from his Uncle Bill and issues to Uncle Bill a note for $1,000, payable to bearer. Upon Marty's graduation from college, Uncle Bill, in a generous mood, rips up the note. Shortly thereafter, alas, Aunt Alice, who never liked Marty, found out about the note and persuaded Uncle Bill to change his mind, causing him to sue Marty on the note. Who should win? voluntary destruction

4. *Discharge on Refusal of Tender of Payment*

Pursuant to § 3-603(c), if a person who is obligated on an instrument tenders payment to a PETE, and the PETE refuses to take it, the person's obligation to pay interest on the amount tendered after the due date of the instrument is discharged. In addition, under § 3-603(b), if someone who is obligated to pay an instrument tenders payment to a PETE, and the tender is refused, anyone with a "right of recourse" as to the obligation is discharged to the extent of the amount tendered. The UCC does not define the phrase, "right of recourse." Nonetheless, it refers to situations in which one party to an instrument, A, has the right, upon his payment of the instrument to a PETE, to enforce the instrument against another party, B. Consequently, parties who have rights or recourse are accommodation parties and indorsers.

PROBLEM 8.16

Chico borrows $1,000 from Margaret and issues a note to her for $1,000, plus 10 percent interest, payable on April 1, 2004. Aware of Chico's unreliability, Margaret lends the money only after requiring that Groucho sign as an accommodation maker. On the due date, Chico tenders the entire amount due, but Margaret tells him to come back next month. Assume Chico, in fact, never comes back — and cannot be found. Margaret sues Groucho on his maker's obligation. What result? Would the result be any different if on the due date, Chico had tendered only $400? What if, six months after the tender of $400 had been refused, Chico was found. Could Margaret successfully sue Chico and, if so, how much could she recover?

What if on the due date, Groucho had tendered the full amount due and Margaret refused to accept it? Six months later can she sue Groucho? If so, for how much? Can she sue Chico? If so, for how much?

5. Section 3-605 Provisions

The 2002 Revisions to Article 3 made substantial changes to § 3-605. We will first consider the pre-2002 Revision Approach and then examine the 2002 Revisions.

Pre-2002 Revision Version of § 3-605 (found in Appendix 4)

The pre-2002 Revision version of § 3-605 provides for the possible discharge, in whole or in part, of a party's liability when, without that party's consent, a PETE (1) extends the due date of an instrument, otherwise (2) modifies an instrument, or (3) impairs the collateral securing payment of an instrument. Although § 3-605 is entitled, "Discharge of Indorsers and Accommodation Parties," its provisions can also operate to discharge, at least in part, the obligation of others, such as non-accommodation parties who are jointly and severally liable on an instrument, such as non-accommodation co-makers.

Whether, and to what extent, a person's obligation is discharged under pre-2002 § 3-605 depends, among other things, on: (1) the loss the person suffered because of the PETE's conduct; and (2) as to the obligation of an accommodation party, whether the PETE knew of the person's accommodation status. *See* § 3-605(h).

In addition, there are two major constraints on a party's ability to successfully defend itself in a suit on an instrument by arguing that its obligation was discharged. First, pre-2002 § 3-605(i) provides that a party's obligation is not discharged if: (1) the party consents to the event or conduct that purportedly gives rise to the discharge; or (2) the instrument or a separate agreement of the party "either specifically or by general language" waives these grounds for discharge or waives "defenses based on suretyship or impairment of collateral." Many commercial notes contain boilerplate language which waives many, if not all, of these defenses.

Second, even if a PETE's conduct gives rise to a discharge that was not waived, pre-2002 § 3-601(b) prevents any discharge from being successfully asserted against a plaintiff who acquired the rights of a holder in due course without notice of the discharge. Assume, for instance, that a PETE modified an agreement without an accommodation party's consent and this modification caused the accommodation party a loss. If the PETE subsequently negotiated the instrument to a holder in due course who was unaware of the unapproved modification, the holder in due course could enforce the instrument against the accommodation party.

PROBLEM 8.17

Marty Maker borrows $5,000 from Fast-Talk Finance, Inc. (FTF), and issues to FTF a note payable to its order on May 3, 2004. Ima N. Dorser, Marty's friend, signs as an indorser. The note is negotiated to Big Bank (BB) shortly after it is issued. On April 30, 2004, Marty, while still solvent, asks for and receives from BB an extension of the due date on the note to September 3, 2004. On August 12, Marty loses all of his life's savings at the track and files for bankruptcy. Suppose when the note goes unpaid on September 3, BB gives timely notice of dishonor to Ima and sues Ima on her indorser's obligation. What will Ima have to prove in order to establish that her obligation was discharged? Would your answer be different if Ima had signed as an accommodation co-maker rather than as an indorser? See pre-2002 §§ 3-605(c), (h).

PROBLEM 8.18

Groucho borrows $10,000 from Fast-Talk Finance, Inc ("FTF"), and issues to it a promissory note payable to bearer in the amount of $10,000, plus interest at 8%, on July 2, 2004. Chico and Harpo sign as accommodation indorsers. Groucho asks FTF to extend the due date until December 1, 2004, and FTF is only willing to do so if Groucho agrees to raise the interest rate from 8% to 12%. Groucho agrees, and the note is amended to extend the due date and alter the interest rate. When the due date arrives, Groucho is nowhere to be found. FTF gives timely notice of dishonor to Chico and Harpo, and sues them as indorsers. They assert that their obligations as indorsers have been discharged. What must happen if FTF is to prevail? See pre-2002 § 3-605(d).

The most difficult parts of pre-2002 § 3-605 deals with a PETE's impairment of the PETE's interest in "collateral." In order to convince someone to lend money or provide credit, often a person must not only sign a promissory note but also provide the creditor with a security interest or other lien in property the person owns. The property in which the creditor's interest reposes is called "collateral." If the debt is not paid, the creditor can foreclose on its interest in the collateral, sell the collateral, and keep the net proceeds of the sale to the extent necessary to pay itself the debt owed it. Similarly, if a party other than the principal debtor, who has a right of recourse against the debtor, is required to pay the instrument, that party could seek reimbursement by asserting an interest in the collateral and taking actions similar to those available to the creditor.

Pre-2002 § 3-605(e) states that if a PETE does something which reduces the value of its interest in collateral (impairs the collateral) owned by a party to an instrument, this may, in whole or in part, discharge the obligation of any other party with a right of recourse against the owner of the collateral.

Pre-2002 § 3-605(g) provides a non-exclusive list of ways in which a PETE could be guilty of impairing the value of an interest in collateral, and § 3-605(e) sets forth two formulas to be used to calculate the extent to which such impairment has occurred. Use these provisions to answer the following problem.

PROBLEM 8.19

On March 1, 2003, Marty Maker borrows $100,000 from First Insatiable Bank ("FIB"), signs a $100,000 promissory note due, with one balloon payment of principal and interest, on March 1, 2006, and, to secure repayment of this note, gives FIB a mortgage in real property worth $180,000 that Marty owns. On March 1, 2003, Naive Ned signs the promissory note as an accommodation indorser. On August 1, 2005, however, Marty files bankruptcy, and, as it tries to participate in the bankruptcy proceeding, FIB realizes that it never recorded its mortgage in Marty's property. Another party, however, which lent Marty money after FIB but before the bankruptcy, did perfect an interest on Marty's property and, as a result, the entire value of the property was used to pay that lender. Marty has no other money from which FIB is able to recover payment on the note. Consequently, FIB sues Ned. Ned asserts that his obligation on the note has been discharged. How should the court rule? Suppose that, at all times relevant to this property, the value of Marty's property had been only $90,000 instead of $180,000. How would this change your answer?

Pre-2002 § 3-605(f) provides that a PETE's impairment of its interest in collateral can also cause the partial discharge of the obligation of a party who has a "right of contribution" against the owner of the collateral. What is a right of contribution? Unless an instrument specifies otherwise, when two or more people sign in the same capacity on an instrument — as co-makers, co-indorsers, etc. — they are "jointly and severally liable" on the instrument. § 3-116(a). This means that a PETE can sue them singly or in any combination, although he cannot recover more than the full value of the note. If the PETE collects all of the note from one of these parties, does this party have any rights against the others who were jointly and severally liable with it? According to Section 3-116(b), if none of these parties were accommodation parties for each other, then each of them has a "right of contribution" against the other "in accordance with applicable law." This means that if any of these parties has paid more than its pro rata share of the note, it can recover the excess from the other parties, up to such other parties' pro rata shares. When a party asserts its right of contribution, it can also enforce the interest in collateral that was given to the PETE. If that interest has been impaired, then the party with the right of contribution is discharged to the extent that the impairment prevents it from recovering on its right of contribution.

PROBLEM 8.20

Clark and Lois sign a note for $1,000 as co-makers, neither being an accommodation party. Clark grants a security interest in Clark's property to secure the note, the collateral being worth more than $1,000. Payee fails to perfect the security interest before Clark files in bankruptcy so that the interest in the property is not enforceable. Payee sues Lois for the $1,000. Lois asserts a defense under §

3-605. Identify her best argument and explain whether she should succeed. See UCC Comment 7 to pre-2002 § 3-605. Explain whether your answer would have been any different if Lois had been an accommodation party for Clark and Payee had known this all along. Would your answer be different if Payee had not known about Lois' accommodation party status until after Clark had filed bankruptcy?

The Rules Under Revised 2002 § 3-605

Revised 2002 § 3-605 uses various terms introduced and defined by Revised 2002 § 3-103(a):

> (11) "Principal obligor," with respect to an instrument, means the accommodated party or any other party to the instrument against whom a secondary obligor has recourse under this article;
>
> . . . .
>
> (17) "Secondary obligor," with respect to an instrument, means (a) an indorser or an accommodation party, (b) a drawer having the obligation described in Section 3-414(d), or (c) any other party to the instrument that has recourse against another party to the instrument pursuant to Section 3-116(b).

Section 3-116(b) deals with situations in which one person who is jointly and severally liable with another has a claim against such other for contribution.

Revised 2002 § 3-605(a) deals with how the a PETE's release of the obligation of a principal obligor affects the rights of a secondary obligor. Pre-2002 Revision § 3-605(b) essentially provided that a PETE's discharge of one party did not discharge the obligation of an indorser or accommodation party having a right of recourse against that party. In other words, using 2002 Revision terminology, the pre-Revision § 3-605(b) stated that a PETE's discharge of a principal obligor did not discharge the obligation of a secondary obligor. Revised 2002 § 3-605(a) changes this rule. First, unless the PETE's release provides that he retains the right to enforce the instrument against a secondary obligor, the secondary obligor's obligation is discharged to the same extent as that of the principal obligor. Revised 2002 § 3-605(a)(2). If the instrument is a check, the secondary obligor's obligation is discharged irrespective of the language or circumstances of the release or discharge regarding the principal obligor. In all such cases, the obligation of the secondary obligor is discharged to the extent of any consideration that was given by, or on behalf of, the principal obligor in exchange for the release and to the extent that the release would otherwise cause the secondary obligor a loss. Revised 2002 § 3-605(a)(3). Revised 2002 § 3-605(a) also provides that, unless the terms of a release specifies otherwise, the release of the principal obligor releases that principal obligor from any liability to the secondary obligor based on the secondary obligor's subsequent payment of the instrument. *See* Comment 4 to Revised 2002 § 3-605.

PROBLEM 8.21

Baker borrows $10,000 from Able and, in return, issues a $10,000 promissory note payable to the order of Able. Carter is an accommodation indorser on this note. As the due date of the note draws near, Able sees that Baker, who is in dire financial straights, will be unable to pay. Consequently, Able releases Baker from liability on the note in exchange for a $1,000 cash payment from Baker.

a. *Suppose the release does not mention anything about Carter's liability on the note, and Able subsequently sues Carter for $9,000. Under Revised 2002 § 3-605, who wins? See Comment 4, Case 1 to Revised 2002 § 3-605. Who would win under the pre-2002 Revision version?*

b. *Suppose Carter had signed as an accommodation co-maker rather than as an accommodation indorser, and Able knew from the beginning about Carter's accommodation party status. Would you answer to "a," above, be any different?*

c. *Suppose that the release expressly retained Able's right to enforce the note against Carter, and Able sues Carter to enforce the note. If Carter pays the note, will Carter be able to sue Baker, the accommodated party? See Comment 4, Case 2 to Revised 2002 § 3-605. Suppose that Baker had assets that Able did not know about and that, if, after paying the note, Carter had been legally permitted to sue Able, he would have been able to obtain full reimbursement. Does this fact affect Able's ability to enforce the note against Carter? See Comment 4, Case 2 to Revised 2002 § 3-605.*

Revised 2002 § 3-605(b) addresses the effect of a PETE's granting a principal obligor an extension of time. Unless the extension of time preserves the secondary obligor's right of recourse against the principal obligor, the extension extends the time for performance by the secondary obligor as well. Revised 2002 § 3-605(b)(1). To the extent that the extension of time would cause the secondary obligor a loss, the secondary obligor is discharged. Revised 2002 § 3-605(b)(2). If the secondary obligor's liability is not discharged, then, unless the extension specifically retains the right to enforce the instrument against the secondary obligor as if there had been no extension, the secondary obligor can choose to pay either according to the original due date or at the new, extended due date.

Revised 2002 § 3-605(c) involves the effect of a modification (other than a complete or partial release or an extension of due date), with or without consideration, of the principal obligor's obligation on an instrument. The modification modifies any obligations owed by the principal obligor to the secondary obligor, except as such obligations pertain to any previous payments made by the secondary obligor. To the extent that the modification would cause the secondary obligor a loss, the unperformed portion of the secondary obligor's obligation is discharged. Revised 2002 § 3-605(c)(2). To the extent the secondary obligor's obligation is not discharged, the secondary obligor has the choice to perform in accordance with the unmodified or in accordance with the modified terms of the instrument. Revised 2002 § 3-605(c)(3).

Many of the remaining portions of Revised 2002 § 3-605 are similar to those of pre-Revision § 3-605. Among the differences, however, is that Revised 2002 § 3-605(h) generally imposes on the secondary obligor the burden of persuasion "both with respect to the occurrence of the facts alleged to harm the secondary obligor and loss or prejudice caused by those acts." Revised 2002 § 3-605(h). Revised 2002 § 3-605(i) provides an exception, however, where the secondary obligor proves prejudice based on impairment of its right of recourse, but the amount of loss is not "readily susceptible of calculation or requires proof of facts that are not ascertainable." In such a case, the burden of persuasion "as to any lesser amount of the loss is on the person entitled to enforce the instrument."

6. Discharge Due to Late Presentment or Notice of Dishonor

As previously discussed in Chapter 5, if a check, and only a check, is not presented for payment or given to a depository bank for collection within 30 days after an indorsement is made, the liability of the indorser is discharged. Section 3-415(e). An indorser on any instrument is also discharged if notice of dishonor is neither excused pursuant to § 3-504 nor timely given. On the other hand, drawers on a check are discharged for late presentment only when the following circumstances occur: (1) the drawee suspends payments without paying the check, (2) the suspension deprives the drawer of funds with which to cover the check and (3) the drawer assigns his rights to such funds to the person entitled to enforce the check. See § 3-414(f) and discussion in Chapter 5. Remember a drawer of a check is not entitled to notice of dishonor.

7. Discharge on an Accepted Draft (Including Certified Check)

If a draft is accepted by a bank, the drawer and those indorsers who signed *prior* to the acceptance are discharged. Sections 3-414(c), 3-415(d). This would, of course, include all certified checks, which by definition are accepted by a bank. The drawer is discharged, regardless of when or by whom acceptance was obtained. *See* § 3-414(c).

If a draft is accepted by a party other than a bank, the drawer remains personally liable, but the liability is the same as that of an indorser on any other instrument. As such, he is entitled to be given proper notice of dishonor, and failure to do so will result in his discharge. *See* §§ 3-414(d), 3-415(a), 3-415(c).

If a draft is presented for acceptance and the holder assents to an acceptance that varies the terms of the draft, the obligation of each drawer and indorser that does not expressly assent to the acceptance is discharged. *See* § 3-410(c)

PROBLEM 8.22

a. Harry Dresser purchases a used Harley-Davidson motorcycle from Angel Heller for $11,000 and gives Angel his personal check for that amount drawn on his bank, Times Square Savings and Loan. Angel wishes to use the check as a partial payment on a new bike, but the dealer from whom he wants to purchase the bike refuses to take a third-party check unless it is certified. Angel takes the check to Times Square, which does, in fact, certify the check. Angel then indorses the check over to Dealer who takes it, along with Angel's personal check for the balance of the amount due. When Dealer presents the check to Times Square, the check is dishonored. Can dealer enforce the check against Harry? Can dealer enforce the check against Angel after giving Angel notice of dishonor?

b. Assume the same set of facts as in "a" except that instead of a check, Harry gives Angel a draft drawn on the Redline Company, a customer of Harry's who owes him money. Assume again that Angel has the draft accepted by Redline and then indorses it over to dealer. If Redline refuses to pay upon presentment, can Dealer enforce the draft against Harry? Can dealer enforce the check against Angel after giving Angel notice of dishonor? If Dealer can sue Harry, does he need to give Harry notice of dishonor? What if Redline was willing to only commit to pay $10,000 and Dealer agreed to Redline's acceptance for that amount?

8. Discharge Due to a Fraudulent Alteration

a. Generally

An alteration includes an unauthorized change in an instrument that purports to modify the obligation of a party or an unauthorized addition of words or numbers to an incomplete instrument. An alteration *fraudulently* made discharges any party whose obligation is affected by the alteration, unless that party assents or is precluded from asserting the alteration. See the discussion of preclusion in Chapter 17. There is no discharge if the alteration is innocently made, such as by filling in a blank in the honest belief it was authorized, or if a change is made with a benevolent motive, such as a desire to give the obligor the benefit of a lower interest rate. If the alteration is not fraudulent, the instrument may be enforced in accordance with its original terms. Section 3-407(b).

PROBLEM 8.23

Bill and Tim enter into an agreement by which Bill agrees to purchase lamps from Tim at $50 each. The lamps are to be picked up at Tim's apartment while Tim is not at home. Bill takes three lamps and leaves a check for $150. When Tim comes home, he notes that four lamps have been taken, so he assumes in good faith that Bill has made an error and changes the amount of the check to $200. Unbeknownst to Tim, his wife had given a lamp away to one of her friends.

When Tim presents the check to Bill's bank, the bank dishonors it. When Tim presents the check to Bill, Bill refuses to pay it at all, citing the alteration. If Tim sues Bill to enforce the check, how should the court rule?

b. Exceptions

The discharge because of a fraudulent alteration is not effective with respect to a payor bank or drawee who pays the instrument or a person who takes it in good faith and for value without notice of the alteration. Those parties may enforce rights with respect to the instrument according to its original terms or, in the case of an incomplete instrument altered by an unauthorized completion, according to the terms as completed. § 3-407(c).

PROBLEM 8.24

Dan Drawer writes a check for $200 payable to Simon Sleaze, who expertly changes the amount to $2,000. Simon takes the check to the Big Screen TV store where he purchases a 54" TV, priced at exactly $2,000. Simon indorses Dan's check over to Big Screen TV, which takes it as full payment for the set. When the check is presented to Dan's Bank, it is dishonored. Big Screen then initiates suit against Dan on his drawer's obligation. What will Dan assert in his defense? What result?

What result if Simon had not used the check to purchase a TV, but instead had given it to his niece as a generous graduation gift and the niece tried to enforce it against Dan?

Going back to the original problem, suppose Dan had given Simon a blank check with the understanding that Simon would fill in $200 as the sum payable, but Simon instead filled in $2,000. Would this affect your answer as to whether, or as to by how much, Big Screen could recover from Dan?

C. *Your Client May Be Able to Assert a Third Person's Claim to the Instrument, Claim in Recoupment, Defense or Discharge*

If your client is an accommodation party who is sued on an instrument, then, despite the fact that he may have no defense of his own, he may be able to assert a claim in recoupment, defense or discharge that the accommodated party would be able to assert. Use § 3-305(d) to answer the next three problems.

PROBLEM 8.25

Marty Maker enters into a contract with Fraudulent Fred to have Fred build an extension on Marty's house for $50,000. Fred, who had no intention to build anything, lied about this to Marty and even convinced him to issue in advance a promissory note for the $50,000. In fact, pretending to be concerned about Marty's creditworthiness, Fred required that Marty get his Rich Uncle Robert to sign as an accommodation party. Rich Uncle Robert signed the note without talking to Fred and without asking Marty any questions about why the note was being issued. Although Fred does not do any work on Marty's house, when the note falls due, he sues Rich Uncle Robert. What claims or defenses, if any, can Rich Uncle Robert assert? fraud or lack of consideration

PROBLEM 8.26

When Mary Maker borrowed $15,000 from Fast-Talk Finance, Inc. ("FTF"), she issued to FTF a promissory note for $15,000 due on June 1, 2004. Mary's Aunt Sally signed as an accommodation indorser. In March, 2004, Mary filed bankruptcy and obtained a discharge of personal liability to FTF. When the debt falls due, FTF gives timely notice of dishonor to Aunt Sally and sues her on her indorser's obligation. Can Aunt Sally assert in her own defense the fact that Mary's obligation was discharged in bankruptcy?

But suppose your client is not an accommodation party. If your client is sued, can he assert a claim to the instrument, a claim in recoupment, defense or discharge of some other party to the instrument? The general rule is that he cannot. But § 3-305(c) provides some exceptions.

PROBLEM 8.27

Marty Maker writes a note payable to his friend Paul for $650 to pay off an old loan. Paul orders a used car from Fraudulent Fred and pays for it by indorsing the note in blank and giving it to Fred. Fred, however, fails to delivers the car.

Paul calls Marty and asks him not to pay the note. Fred sues Marty on his maker's obligation. What must Marty do to be able to assert Paul's claim?

[handwritten: Join Paul, have him assert own claim]

PROBLEM 8.28

Dan Drawer writes a check payable to his friend Lucky Louie for $650 in exchange for a set of used high quality golf clubs. Lucky indorsed the check in blank and put it in his back pocket and went to the track to make some investments in the fortunes of some thoroughbreds. Unfortunately, Lucky was relieved of his check before he could even place a bet on a horse, by a petty thief named Lightfingers Larry. When Lucky realized what had happened he immediately called Dan and told him to put a stop order on the check (i.e., to tell Dan's bank not to pay it). When Larry tried to cash the check at Dan's bank, the check was dishonored. Now Larry is suing Dan on his drawer's obligation. Must Dan pay the amount of the check to Larry? What would happen if Larry, instead of cashing the check, gave it over to SnapShotz Camera Supplies in exchange for a digital camera, and SnapShotz (a "holder in due course") sued Dan on the check?

[handwritten left margin: not if he knows its stolen]

Chapter 9

THE HOLDER IN DUE COURSE DOCTRINE

When a person entitled to enforce an instrument actually tries to enforce it, the defendant has the opportunity to raise a number of defenses to ultimate liability, as discussed in Chapter 8. These include (a) defenses listed in § 3-305(a)(1)("real defenses"); (b) defenses explicitly created by particular provisions of Revised Article 3; and (c) other defenses ("personal defenses") that would be available if the person entitled to enforce the instrument was attempting to enforce a right to payment under a simple contract (e.g., fraud, misrepresentation, or mistake in the inducement). How successful these defenses may be depends partly on the plaintiff's status, because if the plaintiff is what is called a "holder in due course," she is going to be awfully tough to beat. Specifically, a holder in due course generally takes free of all but real defenses.

As also discussed in Chapter 8, a person's obligation on an instrument may be discharged under certain circumstances. A holder in due course who acquires an instrument without notice of a discharge is not subject to that discharge. Section 3-601(b). She is subject only to discharges of which she had notice or that she caused. In addition, a holder in due course takes an instrument free from any claims third parties may have in the instrument, see § 3-306, and from any claims in recoupment an obligor may have against a party other than the holder in due course, see § 3-305(b).

The purpose of providing a holder in due course with such special rights is to facilitate the transferability of negotiable instruments. A party will be more willing to take an instrument in exchange for an obligation when she can enforce the instrument despite an unknown irregularity in the underlying transaction for which the instrument was issued. Given the value of the holder in due course status, it is not surprising that the bulk of negotiable instruments litigation concerns whether one meets the criteria and thus qualifies to reap the benefits of being a holder in due course.

Acquiring Holder in Due Course Status

Under Article 3, there are two basic ways in which a person may acquire the *rights* of a holder in due course. The first is to satisfy all of the requirements of § 3-302. The second is for a transferee to acquire holder in due course status simply because the transferor had such status. This is commonly referred to as the "shelter doctrine."

Holder in Due Course Requirements Generally (§ 3-302)

The requirements one must satisfy in order to be a holder in due course are set forth in § 3-302(a), which states:

> **Subject to subsection (c) and Section 3-106(d), "holder in due course" means the holder of an instrument if:**
>
> **(1) the instrument when issued or negotiated to the holder does not bear such apparent evidence of forgery or alteration or is not otherwise so irregular or incomplete as to call into question its authenticity, and**
>
> **(2) the holder took the instrument (i) for value, (ii) in good faith, (iii) without notice that the instrument is overdue or has been dishonored or that there is an uncured default with respect to payment of another instrument issued as part of the same series, (iv) without notice that the instrument contains an unauthorized signature or has been altered, (v) without notice of any claim to the instrument described in Section 3-306, and (vi) without notice that any party has a defense or claim in recoupment described in Section 3-305(a).**

In order to become a holder in due course according to § 3-302(a), then, one must (1) be a holder of (2) a negotiable instrument (3) whose authenticity is not called into question by apparent evidence, (4) that was taken for value, (5) was taken in good faith, and (6) was taken without notice that it was overdue or of any claims or defenses against it.

The Requirements:

The Instrument Must Be Negotiable

Clearly, a party may not acquire holder in due course status of an instrument that is not a negotiable instrument. In order to be negotiable, an instrument must satisfy the requirements of § 3-104.

The Individual Must Be a Holder

A holder of a negotiable instrument is (1) if the instrument is payable to bearer, the person in possession, or (2) if the instrument is payable to an identified person, that person, if he is in possession of the instrument. *See* § 1-201(20).

The Instrument Must Not on Its Face Be of Questionable Authenticity

Under § 3-302, if the holder of the instrument is to qualify as a holder in due course, the instrument in question must not have borne such apparent evidence of forgery or alteration, or otherwise been so irregular or incomplete, at the time it came into his possession as to call into question its authenticity. Under Former Article 3, apparent evidence of forgery, alteration, irregularity, or incompleteness that called an instrument's authenticity into question was deemed to have given the holder notice of a claim or defense to the instrument. The drafters of the 1990 Revised Code, however, felt that "it was not clear from that provision [pre-1990 § 3-304(1)] whether the claim or defense had to be related to the irregularity or incomplete aspect of the instrument." *See* UCC Comment 1 to § 3-302. Accordingly, the drafters decided to include the "authenticity test" as a separate requirement to obtain holder in due course status under § 3-302. The term "authenticity" is used to make it clear that the irregularity or incompleteness must indicate the instrument is not what it purports to be.

The Instrument Must Be Taken for Value

The question whether an instrument is taken for value is governed by § 3-303.

An Executory Promise Is Usually Not Value

Subject to the exception regarding irrevocable promises to third parties, an executory promise (i.e., a promise that is not yet performed) does not constitute value. A promise to perform constitutes value only to the extent the promise already has been performed. Even though an executory promise constitutes valid consideration to support a simple contract, it does not constitute value for determining if one is a holder in due course.

The reason given for this rule is that a holder who gives an executory promise of performance does not need holder in due course status to avoid a loss. *See* UCC Comment 2 to § 3-303. If, at the time the instrument is dishonored, the holder has not performed the promise, the dishonor excuses the holder from performing the promise, and, therefore, the holder suffers no out-of-pocket loss. *See* UCC Comment 2 to § 3-303. Of course, the holder would need holder in due course status to become entitled to any *gain* he anticipated from her acquisition of the instrument. The Code, however, does not deprive the obligor of his personal defenses and does not deprive other parties of their claims to the instrument in order to grant the holder such anticipated gain.

PROBLEM 9.1

On January 15, after Norm fraudulently convinces Rebecca to issue a check to him for $5,000, as a down payment on property in Florida that does not exist, Norm indorses the check in blank and gives it to his wife, Vera, who uses it to pay for a linoleum floor she has picked out at Larry's Linoleum Outlet. The pattern Vera wants, however, is temporarily out of stock, but is on order, and the new shipment is scheduled to arrive on February 1. When he takes the check from her, Larry promises to deliver the flooring on February 3. Beforehand, however, on January 19, Larry presents the check at Rebecca's bank, Cheers National Bank, which refuses to pay it because Rebecca issued a stop order upon learning of Norm's fraud. Will Rebecca be able to successfully assert her defense of Norman's fraud against Larry or is Larry a holder in due course who takes free of her defense?

executory promise *no value*

PROBLEM 9.2

Sam Seller contracts to deliver 4,000 widgets to Bob Buyer in two installments for a total purchase price of $1,000 payable at the time of the first delivery. He delivers the first installment of 2,000 widgets on May 1. On that date Bob indorses a $1,000 check payable to Bob from Dan Drawer over to Sam. The second delivery is to be made on May 15, but on May 3, Sam presents the check to Dan's bank, and it is dishonored. Sam sues Dan for the amount of the check, but Dan asserts the personal defense that he was fraudulently induced to issue the check to Bob. Can Sam recover the total amount of the check from Dan? If not, can he recover any amount? If Sam cannot recover the entire amount, what should he do?

An Irrevocable Commitment to a Third Party Is Value

If, in exchange for the issue or transfer of an instrument, a person incurs an irrevocable obligation to a third party, the person incurring the obligation has given value even before he performs that obligation (i.e., while his promise to perform the obligation is still executory). Why? Because even if the instrument is dishonored, the holder-promissor is unavoidably liable to the third party to fulfill his promise to perform. Consequently, he will suffer a loss unless he is accorded holder in due course status.

PROBLEM 9.3

Assume in Problem 9.1, that the floor that Vera ordered was not a standard one, but instead was to be custom designed and made by Larry's supplier. Larry had placed the order with that supplier on the same day that Vera was in his *store telling him what she wanted and work had actually begun on the floor. The supplier had required Larry to put down a non-refundable deposit and to sign a contract that would not allow him to cancel his order once work began. Do these facts change the result in Problem 9.1?*

Discounted Notes and Partial Performance

Often, promissory notes, especially those that will be paid over a period of time, will be sold for less than their face value because the payee would rather have the cash at an earlier date than that called for in the notes or because of the inherent risk that intervening circumstances before the due date may impede the ability to collect the amount due. Since the party to whom the note is transferred will now have to incur that risk, it is only fair that he pay a discounted amount (i.e., less than face value) for the instrument. When the agreed-upon amount has been paid, the holder will have given value and, assuming he meets all other requirements, will he be a holder in due course for the full amount of the note.

PROBLEM 9.4

a. On February 1, Mary Maker issues a $ 1,000 note payable to the order of Paul Payee that is due June 1 . On February 15, Paul agrees to sell the note to Harry Holder for $800. Thereupon, Harry gives Paul $800 cash, and Paul indorses the note over to Harry. When Harry sues Mary to enforce the note, Mary asserts a lack of consideration defense that would have worked against Paul. What, if anything, can Harry recover?

b. Assume once again that on February 15. Payee sells the $1,000 note to Harry for an agreed-upon $800. This time, however, Harry pays $400 cash and promises to pay the other $400 on June 15. When the note becomes due on June 1, Harry presents it to Maker for payment, but she refuses to pay. When Harry sues Mary to enforce the note, Mary asserts a lack of consideration defense that would have worked against Paul. What, if anything, can Harry recover? See § 3-302(d)

Acquiring a Security Interest or Lien Is Value

Section 3-303(a)(2) defines "value" as including the obtaining of a security interest or a nonjudicial lien in the instrument. The term "security interest" includes cases in which an instrument may be taken as collateral under Article 9 of the UCC.

UCC Comment 3 to § 3-303 makes clear that an attaching creditor or other person who acquires a lien by judicial proceedings does not give value for the purposes of § 3-303(a)(2). Holder in due course status is intended to persuade persons to be willing to take a negotiable instrument voluntarily in satisfaction of an underlying obligation. There is no need to provide holder in due course status as an incentive to a creditor seeking to obtain satisfaction of a judicial lien. Such a creditor is satisfied to obtain whatever asset it can obtain.

Section 4-211 restates the general rule as it applies to banks by providing that a bank has given value to the extent it obtains a security interest in an item. Section 4-210 describes circumstances under which a bank acquires a security interest in an item. The bank has a security interest to the extent to which (a) credit given for a deposited item has in fact been withdrawn or applied, (b) the bank made an advance on or against the item, or (c) the customer has the legal right to withdraw such credit.

When, before depositing an item, the customer had a zero balance in his account, it is relatively easy to determine whether credit given for the item has been withdrawn or applied. If, however, there is a previous balance, some specific rule must be used to determine whether the money withdrawn was from the previous balance or from credit on the new item deposited. Section 4-210(b) continues the former UCC's adoption of the first-in, first-out (FIFO) rule for determining which credits have been withdrawn when.

PROBLEM 9.5

a. Dick Depositor deposits a check drawn to him by Dan Drawer for $2,000 into an account in which Dick has a zero balance. The Depository Bank credits his account for $2,000, and the following day Dick withdraws $500. If Dick's bank tries to enforce the check against Dan Drawer, who has a valid personal defense, what amount, if any, will the bank be able to recover? 500

b. Assume that in the example above Dick already had $500 in his account when he deposited Dan's check for $2,000. Then assume, as above, Dick withdraws $500 the following day. If again, Dick's bank tries to enforce the check against Dan Drawer, who has a valid personal defense, what amount, if any, will the bank be able to recover?

c. Assume now that Dick had withdrawn $1,000 under the facts as set forth in "b," above. If again, Dick's bank tries to enforce the check against Dan Drawer, who has a valid personal defense, what amount, if any, will the bank be able to recover?

The FIFO rule, however, does not help when several items are deposited at the same time. Section 4-210(b), which is designed to address this situation, is unclear. It states:

If credit given for several items received at one time or pursuant to a single agreement is withdrawn or applied in part,

the security interest remains upon all the items, any accompanying documents or the proceeds of either.

UCC Comment 2 to 4-210(b) "explains" that this provision "spreads the security interest of the bank over all items in a single deposit or received under a single agreement and a single giving of credit." The ambiguity of § 4-210(b) and UCC Comment 2 thereto can be best appreciated based on the following fact pattern:

PROBLEM 9.6

Dick Depositor, a dentist, makes a deposit of three checks, all drawn by his patients and made payable to him, into his account at First National Bank. One check, for $100, was drawn by Tom Toothache. Another, for $200, was drawn by Buck Teeth. The last, for $300, was drawn by Ruth Canal. The deposit slip for $600 listed all three checks. First National allowed Dick to withdraw $100 immediately, and he did so. The checks drawn by Buck and Ruth were honored. When First National presented Tom's check to his drawee bank, however, the check was dishonored. First National then sued Tom on his drawer's obligation, and Tom raised a valid personal defense. To the extent that First National is a holder in due course, however, it may prevail against Tom despite Tom's personal defense. Is First National a holder in due course and, if so, to what extent?

In the case of an item for which the bank has given credit available for withdrawal as of right, a bank has a security interest to the extent of the credit given, regardless of whether the credit has been drawn on by the customer or the bank has a right to charge back the amount of the credit given for the item to the customer's account. *See* § 4-210(a)(2).

Section 4-215(e) provides that credit given by a bank becomes available for withdrawal as of right:

(1) if the bank has received a provisional settlement for the item, when such settlement becomes final and the bank has had a reasonable time to receive return of the item but the item has not been received within that time;

(2) if the bank is both the depositary bank and the payor bank, and the item is finally paid, at the opening of the bank's second banking day following receipt of the item

A customer may also have a legal right to withdraw such credit based on § 4-215, on a special contractual arrangement with the bank, or on state or federal statutes governing the collection of funds. See Chapter 15 for a discussion of one such statute, the federal Expedited Funds Availability Act.

Antecedent Debts Constitute Value

Section 3-303(a)(3) states that an instrument is transferred for value if it is transferred as payment of or security for an antecedent claim against any person. This is so even if there is no concession, such as an extension of time to pay the debt, and regardless of whether the claim has come due.

PROBLEM 9.7

Marty Maker has owed Paula Payee $1,000 since January 1, 2005, and has promised to pay her back by January 1, 2006, but the debt is not represented by a note. On March 15, 2005, Marty issues a note to Paula in that amount payable on January 1, 2006, but receives no concessions from Paula for doing so.

    a. *Under traditional contract law was there consideration for Marty's promise of March 15, 2005?*

    b. *Has Marty's note been issued for value under Article 3?*

    c. *Can Paula be a holder in due course of this note?* Yes

    d. *If Marty is sued on his obligation on this note, may he raise the defense that there was no consideration given in exchange for his promise to pay?*

                   No – value of debt was consideration

Negotiable Instruments Are Value

An instrument issued or transferred in exchange for another negotiable instrument is also said to be issued or transferred for value, § 3-303(a)(4), even though the negotiable instrument, if payable in the future, appears to be an executory promise. A negotiable instrument is value because it may be negotiated to a holder in due course and, if it is so negotiated, the obligor could not avoid paying it.

The Instrument Must Be Taken in Good Faith

In dealing with questions of "good faith," courts and legislatures struggled for centuries over whether to apply an objective test (e.g., whether the person acted as a reasonably prudent person would have acted under the circumstances) or a subjective test (i.e., whether the person acted honestly, however stupid or negligent his behavior may have been). The UCC approach has evolved over time. Initially, its definition of good faith, set forth in Former § 1-201(19), merely required "honesty in fact and in the conduct or transaction concerned." The majority view construed Former § 1-201(19) as requiring only subjective good faith, employing an approach sometimes called the "white heart and empty head test" of good faith. Later on, the UCC adopted a special definition of good faith for purposes of Articles 3 and 4, which was two-tiered. It retained the "honesty in fact" requirement, but added that an act would not be characterized as having been taken in good faith unless it was done in "the observance of reasonable commercial standards of fair dealing." *See* § 3-103(a)(4). In the 2001 revisions to UCC Article 1, the NCCUSL adopted this two-tiered test as its general definition of "good faith" as new § 1-201(20).

Nevertheless, even courts applying the subjective test of good faith recognized certain "exceptions." Thus, if the suspicious circumstances were very substantial, a person who failed to inquire was sometimes said to have acted in bad faith by closing its "eyes and mind to any defects in or defenses to the transaction." *See General Investment Corp. v. Angelini*, 58 N.J. 396, 278 A.2d 193 (1971). *See also Community Bank v. Ell*, 278 Or. 417, 564 P.2d 685 (1977); *Hollywood National Bank v. International Business Machines Corporation*, 38 Cal.App. 3d 607, 113 Cal.Rptr. 494 (1974); *Mid-Continent National Bank v. Bank of Independence*, 523 S.W.2d 569 (Mo.App. 1975). Thus, a "guilty" failure to inquire by a person who subjectively suspected such defenses was bad faith — while a mere negligent failure to suspect the defenses was not. *See, e.g., Northwestern National Insurance Co. v. Maggio*, 976 F.2d 320 (7th Cir. 1992) (deliberate avoidance of inquiry by person who fears what inquiry will reveal is bad faith). Objective evidence as to the nature of the surrounding circumstances was allowed in order to raise an inference regarding a party's subjective state of mind. *See, e.g., Funding Consultants, Inc. v. Aetna Casualty & Surety Co.*, 187 Conn. 637, 447 A.2d 1163 (1982).

One factor frequently cited as significant was the type of relationship, if any, that existed between the original payee and the purchaser of the instrument. When it was found that a close and confidential relationship existed between them, the "close connection doctrine," originally set forth in *Unico v. Owen*, 50 N.J. 101, 232 A.2d 405 (1967), prevented the purchaser from asserting holder in due course status. *See also Stotler v. Geibank Indus. Bank*, 827 P.2d 608 (Colo.App. 1992); *Myers v. College Manor*, 587 So.2d 820 (La.App.3d Cir. 1991); *Johnston III v. Bumba*, 764 F.Supp. 1263 (N.D. Ill. 1991); *Kaw Valley State Bank & Trust Co. v. Riddle*, 219 Kan. 550, 549 P.2d 927 (1976); *Morgan v. Reasor Corp.*, 69 Cal.2d 881, 447 P.2d 638 (1968). *But see Christinson v. Venturi Construction Co.*, 109 Ill App.3d 34, 440 N.E.2d 226, 64 Ill.Dec. 674 (5th Dist. 1982) (limiting close connection doctrine to consumer financing transactions — "where a transaction does not involve a consumer as a party . . . the bald conclusion that two entities are closely connected, without more, provides no reason for denying the holder of an instrument the favored status of a holder in due course"). *See also Annot.*, 39 A..R.3d 518 (1971).

The Code provides little guidance as to the likely effect of expanding the definition of good faith to include "the observance of reasonable commercial standards of fair dealing." UCC Comment 4 to § 3-103 expressly states that the new language is concerned with *fairness* not *negligence*. It asserts that the failure to exercise ordinary care is entirely different from the failure to deal fairly and, although each is to be judged in light of reasonable commercial standards, those standards are directed to different aspects of commercial conduct. *See, generally, Any Kind Checks Cashed, Inc. v. Talcott*, 830 So.2d 160 (D.Ct.Ap. Fla. 2002) *and Gerber v. Gerber, P.C. v. Regions Bank*, 2004 WL 287347, S.E.2d .

The following case contains an excellent discussion of both the "honesty in fact" and the "observance of reasonable commercial standards of fair dealings" elements of "good faith":

MAINE FAMILY FEDERAL CREDIT UNION v. SUN LIFE ASSURANCE COMPANY OF CANADA et al.
Supreme Judicial Court of Maine
199 Me. 43, 727 A.2d 335, 37 UCC Rep.Serv.2d 875 (1999)

SAUFLEY, J.

We are called upon here to address the concept of "holder in due course" as defined by recent amendments to the negotiable instruments provisions of the Maine Uniform Commercial Code. We conclude that, pursuant to those amendments, the Superior Court (Cumberland County, *Calkins,* J.) did not err when it entered a judgment based on the jury's finding that the Maine Family Federal Credit Union was not a holder in due course. Because we find, however, that Sun Life Assurance Company was not entitled to raise a third party's defense of fraud to its liability as drawer of the instruments, we vacate that portion of the judgment entered in favor of Sun Life and against the Credit Union.

I. Facts

Daniel, Joel, and Claire Guerrette are the adult children of Elden Guerrette, who died on September 24, 1995. Before his death, Elden had purchased a life insurance policy from Sun Life Assurance Company of Canada, through Sun Life's agent, Steven Hall, and had named his children as his beneficiaries. Upon his death, Sun Life issued three checks, each in the amount of $40,759.35, to each of Elden's children. The checks were drawn on Sun Life's account at Chase Manhattan Bank in Syracuse, New York. The checks were given to Hall for delivery to the Guerrettes.

The parties have stipulated that Hall and an associate, Paul Richard, then fraudulently induced the Guerrettes to indorse the checks in blank and to transfer them to Hall and Richard, purportedly to be invested in "HER, Inc.," a corporation formed by Hall and Richard. Hall took the checks from the Guerrettes and turned them over to Richard, who deposited them in his account at the Credit Union on October 26, 1995. The Credit Union immediately made the funds available to Richard.

The Guerrettes quickly regretted having negotiated their checks to Hall and Richard, and they contacted Sun Life the next day to request that Sun Life stop payment on the checks. Sun Life immediately ordered Chase Manhattan to stop payment on the checks. Thus, when the checks were ultimately presented to Chase Manhattan for payment, Chase refused to pay the checks, and they were returned to the Credit Union.

The Credit Union received notice that the checks had been dishonored on November 3, 1995, the sixth business day following their deposit. By that time, however, Richard had withdrawn from his account all of the funds represented by the three checks. The Credit Union was able to recover almost $80,000 from Richard, but there remained an unpaid balance of $42,366.56, the amount now in controversy.

The Credit Union filed a complaint against Sun Life alleging that Sun Life was liable as drawer of the instruments, and that Sun Life had been unjustly enriched at the Credit Union's expense. Although it could have done so, the Credit Union did not originally seek any recovery from the Guerrettes. Sun Life, however, filed a third-party complaint against Daniel Guerrette and Paul Richard, whose signatures appeared on the back of one of the checks. The Credit Union then filed a cross-claim against third-party defendants Guerrette and Richard, alleging that they were liable as indorsers of the checks, and Daniel Guerrette filed cross-claims against the Credit Union and against Sun Life. Finally, Sun Life eventually filed third- party complaints against Joel and Claire Guerrette.

The Credit Union moved for summary judgment. The Superior Court held, as a matter of law, that Daniel Guerrette had raised a "claim of a property or possessory right in the instrument or its proceeds," 11 M.R.S.A. § 3-1306 (1995), and therefore that Sun Life was entitled to assert that claim as a "defense" against the Credit Union. *See* 11 M.R.S.A. § 3- 1305(3) (1995). The court found, however, that a genuine issue of material fact remained as to whether the Credit Union had acted in "good faith" when it gave value for the checks — a fact relevant to determining whether the Credit Union was a holder in due course. *See* 11 M.R.S.A. § 3- 1302(1)(b)(ii) (1995). Accordingly, the court denied the Credit Union's motion for summary judgment, and the matter proceeded to trial.

At trial, the only issue presented to the jury was whether the Credit Union had acted in "good faith" when it gave value for the checks, thus entitling it to holder in due course status. At the close of evidence, the Credit Union made a motion for a judgment as a matter of law, which the Superior Court denied. The jury found that the Credit Union had not acted in good faith and therefore was not a holder in due course. Therefore, the Superior Court entered judgment in favor of Sun Life, Daniel, Joel, and Claire, and against the Credit Union. The court denied the Credit Union's renewed motion for judgment as a matter of law and motion to amend the judgment, and the Credit Union filed this appeal.

II. Obligations of the Parties

At the heart of the controversy in this case is the allocation of responsibility for the loss of the unpaid $42,366.56, given the fact that Paul Richard and Steven Hall, the real wrongdoers, appear to be unable to pay. Maine, like the other forty-nine states, has adopted the Uniform Commercial Code. Under the Maine U.C.C., Articles 3-A and 4 deal with "Negotiable Instruments" and "Bank Deposits and Collections." *See* 11 M.R.S.A. §§ 3-1101, 4-101 (1995). It is these statutes that govern the parties' dispute.

Pursuant to Article 4 of the Maine U.C.C., the Credit Union, as a depositary bank, is a "holder" of the instruments, see 11 M.R.S.A. § 4-205(1) (1995), making it a "person entitled to enforce" the instrument under Article 3-A. *See* 11 M.R.S.A. § 3-1301(1) (1995). Upon producing an instrument containing the valid signature of a party liable on the instrument, a person entitled to enforce the instrument is entitled to payment, unless the party liable proves a defense or claim in recoupment, see 11 M.R.S.A. § 3-1308(2) (1995), or a possessory claim to the instrument itself. *See* 11 M.R.S.A. § 3-1306.

Because their signatures appear on the backs of the checks, Daniel, Joel, and Claire are "indorsers" of the checks. *See* 11 M.R.S.A. § 3-1204(1), (2) (1995). As indorsers, they are obligated to pay the amounts due on each dishonored instrument "[a]ccording to the terms of [each] instrument at the time it was indorsed." 11 M.R.S.A. § 3-1415(1)(a) (1995). This obligation is owed "to a person entitled to enforce the instrument or to a subsequent indorser who paid the instrument under this section." *Id.*

As drawer of the checks, Sun Life is obligated to pay each dishonored instrument "[a]ccording to its terms at the time it was issued." 11 M.R.S.A. § 3-1414(2)(a) (1995).

Unless the Credit Union is a holder in due course, its right to enforce the obligations of the drawer and indorsers of the instruments is subject to a variety of defenses, including all those defenses available "if the person entitled to enforce the instrument[s] were enforcing a right to payment under a simple contract." *See* 11 M.R.S.A. § 3-1305(1)(b) (1995). In addition, its right to enforce is subject to any claims in recoupment, see 11 M.R.S.A. § 3-1305(1)(c) (1995), or claims to the instruments themselves. *See* 11 M.R.S.A. § 3-1306. If, however, the Credit Union establishes that it is a "holder in due course," it is subject to only those few defenses listed in section 3-1305(1)(a). *See* 11 M.R.S.A. § 3-1305(2) (1995). None of those specific defenses is applicable here. Thus, the Credit Union argues that because it is entitled as a matter of law to holder in due course status, it is entitled to enforce the instruments against the Guerrettes and Sun Life.

III. Holder in Due Course

A. Burden of Proof and Standard of Review

A holder in due course is a holder who takes an instrument in good faith, for value, and without notice of any claims or defenses. *See* 11 M.R.S.A. § 3-1302(1) (1995). Once the persons who may be liable on the instruments have raised a recognized defense to that liability, the burden is on the holder to prove by a preponderance of the evidence that it is a holder in due course. *See New Bedford Inst. for Sav. v. Gildroy*, 36 Mass.App.Ct. 647, 634 N.E.2d 920, 925 (1994).

[FN14] If it fails in that proof, the persons otherwise liable on the instruments may avoid liability if they prove a defense, claim in recoupment, or possessory claim to the instrument. *See* 11 M.R.S.A. §§ 3-1305(1)(b), 3-1308(2).

The issue of whether a party is a holder in due course is usually one of fact, although "where the facts are undisputed and conclusive, [a court] can determine . . . holder in due course status as a matter of law." *See Triffin v. Dillabough*, 552 Pa. 550, 716 A.2d 605, 611 (1998). In this case, the Superior Court declined to decide the holder in due course issue as a matter of law, and submitted the question to the jury. The jury found that the Credit Union was not a holder in due course, implicitly because the Credit Union did not act in good faith. . . .

B. Good Faith

We therefore turn to the definition of "good faith" contained in Article 3-A of the Maine U.C.C.[1] In 1990, the National Conference of Commissioners on Uniform State Law recommended substantial changes in the U.C.C. The Maine Legislature responded to those recommendations in 1993 by repealing the entirety of Article 3 and enacting a new version entitled Article 3-A, which contains a new definition of "good faith." While the previous version of the good faith definition only required holder to prove that it acted with "honesty in fact," the new definition provides:

"Good faith" means honesty in fact *and the observance of reasonable commercial standards of fair dealing.*

11 M.R.S.A. § 3-1103(1)(d) (1995) (emphasis added). Because the tests are presented in the conjunctive, a holder must now satisfy both a subjective and an objective test of "good faith."[2]

1. Honesty in Fact

Prior to the changes adopted by the Legislature in 1993, the holder in due course doctrine turned on a subjective standard of good faith and was often referred to as the "pure heart and empty head" standard. *See* M.B.W. Sinclair, *Codification of Negotiable Instruments Law: A Tale of Reiterated Anachronism,*

---

[1] [15] We reject the Credit Union's argument that the good faith element of holder in due course status was not intended to encompass the giving of value for the check. Unless the depositary bank has given value, it cannot become a holder in due course, and its conduct is not scrutinized for compliance with section 3-1302. To determine whether a holder is a holder in due course, the factfinder must determine whether the holder acted with good faith when it took the checks and gave value for them.

[2] [16] The U.C.C. Prefatory Note of National Conference of Commissioners on Uniform State Laws and the American Law Institute lists the new definition of "good faith" among the "benefits to users" of the revised Article 3. The Notes states that:

The definition of good faith . . . is expanded to include observance of reasonable commercial standards of fair dealing. This objective standards for good faith applies to the performance of all duties and obligations established under Articles 3 and 4.

21 U. TOL. L.REV. 625, 654 (1990); see also *Seinfeld v. Commercial Bank & Trust Co.*, 405 So.2d 1039, 1042 (Fla.Dist.Ct.App.1981) (noting that the U.C.C. "seem[s] to protect the objectively stupid so long as he is subjectively pure at heart"). That standard merely required a holder to take an instrument with "honesty in fact" to become a holder in due course.[3]

Courts interpreting this language have routinely declared banks to be holders in due course, notwithstanding the failures of these banks to investigate or hold otherwise negotiable instruments, when they took the instruments with no knowledge of any defects, defenses, or stop payment orders. *See, e.g., UAW-CIO Local # 31 Credit Union v. Royal Ins. Co.*, 594 S.W.2d 276, 279 (Mo.1980) (en banc); . . . . This approach has been understood to promote the negotiability of instruments, particularly checks, in the stream of commerce. Rejecting a contrary approach, one court put it bluntly:

> The requirement urged by defendant would bring the banking system to a grinding halt. A stop payment order issued by the drawer to the drawee which is unknown to the paying-collecting bank cannot fasten upon the paying bank any legal disability; particularly it cannot reduce the status of the collecting bank to a mere assignee of the instrument or a holder of a non-negotiable instrument, or a mere holder of a negotiable instrument.

Mellon Bank, N.A. v. Donegal Mutual Ins. Co., 29 UCC Rep.Serv. (CBC) 912, 1980 WL 98414 (Pa. Ct. C.P. Alleghany County, Jan. 8, 1980).

Although courts were often urged to engraft an objective reasonableness standard onto the concept of "honesty in fact," most refused to do so.[4] Their refusals recognized that: "[T]he check is the major method for transfer of funds in commercial practice. The maker, payee, and endorsers of a check naturally expect it will be rapidly negotiated and collected . . . . The wheels of commerce would grind to a halt [if an objective standard were adopted]." *Bowling Green, Inc. v. State St. Bank & Trust*, 425 F.2d 81, 85 (1st Cir.1970).

Moreover, under the purely subjective standard, a bank was not expected to require the presence of offsetting collected funds in the customers' account in order to give value on newly deposited checks: "A bank's permitting its customers to draw against uncollected funds does not negate its good faith." *Asati, Inc.*, 15 UCC Rep.Serv.2d at 521; *accord Vail Nat'l Bank v. J. Wheeler Constr. Corp.*, 669 P.2d 1038, 1039-40 (Colo.Ct.App.1983), ...

---

[3] [17] ecause we are required to interpret the current definition of "good faith" for purposes of holder in due course status — a definition which is not without ambiguity — we look to the history of the definition for guidance. "When the language of a statute is ambiguous, we 'look beyond the words of the statute to its history, the policy behind it, and other extrinsic aids to determine legislative intent.' " *Arsenault v. Crossman*, 1997 Me. 92, ¶7, 696 A.2d 418 (1997)(quoting *State v. Fournier*, 617 A.2d 998, 1000 (Me. 1992)); accord *Salenius v. Salenius*, 654 A.2d 426, 429 (Me. 1995).

[4] [18]*But see, e.g., Seinfeld*, 405 So.2d at 1042 n.4 (applying what many have viewed as an objective standard of good faith).

Application of the "honesty in fact" standard to the Credit Union's conduct here demonstrates these principles at work. It is undisputed that the Credit Union had no knowledge that Richard obtained the Sun Life checks by fraud. Nor was the Credit Union aware that a stop payment order had been placed on the Sun Life checks. The Credit Union expeditiously gave value on the checks, having no knowledge that they would be dishonored. In essence the Credit Union acted as banks have, for years, been allowed to act without risk to holder in due course status. The Credit Union acted with honesty in fact.

Thus, had the matter at bar been decided before the Legislature's addition of the objective component of "good faith," there can be little question that the Credit Union would have been determined to have been a holder in due course. Because it took the instruments without notice of any possible dishonor, defect, fraud, or illegality, it could have given value immediately and yet have been assured of holder in due course status. *See Mellon Bank*, 29 UCC Rep.Serv. at 912; *Industrial Nat'l Bank of Rhode Island v. Leo's Used Car Exchange, Inc.*, 362 Mass. 797, 291 N.E.2d 603, 606 (1973); *New Bedford Inst.*, 634 N.E.2d at 925; *Triffin*, 716 A.2d at 611. Today, however, something more than mere subjective good faith is required of a holder in due course.

2. Reasonable Commercial Standards of Fair Dealing

We turn then to the objective prong of the good faith analysis. The addition of the language requiring the holder to prove conduct meeting "reasonable commercial standards of fair dealing" signals a significant change in the definition of a holder in due course.[5] While there has been little time for the development of a body of law interpreting this new objective requirement, there can be no mistaking the fact that a holder may no longer act with a pure heart and an empty head and still obtain holder in due course status.[6] The pure heart of the holder must now be accompanied by reasoning that assures conduct comporting with reasonable commercial standards of fair dealing.

The addition of the objective element represents not so much a new concept in the doctrinal development of holder in due course status, but rather a return, in part, to an earlier approach to the doctrine. *See* James J. White & Robert S. Summers, Uniform Commercial Code § 14-6, at 62829 (3d ed.1988) (discussing the objective test of good faith in England, first applied by the King's Bench in *Gill v. Cubitt*, 3 B & C 466, 107 Eng.Rep. 806 (K.B.1824)). The concept of an objective component of good faith has been part of the discussion regarding the holder in due course doctrine since the first enactment of the U.C.C. *See id.* (not-

---

5 [19] "The new definition of good faith *substantially affects* . . .the requirements for holder in due course status." Hawkland & Lawrence UCC Series § 3-103:05 (Rev Art 3)(emphasis added).

6 [20] The objective requirement, however, has generated a number of articles and commentaries on the reason, meaning, and anticipated interpretations of the changes. *See, e.g.,* Patricia L. Heatherman, Comment, *Good Faith in Revised Article 3 of the Uniform Commercial Code: Any Change? Should There Be?* 29 WILLAMETTE L. REV. 567 (1993); Kerry Lynn Macintosh, *Liberty, Trade, and the Uniform Commercial Code, When Should Default Rules be Based on Business Practices?* 38 WM. & MARY L. REV. 1465, 1466 (1997).

ing that "[t]he good faith requirement has been the source of a continuing and ancient dispute"). The early drafters debated the need and wisdom of including such an objective component and ultimately determined *not* to include it in the definition of good faith because of its potential for freezing commercial practices. *See Sinclair, supra,* at 653-54 (noting, in particular, the objection by the banking industry to the addition of an objective good faith component). The "new" element of good faith requiring the holder to act according to reasonable commercial standards of fair dealing is actually a more narrow version of the "reasonable person" standard considered and rejected by the drafters of the 1962 Code.

The new objective standard, however, is not a model of drafting clarity. Although use of the word "reasonable" in the objective portion of the good faith test may evoke concepts of negligence, the drafters attempted to distinguish the concept of "fair" dealing from concepts of "careful" dealing:

> Although fair dealing is a broad term that must be defined in context, it is clear that it is concerned with the fairness of conduct rather than the care with which an act is performed. Failure to exercise ordinary care in conducting a transaction is an entirely different concept than failure to deal fairly in conducting the transaction.

U.C.C. § 3-103 cmt. 4 (1991).

Unfortunately, the ease with which the distinction between "fair dealing" and "careful dealing" was set forth in the comments to the U.C.C. revisions belies the difficulty in applying these concepts to the facts of any particular case, or in conveying them to a jury. The difficulty is exacerbated by the lack of definition of the term "fair dealing" in the U.C.C.[7] The most obvious question arising from the use of the term "fair" is: fairness to whom? Transactions involving negotiable instruments have traditionally required the detailed level of control and definition of roles set out in the U.C.C. precisely because there are so many parties who may be involved in a single transaction. If a holder is required to act "fairly," regarding all parties, it must engage in an almost impossible balancing of rights and interests. Accordingly, the drafters limited the requirement of fair dealing to conduct that is reasonable in the commercial context of the transaction at issue. In other words, the holder must act in a way that is fair according to commercial standards that are themselves reasonable.

The factfinder must therefore determine, first, whether the conduct of the holder comported with industry or "commercial" standards applicable to the transaction and, second, whether those standards were reasonable standards intended to result in fair dealing. Each of those determinations must be made in the context of the specific transaction at hand. If the factfinder's conclusion

---

[7] [21] One commentator has suggested that fair dealing refers to "playing by the rules." *See Heatherman, supra,* at 585. Yet "the rules" ordinarily define the parameters of reasonable conduct, a concept which sounds much like a negligence analysis.

on each point is "yes," the holder will be determined to have acted in good faith even if, in the individual transaction at issue, the result appears unreasonable. Thus a holder may be accorded holder in due course status where it acts pursuant to those reasonable commercial standards of fair dealing — even if it is negligent — but may lose that status, even where it complies with commercial standards, if those standards are not reasonably related to achieving fair dealing.

Therefore the jury's task here was to decide whether the Credit Union observed the banking industries' commercial standards relating to the giving of value on uncollected funds, and, if so, whether those standards are reasonably designed to result in fair dealing.

The evidence produced by the Credit Union in support of its position that it acted in accordance with objective good faith included the following: The Credit Union's internal policy was to make provisional credit available immediately upon the deposit of a check by one of its members. In certain circumstances — where the check was for a large amount and where it was drawn on an out-of-state bank — its policy allowed for a hold to be placed on the uncollected funds for up to nine days. The Credit Union's general written policy on this issue was reviewed annually — and had always been approved — by the National Credit Union Administration, the federal agency charged with the duty of regulating federal credit unions. *See* 12 U.S.C.A. § 1752a (Law.Co- op.1996). In addition, the policy complied with applicable banking laws, including Regulation CC. *See* 12 C.F.R. §§ 229.12(c), 229.13(b) (1998).

The Credit Union also presented evidence that neither Regulation CC nor the Credit Union's internal policy *required* it to hold the checks or to investigate the genesis of checks before extending provisional credit. It asserted that it acted exactly as its policy and the law allowed when it immediately extended provisional credit on these checks, despite the fact that they were drawn for relatively large amounts on an out-of-state bank.[8] Finally, the Credit Union presented expert testimony that most credit unions in Maine follow similar policies.

In urging the jury to find that the Credit Union had not acted in good faith, Sun Life and the Guerrettes argued that the Credit Union's conduct did not comport with reasonable commercial standards of fair dealing when it allowed its member access to provisional credit on checks totalling over $120,000 drawn on an out-of-state bank without either: (1) further investigation to assure that the deposited checks would be paid by the bank upon which they were drawn, or (2) holding the instruments to allow any irregularities to come to light.

The applicable federal regulations provide the outside limit on the Credit Union's ability to hold the checks. Although the limit on allowable holds estab-

---

[8] [22] The Credit Union could also have withheld provisional credit under the law and its own internal policy if there were other reasons to doubt the validity of the checks. *See* 12 C.F.R. § 229.13(e) (1998).

lished by law is evidence to be considered by the jury, it does not itself establish reasonable commercial standard of fair dealing. The factfinder must consider all of the facts relevant to the transaction. The amount of the checks and the location of the payor bank, however, are relevant facts that a bank, observing reasonable commercial standards of fair dealing, takes into account when deciding whether to place such a hold on the account. The jury was entitled to consider that, under Regulation CC, when a check in an amount greater than $5,000 is deposited, or when a check is payable by a nonlocal bank, a credit union is permitted to withhold provisional credit for longer periods of time than it is allowed in other circumstances. *See* 12 C.F.R. § 229.13(b), (h) (1998). Therefore, the size of the check and the location of the payor bank are, under the objective standard of good faith, factors which a jury may also consider when deciding whether a depositary bank is a holder in due course.

The Credit Union's President admitted the risks inherent in the Credit Union's policy and admitted that it would not have been difficult to place a hold on these funds for the few days that it would normally take for the payor bank to pay the checks. He conceded that the amount of the checks were relatively large, that they were drawn on an out-of-state bank, and that these circumstances "could have" presented the Credit Union with cause to place a hold on the account. He also testified to his understanding that some commercial banks followed a policy of holding nonlocal checks for three business days before giving provisional credit.[9] Moreover, the Credit Union had no written policy explicitly guiding its staff regarding the placing of a hold on uncollected funds. Rather, the decision on whether to place a temporary hold on an account was left to the "comfort level" of the teller accepting the deposit. There was no dispute that the amount of the three checks far exceeded the $5,000 threshold for a discretionary hold established by the Credit Union's own policy.

On these facts the jury could rationally have concluded that the reasonable commercial standard of fair dealing would require the placing of a hold on the uncollected funds for a reasonable period of time and that, in giving value under these circumstances, the Credit Union did not act according to commercial standards that were reasonably structured to result in fair dealing.

We recognize that the Legislature's addition of an objective standard of conduct in this area of law may well have the effect of slowing the "wheels of commerce."[10] As one commentator noted:

> Historically, it was always argued that if negotiable instruments were to be usefully negotiable a subsequent holder should not have to investigate the

---

[9] [23] There was evidence that, on the second business day after he deposited the checks, Paul Richard notified the Credit Union that there may have been a problem with his deposit.

[10] [24] The new definition of "good faith" has been forecasted by some to bring possible "undesirable changes" to the law of negotiable instruments. *See* Henry J. Bailey, *New 1990 Uniform Commercial Code: Article 3, Negotiable Instruments, and Article 4, Bank Deposits and Collections,* 29 WILLAMETTE L. REV. 409, 415 (1993).

transaction giving rise to the paper. The paramount necessity of negotiability has dominated thinking and legislation on negotiable instruments law. Drafts and promissory notes, it has been believed, must be able to change hands freely, without investigation beyond the face of the instrument, and with no greater requirement than the indorsement of the holder.

Sinclair, supra, at 630 (footnotes omitted). Notwithstanding society's oftcited need for certainty and speed in commercial transactions, however, the Legislature necessarily must have concluded that the addition of the objective requirement to the definition of "good faith" serves an important goal. The paramount necessity of unquestioned negotiability has given way, at least in part, to the desire for reasonable commercial fairness in negotiable transactions . . . .

PROBLEM 9.8

A man, who identifies himself as John Walker enters a check-cashing store, CashNow, Inc. ("CashNow") and tries to cash a $10,000 check that was made payable to him. The CashNow cashier tells Walker that she was not authorized to cash such large checks. Walker explains that he is a financial advisor, and that the drawer of the check is an investor who sent the check to him by mail. Walker even shows the cashier the envelope in which he says he received the check. The cashier goes ahead and, after having Walker indorse the check in blank, cashes the check, charging $500 (5%) as the fee for doing so. When CashNow presents the check, the drawee bank refuses to pay it, saying that the drawer had executed a stop payment order. CashNow sues the drawer, a 93-year old man who asserts a personal defense of fraudulent inducement. Assuming the trier of fact believes the defense, who should win and why? Cash Now won if HIDC
L not HIDC → unreas.

The Instrument Must Be Taken Without Notice

In order to be a holder in due course, the holder must have taken the instrument without notice of certain facts indicating that he might encounter some difficulty in enforcing the instrument. *See* § 3-302(a)(2). [Note: The Chemical Bank case, above, applied New York's version of the UCC, which used the word "knowledge" rather than "notice."] The facts that, if known, preclude one from becoming a holder in due course are set forth in § 3-302 and discussed in the text below.

In order to understand the rationale for this requirement, it is important to remember that the holder in due course doctrine was developed to ensure that innocent unsuspecting parties who purchased instruments or provided services or goods in exchange for them would be protected against other parties who had claims to the instruments or defenses to their liability on them. If a holder knew or had reason to know of such facts before his purchase or exchange, he would have had the opportunity to protect himself by simply not taking the instrument. If the holder nevertheless took the instrument with such notice, the holder would no longer be the entirely innocent, unsuspecting party who should be entitled to defeat a prior owner or third party having a valid claim to the instrument or an obligor with a legitimate defense to his liability.

Facts That Preclude Holder in Due Course Status

A holder cannot be a holder in due course if he has notice that the instrument he is taking is overdue, or had been dishonored before being transferred to him.

PROBLEM 9.9

Use Section 3-304 to determine whether the following instruments provide notice to the holders that the instruments are overdue and thus prevent the holders from being holders in due course.

a. *The holder receives a check on May 3, 2005 that is dated January 14, 2005;*

b. *The holder receives an undated check on May 3, 2005, that was actually drawn 5 months earlier;*

c. *The holder is given a check by a friend who had tried unsuccessfully to cash it at the friend's own bank 3 days earlier (does it matter whether the holder was aware of that fact?);* not necessarily a dishonor

d. *On June, 1, 2005, the holder is given a promissory note with a due date of May 15, 2005;*

e. *The holder is given a note payable in monthly installments. On the face of the note, it says, "First interest payment due on May 1, 2005, WAS NOT PAID";* Not overdue (principal only)

f. *On April 17, 2005, the holder is given a note due on May 15, 2005. Unbeknownst to the holder, the note had been accelerated, so as to be due on April 15, 2005.* no notice = HIDC

A holder also cannot be a holder in due course if he has notice that there is an uncured default with respect to the payment of another instrument issued as part of the same series, that the instrument contains an unauthorized signature or has been altered or that any party has a claim to the instrument under § 3-306 or a defense or claim in recoupment described in § 3-305(a).

What Constitutes "Notice" of These Facts

A person has "notice" of a fact not only when he has actual knowledge or has received a notice or notification of it but also when he has *reason to know* that it exists. See pre-2001 revision § 1-201(25) and post-2001 revision § 1-202(a). Under pre-2001 revision § 1-201(26), whether one has reason to know that a fact exists depends on all the facts and circumstances known to him at the time in question.

Under Former Article 3, some courts applied a subjective test, much like that used for "good faith," to determine whether one had "notice" that would prevent her from being a holder in due course. In these jurisdictions, it was not what a reasonable person would have known that matters, it was what the particular person subjectively knew. Others argued that the notice test, as opposed to the good faith test, was objective. But even those courts applying an objective test, sometimes held that knowledge of suspicious circumstances did not give rise to notice of a defense, since what was important were the *facts*, not the suspicions, that could be objectively inferred from the information known. As such they held that the *negligent* failure to investigate did not constitute notice of facts that an investigation might have disclosed. *See, e.g., Eldon's Super Fresh Stores, Inc. v. Merrill Lynch, Pierce, Fenner & Smith, Inc.*, 296 Minn. 130, 207 N.W. 282 (1973); *The Unbank Co. v. Dolphin Temporary Help Services, Inc.*, 485 N.W.2d 332 (Minn.App. 1992) (failure to inquire about a fact is not the same as knowledge of the fact). On the other hand, courts would nonetheless refuse to allow parties to *purposely* avoid making an inquiry when such parties subjectively suspect they might uncover evidence of a defense.

Time at Which To Determine Whether There Is Notice

The crucial time for determining whether a holder has notice is the time of negotiation of the instrument to the holder. Subsequent knowledge of a defense to an instrument will not impair holder in due course status. This is because once the transaction has been completed there is nothing the holder can do to protect his investment in the instrument. To say, however, that holder in due course status is solely determined at the time of negotiation and that subsequent notice is irrelevant is somewhat misleading. If an instrument is taken by someone who, at the time of taking, had no notice of a claim or defense, but who subsequently acquires such notice before giving the promised value for the instrument, that person does not become a holder in due course. *See* UCC Comment 2 to § 3-303. In short, notice that is received before *either* negotiation *or* the giving of value prevents a person from becoming a holder in due course. Notice that is received after *both* negotiation and the giving of value does *not* prevent a person from being a holder in due course. Finally, in some instances, a person may actually have prior notice of a defense and yet still *become* a holder in due course. This is because § 3-302(f) states that, "[t]o be effective, notice must be received at a time and in a manner that gives a reasonable opportunity to act on it.

PROBLEM 9.10

a. *Sam Slime sells Sally Sincere a worthless piece of glass, convincing her that it is a valuable gem. Sally gives him a $1,000 check, which he negotiates to Harry Holder in exchange for computer equipment. The day after taking the check Harry learns that Sam had defrauded Sally. When Harry subsequently tries to enforce the check against Sally, will she be able to successfully assert her defense against him?*

b. *Assume instead that Sam Slime negotiates the check to Harry in exchange for computer equipment which is to be delivered in two weeks. Again, at the time of the negotiation, Harry was unaware that Sam had defrauded Sally, but the day after taking the check, Harry learns that Sam had defrauded Sally. If Harry delivers the computer equipment two weeks later and then attempts to enforce the check against Sally, will Sally be able to successfully assert her defense against Harry?*

c. *Assume this time that Slime gives Harry the check from Sally in exchange for computer equipment that Harry turns over to Sam, but Sam failed to indorse the check. Harry brings the check to Sally's bank to present it for payment, but is told that Sally has ordered the bank not to pay the check because of Sam's fraud. Before filing suit to enforce the check against Sally, Harry realizes the check has not been indorsed and pursuant to his right under § 3-203(c), requires Sam to supply the missing indorsement. When Harry meets Sally in court, will she be able to successfully assert her defense against him?*

Specific Statutory Notice Provisions

(1) Notice of Breach of Fiduciary Duty

Section 3-307 states rules for determining when a person taking an instrument from a fiduciary is deemed to have notice of a breach of fiduciary duty that arises as a result of that transaction. Having notice of such a breach precludes that person from becoming a holder in due course of the instrument since it constitutes notice of a claim to the instrument. *See* § 3-307(b)(1).

Read § 3-307 and then do the following problem.

PROBLEM 9.11

a. *A. Gent is a party known by Sam Seller to be the corporate treasurer of the Victor Principal Corporation ("VPC"). On January 7, 2005, Gent gives Sam a check made payable to VPC, which was indorsed in blank by Gent purportedly on behalf of VPC, to pay off the amount owed by Gent on a red sports car Gent had bought for his wife. When VPC makes a claim to the instrument on the grounds that Gent had breached his fiduciary duty, may Sam assert holder in due course status?* ,

b. *Adam Minister is the executor of the estate of Rigor Mortis. He maintains two accounts at State National Bank, one of which is in his name as executor of the estate and one of which is in his name as president of a small advertising agency. He brings a check made out to him as the executor of the estate but deposits it in his advertising agency account and withdraws the amount of the* **commingling** *check two days later. When the estate makes a claim to the instrument on the grounds that Minister had breached his fiduciary duty, may State National Bank assert holder in due course status?* No notice

c. *Terry Tyler, trustee of a fund established for her nine-year-old nephew, writes a check from the account of that fund to the C. U. Later Travel Agency to buy a single ticket on a Caribbean cruise. Terry asks the agent to issue the ticket with the name left blank. Terry then proceeds to go on the cruise and has a great time. When a claim to the check is made on behalf of the nephew on the grounds that Terry had breached her fiduciary duty, can the travel agency assert holder in due course status?*

(2) *Notice of a Discharge Is Not Notice of a Defense*

A holder who knows that a party to the instrument has been discharged can still be a holder in due course of the instrument. Section 3-302(b) provides that notice of a discharge, other than a discharge in an insolvency proceeding, is not the same as notice of a defense. The discharge is effective, however, against one who became a holder in due course with notice of the discharge.

PROBLEM 9.12

Mary Maker issues a promissory note payable to the order of Paul Payee. Paul negotiates the instrument by special indorsement to Eric Indorser. Eric indorses it over to Fran Friend, who discharges Eric's obligation by striking out Eric's signature (§ 3-604). Fran then negotiates the instrument for value to Harry Holder. Assuming that Harry took the instrument for value, in good faith and without notice of anything other than what could be seen on the face and back of the instrument itself, what result when Harry seeks to enforce the instrument against Paul and Paul raises a valid personal defense? What if Harry seeks to enforce the instrument against Eric and Eric claims that he has been discharged? What if Eric's indorsement had not been struck out but he had in fact been discharged by Fran pursuant to an agreement in a signed writing of which Harry had no notice?

(3) Public Filing Does Not Constitute Notice

Unlike provisions in some other bodies of law which provide that, for certain purposes, the filing of a claim provides constructive notice of that claim, § 3-302(b) states that "[p]ublic filing or recording of a document does not of itself constitute notice of a defense, claim in recoupment, or claim to an instrument."

Can the Payee Be a Holder in Due Course?

Former § 3-302(2) specifically provided that "a payee may be a holder in due course." Although the current version has deleted this statement "because it is surplusage and may be misleading," the drafters intended no change in the law. *See* UCC Comment 4 to § 3-302. UCC Comment 4 does point out, however, that the use of the holder in due course doctrine by the payee is not the normal situation. Since holder in due course status is of most significance when the obligor has a defense or claim in recoupment, usually arising from the transaction in which the instrument was issued, a payee will typically not qualify as a holder in due course either because he has notice of the facts that created the claim or defense or because it is the value he gave that has failed.

The UCC Comments to both the former and revised versions of § 3-302 contain several examples of when the payee can be a holder in due course. For the most part, the payee in these examples is (1) a third-party beneficiary who did not play a direct role in the underlying transaction nor deal directly with the obligor asserting the defense or (2) one who has given value to a person committing a fraud against the obligor of the instrument.

The Holder in Due Course Doctrine in Consumer Transactions

Courts and legislators have been particularly concerned by the potentially harsh effects of the holder in due course rule in consumer transactions. The all-too-common scenario involves a consumer purchasing goods or services from a seller who then assigns or sells the consumer's obligation to pay to a third party. The consumer is then obligated to pay even when the seller fails to live up to the agreement because the creditor is a holder in due course immune to the defenses and claims that the consumer could raise against the seller, including misrepresentation, breach of warranty, breach of contract, and fraud. The consumer thus loses the most effective weapon against wrongdoing by the seller — nonpayment — and is obligated to pay in full despite not getting the benefit of the bargain.

As discussed earlier, the judicial response to this problem was to engage in very close scrutiny of whether the third-party holder was in fact a holder in due course. This involved a case-by-case inquiry into the alleged good faith of the transferee and its relative knowledge of the underlying circumstances of the original transaction or of the general business practices of the seller. Courts would look to the relationship between the seller and the subsequent holder to determine if they were "closely connected." If such a connection was established, the court would deny holder in due course status to the transferee on the theory that it did not take the instrument in good faith or did so with notice of a claim or defense. *See, e.g., Unico v. Owen*, 50 N.J. 101, 232 A.2d 405 (1967)

The FTC Holder in Due Course Rule

In 1976, the Federal Trade Commission (FTC) further attempted to remedy the situation by promulgating a trade regulation rule that in most consumer credit transactions, other than those involving real estate, would make the creditor contractually subject to all claims and defenses the debtor could assert against the seller. When applicable, the FTC rule effectively abrogates the holder in due course doctrine.

The FTC rule, 16 C.F.R. Part 433, provides that it is an unfair or deceptive practice for a seller to take or receive a consumer credit contract that fails to include a provision that reads as follows:

NOTICE

ANY HOLDER OF THIS CONSUMER CREDIT CONTRACT IS SUBJECT TO ALL CLAIMS AND DEFENSES WHICH THE DEBTOR COULD ASSERT AGAINST THE SELLER OF GOODS OR SERVICES OBTAINED PURSUANT HERETO OR WITH THE PROCEEDS HEREOF. RECOVERY HEREUNDER BY THE DEBTOR SHALL NOT EXCEED AMOUNTS PAID BY THE DEBTOR HEREUNDER. 16 C.F.R. § 433.2

This notice must appear even on negotiable instruments since the definition of a "consumer credit contract" includes "[a]ny instrument which evidences or embodies a debt arising" from the consumer transactions to which the FTC rule applies. 16 C.F.R. § 433.1(i).

For purposes of the FTC rule, a covered consumer credit transaction is one in which a natural person acquiring goods or services for personal, family, or household use becomes obligated to pay the seller on a deferred payment basis in more than four installments or to pay a "finance charge," as defined by the Truth in Lending Act (15 U.S.C. § 1601, *et seq.*) and Regulation Z (12 C.F.R. Part 226) on the amount of credit extended.

The FTC rule also requires virtually identical language to be included in any consumer credit contract or note evidencing a "purchase money loan," which is defined as a

cash advance which is received by a consumer for a "Finance Charge," within the meaning of the Truth in Lending Act and

> Regulation Z, which is applied . . . to a purchase of goods or
> services from a seller who (1) refers consumers to the creditor or
> (2) is affiliated with the creditor by common control, contract, or
> business arrangement. 16 C.F.R. § 433.1(d).

This requirement is designed to ensure that sellers cannot avoid the purpose of
the rule by arranging for the extension of credit with others rather than extending the credit themselves. Thus, the seller may not accept money that a consumer obtained from a lender to whom the seller referred the consumer or with
whom the seller is affiliated unless the credit contract made in connection with
the sale contains the required notice.

PROBLEM 9.13

Determine whether the FTC notice is required in the following transactions:

a. *Nat Person goes to Creditor Motors and purchases a brand new Honda for
   $17,000. He puts $5,000 down and agrees to finance the remaining amount
   at 1.5% by making monthly installments for the next three years. He signs
   an agreement with Creditor Motors to that effect, also agreeing to pay a
   finance charge on the amount owed. He is also asked to sign a promissory
   note payable to Creditor that evidences the debt owed. Must the FTC notice
   appear on the financing agreement? On the promissory note? On both?*

b. *What if, instead, Nat is able to get 0% financing on the same 3 year agreement as in "a"?*

c. *What if Nat is a landscaper, with his own business, and instead of buying
   a Honda, he purchases a truck to be used exclusively to transfer large trees
   from his suppliers to his customers. Assume again, he puts money down and
   signs a an agreement and a promissory note to pay the remaining amount
   in monthly payments at a specified interest rate?* No, business purpose

d. *What if this time Nat goes to a car dealer to buy the Honda that offers no
   financing itself but refers all its customers to the Friendly Finance Company down the street. Nat's application for a loan is approved, and he is
   given a $12,000 loan after signing a promissory note on which he agrees to
   pay interest on the amount owed?*

e. *What if instead Nat goes to the credit union at his place of employment to
   get a new car loan. Nat's application is approved, and he is given a $12,000
   loan after signing a promissory note on which he agrees to pay interest on
   the amount owed?* No, regular loan initiated by consumer

f. *What if Nat instead buys a new home from a construction company that
   does its own financing and he signs a promissory note to repay the balance
   of the amount owed in monthly installments over a 7 year period at 6.75%?*

not goods or services

Once the required notice is inserted in the contract, it becomes part of the agreement between the consumer and any holder of the contract. It is the inclusion of the notice that gives the debtor the right to assert claims and defenses against the holder and prevents that holder from becoming a holder in due course. The FTC rule itself provides no substantive or procedural rights. A seller who fails to comply with the rule is in violation of the Federal Trade Commission Act (15 U.S.C. § 41, *et seq.*) and may be subject to civil penalties, but there is no private cause of action for the consumer under that Act. Thus, without the required notice, the consumer has no guaranteed right to assert claims or defenses against the holder. However, one may be able to argue that some third parties who take an instrument knowing or having reason to know that it arose out of a consumer transaction would be unable to meet the requirements of a holder in due course since they may have reason to know that the instrument was in violation of the FTC rule.

When the notice is included, the consumer is not only entitled to assert any defenses he may have against the seller in an action brought by the creditor, he can also "maintain an affirmative action against a creditor who has received payments for a return of monies paid on account." 40 Fed.Reg. 53,524 (1975). In its Statement of Basis and Purpose supporting the rule, the FTC noted that if the consumer was limited to a purely defensive position, the creditor-assignee may elect not to sue for the balance due when the consumer's defenses have some merit and the seller is judgment-proof. Under the FTC rule, therefore, consumers may assert a warranty claim against a creditor irrespective of whether the creditor has filed a lawsuit against them or recover for fraud engaged in by the seller. *See Eachen v. Scott Housing Systems, Inc.*, 630 F.Supp. 162 (M.D.Ala. 1986); *Armstrong v. Edelson*, 718 F.Supp. 1372 (N.D.Ill. 1989).

Recovery for claims affirmatively asserted against the creditor, however, is limited to amounts paid in by the debtor and is available only when a seller's breach is so substantial that a court is persuaded that rescission and restitution are justified under applicable state law. *See Felde v. Chrysler Credit Corp.*, 219 Ill.App.3d 530, 580 N.E.2d 191, 162 Ill.Dec. 565 (2d Dist. 1991).

Effect of Revised 2002 § 3-305(e)

Revised 2002 § 3-305(e) introduces a new pro-consumer rule. It deals with consumer transactions in which applicable law other than UCC Article 3 requires that an instrument contain a statement that the rights of a holder or transferee are subject to any claim or defense that the issuer could assert against the original payee. Revised 2002 § 3-305(e) provides that if the instrument does not comply with such law and contains no such statement, the instrument has the same effect as if it did contain the statement. Consequently, to the extent that an issuer could have asserted such claim or defense if the statement had been included in the instrument, the issuer can still assert the claim or defense even though the statement was omitted.

State Consumer Protection Statutes

Various states have enacted laws to protect consumers in particular types of transactions. Some statutes specifically provide that personal defenses will be effective against a holder in due course. *See, e.g.*, Connecticut, C.G.S.A. § 52-572g; Georgia, Code, 10-1-393.2 (instruments in connection with health spas); South Dakota, SDCL, § 57A-3A-104; West Virginia, Code 46A-2-102. *See also, State of West Virginia v. Scott Runyan Pontiac-Buick, Inc.*, 461 S.E.2d 516, 1995 WL 425114 (W.Va.); *One Valley Bank of Oak Hill, Inc. v. Bolen*, 188 W. Va. 687, 425 S.E.2d 829 (1992). Sometimes these statutes also impose penalties when excess charges have been exacted from consumers. *See, e.g., State of West Virginia, supra.* Others regulate the types and forms of instruments that may be used in consumer transactions. *See, e.g.*, Illinois Retail Installment Sales Act, 815 ILCS 405/1, et seq.; Illinois Consumer Fraud and Deceptive Practices Act, 815 ILCS 505/1 et seq.; Oklahoma Health Spa Act, 59 Okl.St.Ann. § 2005; Rhode Island, Gen. Laws 1956, § 6-27-5. To some extent, such laws may be preempted by the FTC rule.

The Shelter Doctrine

A party who does not meet all the requirements to become a holder in due course nevertheless can have the rights of a holder in due course under what has come to be known as the shelter doctrine. Section 3-203(b) provides that the transfer of an instrument vests in the transferee any right of the transferor to enforce the instrument, including any right as a holder in due course. The purpose of this provision is to ensure that the holder in due course has a free market for the instrument.

The shelter doctrine essentially allows the transferee to step into the shoes of the transferor. Thus, the shelter doctrine gives the transferee the same rights against obligors that the transferor had. The shelter doctrine *does not* give the transferee any special rights against the transferor himself. Thus, if a transferor who was a holder in due course transfers an instrument as a gift, the transferee does not have holder in due course rights against the transferor. Consequently, if the transferee tries to enforce the instrument against the transferor, the transferor will be entitled to assert lack of consideration as a defense even though that defense would not be effective against one who was a holder in due course or who had the rights of a holder in due course.

The shelter doctrine is operative even if the transfer is not a negotiation. Thus, if an item is delivered to a transferee without a necessary indorsement, the transferee, who is not a holder because the transferor did not indorse, is nevertheless a person entitled to enforce the instrument if the transferor was a holder at the time of transfer. Under the shelter doctrine, this transferee obtains the same rights to enforce the instrument (but *not* the right to negotiate it) that the transferor enjoyed. Nevertheless, the transferee must prove those rights by offering proof of the transfer. Because the transferee is not a holder, he is not aided by the presumption under § 3-308 that he is entitled to payment.

PROBLEM 9.14

a. Harriet Holder is a holder in due course of a check for $150 drawn by Dan Drawer. She indorses the check and gives it as a gift to Gwen Friend. When Gwen tries to cash the check at Dan's bank, she finds out that Dan had stopped payment on the check, because the person he had originally made it payable to had never delivered the goods Dan had ordered. Gwen sues Dan on his drawer's contract and Dan asserts that he has a defense of failure of consideration. What result?

b. What if Gwen, after learning of the non-delivery of the goods at the bank when she tried to cash the check, tells her niece Barbara exactly what happened at the bank, and then indorses the check over to Barbara and gets nothing in return. What result when Barbara sues Dan on his drawer's contract and Dan asserts that he has a defense of failure of consideration? What result if Barbara, instead of suing Dan on his drawer's contract sues Harriet on her indorser's liability?

c. Assume instead that Barbara uses the check to purchase groceries from the Acme Market, mentioning nothing about the check's derivation. Acme tries to cash the check, is unsuccessful in doing so and sues Harriet on her indorser's obligation. Will Acme be successful in recovering $150 from Harriet?

d. Assume instead that the manager for Acme indorses the check in blank in the company name and gives it, with several other checks, to a clerk, to bring to the bank to deposit. On the way to the bank, the clerk drops the check and it is found by Lucky Larry. Lucky attempts to enforce the check against Dan Drawer, and Dan asserts that he has a defense of failure of consideration. What result?

Incidentally, § 3-203(c) provides that if an instrument made payable to the order of, or specially indorsed to, the transferor is transferred for value, the transferee, absent a contrary agreement, has a specially enforceable right to the transferor's unqualified indorsement. The indorsement must provide for full liability of the transferor, and the transferee's right will not be satisfied by an indorsement "without recourse" unless so agreed by the parties. Section 3-203(c) further provides that there is no negotiation of the instrument until the indorsement is made by the transferor. Until that time, the transferee does not become a holder, and if notice of a claim or defense is received, the transferee cannot become a holder in due course in his own right. If the transferor was a holder in due course, however, the transferee would be the recipient of his holder in due course rights under the shelter doctrine.

PROBLEM 9.15

Harry Holder was in possession of a note made payable to his order by the maker, Josephine Maker. Harry then sold the note to Paul Purchaser, who took it for value, in good faith and without notice of the circumstances under which the note was issued. The note was delivered to Paul but did not include Harry's indorsement. Paul presented the note to Josephine who claimed that the goods she had ordered had never been delivered as per the contract pursuant to which the note was issued. Prior to filing his lawsuit against the maker, Paul noticed that the instrument did not contain Harry's indorsement and specifically demanded that Harry sign it. Once indorsed, Paul filed suit to enforce the maker's obligation. What result?

The one exception to the doctrine that the transferee has the rights of the transferor to enforce the instrument, including any holder in due course rights, is that the transferee cannot acquire rights of a holder in due course if the transferee engaged in fraud or illegality affecting the instrument. This provision prohibits a party who has engaged in fraud from passing the instrument through the hands of an innocent purchaser for value in order to obtain superior rights.

Chapter 10
WARRANTY LIABILITY

As mentioned in Chapter 5, there are two principal ways in which someone can become liable with respect to an instrument even if he never became a party to it: by making warranties with respect to the instrument or by converting the instrument. This Chapter deals with warranty liability, while Chapter 11 addresses conversion liability.

This Chapter examines the transfer and presentment warranties set forth in §§ 3-416, 3-417, 4-207 and 4-208. Although the check collection process is governed not only by Article 4 but also by Federal Reserve regulations, such as Regulation CC, these additional wrinkles, to the extent covered by this casebook, are discussed in Chapters 15, 17-20.

In analyzing whether one party, A, may successfully sue another party, B, for breach of warranty, it is useful to apply a six-step analysis:

1. Did B make any warranties to anyone? If B did not, then B cannot be liable for breach of warranty.

2. If B did make warranties, did B make warranties to A? If B did not make warranties to A, then B cannot be liable to A for breach of warranty.

3. If B did make warranties to A, what were those warranties?

4. Were any of the warranties B made to A breached?

5. If any such warranties were breached, did the breach proximately cause any injury?

6. If there was such an injury, what damages may A recover?

This six-step analysis can be applied whether the warranties in question are transfer warranties or presentment warranties.

I. TRANSFER WARRANTIES

Two principal provisions govern transfer warranties: §§ 3-416 and 4-207. Section 3-416 applies generally to transfers from one person to another. Section 4-207 applies when a customer of a bank transfers an instrument to his bank or when a collecting bank transfers an instrument to another collecting bank.

Step 1: Who Makes Transfer Warranties?

When a person transfers a negotiable instrument, that transfer typically carries with it certain implied warranties about the transferor and the instrument itself. Briefly stated, transfer warranties are ordinarily made by one who transfers an instrument for consideration or, in the case of an instrument deposited in a collecting bank, for a "settlement," i.e., a credit to the transferor's account. Therefore, if a particular transferor does not transfer for consideration or settlement, but, instead, gives the instrument as a gift, the transferor does not make any transfer warranties. §§ 3-416(a), 4-207.

In order to better understand who makes transfer warranties, we must briefly review what it means (1) to "transfer an instrument" and (2) to receive "consideration" or settlement in exchange for the transfer.

A transfer occurs when an instrument "is delivered by a person other than its issuer for the purpose of giving to the person receiving delivery the right to enforce the instrument." § 3-203(a). Delivery involves a voluntary transfer of possession. § 1-201(14). The initial issue of an instrument is not a "transfer" because it involves delivery by the issuer, namely the maker, in the case of a note, or the drawer, in the case of a draft. § 3-105. Similarly, presentment of an instrument for acceptance or payment is not a "transfer," because the purpose of a presentment is not to give the person receiving delivery the right to enforce the instrument. § 3-501. As such, neither a maker, drawer or person presenting an instrument for payment or acceptance makes transfer warranties.

PROBLEM 10.1

D. Rohr writes a check for $500 payable to bearer and gives the check to M. Ployee in exchange for M's promise to do certain work. Has D made any transfer warranties to M? Suppose M takes the check and hands it to the cashier at the local Currency Exchange in exchange for $495. Has M made any transfer warranties? Suppose, instead, that, on the way to the Currency Exchange, M is robbed at gunpoint by Ima Crook and is forced to give Crook the check. Has M made any transfer warranties? Identify all of the reasons for your answers.

"Consideration" is defined in § 3-303(b) as "any consideration sufficient to support a simple contract." The transferor must receive consideration in order to make a transfer warranty.

The word "settlement" is not separately defined, but § 4-104(a)(11) uses it in defining "settle": "'Settle' means to pay in cash, by clearing house settlement, in a charge or credit or by remittance, or otherwise as agreed. A settlement may be either provisional or final."

PROBLEM 10.2

Suppose M. Ployee, from Problem 10.1, does not take the $500 check to Currency Exchange and is not robbed. Instead, he contracts for Sally Swindler to build him a swimming pool for $5,000, and gives her the check as a 10% down payment. Before he gave Swindler the check, M indorsed it in blank. Swindler, who never intended to build a swimming pool, cashes the check at her own bank, Last National, for $500 and disappears. Did M make any transfer warranties to Swindler? Did Swindler make any transfer warranties to Last National Bank? Suppose Swindler brought the check to the bank at which D. Rohr has an account and cashed the check? Has she made a transfer warranty to that bank?

Section 3-416(c) expressly states that a transferor may not disclaim warranties with respect to a check. This is because in the check collection process, which is largely automated, the banking system relies on those warranties. Section 3-416(c) implies, however, and UCC Comment 5 clearly states that a disclaimer is effective as to other instruments. Specifically, UCC Comment 5 provides that a disclaimer between the immediate parties "may be made by agreement." As to other parties, the disclaimer must be in the indorsement "with words such as 'without warranties' or some other specific reference to warranties." *Id*. **The term, "without recourse" is not sufficient to disclaim transfer warranties. See comment 3 to § 3-416.**

Step 2: To Whom are Transfer Warranties Made?

Even if a person transfers an instrument for consideration and makes transfer warranties, the question arises as to whom he has made them. When made, such warranties are always made to the transferor's immediate transferee. Furthermore, if a transferor indorses the instrument when he transfers it, he also makes transfer warranties to all subsequent transferees. By contrast, if a transferor does not indorse the instrument, then his transfer warranties are made only to his immediate transferee. § 3-416(a). There is an exception, however, when an instrument is transferred to a bank for collection. Thus, if a customer of a bank transfers an instrument to a bank, such as when he deposits a check into his bank account, or if a collecting bank transfers an instrument to another collecting bank, then, whether or not the transferor indorsed the instrument, the transferor makes transfer warranties not only to his immediate transferee but to all subsequent collecting banks to whom the instrument is transferred. § 4-207(a).

PROBLEM 10.3

Dr. Andrew Werr writes a check payable to bearer for $100 which he gives to his son, Alan, to buy books for law school. Alan uses the check to buy a used con-

tracts book and a used torts book from a second year student named Hope Tupas. Alan does not indorse the check. Hope then cashes the check at the grocery store who requires her indorsement on the back of the check. The grocery store deposits the check in its account at the Harris Bank, which then presents the check to Dr. Werr's bank for payment. To whom, if anyone, does Dr. Werr make a transfer warranty? To whom, if anyone, does Alan make a transfer warranty? To whom does Hope make a transfer warranty? To whom does the grocery store make a transfer warranty?

Steps 3 & 4: What are the Transfer Warranties and What Constitutes a Breach?

There are five basic transfer warranties:

1. The transferor is a person entitled to enforce the instrument.

2. All signatures appearing on the instrument are authentic and authorized. This warranty is made as to all signatures on the instrument, including those of the maker or drawer, not just as to those necessary for the transferor to be a person entitled to enforce the instrument.

3. The instrument has not been altered. See § 3-407 for a discussion of what constitutes an "alteration."

4. The instrument is not subject to a defense or claim in recoupment of any party which can be asserted against the transferor. UCC Comment 3 to § 3-416 states that the transferor breaches this warranty even when the defense is ineffective against the transferee, such as when the transferee is a holder in due course. *See, generally,* Chapter 9. This is because the transferee does not intend to buy a lawsuit against a party with whom she has not dealt. She is instead given the option to sue the transferor for breach of warranty rather than to litigate the issue of her holder in due course status against the obligor.

5. The transferor has no knowledge of any insolvency proceeding initiated as to the maker or acceptor or as to the drawer of an unaccepted instrument.

The first four warranties are "strict liability" warranties. The transferor makes these warranties about objective facts and, if they are untrue, the transferor faces liability even if he is not responsible for their being untrue and even if he made the warranties in good faith. The fifth warranty is different, because it involves only a warranty as to the transferor's own state of mind, not external facts. Consequently, even if the relevant parties are involved in insolvency proceedings, the warranty is not breached so long as the transferor had no knowledge of such proceedings. The transferor makes no warranty regarding the difficulty of collection or the state of the obligor's credit or solvency. It is the transferee's responsibility to determine such questions before taking the instrument. However, if insolvency proceedings have been instituted against the party obligated to pay *and* the transferor knows it, the transferor's passive concealment of that fact is considered a type of fraud on the transferee; warranty liability is the transferee's remedy. *See* UCC Comment 4 to § 3-416.

PROBLEM 10.4

Martha draws a check for $250 payable to bearer and gives it to George as a birthday gift. Felonious Frank picks George's pockets, goes to the Local Currency Exchange, and asks it to cash the check for him. Local Currency Exchange asks Frank for identification, and he shows it George's credit card. Local Currency Exchange then asks that Frank indorse the check, and he signs George's name. In exchange for the check, Local Currency Exchange gives Frank $245. Identify any and all transfer warranties that Frank has violated.

PROBLEM 10.5

Tom draws a check for $100 payable to John and gives it to him as a birthday present. John uses the check to purchase clothing at Harry's retail shop by indorsing it over to Harry. When Harry presents the check to Tom's bank for payment, Harry learns that Tom has issued a stop payment order on the check because of a disagreement he has had with John. The check is therefore dishonored by Tom's bank. Has John violated any transfer warranty?

In determining whether a particular transferor's warranties were breached, it is important to consider the facts as of the time the warranty was made. Even though a transferor by indorsement may make warranties not only to his immediate transferee but also to all subsequent transferees, the warranties are made only as of the time that the particular transferor transferred the instrument.

PROBLEM 10.6

On January 10, 2004, Mayberry Milton issues a promissory note to the order of Lender Larry for $1,000 plus 10% interest, due on January 10, 2006, in exchange for a loan of $1,000. On March 15, 2005, Larry negotiates the note to Finnagler's Finance in exchange for cash. Finnagler's Finance alters the note so that it appears to be for $10,000 plus interest, rather than for $1,000 plus interest, and, on May 1, 2005, negotiates the note to Naive National Bank for $10,500. Did Finnagler's make transfer warranties to Naive National Bank? If so, did it breach any of those warranties? Did Larry make any transfer warranties to Naive National Bank? If so, did he breach any of those warranties?

Revised 2002 §§ 3-416 and 4-207

Revised 2002 §§ 3-416 and 4-207 introduce a sixth transfer warranty as to a "remotely-created consumer item," which Revised 2002 § 3-103(a)(16) defines as:

an item drawn on a consumer account, which is not created by the payor bank and does not bear a handwritten signature purporting to be the signature of the drawer.

Such items may, for instance, be produced, and then submitted to payor banks, by telemarketers after they obtain a customer's consent over the phone. Revised 2002 §§ 3-416 and 4-207 state that someone who makes transfer warranties also makes, as to a remotely-created consumer item, a warranty that "the person on whose account the item is drawn authorized the issuance of the item in the amount for which the item is drawn." The basis for this rule is the belief that depositary banks, rather than payor banks, are best able to control fraud relating to such items.

Steps 5 & 6: Was there Proximate Cause and, if so, How Much May the Transferee Recover?

Whether the breach was the proximate cause of the injury, and, if so, the amount of any damages are fact questions to be determined in each case. Nevertheless, there are three limitations on a plaintiff's ability to recover damages for breach of transfer warranty. First, only transferees who take an instrument in good faith can sue for breach of a transfer warranty. §§ 3-416(b), 4-207(c). (Incidentally, the transferor's good faith is not a defense to warranty liability.) Second, while the transferee may recover an amount equal to the loss suffered as a result of the breach, she may not recover more than the amount of the instrument plus expenses and interest. See §§ 3-416(b), 4-207(c). Comment 6 states that attorneys' fees might be recoverable as "expenses," but that the intention of § 3-416 was to leave this issue to state courts. Third, if the beneficiary of the breached transfer warranty fails to give the warrantor notice of the breach within 30 days after the claimant has reason to know of both the breach by and the identity of the warrantor, the warrantor's liability, to the extent caused by the delay in giving notice, is discharged. §§ 3-416(c), 4-207(d). It is important to recognize that this is a notice requirement, not a statute of limitations. The transferee need not file suit within the said 30 days. Obviously, a transferee's claim will be barred if the transferee fails to file suit within the applicable statute of limitations. Pursuant to § 3-118(g), an action for breach of warranty must be commenced within three years after the cause of action accrues. A cause of action for breach of transfer warranty arises when the transferee "has reason to know of the breach." See § 3-416(d).

PROBLEM 10.7

William draws a check payable to the order of Hillary for the amount of $500. Hillary puts the check into her purse, and then leaves her purse on an airplane. Deidre finds the purse, forges Hillary's name to the check, and transfers it to her friend, Albert, who does not realize that Hillary's signature was forged, for $480 cash. Deidre persuasively explains that it's worth $20 to her to save the hassle of going to get the check cashed. On 1/2/2004, Albert, in good faith, goes to the Local Currency Exchange and cashes the check, receiving $500. Local Currency Exchange discovers the forgery of Hillary's signature on 1/10/2004, when William's bank refuses to pay the check, telling Local that William placed a stop payment order on it. Due to a mixup, Local Currency Exchange does not tell Albert of the forgery until 5/10/2004. Explain whether Albert has violated any transfer warranties and, if so, whether Local Currency Exchange will be able to recover any damages from him.

COMPARING SECTION 3-416 AND SECTION 4-207

While § 3-416 applies generally to all transfers of instruments, § 4-207 is tailored to apply to transfers as part of the bank collection process. If there is a conflict between §§ 3-416 and 4-207, the rules of § 4-207 govern. *See* § 3-102(b).

Section 3-416 provides that transfer warranties are made by persons that transfer instruments for "consideration;" § 4-207 states that transfer warranties are made by each bank "customer" or collecting bank that transfers an "item" and receives a settlement or other consideration for it. For purposes of § 4-207, the word "customer" is generally construed as referring to a person for whom the bank "has agreed to collect items." The word, "item," can refer to something that is not a "negotiable instrument." *Cf.* UCC Comment to § 4-208. However, an item is not a payment order under revised Article 4A or a credit or debit card slip. *See* § 4-104(a)(9).

Section 3-416 states that when a person transfers an instrument for consideration, he always makes transfer warranties to his immediate transferee. He only makes these warranties to subsequent transferees if he indorsed the instrument. By contrast, a person who makes transfer warranties under § 4-207 always makes them not only to the immediate transferee but also to all subsequent collecting banks to whom the item is transferred, regardless of whether he indorsed the instrument.

PROBLEM 10.8

Bob receives a paycheck payable to his order from his employer. Lightfingers Louie lifts the check from Bob's pocket, indorses Bob's name on the check, and transfers the check for consideration to Patrick. Patrick then transfers the check for consideration to Sally, who deposits the check in her bank, First Insatiable Bank ("FIB"), and receives a "settlement" or credit to her account for the amount of the check. FIB transfers the check to Second National Bank, which gives FIB a "settlement" for the amount of the check and then presents the check for payment to Drawee Bank. Drawee Bank dishonors the check. As to each person who made transfer warranties, identify: (1) to whom the warranties were made, and (2) whether the warranties would be governed by § 3-416 or § 4-207.

The transfer warranties made under § 4-207 are identical to those made under § 3-416. *See* § 4-207(a). In fact, most of the remaining provisions of § 4-207 are the same as those of § 3-416. *See* UCC Comment to § 4-207. There is, however, one significant difference. Section 4-207 imposes on a transferor, strict liability in the event the item is for any reason dishonored. Section 4-207(b) provides that if an item is dishonored, the customer or collecting bank that transferred it and received settlement or consideration for it must pay to the transferee suffering the loss the amount due on the item at the time it was transferred. If the item was incomplete when transferred but was subsequently completed, the warrantor must pay the item as completed to the transferee or to any subsequent collecting bank that takes the item in good faith.

This obligation to pay the instrument if it is dishonored sounds much like indorser's liability, but it arises even if there is no indorsement by the customer or collecting bank. Furthermore, unlike an indorser's liability, the obligation arising under § 4-207 cannot be avoided by use of "without recourse" language or any other terms purporting to disclaim liability. *See* § 4-207(b).

II. PRESENTMENT WARRANTIES

Sections §§ 3-417 and 4-208 apply to presentment warranties. Historically, the predecessor to § 3-417 applied to presentment warranties generally, while the predecessor to § 4-208 applied only to presentment warranties made in bank collection transactions. Although there is some ambiguity as to the respective scopes of these current provisions, when there is a conflict between the provisions of §§ 3-417 and 4-208, § 4-208 governs. *See* §§ 3-102(b), 4-102(a). Nevertheless, §§ 3-417 and 4-208 are virtually identical. (Although § 3-417(a)(3) refers to "drawer" while § 4-208(a)(3) refers to "purported drawer," this difference appears inadvertent and insignificant.) In one way, § 4-208(a) is broader than § 3-417(a) because the word "draft" — which appears in both §§ 3-417(a) and 4-208(a) — is defined in Article 4 to include even nonnegotiable drafts. *See* UCC Comment to § 4-208.

Briefly stated, presentment warranties are made if some party has presented or purportedly presented an instrument for acceptance or payment, and the party to whom to it was so presented in fact accepted it or paid it in good faith. The phrase "purportedly presented" is used because of an apparent inconsistency in the provisions of Article 3. Although §§ 3-417 and 4-208 indicate that no presentment warranties are made unless a presentment has been made by some party, § 3-501(a) defines "presentment" as "a demand made by or on behalf of a person entitled to enforce an instrument." Yet case law makes it clear that if a party who is not entitled to payment demands payment and is paid, that party has violated a presentment warranty. Consequently, the references in §§ 3-417 and 4-208 should be to either "purported" (or "apparent") presentments *or* "actual presentments" — and not merely "presentments" as defined in § 3-501. For convenience, however, the text shall from now on refer only to "presenter" and "presentment" and not to "purported presenter" or "purported presentment."

Presentment warranties are only made if a particular presentment is "successful," i.e., if an instrument presented for payment is paid or an item presented for acceptance is accepted. Where there is a successful presentment, presentment warranties are made not only by the party that made the presentment, but also by all prior transferors of the instrument, whether or not such prior transferors received consideration or indorsed the instrument.

Presentment warranties are made only to the party who accepted or paid the instrument. It is perhaps useful to think of presentment warranties as the warranties that are made to presentees, while transfer warranties are the warranties that are made to transferees.

The specific warranties made depend on the nature of the instrument that was presented and whether the instrument had previously been accepted or dishonored. Although a party may generally disclaim its warranty liability by express language referring to a disclaimer of warranties, a party may not disclaim presentment warranties in connection with checks. The warrantor's liability is discharged, however, to the extent that a loss is caused by the warrantee's failure to give the warrantor timely notice of the breach. Notice must be given within 30 days after the claimant has reason to know both the claim and the identity of the warrantor. *See* §§ 3-417(e) and 4-208(e). Of course, a warranty claim may be barred by any applicable statute of limitations. Pursuant to § 3-118(g), an action for breach of warranty must be commenced within three years after the cause of action accrues. A cause of action for breach of a presentment warranty accrues when the claimant has reason to know of the breach. Interestingly, there is no requirement that the claimant know the identity of the warrantor.

Each of § 3-417 and § 4-208 set forth two separate rules with respect to presentment warranties.

A. *Presentments of an Unaccepted Draft to the Drawee*

When an unaccepted draft is presented to the drawee for payment or acceptance, and the drawee, in good faith, pays or accepts the draft, presentment warranties are made (a) by the person who made the presentment and (b) by any prior transferor of the instrument. The person presenting the item makes the warranties as of the time of presentment; prior transferors make the warranties as of the time of their respective transfers. A typical example occurs when a party presents an uncertified check to the drawee bank for payment or, even more commonly, when a collecting bank presents a check to the drawee bank for payment.

The warranties made are that:

a. the warrantor is either a person entitled to enforce the draft or is authorized to obtain payment or acceptance of the draft on behalf of a person entitled to enforce it;

b. the draft has not been altered; and

c. the warrantor has no knowledge that the drawer's signature is unauthorized.

Revised 2002 §§ 3-417 and 4-208

Revised 2002 §§ 3-417 and 4-208 introduce a fourth presentment warranty as to a "remotely-created consumer item," as defined by Revised 2002 § 3-103(a)(16). Specifically, these sections state that if someone successfully presents to a drawee such a remotely-created consumer item, that person — and all prior transferors of the item — also warrant to the presentee that "the person on whose account the item is drawn authorized the issuance of the item in the amount for which the item is drawn." The basis for this rule is the belief that depositary banks, rather than payor banks, are best able to control fraud relating to such items.

PROBLEM 10.9

Dan Drawer issues a check for $100 drawn on his bank, First National, payable to the order of Paula Payee. Paula indorses the check over to Harry, who in turn indorses it over to Judy. Judy then takes the check to First National, presents it for payment, and is given $100 cash. Explain whether Dan, Paula, Harry and / or Judy have made presentment warranties. As to Paula or Harry, does it matter whether they received consideration when they transferred the check?

PROBLEM 10.10

Dan Drawer issues a check for $100 drawn on his bank, First National, payable to the order of Paula Payee. Devious Donna picks Paula's pocket, forges Paula's name to the check, and transfers it to Harry, who in turn indorses it over to Judy. Judy then takes the check to First National, presents it for payment, and *is given $100 cash. Explain whether Dan, Paula, Donna, Harry and/or Judy have made presentment warranties.*

In the case of a breach of a presentment warranty, if a drawee pays an unaccepted draft presented to it or a drawee pays a previously unaccepted draft that it accepted after presentment to it, the drawee may recover from any warrantor:

a. damages equal to the amount paid by the drawee minus the amount the drawee received or is entitled to receive from the drawer as a result of the payment; and

b. compensation for consequential expenses and loss of interest.

The failure by the drawee to exercise ordinary care in making payment does not affect its right to recover damages for breach of presentment warranty. *See* § 3-417(b). Nevertheless, if a drawee alleges a breach of warranty under § 3-417(a) based on an unauthorized indorsement or alteration, a warrantor may defend by:

a. proving the indorsement is effective under § 3-404 or § 3-405; or

b. proving the drawer is precluded under § 3-406 or § 4-406 from asserting that the indorsement or alteration was unauthorized. *See* § 3-417(c).

These provisions will be discussed later in Chapter 17.

B. Presentment of Dishonored Drafts and Other Instruments

If a party presents a dishonored draft to the drawer or an indorser for payment, or presents for payment any other item to a person obligated to pay it (e.g., a promissory note to the maker or an accepted draft to the acceptor) and the instrument is paid in good faith, a presentment warranty is made by the party who made the presentment and by any prior transferors to the party making payment in good faith. The party making the presentment makes the warranty as of the time of the presentment. Prior transferors make the warranty as of the time of their transfer. The warranty made is that the warrantor either is a person entitled to enforce the instrument or is authorized to obtain payment on behalf of such a person.

PROBLEM 10.11

Dan is the maker of a promissory note payable to the order of Yvette. Yvette negotiates the note to Cheryl. Cheryl presents the note to Dan for payment and Dan pays it. Has Cheryl made any presentment warranties to Dan and, if so, what are they? Has Cheryl made any transfer warranties to Dan? Has Yvette made any presentment warranties to Dan? Has Yvette made any warranties to Cheryl?

PROBLEM 10.12

Jean draws a check to Contractor on her account at Drawee National Bank ("DNB"), has the check certified, and gives it to Contractor. Contractor deposits the check in its account at First State Bank ("FSB"), and FSB presents the check to DNB, which pays it. What presentment warranties have been made to DNB, and who has made them?

PROBLEM 10.13

DrawCo is the drawer of a draft instructing Customer to pay $1,500 to the order of Supplier. Supplier negotiates the draft to Moneybags Company. Nevertheless, when Moneybags presents the check to Customer, Customer dishonors it. Moneybags then presents the draft to DrawCo, which pays it. What warranties has Moneybags made to DrawCo?

The presentment warranty made to the maker of a note, to the acceptor or drawer of a draft, or to an indorser of either instrument (§ 3-417(d)) involves only the status of the person who is presenting or who has transferred the instrument (i.e., that he is entitled to enforce the instrument). Unlike the presentment warranty made to the drawee (§ 3-417(a)), there are no warranties that pertain to the instrument itself (i.e., no alterations or no knowledge of a forged drawer's signature on the instrument). This is because each of the parties to whom presentment is made under § 3-417(d) has already seen the instrument and is therefore in a position to know if it has been altered or if it contains a forged drawer's signature.

III. REMEDIES FOR BREACH OF WARRANTIES

All usual warranty remedies should be available in the event of a breach of warranty. UCC Comment 1 to Former § 3-417 (which dealt with both transfer warranties and presentment warranties) stated:

> **Warranty terms, which are not limited to sale transactions, are used with the intention of bringing in all the usual rules of law applicable to warranties and in particular the necessity of reliance in good faith and the availability of all remedies for breach of warranty, such as rescission of the transaction or an action for damages.**

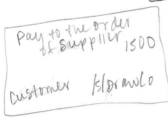

UCC Comment 1 to Former § 4-207 (which dealt with both transfer warranties and presentment warranties) referred the reader to the UCC Comments to Former § 3-417. Nothing in the UCC Comments to §§ 3-416, 3-417, 4-207, or 4-208 indicates a change in this regard.

If a drawee rescinds its acceptance based on breach of a presentment warranty, the drawee will have a defense to liability on the instrument. If a party that paid the instrument or took it for consideration rescinds a transfer based on a breach of presentment or transfer warranty, that party should recover the amount it paid or the consideration it gave.

When a party elects to sue for damages, however, the amount of damages recoverable is less clear. There are three *principal* alternatives. *See* Note, *Measure of Damages for Breach of Implied Warranty by Transferor of a Negotiable Instrument*, 25 Albany L.Rev. 110 (1961); Note, *Warranties on the Transfer of a Negotiable Instrument — UCC 3-417(2)*, 17 Stan.L.Rev. 77 (1964). Prior to enactment of *Former* Article 3, the majority view was to allow the transferee to recover the amount it paid for the instrument. 25 Albany L.Rev. at 110 (citing, among other cases, *Raplee v. Morgan*, 3 Ill. 561 (1840)); 17 Stan.L.Rev. at 87-88. A second alternative is to allow recovery from a particular defendant equal to the consideration that particular defendant received when she transferred the instrument. A third approach, one used in UCC Article 2 regarding the sale of goods, would allow the plaintiff to recover the value the instrument would have had to the plaintiff if the warranty had not been breached, usually the face value of the instrument.

PROBLEM 10.14

On May 1, 2003, Paula Payee fraudulently promised to deliver goods to Mary Maker, thereby inducing Mary to issue to Paula a promissory note payable to her order for $500, due on June 30,2004. On May 15, 2003, Paula transferred the note by indorsement to Harriet for $400. Harriet took the instrument in good faith but knew of Mary's allegation of fraud. On June 15, 2003, Harriet transferred the note to Nancy for $450. Nancy took the instrument in good faith and without notice of Mary's alleged defense. Paula and Harriet have each breached the § 3-416(a)(4) warranty that "the instrument . . . [was] not subject to a defense . . . of any party which . . . [could] be asserted against the warrantor." Assume Nancy sues Paula, as a prior transferor who indorsed the instrument, for breach of warranty. Under the three alternative approaches, how much could Nancy recover?

Former § 4-207 selected a modified version of the second standard by stating:

Damages for breach of such [transfer or presentment] warranties . . . shall not exceed the consideration received by the

customer or collecting bank responsible plus finance charges and expenses related to the item, if any.

By contrast, Former § 3-416 was silent as to the amount of recoverable damages, and it is unclear whether this silence was meaningful.

Sections 4-207, 4-208, 3-416, and 3-417 adopt various approaches regarding the extent of recoverable damages. Section 4-207 no longer refers to the amount of consideration the warrantor received. Instead, it states that one may recover "an amount equal to the loss suffered as a result of the breach, but not more than the amount of the item plus expenses and loss of interest incurred as a result of the breach." It is not entirely clear, however, whether this provision, while allowing the plaintiff to recover expenses and lost interest, basically follows the first approach (with "loss" referring to the plaintiff's out-of-pocket loss) or the third approach (with "loss" referring to the plaintiff's expectation loss). Section 3-416 uses the same language as § 4-207.

The presentment warranty provisions, §§ 3-417(b), 3-417(d), 4-208(b), and 4-208(d), more clearly follow the first alternative. Sections 3-417(b) and 4-208(b) state that a drawee making payment may recover, in addition to expenses and lost interest, damages "equal to the amount paid by the drawee less the amount the drawee received or is entitled to receive from the drawer because of the payment." Sections 3-417(d) and 4-208(d) state that one making payment may recover "an amount equal to the amount paid plus expenses and loss of interest resulting from the breach."

All of the warranty provisions allow for the recovery of "expenses" but make no express provisions for attorneys' fees. Instead the Comments indicate that whether attorneys' fees are to be recoverable as "expenses" depends on local law. *See* UCC Comment 6 to § 3-416; UCC Comment 5 to § 3-417. As to attorneys' fees that were incurred in an action against the warrantor, the courts are split. *Compare, e.g., Vectra Bank of Englewood v. Bank Western*, 890 P.2d 259 (Colo.App. 1995); *E.S.P., Inc. v. Midway National Bank of St. Paul*, 466 N.W.2d 417 (Minn.App. 1991); *McAdam v. Dean Witter Reynolds, Inc.*, 896 F.2d 750 (3rd Cir. 1990)(applying N.J. law); *Bagby v. Merrill Lynch, Pierce, Fenner & Smith, Inc.*, 491 F.2d 192 (8th Cir. 1974) (no attorneys' fees allowed in action against warrantor) *with First Virginia Bank-Colonial v. Provident State Bank*, 582 F.Supp. 850 (D.Md. 1984); *First National Bank of Neenah v. Security National Bank of Springfield*, 32 UCC Rep.Serv. 926, 1981 WL 138022 (D.Mass. 1981); *Guaranty Bank & Trust Co. v. Federal Reserve Bank of Kansas City*, 454 F.Supp. 488 (S.D.Okl. 1977); *National Bank v. National Bank of North America*, 17 UCC Rep.Serv. 486, 1975 WL 22876 (N.Y.City Civ.Ct. 1975) (attorneys' fees granted).

Sometimes, however, the beneficiary of a warranty sues to enforce an instrument against a purported obligor but is unsuccessful because of the warrantor's breach of warranty. Similarly, the beneficiary, in reliance on the warranty, may defend itself against a payee's suit for conversion of the instrument or a customer's suit to have his account recredited. Under Former Articles 3 and 4, cases generally held that the beneficiaries of such warranties could recover as "expenses" the attorneys' fees incurred in unsuccessful suits. *See, e.g., Hoppe v. First Midwest Bank of Poplar Bluff*, 899 S.W.2d 879 (Mo.App. 1995) (attorneys' fees incurred in defending payee's conversion action); *Garnac Grain Company, Inc. v. Boatmen's Bank & Trust Company of Kansas City*, 694 F.Supp. 1389 (W.D.Mo. 1988); *Lund v. Chemical Bank*, 675 F.Supp. 815 (S.D. N.Y. 1987); *First Virginia Bank-Colonial v. Provident State Bank*, 582 F.Supp. 850 (D.Md. 1984); *Perkins State Bank v. Connolly*, 632 F.2d 1306 (5th Cir. 1980).

PROBLEM 10.15

Dan Drawer issues a check on his account at Drawee Bank payable to the order of Patty Payee. Sinister Sue steals the check from Patty, forges Patty's signature and transfers it to Grocer for value. Grocer cashes the check at Currency Exchange. Meanwhile Patty advises Dan that the check was stolen and he orders Drawee Bank to stop payment. When Drawee Bank stops payment, Currency Exchange sues Dan on his drawer's obligation. But because Patty's indorsement is forged, the check is still order paper payable to Patty, and Currency Exchange is not a person entitled to enforce the instrument. Consequently, the court rules for Dan. Can Currency Exchange successfully sue Grocer and, if so, can it collect for the attorneys' fees it expended in its lawsuit against Dan?

Chapter 11

CONVERSION LIABILITY

UCC Article 3 also provides that a person, even without ever becoming a party to an instrument, can become liable for the instrument by converting it. Four principal questions arise regarding conversion:

A. What constitutes conversion?

B. Who may sue for conversion?

C. Who may be sued for conversion?

D. What is the measure of damages available to one who successfully sues for conversion?

A. *What Constitutes Conversion?*

An instrument can be "converted" in any of five basic ways. Four of them are mentioned in UCC § 3-420, and one is set forth in UCC § 3-206(d). We will briefly identify each of these ways and then examine them one by one.

1. The "law applicable to conversion of personal property" applies also to negotiable instruments. *See* UCC § 3-420(a).

2. A person also commits conversion when he takes an instrument by transfer other than by a negotiation from someone who is not a person entitled to enforce the instrument (a "PETE"). *See* UCC § 3-420(a).

3. A bank commits conversion when it obtains payment of an instrument for someone who is not a PETE. *See* UCC § 3-420(a).

4. A bank also commits conversion when it pays an instrument to someone who is not a PETE. *See* UCC § 3-420(a).

5. Certain persons commit conversion when they act inconsistently with particular restrictive indorsements that appear on an instrument. *See* UCC § 3-206(c).

1. *"Law Applicable to Conversion of Personal Property"*

By "law applicable to conversion of personal property," UCC § 3-420(a) means the tort of conversion of personal property. This tort is committed when one person exercises wrongful dominion, either temporarily or permanently, over the property of another. The exercise of such dominion is wrongful when it is done

161

in denial of, or in a manner inconsistent with, the rights of the person to whom the property belongs.

PROBLEM 11.1

Determine whether the following constitutes conversion under § 3-420(a):

a. *Paul Payee is robbed at gunpoint. The thief takes Paul's watch, his money and a check made payable to Paul from Paul's employer.* Y

b. *A check made payable to bearer drops out of Paul's pocket. Lucky Eddie sees it fall, picks it up and takes it to the nearest Currency Exchange where he cashes it.* Y

c. *Paul Payee takes a check made payable to him to the drawee bank and presents it for payment over the counter. The teller takes the check from Paul, goes back to his desk and returns with neither cash nor Paul's check. He tells Paul that the check will not be cashed. When Paul asks for the check to be returned to him, the teller refuses to give it back.* Y

2. *Taking an Instrument by Transfer, but Not by Negotiation, from a non-PETE*

A person converts an instrument if he (a) takes it by transfer, but not by negotiation, (b) from someone who is not a PETE. As to (a), an instrument is transferred when it is voluntarily delivered by one person to another. *See* § 3-203(a). The transfer is not a negotiation unless it results in the transferee becoming a holder. Thus, where an instrument is transferred without a necessary indorsement, the transferee does not become a holder and the transfer is not a negotiation. As to (b), if the person who transferred the instrument in such a way, was also not a PETE, the transferee taking the instrument has committed conversion.

PROBLEM 11.2

In Problem 11.1b, above, is the Currency Exchange that cashed the check liable for conversion? No

PROBLEM 11.3

Suppose Bonnie issues a check to Frank for $250 payable to his order. Without indorsing the check, Frank puts it in his wallet. Mark then picks Frank's pocket and takes the wallet.

a. *Mark buys groceries and pays for them by indorsing the stolen check in Frank's name and giving it to Grocer. Suppose Grocer still has the check and has not presented it for payment. Has Grocer converted the check?*

b. *Suppose that, instead of transferring the check to Grocer, Mark had given it to Niece as a gift. Would Niece be liable for converting the check? Does it matter whether or not Mark forged Frank's signature before giving the check to his niece?* Y

c. *Suppose that Frank had indorsed the check in blank before putting it into his wallet. Would that change your answers to "a" and/or "b"?*

PROBLEM 11.4

Suppose Bonnie issues a check to Frank for $250 payable to his order. Frank asks his friend, Mike to cash the check for him. Mike gives Frank $250, and Frank, without indorsing the check, gives it to Mike. Has Mike converted the check? Why or why not? Ns

3. Banks Obtaining Payment for a Non-Pete

A bank that obtains payment of an instrument for a person not entitled to enforce it is liable for conversion. This part of § 3-420(a) seems to apply to depositary banks and collecting banks. Frankly, this language seems unnecessary because depositary and collecting banks are also transferees of the persons for whom they obtain payment. If such persons are not entitled to enforce the instrument, the depositary and collecting banks might be liable for conversion as soon as they take the checks, because they would be taking checks by transfer, other than by negotiation, from non-PETEs, as discussed above. Nevertheless, there was considerable controversy under Former § 3-419 as to whether depositary banks could be liable for conversion. This language in § 3-420 makes it clear that depositary banks can be liable for conversion, which is probably the reason why the language was included.

PROBLEM 11.5

Felonious Frank snatches a wallet from Clueless Cary that contains a check made payable to Cary for $500. The check is drawn on a bank in another part of the country. On the back of the check Frank writes "Pay to Felonious Frank" and forges Cary's signature as an indorsement. Frank then deposits the check into Frank's account at First National Bank. First National sends the check to a local Federal Reserve Bank (FRB 1), which then forwards the check to another Federal Reserve Bank (FRB 2) in the state in which the drawee bank is located. FRB2 presents the check to the drawee bank and the check is paid. The proceeds of the check are then sent bank to First National Bank, which credits Frank's account. Several days later, Frank withdraws all the money in his account at First National. Is First National liable for conversion? Are FRB1 and FRB2 also liable for conversion? Be sure to read § 3-420(c) carefully.

PROBLEM 11.6

After his appearance at the opening of a feed store in central Texas, a $10,000 check made payable to Bronco Billy, a world famous rodeo star, is given to his agent, Arliss Michaels for safekeeping. Arliss, who has authority to sign checks on Billy's behalf, signs Billy's name on the back of the check and then signs his own name and deposits the check in Arliss's account at Highland Bank of Oregon ("HBO"). HBO obtains payment from the drawee bank and credits Arliss' account. Arliss subsequently withdraws the money and uses it to purchase a used motorcycle for his personal use. Is Arliss liable for conversion? Is HBO liable for conversion?

4. Banks Paying Instruments to a non-PETE

A payor bank that pays an instrument for one not entitled to enforce it is also liable for conversion. With one exception, this means that whenever a check previously converted under § 3-420 as a result of its transfer is paid by the payor bank, the payor bank will also be liable for conversion. Why? Because the previous conversion was based on the fact that the a transferor was a non-PETE. The transferor's status as a non-PETE was based on the fact that he was not a holder in his own right because a necessary indorsement was missing and he did not have rights of a holder under the shelter doctrine because no PETE had transferred the instrument to him. Consequently, unless the necessary indorsement was somehow added to the instrument before the payor bank paid the item, the payor bank would be making payment to a non-PETE. The exception, obviously, would be if the needed indorsement were added to the instrument before the payor bank paid the item. Of course, payor banks can also commit conversion under § 3-420 even as to items that were never previously transferred.

PROBLEM 11.7

Suppose Bonnie issues a check to Frank for $250 payable to his order. The check is drawn on Bonnie's account at First Insatiable Bank ("FIB"). Without indorsing the check, Frank puts it in his wallet. Mark then picks Frank's pocket and takes the wallet. He then forges Frank's indorsement, walks into FIB, goes up to a teller, hands the teller the check and asks for the $250. The teller gives him the $250. Has FIB converted the instrument? *yes, paid non-PETE*

PROBLEM 11.8

c – A – abe

Crestwood Investors, Inc., issued a check on its account at First Insatiable Bank ("FIB") for $15,000 payable to Affluent Alfred. Alfred brought the check with him when he met with his financial advisor, Honest Abe, a partner at Phoenix Fraudulent Advisors ("PFA"), and inadvertently left the check in Abe's office. Abe, who is not authorized to sign for Alfred, forged Alfred's indorsement and deposited it his own account at Illinois State Bank ("ISB"). ISB presents the check to FIB, which pays it. Identify any and all persons who are liable for conversion. Would your answer be any different if Abe had deposited the check without bothering to forge Alfred's indorsement? See Schmitz v. Firstar Bank Milwaukee, 262 Wis.2d 672 (2003), 664 N.W.2d 594, 50 UCC Rep.Serv.2d 1143.

abe
ISB

When an instrument is drawn to two or more persons *not alternatively*, it may be negotiated or enforced only by *all of the payees* acting jointly. Thus, any one of the payees acting without the consent of the others is not a person entitled to enforce the instrument. Consequently, any party or bank who takes the instrument by transfer or for deposit with less than all of the payees' indorsements or any payor bank that pays such an instrument is liable in conversion to the payee or payees who have not indorsed the instrument. *See* UCC Comment 1 to § 3-420.

PROBLEM 11.9

Bob drew a check payable to the order of Ted and Alice and gave it to Ted when he and Ted played golf together. Unbeknownst to Bob, Ted and Alice were having some marital difficulties. Ted indorsed the check in his name only and deposited in a secret account he had opened at Cheaters National Bank. Cheaters took the check and presented it for payment at the drawee bank, First National Bank. First National paid the check. Has the instrument been converted, and if so, by whom? What result if Ted, without the authority to do so, signed Alice's name?

Ted

5. Non-Compliance with Restrictive Indorsements

Section 3-206(c) discusses restrictive indorsements, such as "pay any bank," "for deposit," or "for collection," which indicate that an instrument is to be collected by a bank for the benefit of the indorser or a particular account. Under § 3-206(c), a person who purchases an instrument so indorsed converts it unless the amount paid is received by the indorser or applied in accordance with the indorsement. § 3-206(c)(1). A depositary bank that purchases such an instrument or takes it for collection also converts it unless the amount paid by the bank is received by the indorser or applied in accordance with the indorsement. § 3-206(c)(2). A payor bank that is also the depositary bank or that takes such an instrument for payment over the counter from someone other than a collecting bank converts the instrument unless the proceeds are received by the indorser or applied in accordance with the indorsement. § 3-206(c)(3).

PROBLEM 11.10

Alexis Employer issues a check for $500 payable to the order of Patricia Payee. Patricia indorses it "For Deposit Only /s/ Patricia Payee" and gives it to her friend Gail to deposit for her in Patricia's account at First State Bank. Gail takes the check to First State Bank ("FSB") but, instead of depositing it into Patricia's account, she asks FSB to give her the $500, which it does. Identify any and all persons who have converted the instrument.

B. Who May Sue for Conversion

Section 3-420 does not explicitly identify the parties who may sue for conversion. However, it does state that neither (a) "the issuer or acceptor of the instrument," nor (b) a payee or indorsee to whom the instrument was neither directly nor indirectly delivered, may bring "an action for conversion of an instrument."

1. Issuers may not sue for conversion

The term "issuer" means the maker of an issued or unissued note or the drawer of an issued or unissued draft. Section 3-105. Before § 3-420 was implemented, there was a split in authority among the jurisdictions as to whether a drawer could sue for conversion. Section 3-420(a) resolves this issue by explicitly stating that a drawer *may not* sue for conversion. UCC Comment 1 to § 3-420 cites two reasons for this change. First, it states that the check represents the drawer's obligation and not the drawer's "property." Second, Comment 1 states that the drawer has an adequate remedy against the payor bank since the drawer can seek re-credit of the drawer's account of an unauthorized payment using § 4-401.

PROBLEM 11.11

Donna Drawer writes a check payable to her friend Penny Payee for $500 and leaves it on her desk with the intention of giving it to Penny the next day. That evening, Terry Thief breaks into Donna's house and steals the check. He forges Penny's indorsement and brings the check to the 4th Avenue Currency Exchange where he is able to cash it for the full amount. The 4th Avenue Currency Exchange deposits the check into its account at Fifth Third Bank which then presents it to Donna's Bank for payment and it is paid. Which of these parties have converted the check? Which of these parties can Donna sue for conversion?

2. *Payee and Indorsees May Only Sue for Conversion After Delivery*

Neither a payee nor an indorsee acquires any proprietary rights in an instrument until the instrument is delivered to him. Consequently, until such delivery, the payee and indorsee are not proper parties to sue for conversion. *See* § 3-420(a). This represents a change from a number of decisions under Former § 3-419, the pre-1990 UCC provision, which held that a payee could sue for conversion provided that it was simply "entitled" to possession. *See, e.g., See Lund's Inc. v. Chemical Bank*, 870 F.2d 840 (2nd Cir. 1989); *Sony Corp. of America v. American Express Co.*, 115 Misc.2d 1060, 1061, 455 N.Y.S.2d 227, 230-31 (Civ.Ct.1982); *Burks Drywall, Inc. v. Washington Bank & Trust Co.*, 110 Ill.App.3d 569, 442 N.E.2d 648, 66 Ill.Dec. 222 (2d Dist. 1982).

PROBLEM 11.12

Under the facts of Problem 11.11, could Penny bring a cause of action against all those parties who converted the check?

Comment 1 to § 3-420 suggests that the reason a payee may not sue in conversion unless he has received the check is that a payee who has not received the check is not harmed by the conversion. If the check was going to be given to the payee as payment for an underlying obligation between the drawer and the payee, the payee can still enforce the underlying obligation. Comment 1 also says that the situation is different if the check is delivered to the payee. If the check is taken for an obligation owed to the payee, the last sentence of Section 3-310(b)(4) provides that the underlying obligation may not be enforced to the extent of the amount of the check. The payee's rights are restricted to enforcement of the payee's rights in the instrument. In this event, the payee is injured by the theft and has a cause of action for conversion.

Interestingly, there appears to be a problem with this rationale. Section 3-310, refers to a case in which an instrument *"is taken"* for an underlying obligation, *i.e.*, where a payee voluntarily *takes* a preferred instrument for an underlying obligation. When that *taking* occurs, the payee's rights to sue on the underlying obligation are restricted by § 3-310(b)(4). The discussion of whether the payee or indorsee can sue for conversion found in the comment cited above, as well as in the statutory language of § 3-420, focuses instead on the *delivery* to the purported plaintiff. Read the discussion of delivery in Comment 1 to § 3-420 carefully and then do the following problem to see why we believe the rationale is flawed.

PROBLEM 11.13

Dan Drawer owes $250 to Peter Payee and, without getting Peter's consent to pay by check, mails Peter a check for $250, drawn on Dan's account at First State Bank ("FSB") as payment. The postal carrier places the check in Peter's mailbox, but it is stolen from the mailbox by Stickyfingers Sam, who forges Peter's indorsement, and presents the check to FSB, which pays it. Looking at the discussion of delivery in Comment 1 and then to § 3-310(b)(4) can Peter sue Dan on the underlying obligation or must he sue the drawee bank in conversion?

PROBLEM 11.14

Homeowner Nancy owes $750 to Fred and Barney for work they have done on her house. She draws a check on her account at First National Bank ("FNB"), payable to Fred and Barney as joint payees and hands the check to Fred. Fred, without telling Barney anything about the check, signs his own name and forges Barney's to the back of the check, and successfully presents it for payment to FNB. May Barney sue anyone for conversion of the check? If so, whom may he sue? Would your answer be any different if Fred had signed only his name to the bank of the check and not forged Barney's and yet the instrument was paid?

C. Who May Be Sued for Conversion

As we have already seen, a § 3-420 conversion action may be brought against (a) any person who takes an instrument from someone who was not entitled to enforce the instrument or (b) any bank, including depositary and collecting banks, that makes or obtains payment for someone not entitled to enforce the instrument. Of course, anyone who steals an instrument is also liable in conversion under the law of conversion relating to personal property.

Section 3-420(c) protects representatives, except for depositary banks, who deal in good faith with an instrument or its proceeds on behalf of a person who is not a PETE. Such representatives can only be liable in conversion to the extent of any proceeds that they have received and not yet paid out. The fact that depositary banks are denied such protection is a welcome departure from the pre-1990 § 3-419. The efficiency of this change may be illustrated by an example. Suppose a dentist has ten customers who use ten different banks. Each of these customers paid the dentist on Monday by checks drawn on the ten different drawee banks. A burglar breaks into the office Monday night, steals the ten checks, forges the dentist's name, and deposits the checks into the burglar's own account at Depositary Bank, and Depositary Bank successfully presents the checks to each of the ten drawee banks. If the dentist were not entitled to sue Depositary Bank for conversion, the dentist would have to sue each of the ten drawee banks in separate lawsuits — and, depending on jurisdictional technicalities, possibly in separate courts. Each of the drawee banks would then have a successful cause of action against Depositary Bank for breach of its presentment warranty that it was a PETE. This would involve considerable transaction costs and inconvenience. Under § 3-420, however, the dentist may sue Depositary Bank in one suit as to all ten checks.

D. *Measure of Damages*

Section § 3-420(b) provides that, although the measure of damages for conversion is presumed to be the amount payable (which should include any applicable interest) on the instrument in all cases, this presumption may be rebutted, and "recovery may not exceed the amount of the plaintiff's interest in the instrument." This § 3-420(b) rule obviously applies to the forms of conversion expressly enumerated in § 3-420(a). Presumably, it also applies to conversion under § 3-206(c) for failing to act consistently with a restrictive indorsement.

Although Former § 3-419 did not refer to a bank's ability to assert common law defenses to liability for conversion, courts frequently permitted such defenses. Thus, where the proceeds of a check were ultimately received by or benefitted the intended payee, courts reasoned that enabling the payee to recover for conversion would result in unjust enrichment. *See, e.g., O'Petro Energy Corporation v. Canadian State Bank*, 837 P.2d 1391 (Okla. 1992). Unjust enrichment was also used as a defense when a named payee was not actually intended to receive any interest in an instrument. *See, e.g., Midwest Industrial Funding v. First National Bank*, 973 F.2d 534 (7th Cir. 1992) (citing a variety of cases in which common law defenses were allowed). *See, generally, Twellman v. Lindell Trust Co.*, 534 S.W.2d 83 (Mo.App. 1976) (drawer of draft improperly paid over forged indorsement not entitled to recover full face value where he had been partially reimbursed for his loss); *Century Mortgage Company, Inc. v. George*, 1993 WL 12144 (Conn. Super.). These common law defenses should be available under § 3-420 as well. Similarly, in *National Accident Insurance Underwriters, Inc. v. Citibank, F.S.B.*, 243 F.Supp.2d 769, 50 UCC Rep.Serv.2d 867 (N.D.Il. 2003), the federal district court for the northern district of Illinois held that a defendant in a § 3-420 action may assert affirmative defenses such as failure to join necessary parties, laches, unclean hands, and failure to mitigate damages.

Section 3-420 does not refer to the availability of punitive damages. Under Former § 3-419, a number of courts held that punitive damages could be awarded if a defendant's conduct was reckless or malicious. *See, e.g., Flavor-Inn, Inc. v. NCNB National Bank of South Carolina*, 424 S.E.2d 534, 19 UCC Rep.Serv.2d 1116 (Ct.App. 1992); *Sherrill White Constr., Inc. v. South Carolina Nat'l Bank*, 713 F.2d 1047, 1051-52 (4th Cir.1983); *McAdam v. Dean Witter Reynolds, Inc.*, 896 F.2d 750, 772 (3d Cir.1990) (applying New Jersey law); *D & G Equip. Co. v. First Nat'l Bank*, 764 F.2d 950, 957 note 6 (3d Cir.1985); *Mohr v. State Bank*, 241 Kan. 42, 734 P.2d 1071, 1082 (1987). *See also Louis v. Citi-*

zens & Southern Bank, 189 Ga.App. 164, 375 S.E.2d 82 (1988) (court held that testimony regarding bank's alleged "bad faith" was relevant given demand for punitive damages for conversion under the Code). Nothing in § 3-420 should affect future application of these cases.

Chapter 12

THE BANK-CUSTOMER RELATIONSHIP

A variety of issues regarding negotiable instruments arise between banks and their customers. Although Article 3 applies to some of these matters, Article 4 specifically governs the bank-customer relationship. If there is a conflict between a provision of Article 4 and Article 3, Article 4 controls. *See* § 3-102(b).

A. *Agency Relationship*

The relationship between a bank and its customer is that of agent to principal. By drawing a draft, such as a check, the customer orders the bank, as drawee, to pay according to the draft's terms. In paying the draft, the bank acts as the customer's agent. When the bank pays a check in accordance with its terms, the bank is entitled to debit the customer's account. This right is reflected in § 4-401, which provides that if a bank pays an "item," such as a check, that is "properly payable," the bank may charge the amount of the item against the customer's account.

An "item is defined in § 4-104(a)(9) as "an instrument or a promise or order to pay money handled by a bank for collection or payment. The term does not include a payment order governed by Article 4A or a credit or debit card slip." Consequently, a bank customer may be the drawer of an item or the maker of an item. Similarly, the bank may be a drawee or may otherwise be responsible for paying the instrument. Thus, various provisions in Article 4 refer to "payor banks" rather than to "drawees." For the sake of simplicity, however, we usually refer to bank customers as "drawers" and to payor banks as "drawees." Similarly, we often refer to instruments or checks even though the term "item," used with respect to customer-bank relations, is more comprehensive.

If a bank pays an item that is *not* properly payable, the rule, implicit in § 4-401, is that the bank may not debit its customer's account. Nevertheless, for various policy reasons, Article 4 provides some implicit and explicit exceptions to this rule. This chapter initially explores when an item is properly payable. It then discusses contexts in which a bank may debit an account even though it paid an item that was *not* properly payable.

B. *What is "Properly Payable"?*

Section 4-401(a) states that an item is "properly payable" against an account if it is "authorized by the customer and is in accordance with any agreement between the customer and bank."

it is authorized
by client & doesn't
violate any terms below

PROBLEM 12.1

Cosmo Kramer, who has $250 in his account at Seinfeld National Bank (SNB), writes a check to his friend George for $300 to pay George for World Series tick-ets to a game at Yankee Stadium. Is Kramer's check for $300 properly payable by SNB? Absent an agreement, does SNB have to honor the check? If Kramer is mar-ried and this is a joint account with his wife, would his wife be liable to SNB for the amount in excess of funds available in the account if SNB pays the full amount of the check? Would it matter whether or not she goes to the game? N D
N b *Would it matter whether the team she roots for wins? See § 4-401 and the acc-companying comments.*

Unless different terms are specifically agreed on, the "properly payable" rule generally requires that for a check to be properly payable:

1. the drawer's authorized signature must appear on the check;

2. the check must be paid to a party entitled to enforce it;

3. the check must not have been altered;

4. an incomplete check must not have been completed by the addition of unauthorized terms;

5. the check must be paid on or after the date of the check; *and*

6. the drawer must not have issued an effective stop payment order.

1. Authorized Drawer's Signature

If the drawer's signature is unauthorized or missing, the item does not con-tain an order by the drawer and is not properly payable from her account. Often the unauthorized signature is a forgery. UCC Comment 1 to § 4-401 states: "An item containing a forged drawer's signature . . . is not properly payable." Of course, it may be that the signature was made by someone who mis-takenly believed she had authority to sign for the drawer. In this case, too, the item lacks the customer's authorized signature and, if the bank pays the check, it is ordinarily not allowed to charge the customer's account.

There are situations, however, in which a purportedly unauthorized signature may be treated as "authorized" for purposes of § 4-401(a), thereby allowing the bank to debit the customer's account. See the following problem

PROBLEM 12.2

As to each of the following cases, explain whether the "implicit" rule of § 4-401 permits the drawee to charge its customer's account:

a. *Willy Weasel, known to be the attorney for Victor Principal, tells a business associate of Victor's that he has authority to sign checks in Victor's name. Willy writes a check from Victor's account at First National Bank for $500 to the business associate and the check is paid. Willy did not have actual authority to sign checks in Victor's name. See §§ 3-401, 3-402.*

b. *Frank Forger steals Richie Rich's checkbook and goes to a fancy clothing store where he presents himself as Richie Rich and buys $5,000 worth of expensive clothing. He writes a check on Richie's account at First National Bank to the clothing store for $5,000 and signs it "Richie Rich." When the check is presented, First National Bank pays it.* no authorized sig.

2. Payment to a "Person Entitled To Enforce"

A drawer wants her obligation as drawer to be extinguished when the drawee pays the check. This is accomplished when the bank pays a "person entitled to enforce" the instrument, i.e., a PETE. *See* §§ 3-301, 3-602. If, however, the drawee bank pays a non-PETE, the drawer's liability is not extinguished, and the PETE may still enforce it. The PETE may (a) replevin the instrument and enforce it, or, (b) if it is impossible or infeasible to recover possession of the instrument, the PETE may enforce it pursuant to § 3-309, which deals with lost, stolen, or destroyed instruments. Therefore, if a drawee paying a non-PETE were allowed to debit the customer's account, the customer might end up being liable for the amount of the check twice. Consequently, a drawee bank may not charge the customer's account if it pays a person who is not entitled to enforce the item. The item must be "properly payable" to the party the bank pays.

PROBLEM 12.3

Diana Drawer issues a check for $100 payable to Pete Payee and drawn on Naive National Bank ("NNB"). Before Pete indorses the check, however, Tricky Ted steals it. Ted expertly forges Pete's name and presents the check to NNB, and NNB pays Ted the $100 in good faith and in the exercise of ordinary care. May NNB debit Diana's account for the $100 it paid? No.

Ted forges

Payable to order of Pete $100
Naive /s/ Diana

PROBLEM 12.4

Dan Drawer gives Paula Payee a check drawn on Naive National Bank ("NNB"), payable to bearer for $100. Paula specially indorses the check by writing on the back "Pay to Janet Jones, /s/ Paula Payee" and gives the check to Janet as a graduation gift. Before Janet indorses the check, Wilma Wrongdoer steals the check, forges Janet's indorsement, and presents the check to NNB for payment. NNB pays Wilma the $100 in good faith and in the exercise of ordinary care. May NNB debit Don's account for the $100 it paid? No

Pay to bearer $100
Naive /s/ Dan

Paula = PETE
Janet = PETE
Wilma = NOT PETE

PROBLEM 12.5

Diana Drawer issues a check for $100 payable to Pete Payee and drawn on Naive National Bank ("NNB"). Pete needs the cash right away and is not anywhere near a bank, so he asks his friend Charlie to cash the check for him. Charlie gives Pete $100, and Pete gives Charlie the check, but forgets to indorse it. Charlie presents the check for payment to NNB, and NNB pays the check, negligently failing to notice that Pete's indorsement was missing. May NNB debit Diana's account for the $100 it paid?

3. Alterations

Section 3-407(a) defines "alteration" as

> **(i) an unauthorized change in an instrument that purports to modify in any respect the obligation of a party to the instrument, or (ii) an unauthorized addition of words or numbers or other change to an incomplete instrument relating to the obligation of any party to the instrument.**

Since an item is properly payable only if it is authorized by the customer, it follows that a check containing an "alteration" — an unauthorized change or completion — is not properly payable. It does not represent the customer's order to the bank.

4. *Payment on or After Any Stated Date*

The general rule is that an instrument that is payable on demand is not properly payable before its stated date or, if no date is stated: (a) its date of issue, if the instrument was issued; or (b) the date it first comes into the possession of a holder, if the instrument was not issued. *See* § 3-113. According to this rule, if a drawer issued a post-dated check and the drawee paid it prior to the date on the check, the bank would not have paid a properly payable item. The agency principle underlying the customer-bank relationship would seem to provide that the bank would not be able to debit the drawer's account, because the bank did not properly fulfill the drawer's order, which was not to pay the check until its stated date. Nevertheless, § 4-401(c) statutorily supercedes this principle and states that a bank that pays a check that is properly payable but for the fact that it was paid prior to the date of the check *may* debit the customer's account, subject to one exception. The reason for this rule is that bank's handle a great many checks, and the technological processes which they employ for this purpose are not designed to efficiently catch the fact that a check has been post-dated.

The exception is if the customer gave the bank notice of the postdated check, describing the check with reasonable certainty, and this notice is received by the

bank at a time and in a manner which provided the bank a reasonable opportunity to act on the notice before taking any other action with respect to the
check. Such notice, if given in writing, is effective for six months, and can be
renewed for an additional six-month periods. If the notice is oral, it is only
valid for fourteen days, unless, within such fourteen days, it is confirmed by a
writing. *See* §§ 4-401(c), 4-403. By providing such notice and making it feasible
for the post-dated check to be identified and treated individually, the customer
is entitled to insist that it not be paid before its date.

PROBLEM 12.6

Imprudent Insurance Company ("IIC") is a customer of First State Bank ~~post-dated~~
("FSB"). On May 1, 2005, IIC issues to Icabod Insured a check dated November
1, 2005 for $15,000. Icabod presents the check to FSB for payment on August 15,
2005, and FSB pays it. Can IIC prevent FSB from debiting its account by argu-
ing that the check, when paid, was not properly payable? No, must give bank notice

5. Stop Payment Orders

Section 4-403 allows a customer or any other person authorized to draw on the
account to stop payment on any item drawn on that account. If the stop order
is made at a time and in a manner that affords the bank an opportunity to act
on the order, the item is no longer properly payable. For a more complete discussion of stop payment orders, see Chapter Thirteen.

C. Bank's Right To Charge for Items Not Properly Payable

A bank may argue that a check was properly payable by establishing that certain conduct by the drawer precludes the drawer from asserting that his signature, that of an indorser or an alteration on the instrument was unauthorized.
These preclusions, found in §§ 3-406 and 4-406, will be discussed in Chapter 17.
Additionally, §§ 3-404 and 3-405, also discussed in Chapter 17, provide for certain circumstances where indorsements that would not otherwise seem to be
authorized are said to be "effective." In all these situations, the instrument is
said to be properly payable and the bank may charge the customer's account.
Also, as already discussed in this Chapter, § 4-401(c) may permit a bank to
debit a customer's account if it pre-pays a post-dated check. In addition, there
are at least seven other statutory provisions that may permit a bank to debit a
customer's account for an item that was arguably not properly payable: (1) § 4-
401(d), (2) § 3-407, (3) § 4-403, (4) § 4-404, (5) § 4-405, (6) § 4-407, and (7) § 1-103.

1. *Section 4-401(d)*

When a bank pays a check that was not properly payable because it was altered or completed in an unauthorized manner, § 4-401(d) allows the bank to charge its customer's account, at least partially, if payment was made (a) in good faith and (b) to a holder. If the check was altered, the bank may charge the drawer's account according to the *original, unaltered* amount of the check. Thus, if the alteration increased the amount of the check, the bank must bear the loss between the original amount of the check and the increased, altered amount it paid, unless the customer is precluded from asserting the alteration pursuant to one of the other exceptions.

If a drawer signed an incomplete check, § 4-401(d) provides the bank with still greater protection. In such a case, even if the bank knew that the check was completed after the drawer signed it, the bank may charge the drawer's account according to the terms of the check *as completed*, provided that the bank did not have notice that the completion was improper.

PROBLEM 12.7

Don Drawer owed Fraudulent Fred $100. Don Drawer gave Fred a check but left the amount payable blank. Fred went to Drawee Bank and, in front of the teller, filled in $500 as the amount payable. May Drawee Bank debit Don's account and, if so, for how much? yes

PROBLEM 12.8

Don Drawer issues to Paul Payee a check payable to Paul's order in the amount of $100. The check is stolen from Paul by Cary Crook, who changes the amount of the check to $500 and forges Paul's signature on the back of the check. Cary then transfers the check to Honest Harry as payment for a new 25-inch television set. Harry takes the instrument without notice that Paul's indorsement has been forged and presents it to the drawee bank, First National Bank ("FNB"), for payment. FNB pays the check and debits Don's account for $500. When Don complains, FNB asserts that since it paid the instrument in good faith, it has the right to debit Don's account for the full $500? Is FNB correct? If not, is FNB entitled to debit Don's account for some other amount? No, bank must pay PETE

2. *Section 3-407*

Section 3-407 is very similar to § 4-401(d). Section 3-407(c) states, among other things, that a payor bank or drawee that pays a fraudulently altered instrument in good faith and without notice of the alteration, may enforce rights with respect to the instrument: "(i) according to its original terms, or (ii) in the case of an incomplete instrument altered by unauthorized completion, according to its terms as completed."

PROBLEM 12.9

Compare and contrast § 4-401(d) to § 3-407(c). Identify possible practical differences between the relief these two provisions might provide drawee banks who pay altered instruments.

3. Section 4-403(c)

If a timely stop payment order is properly made as to a check, the check is no longer properly payable. Nevertheless, under § 4-403(c), the customer will not be able to recover from the payor bank unless the customer proves that the payment has caused him a loss. If the person paid had a valid claim against the customer, the customer is not said to have suffered a loss because the bank, when it paid the check, was subrogated to that person's claim pursuant to § 4-407 and, therefore, could debit the customer's account. *See also* UCC Comment 7 to § 4-403. The customer bears the burden of proof as to the fact and amount of the loss.

PROBLEM 12.10

Darlene Drawer issues a $500 check to Sam Sly as a downpayment on land in Florida, which Darlene subsequently learns does not exist. Darlene issues a written stop payment order to her bank, Sloppy State Bank ("SSB"), perfectly identifying the check . Meanwhile, however, Sam transfers the check to Ike Innocent, who is a holder in due course. Ten days after the stop payment order was issued, Ike presents the check and SSB pays it and debits Darlene's account. Did SSB pay an item that was properly payable? If Darlene sues SSB to reverse the debit of her account, will she win?

4. Section 4-404

Section 4-404 provides that although a bank is not obligated to pay an uncertified check presented more than six months after its date (a "stale" check), if it does so in good faith, it may charge the customer's account. If a bank pays such a check without knowledge of its staleness, which is likely to occur with automated processing, it probably can be presumed that it has acted in good faith. In addition, the UCC Comment to § 4-404 points out that even with notice of the check's staleness, a bank may pay a check in good faith if it is in a position to know, as in the case of dividend checks, that the drawer wants payment to be made.

5. *Section 4-405*

Section 4-405 provides that under certain circumstances a bank may pay a check even after its customer's death or incompetence. Section 4-405(a) states that the bank remains authorized to pay a check provided that it does not know of its customer's death or adjudication of incompetence or, if it had such knowledge, it lacked a "reasonable opportunity to act" on that knowledge. In addition, § 4-405(b) specifically provides that even when a bank knows of the customer's death, the bank may pay or certify the customer's checks for ten days after the date of death (not ten days after the bank learns of the death) — even if this is more than enough time for it to have acted on its knowledge of the customer's death — unless someone claiming an interest in the account orders it to stop payment. The bank has no responsibility to determine the validity of such a claim or even whether it is "colorable." UCC Comment 3 to § 4-405.

PROBLEM 12.11

Aged Annie has a checking account at First Insatiable Bank ("FIB"). On May 1, 2004, she issued a check for $1,000 to her niece, Graduating Gwen, as a graduation gift. On May 7, 2004, however, Annie was officially adjudicated as legally incompetent. FIB learned about this adjudication on May 10, 2005. On May 16, 2005, Gwen walked into FIB and presented the check for payment, and FIB paid it and debited Annie's account. Assume that the court-appointed representative of Annie's estate sues FIB, demanding that it recredit the $1,000 to Annie's account. Who should win?

6. *Section 4-407*

Section 4-407 provides, in part, that if a bank pays an item under circumstances giving its customer a basis for objection, the bank is entitled to certain subrogation rights to prevent unjust enrichment to any involved party and to the extent necessary to protect the bank from loss. Thus, if a bank pays an item that was not properly payable, it is subrogated against its customer to the rights of the payee or other holder either on the item or on the transaction from which the item arose.

PROBLEM 12.12

Assume that on September 15, 2004, Dan Drawer mailed a check for $1,000, dated November 15, 2004, payable to Paul Payee, someone to whom Dan owed an uncontested $1,000 debt that was past-due. Assume also that Dan gave appropriate written notice to his bank that he had issued a postdated check. Nevertheless, the bank paid the check on September 30, 2004, and debited Dan's *account. If Dan sues his bank, demanding that it recredit his account, who should win?*

PROBLEM 12.13

Same facts as Problem 12.12, except that Dan issued the check to Paul as a gift. If Dan sues his bank, demanding that it recredit his account, who should win?

7. *Section 1-103*

Section 1-103(b) is a general provision that states that unless "displaced" by specific UCC provisions, the general "principles of law and equity, including the law merchant" and many other bodies of law, "supplement" the particular provisions of the UCC. Consequently, a number of cases have allowed parties to assert common law defenses or causes of action. *See, e.g., Spec-Cast, Inc. v. First National Bank & Trust Co.*, 128 Ill.2d 167, 538 N.E.2d 543. 131 Ill.Dec. 168 (1989) (although drawee ordinarily may not debit customer's account when it pays check unsigned by customer, customer's subsequent conduct gave rise to ratification defense that could be asserted under § 1-103); *Swiss Credit Bank v. Chemical Bank*, 422 F.Supp. 1305 (S.D.N.Y. 1976) (a drawer's negligence, even if it did not contribute to the "making" of an unauthorized signature or alteration, may estop him from asserting the unauthorized signature or alteration as long as the negligence contributed to a loss arising from such signature or alteration); *Ambassador Financial Services, Inc. v. Indiana National Bank*, 605 N.E.2d 746 (Ind. 1992) (equitable defenses, which the Code permits unless specifically precluded, include "mitigation of damages" and the related "intended payee" defense, both intended to prevent the drawer's unjust enrichment); *Bryan v. Citizens National Bank in Abilene*, 628 S.W.2d 761 (Tex.1982) (drawee retains common-law defenses and common-law rights under § 1-103). Nevertheless, since § 1-103 provides that the common law and equitable principles supplement the Code "unless displaced by the particular provisions of the Code," courts often need to examine whether the common law theory contradicts either the language or the policy enunciated by the Code. If so, the common law is inapplicable. *See, e.g., Consolidated Public Water Supply Dist. No. C-1 v. Farmers Bank*, 686 S.W.2d 844 (Mo.App. 1985) where the court wrote "to hold that one may use a common law negligence action to recover in a padded payroll case is to allow § 3-405 to become a virtual nullity." As such, the common law impliedly contradicts that Code section, thereby making § 1-103 inoperative. *See also, Western Cas. & Sur. Co. v. Citizens Bank of Las Cruces*, 676 F.2d 1344, (10th Cir. 1982) (applying New Mexico law); *Bryan v. Citizens National Bank in Abilene, supra* (although a common law right to restitution still exists in a case governed by Articles 3 and 4, the right can only continue in a form that does not conflict with Code provisions).

Chapter 13

STOP PAYMENT ORDERS

As explained in Chapter 12, a bank is its customer's agent and can only properly debit the customer's account when the bank pays items that are properly payable. Even after a customer initially issues an item, however, he can order the bank not to pay it. *See* § 4-403. The basic rule is that if a bank's customer directs the bank not to pay a check he or she has issued and the bank pays it anyway, the bank is liable for any resulting loss. Similarly, if a customer orders the bank to close his or her account and the bank fails to do so, the bank is ordinarily liable for any resulting loss. The policy underlying § 4-403 is that stopping payment or closing an account is a service that bank customers expect and are entitled to receive from a bank notwithstanding its difficulty, inconvenience, or expense. Consequently, any losses that result from a bank's failure to heed such stop payment or close account orders should be borne by the bank as an inherent cost of its banking business. *See* UCC Comment 1 to § 4-403.

There are primarily five issues involving stop payment orders:

a. on what items may payment be stopped;

b. who may stop payment or close an account;

c. how may payment be stopped or an account closed;

d. for how long is a stop payment order effective; and

e. what remedies are available if an item is paid despite a properly made stop payment or close account order.

A. *On What Types of Items May Payment Be Stopped*

1. *Generally — Checks and Notes*

Section 4-403 provides:

> **A customer, or any person authorized to draw on the account if there is more than one, may stop payment of any item drawn on the customer's account or close the account.**

An "item," broadly defined in § 4-104(9) as "an instrument or a promise or order to pay money handled by a bank for collection or payment," includes negotiable and nonnegotiable notes and drafts handled by banks. The phrase "any item drawn on the customer's account" (emphasis added) ostensibly limits the right to stop payment to drafts, not notes and, in fact, stop payments usually involve checks. *See* UCC Comment 3 to § 4-403. Nonetheless, UCC Comment 3 asserts

181

that the right to stop payment extends to notes. Citing § 4-106, the UCC Comment declares that the maker of a note would have a right to stop payment if the maker's position is analogous to that of a drawer, such as where a note is expressly payable at a bank identified in the note. The bank that pays such a note is acting as its customer's — the maker's — agent in paying, and has a right to recover the amount of such payment from its customer. Consequently, it makes sense that the customer, as principal, can order the bank, its agent, not to make payment.

2. *Money Orders*

A money order sold by a bank is usually in the same form as a personal check drawn by the purchaser, except that it may be designated on its face a "money order" and the payment amount is machine impressed. (Money orders of this type are referred to in the cases as "personal money orders.") The payee is sometimes left blank and is filled in by the purchaser. In any event, the purchaser must sign his name as drawer at the lower right-hand corner of the money order for the item to be payable. Thus, although the bank charges the purchaser "up-front" when it impresses the payment amount on the money order and delivers it to the purchaser, the purchaser is formally the drawer and, should the bank not pay, liable on his drawer's obligation. Therefore, in paying the item, the bank is formally acting as the purchaser's agent. Consequently, at least when the bank does not sign the instrument (thereby becoming directly liable on it), courts have treated these personal money orders as drafts and have allowed the purchasers the right to stop payment under Former § 4-403.

A money order sold by a bank may also be in a form in which the bank, rather than the purchaser, has signed the instrument as drawer. As such, the purchaser is now not a party to the instrument. These money orders, which are essentially the same as "cashier's checks," are referred to in the cases as "bank money orders." The bank is directly liable on such money orders; it pays its own obligation, not the obligation of the customer. A purchaser of such a money order has no right to stop payment, because the issuing bank need not impair its reputation for paying its debts simply because the purchaser wants payment stopped. *See* Comment 4 to § 4-403. Technically, § 4-403(a) only authorizes a customer to stop payments drawn on its account, and this type of money order, signed by the bank as drawer, is not drawn on the customer's account. *Id.*

3. *Non-Bank Drafts*

The term "bank" is expansively deemed in § 4-105(1) as "any person engaged in the business of banking, including a savings bank, savings and loan association, credit union, or trust company." Because § 4-403 refers to stopping payment by "an order to the bank," it would appear that there is no right to stop payment on drafts when the drawee is not a bank. Such a conclusion is further supported by the fact that Article 4 is entitled "Bank Deposits and Collections" and is obviously intended to deal with items involving banks. UCC Comment 3 to § 4-403 nonetheless asserts that "[b]y analogy the rule extends to drawees other than banks." Moreover, reported cases have applied Former § 4-403 to non-bank drawees. *See, e.g., Best v. Dreyfus Liquid Assets, Inc.,* 215 N.J.Super. 76, 521 A.2d 352 (1987), even though that section also spoke only about stopping payment "by order to his [the customer's] bank."

4. *Payment Cannot Be Stopped on a Certified Check*

A certified check is a check accepted by the bank on which it is drawn. By certifying the check, the drawee promises to pay it in accordance with its terms. Section 3-413(a). At the same time, the drawer is discharged of any liability on the check. Section 3-414(c). Since the bank is liable on the instrument based on its own promise to pay, and the customer himself no longer has any liability on the instrument, the customer has no right to stop payment. *Cf.* Comment 4 to § 4-403.

Furthermore, to be effective, a stop payment order must be received at a time that affords the bank a reasonable opportunity to act on it before, among other things, the bank accepts or certifies the item. As such, any attempt to stop payment on a check that has been certified is by definition too late. *See* § 4-303.

Although neither customers drawing certified checks nor the drawee banks accepting them can make valid stop payment orders, drawee banks, as an accommodation to their customers, may want to refuse to pay certified checks. Whether such banks may avoid paying such items and whether they will be liable for a plaintiff's damages if they wrongfully refuse to pay them are discussed below.

5. *Payment Cannot Be Stopped on a Cashier's Check*

Section 3-104(g) defines a cashier's check as "a draft with respect to which the drawer and drawee are the same bank or branches of the same bank." Although a bank may use a cashier's check to pay its own obligations, often a cashier's check is purchased by a customer to satisfy an obligation to a creditor who wants assurance that funds will be available when he seeks payment. Nevertheless, the sole liability on a cashier's check is that of the issuing bank as defined in § 3-412. Because the bank is directly liable on the instrument, and the item is not drawn on the purchaser's account, the purchaser of a cashier's check has no right to stop payment. *See* Comment 4 to § 4-403.

Many courts have taken the position that issuing banks also may not stop payment on a cashier's check. Those courts hold that a cashier's check is regarded as accepted by the act of issuance. That is, the bank, by signing the check as drawer, is said to accept the check at the same time as drawee. As such, since a stop order is ineffective after the bank has accepted the item (see § 4-303), a stop order on a cashier's check is by definition always too late. Courts will often also use a policy argument that the public's acknowledgment of cashier's checks as "cash equivalents" supports the notion that the issuing bank may not stop payment on a cashier's check. *See e.g., National Newark and Essex Bank v. Giordano,* 268 A.2d at 329 ("To allow the bank to stop payment on such an instrument would be inconsistent with the representation it makes in issuing the check. Such a rule would undermine the public confidence in the bank and its checks and thereby deprive the cashier's check of the essential incident which makes it useful.")

Although neither customers purchasing cashier's checks nor the banks issuing them can make valid stop payment orders, issuing banks, for their own reasons or as an accommodation to their customers, may want to refuse to pay cashier's checks. Whether such banks may avoid paying such items and whether they will be liable for a plaintiff's damages if they wrongfully refuse to pay them is discussed below.

6. Teller's Checks

A "teller's check" is deemed as a "draft drawn by a bank (i) on another bank, or (ii) payable at or through a bank." *See* § 3-104(h).

As with cashier's checks, a customer who purchases a teller's check has no right to stop payment of the check since the purchaser has no liability on it and the check is not drawn on the customer's account.

However, under the Former Code, courts held that a "teller's check," sometimes also called a "bank draft" was subject to a stop payment order by the drawer bank. Unlike a cashier's check, the drawer is not also the drawee, and thus a "teller's check" is not accepted on issuance. Instead, the issuing bank is a "customer," whose definition includes "a bank carrying an account with another bank," of the drawee bank and thus has a right to stop payment on a check under § 4-403(1).

7. Bank's Refusal to Pay Certified, Cashier's or Teller's Checks

Even when not obligated under § 4-403 by their customers' "orders" to stop payment, banks may want to refuse to pay certified or cashier's checks or want to issue stop payment orders of their own teller's checks. Sometimes banks are motivated by their own pecuniary interests, such as when they were fraudulently induced to certify a check or to issue a cashier's or teller's check or when the consideration the banks received with respect to such checks fails. On other occasions, although the banks themselves bear no financial risk, they may want, as a courtesy, to cooperate with their customers (the drawers of certified checks or the remitters of cashier's or teller's checks) who assert some defense in connection with the transactions which led to issuance of the checks.

When a bank takes such an action two issues generally arise: (1) whether the bank can, in fact, avoid the obligation to pay the instrument; and (2) whether the bank will be liable to the person entitled to enforce the instrument for damages pursuant to § 3-411.

Whether the bank can avoid paying the instrument may depend on the nature of the instrument. As explained above, drawer banks may issue stop payment orders on teller's checks. Of course, persons entitled to enforce such checks can sue drawer banks on their drawer's obligations. If the banks have real defenses, the banks should win. If the banks have only personal defenses, the banks should win only if the persons entitled the enforce the instruments do not have holder in due course rights. If the banks have no defenses, the banks should lose.

When a certified or cashier's check is involved, courts disagree as to the proper result. One approach (the one that the authors think is correct) simply says that Article 3 applies the same way it applies to other instruments. In each case, the bank is obligated as an acceptor (as to cashier's check, the bank is also obligated as the drawer). If a person entitled to enforce the instrument sues, the bank should be able to assert all the defenses that any acceptor could assert. The bank should prevail even against a holder in due course if the bank itself has a real defense. If the bank itself has only a personal defense, it should succeed only against those who do not have holder in due course rights.

A second approach seems to treat cashier's checks as "cash" and asserts that banks issuing cashier's checks cannot assert any defenses, even against parties that are not holders in due course. A third, slightly different approach, while generally preventing banks from asserting defenses to their cashier's checks, permits such defenses in some cases based on equitable considerations.

People tend to consider certified, cashier's or teller's checks as good as cash. They fully expect that these instruments will be paid. *See* Comment 1 to § 3-411. Indeed, this is the reason why, when a creditor takes such an instrument in connection with an underlying obligation, the duty of the underlying obligor is not merely suspended — as is the case when other types of instruments are taken — but the duty is actually discharged. *See* § 3-310(a). It is useful to have instruments such as these that are so routinely and universally taken with confidence.

In order to ensure that people will continue to have such confidence in these instruments, and to protect those that act upon such confidence, § 3-411 imposes liability on a bank that wrongfully: (a) refuses to pay a cashier's check that it issued or any other check that it certified, (b) stops payment on a teller's check that it issued, or (c) refuses to pay a dishonored teller's check that it issued. The provision is clearly designed to discourage banks from stopping payment on teller's checks and refusing to pay certified or cashier's checks (or teller's checks that they issued) as a courtesy to their customers. Read § 3-411 carefully and answer the following:

PROBLEM 13.1

Paula Payee fraudulently induces Dan Drawer to issue to her order a $500 check, drawn on and certified by Payor Bank. She cashes the check at Currency Exchange, which takes it for value, in good faith, and without notice of Paula's fraud. Dan discovers the fraud and asks Payor Bank not to pay it. Thereafter, Currency Exchange presents the check to Payor Bank and demands payment. If Payor Bank refuses to pay the check, does it violate § 3-411? yes

What if the owner of the Currency Exchange, who presents the check for payment, is unable to show any documentation that he is authorized to enforce checks on behalf of the Currency Exchange?

PROBLEM 13.2

Same facts as set forth originally in Problem 13.1 except that, when Paula cashed the check at Currency Exchange, she failed to indorse the check. If Payor Bank refuses to pay the check, does it violate § 3-411? Shelter Doctrine
Currency exchange has same rights as Paula

PROBLEM 13.3

Norman Naive entered into an agreement with Sam Slick wherein Norman agreed to purchase an antique gold watch for $14,000. Sam required Norman to pay with a cashier's check that Norman purchased from his bank, Richman's National Bank (RNB). The check was made payable to Sam and given to him when the watch was delivered to Norman. A few days later, Norman showed the watch to his friend a jeweler, who told Norman that the watch was a fake. Norman quickly called his bank, and asked whether the cashier's check payable to Sam had yet been paid. When bank told him it had not, Norman, a very valuable bank customer, asked the bank not to pay it. Sam, accompanied by an important client, went to the bank the next day to present the check, but the bank refused to pay, stating that Norman had informed them that the watch he had purchased from Sam was a fake. Sam protested vigorously, denying that the watch he had sold Norman was a fake. Sam also pointed out that the woman with him was an important client making a similar purchase. Nevertheless, the bank held firm on its refusal to pay. Sam's client was aghast, told Sam she was no longer interested in purchasing an antique necklace Sam had shown her earlier, and left the bank in a huff. Sam went out, hired an attorney and filed suit against the bank the next day. Assuming Sam can prove that the watch was not a fake, what liability, if any, does the bank have to Sam?

expenses + interest
consequential damages (lost profit)
vs. bank says not from refusal to pay

What result if the watch was a fake, but the bank, when sued, had failed to join Norman in the action?

B. Who May Stop Payment or Close an Account

While Former § 4-403(1) provided only that "[a] customer may by order to his bank stop payment," § 4-403 extends this right to a customer "or any person authorized to draw on the account." In the case of a corporate customer, for instance, § 4-403 makes it clear that any of the authorized signatories can issue a stop payment order. There is no requirement that such an order be formally made by the corporate customer, e.g., by way of a corporate resolution. In the case of a joint checking account in the name of two spouses, either spouse may stop a check issued by the other spouse or may close the account.

Section 4-403 also provides that even if the signature of more than one person is necessary in order to draw on an account, any one of such persons may stop payment or close the account. Effectively, § 4-403 treats the change of mind by one of the signatories as nullifying that person's signature.

A payee or indorsee of an instrument does not have the right to stop its payment. *See* UCC Comment 2 to § 4-403. The only instance when a person not a customer or authorized to draw on the account may issue a "stop payment" order is when the drawer or maker has died. In such a case, any person claiming an interest in the account may issue a stop payment order pursuant to § 4-405. *Id.* In these circumstances, the bank has no responsibility to determine the validity of that person's claim or even to determine whether it is "colorable." *See* UCC Comment 3 to § 4-405.

C. How May Payment Be Stopped or an Account Closed

1. Stopping Payment of an Item

Payment may be stopped by an order to the bank that (1) describes the item "with reasonable certainty" and (2) is received by the bank at a time and in a manner affording the bank "a reasonable opportunity to act on it before any action by the bank with respect to the item" under § 4-303. Those actions specified under § 4-303 include

a. the bank's accepting or certifying the item;

b. the bank's paying the item in cash;

c. the bank's settling for the item without having a right to revoke the settlement under statute, clearinghouse rule, or agreement;

d. the bank's becoming accountable for the amount of the item under § 4-302 (payor's bank responsibility for late return of items): or

e. with respect to checks, the expiration of the bank's cutoff hour.

A stop payment or close account order initially may be given orally, except in Texas, which requires, by statute, that a stop payment order be in writing.

Whether a particular description was sufficient was a question of fact to be determined in each case. The following case provides some historical background on the various approaches the courts have taken on this issue.

ROVELL v. AMERICAN NATIONAL BANK
232 B.R. 38138 UCC Rep.Serv.2d 896 (N.D. Ill. 1998.)

MEMORANDUM AND ORDER

MORAN, Senior District Judge.

Michael Rovell (Rovell), the Debtor, initiated a voluntary petition for reorganization under Chapter 11 of the Bankruptcy Code in October of 1995. American National Bank and Trust Company of Chicago (Bank) filed a Proof of Claim (claim) for $50,081.25, the amount Rovell admittedly owed on his secured line of credit. Rovell, however, filed an Objection (objection) seeking to reduce ANB's claim by an amount equal to the losses he incurred when the bank paid a check over a stop-payment order. After hearing testimony on March 17, 1997, United States Bankruptcy Judge Robert Ginsberg held that Rovell had failed to overcome the *prima facie* validity of the bank's claim and allowed it in full (bench order).

Debtor now appeals from both the bench order denying the objection and from Judge Ginsberg's December 22, 1997 order denying Rovell's motion to reconsider (December order). Although we disagree with one of the bankruptcy court's conclusions, we find that the court did not abuse its discretion when it allowed the claim in full. For the reasons stated herein, the decision of the bankruptcy court is affirmed.

BACKGROUND

Most of the facts regarding the stop-payment dispute are uncontested. In September 1994, Michael Rovell, a lawyer, wrote a check for $38,250 to the Pretty Eyes Detective Agency (check # 1). After conveying the check to Patricia O'Connor, the owner of Pretty Eyes, Rovell discovered that he had overpaid her firm by more than $10,000. He asked his employee, Lisa Fair (Fair), also a lawyer, to contact the Bank and make sure the check had not cleared. At approximately 1:40 p.m. on September 19, 1994, Fair phoned Linda Williams (Williams), the ANB officer who served as Rovell's account representative, and told her that if the check had not been cashed, Rovell wanted to stop payment and issue a replacement check for the correct amount. Fair informed Williams that she was not sure of the check number or the date of issue, but she did know the account number, the check amount, and the payee.

The parties disagree about what the two women said next. At the evidentiary hearing, Fair testified she told Williams that "there were a number of checks taken from the book as [Rovell was] out of town, and that I thought it was possible that it was in the range of checks beginning with approximately 1084, but that I couldn't even be certain of that." Rovell's checkbook had three checks to a page. Fair further testified that she told Williams that the Pretty Eyes check "could possibly be in a range of approximately six checks, because I knew those had been taken by Mr. Rovell and were in his possession. But I didn't even know if it was in that range of six."

Williams remembered their conversation differently. She testified that although Fair had been unsure of the precise check number, Fair "was 95% sure" that it was check number 1084 or 1086. The first thing Williams did, she recalled, was to key in those two check numbers to see if they had cleared. They hadn't and she told this to Fair.

This brings us to the heart of the dispute. Debtor Rovell contends that the message from Williams was that the "Pretty Eyes check" had not cleared. The Bank, on the other hand, claims that Williams merely informed Fair that checks 1084 and 1086 had not cleared. In fact, the parties would later discover that check number 1105, made payable to "Pretty Eyes," in the amount of $38,250.00, cleared that day.

At this point in their conversation Fair instructed Williams to stop payment on the check. Williams recalls issuing electronic stop-payment orders for checks 1084 and 1086, and a record of this transaction was entered into evidence. Fair maintains she was told by Williams that if she provided the account number, payee, and amount of the check, payment could be stopped without the check number. Williams explicitly denied this in her testimony. Both parties, however, remember Williams telling Fair to "wait a couple of days" or "a few days" before issuing a replacement check. Williams also testified that it was her "routine procedure" to tell "all [her] customers that they should wait until they get the check back" and "should check back to make sure if a check has been stopped." She reportedly asked Fair, "Are these people reputable?", referring to the payee.

Working on the assumption that check # 1 had not cleared, Rovell's firm issued a second check to Pretty Eyes (check # 2) in the amount of $27,284.50 and sent it to the private investigator along with a letter explaining that the new check was intended to replace the original. Rovell does not dispute the Bank's contention that neither Rovell nor Fair called Williams back to confirm that check # 1 had not yet cleared. Unfortunately for Rovell, check # 2 was also presented and paid, thereby contributing, Rovell contends, to the substantial overdraft on his ANB checking account.

In the meantime, the Bank apparently sent stop-payment confirmation orders to Rovell for checks 1084 and 1086. Fair does not remember receiving the confirmation forms, but acknowledged in her testimony that she found them in the company files while responding to the Bank's discovery request. The forms include the following statement:

> The check(s) appears not to have been paid since the date of your last statement. If the check should be recovered, please promptly advise us in writing, executed by the required number of authorized signers on the account. Please review all information to ensure its accuracy. If any changes are required, call the telephone number listed above. *The primary information required to stop payment on a check is the account number, check number found on the bottom line of the check and exact dollars/cents amount.* (emphasis added).

Neither party disputes Williams' testimony that under the Bank's technology at the time of the stop-payment request, it was not possible to stop a check without the check number. Nor do they dispute that Williams did not tell Fair of this impossibility.

Thus, there are two principal sources of disagreement: first, whether Fair identified checks number 1084 and 1086 as the likely targets for the stop-payment order or indicated, instead, that the check was in a range of about six checks beginning with 1084; and second, whether Williams affirmatively represented to Fair that a check could be stopped despite the absence of a check number. As indicated in the bench order and again in the December order, the bankruptcy court found both witnesses equally credible. The court suggested that there was "no evidence" tending to show that the recollection of either witness was inaccurate or that either was not telling the truth.

On appeal, Rovell renews his claim that American National Bank breached its agreement to stop payment on check # 1. He also claims that ANB was negligent when it informed his representative that the check had not cleared and that payment could be stopped. Ultimately, Rovell argues that he was damaged in the amount of $38,250 when the first check to Pretty Eyes was cashed, or, alternatively, in the amount of $27,284 when he sent the second check to Pretty Eyes *"in reliance on the bank's assurance that the check had not cleared and could be stopped."* (emphasis added). He asks this court to overturn the judgment of the bankruptcy court and to allow only $11,381.25 or, alternatively, only $22,796.75 of ANB's claim.

DISCUSSION

2. Breach of Contract

Chapter 810 ILCS 5/4-403 codifies the common law right of a depositor to order payment of a check stopped and establishes the requirements in Illinois for an effective stop-payment order. Section 4- 403(a) provides in relevant part:

> A customer . . . may stop payment of any item drawn on the customer's account . . . by an order to the bank describing the item . . . with reasonable certainty received at a time and in a manner that affords the

bank a reasonable opportunity to act on it before any action by the
bank with respect to the item described in Section 4-303

Thus, a bank will not be held liable for failing to stop payment on a check that
was not "described with reasonable certainty," nor will it be liable if the stop-payment order was untimely. Rovell contends that Fair's request to Williams satisfied both criteria. The burden of establishing the fact and amount of loss
resulting from the payment of an item contrary to a stop-payment order is on
the customer, § 403(c), [while] the burden of compliance with a valid stop-payment order is placed squarely on the financial institution. § 4-403, Comment 1.
This is so "notwithstanding its difficulty, inconvenience, or expense. The
inevitable occasional losses through failure to stop should be borne by the banks
as a cost of the business of banking." *Id.* We must determine, therefore, whether
Rovell's stop-payment order was a valid one, such that ANB's failure to comply
would be a breach of its duty under Illinois law.

(a) *Identification*

While there is little case law in Illinois detailing what it means for a stop
order to describe an item with "reasonable certainty," courts in other jurisdictions interpreting identical provisions have employed one of two distinct
approaches. The first assesses the degree to which the customer accurately
specified the five identifying features of an individual check: the check number,
amount, account number, payee, and date of issue. *See, e.g., Sherrill v. Frank
Morris Pontiac-Buick-GMC, Inc.,* 366 So.2d 251 (Ala.1978) (incorrect identification of the check date and payee constituted insufficient notice to bank, even
though depositor accurately provided the check amount); *Thomas v. Marine
Midland Tinkers Nat'l Bank,* 86 Misc.2d 284, 381 N.Y.S.2d 797 (N.Y.City
Civ.Ct.1976) (direction to stop payment correct in all aspects except for single
digit mistake on check number provided bank adequate notice and reasonable
opportunity to act).

The second, more recent approach considers whether the customer *and* the
bank have satisfied their respective responsibilities in the generation of an
effective stop-payment order. Where a bank's system relies exclusively on one or
two elements of the description, a number of courts have imposed a duty on the
bank to give customers notice of these requirements. *See, e.g., Rimberg v. Union
Trust Co.,* 12 UCC Rep.Serv. 527, 1973 WL 21420 (D.C. Super.1973) (bank liable
for payment over stop order because teller failed to inform the depositor that the
bank's computerized system required the exact amount of the check to effectuate a stop order); *Staff Service Associates, Inc. v. Midlantic Nat'l Bank,* 207
N.J.Super. 327, 504 A.2d 148 (L.Ct.1985) ("reasonable opportunity" to act was
present where customer only made single digit error in check amount and bank
never informed customer that exact amount of check was necessary for computer
to pull check); *Hughes v. Marine Midland Bank,* 127 Misc.2d 209, 484 N.Y.S.2d
1000 (N.Y.City Civ.Ct.1985) (customer's order correctly stating account number
and check amount satisfied requirements of § 4-403 where New York Banks had
ample time to design software to meet the *Thomas* expectation of identification

without check number); *Parr v. Security National Bank,* 680 P.2d 648 (Okla.Ct.App.1984) (bank was not relieved of liability merely because bank's computers were programmed to stop payment only if reported amount of check was correct); *Delano v. Putnam Trust Co.,* 33 UCC Rep. Serv. 635, 1981 WL 138011 (Conn.Super.Ct.1981) (bank had a duty to inform its customer of the need for precision in reporting the amount before it could rely on customer's error to relieve it of liability).

Here there is no dispute that Fair correctly identified three of the five identifying elements of check # 1: the payee, the amount, and the account number. There is also no argument that the bank's system required the check number to guarantee an effective stop payment. At issue is whether Williams informed Fair that the Bank would be unable to stop the Pretty Eyes check without an accurate check number (a factual question) and whether she had a duty to do so (a conclusion of law). As to the latter issue, Rovell relies upon those cases finding an affirmative duty to disclose the computer system requirements and contends that William's alleged omission deems Fair's request sufficient to meet the identification requirement, notwithstanding her inability to provide the exact check number. The Bank relies instead on those cases relieving the bank of liability where individual identifiers were sufficiently inaccurate to conclude that the customer had failed to identify the check with "reasonable certainty."

It is surely reasonable to require banks to inform customers of the requirements for an effective stop-order and to hold them accountable for payment over a stop order where the payment occurred because the customer was unaware the missing information was critical. By codifying § 4-403 and adopting the accompanying commentary, the Illinois legislature made it clear that depositors expect to be able to stop payment on a check and are entitled to receive this service. This entitlement would be meaningless without guidance from the bank as to the precise information required for processing a stop-payment order. In *FJS Electronics, Inc. v. Fidelity Bank,* 288 Pa.Super. 138, 431 A.2d 326 (1981), the customer phoned in a stop-payment request correct in all respects except that he misstated the check amount by fifty cents. Because the bank had selected a computer system which relied upon the check amount to identify the item, the customer's error prevented the bank's computer from acting on the stop order. Based on its reading of the official comment to UCC 4-403, the *FJS* court found that any heightened risk of mistaken payments due to the system's exclusive reliance on an *exact* check amount should be borne by the bank, and it held the bank liable for the payment over the order. The Oklahoma Court of Appeals in *Parr v. Security National Bank* subsequently adopted this reasoning, but allowed the bank an affirmative defense if it notified the customer of the required elements at the time the stop order was requested. *Parr,* 680 P.2d at 651; *accord Staff Service Associates, Inc.,* 504 A.2d at 152. We believe this is the correct approach to assess the identification element of 810 ILCS 5/4-403.

Thus, the court agrees with Rovell that the Bank had a duty to make clear that an exact check number was required to effectuate the stop- payment order, and joins those courts in other jurisdictions which have so held. We are left, however, with the bankruptcy court's assessment regarding the witnesses' credibility. Williams testified that she told Fair that she needed the check number, although she did not inform her that she could only stop checks with an exact check number. According to Williams, Fair told her she was 95% sure that the check was number 1084 or 1086, and Williams stopped payment of those checks. The bankruptcy court was in the best position to evaluate the testimony of both women, and we defer to the court's judgment that Williams' testimony was credible and that, under the standard of proof prescribed by § 4-403, Rovell failed to establish that the stop order identified the item with "reasonable certainty." In any event, the stop came too late.

(b) *Timeliness*

The second requirement for a bank to be held liable for payment over a stop-payment order is that the request be received "at a time and in such a manner that the bank has a reasonable opportunity to act." 810 ILCS 5/4- 403. Rovell contends that because the bank advised Fair to wait "a couple of days" before issuing a replacement check, ANB must have considered "two days" sufficient time to respond to the stop-payment order, i.e., a "reasonable opportunity to act." The Bank, on the other hand, argues that the bankruptcy court's finding that check # 1 was cashed before any computer direction to stop payment would have been effective indicates that the order arrived too late for the bank to stop payment.

A payment in violation of an effective direction to stop payment is an improper payment even though it is made by mistake or inadvertence. 810 ILCS 5/4-403, Comment 7. But while the code places the burden of compliance on the bank, it is not expected to perform miracles. *Compare Siniscalchi v. Valley Bank of New York,* 79 Misc.2d 64, 66, 359 N.Y.S.2d 173 (N.Y.Dist.Ct.1974) (bank did not have reasonable time to act upon order where check was cashed Saturday morning and stop order was obtained Monday morning) *with Thomas v. Marine Midland Tinkers Nat'l Bank,* 86 Misc.2d 284, 287, 381 N.Y.S.2d 797 (N.Y.City Civ.Ct.1976) (day and one-half was reasonable notice for bank to enforce stop order on check presented at the same branch). The effective time for determining whether a stop order was received too late to affect payment of an item is "receipt plus a reasonable time to act on any of the communications." Further guidance is provided by the reference in § 4-403 to the ordering of payment responsibilities as set forth in § 4-303. Under this code provision, a stop-payment order comes too late to modify the bank's right or duty to pay a check if it comes after the bank accepts the item or pays the item in cash. (*Citations omitted*) It is undisputed here that any stop-payment order would be effectively programmed into the computer for the opening of business the following day, and by then the check had cleared. Thus, as a matter of law, the order came too late to modify the bank's right or duty to pay the item.

In his reply brief, Rovell argues that under 810 ILCS 5/4-301(a)-(b) and 5/4-104(a)(1) a payor bank has 24 hours to recover or revoke the payment after it is made. "Thus, even if ANB paid the check before the stop-payment got into the system, it *could* have recovered the payment." Perhaps, but the authority given to the bank to revoke a settlement does not change the result that ANB is not liable to Rovell under § 4-403 for any losses arising out of the payment of check #1105.

ANB initially shared the responsibility to create an effective stop- payment order, but as ANB's customer, Rovell had the burden of establishing the fact and amount of loss resulting from payment over the order. He failed to do so when he could not persuade the bankruptcy court as to his version of events. Moreover, the order came too late to modify ANB's right to pay the check and charge his account for the overdraft.

3. *Negligent Misrepresentation*

[The court also dealt with the question of whether the bank employee's fail- ure to inform Rovell that the Pretty Eyes check had cleared and her failure to warn him that a stop-payment would not be effective without the check number, constituted the actionable tort of negligent misrepresentation. While it held that ANB *was* "in the business of supplying information for the guidance of others in their business transactions" and could, therefore, be held liable for a negligent misrepresentation by its agent, it also held that, under the circum- stances, Rovell was not justified in relying on Williams' advice, an essential element of recovery.]

CONCLUSION

The court believes it important to make clear that ANB owed a duty to Rov- ell to clarify any elements of check identification necessary to ensure the gen- eration of an effective stop-payment order. Similarly, we find that ANB was in the business of supplying information to its depositors and thus could have been held liable for a negligent misrepresentation. Ultimately, however, we find that the court correctly placed the liability for Rovell's shortsighted behav- ior with the Debtor himself. As a matter of law, his stop-payment order came too late to make a difference. As a matter of common sense, and in light of Fair's uncertainty about which check had been written to "Pretty Eyes," Rovell should have postponed sending any replacement check until he was certain the first had been properly identified and had not cleared.

The decision by the bankruptcy court is affirmed and Claim No. 31 as sub- mitted by American National Bank is allowed in its entirety.

PROBLEM 13.4

On January 6, 2004 Dan Drawer issued a check for $300 to Phony Felice, who had fraudulently told him that she was raising money to distribute to the poor. When Dan discovered she had deceived him, he called First Insatiable Bank (FIB), the drawee, and told the bank's telephone operator, "I'm Dan Drawer.

Stop payment on the check for $300 I made out today to Phony Felice." After the *Bank must inform customer of req'ts for stop payment* phone call ended, the clerk relayed the message to her boss, who concluded that the information was not sufficient for the bank to act on. After all, Dan had several checking accounts at the bank. On January 8, Phony Felice went to FIB and presented the check, and the check was paid. Should the bank be liable for paying an item over a valid stop order? What if Dan had mistakenly described the check as having been for $200 instead of $300? *No*

2. Agreement Affecting Stop Payment Order Requirements

The excerpted language from UCC Comment 5 to § 4-403 states that the item must be described with reasonable certainty "in the absence of a contrary agreement." This language might mean that by agreement (a) a customer could reduce or eliminate the obligation to describe the item with reasonable certainty, (b) a bank could require that a customer describe this item with actual rather than merely reasonable certainty, or (c) both.

While there is no reason to deny a customer the right to negotiate for itself a broader, less restricted right to stop payment, there is a question as to whether or to what extent a bank can bargain to eliminate or restrict the stop payment right. UCC Comment 1 to § 4-403 states that the policy underlying § 4-403 is that banks should bear the risk of occasional losses through failure to stop payment. Allowing banks to avoid this liability through a contrary agreement with their customers could arguably violate this policy. Banks, of course, could argue that the policy referred to in UCC Comment 1 is stated only in a vacuum and that § 4-103(a) explicitly allows variance of Article 4 rules.

Even if § 4-103 applies, there are some restrictions. Use that section to evaluate whether the following clauses would be enforceable:

PROBLEM 13.5

a. "Should this check be paid through inadvertence, accident or oversight, it *No* is expressly agreed that the bank will in no way be liable." See Thomas v. First National Bank, 376 Pa. 181 (1954), 101 A.2d 910, 911, cited approvingly by Best v. Dreyfus Liquid Assets, Inc., 215 N.J.Super. 76 (1987), 521 A.2d 352.

b. "All requests for stop payment orders must be accompanied by a payment *ok* of $15.00." *reasonable fee*

c. "The information on the stop payment order must be correct, including the *OK* exact amount of the check to the penny, for the stop order to be valid." See Staff Service Associates, Inc. v. Midlantic National Bank, 207 N.J.Super.327 (1985), 504 A.2d 148. *can bargain for more or less certainty*

d. "This bank will not act upon any stop payment order unless or until it is *NO* received in writing." *public policy — r't. to ensure, oral stop payment w/i 14 days*

3. Closing of an Account

An account may be closed by an order to the bank that (1) describes the account "with reasonable certainty" and (2) is received by the bank at a time and in a manner affording the bank "a reasonable opportunity to act on it" before action by the bank under § 4-303. Cases regarding stop payment orders should provide guidance as to the latter requirement.

D. For How Long May Payment Be Stopped or an Account Closed

Presumably, an order to close an account, even if made orally, is permanently effective. As to stop payment orders, however, § 4-403(b) distinguishes between oral and written orders. An oral order lapses after fourteen days unless it is confirmed in writing within that period. A written stop payment order or an oral order confirmed in writing is effective for six months from the date it was made. A new written stop payment order made during the effectiveness of an earlier order is good for six months from its own date of issue.

If one stop payment order expires, a new order may be made. In such a case, however, the new order has no retroactive effect. *See* UCC Comment 6 to § 4-403. Once a stop payment order lapses, it is as though it had never been issued. Consequently, if the item is presented, the payor bank not only *could* pay it without being liable under § 4-403, see, e.g., *MG Sales, Inc. v. Chemical Bank*, 161 A.D.2d 148, 554 N.Y.S.2d 863 (1st Dept. 1990), but *must* pay it or face possible liability for wrongful dishonor.

E. Remedies for Failure to Comply with Stop Payment/Close Order

1. In General

Section 4-403 states that the customer has the burden of proving the fact it suffered a loss because an item was paid contrary to a stop payment or close account order and of proving the amount of the loss. Section 4-403, therefore, implicitly provides that if the customer presents such proof, the bank will be liable for the loss. Some of the questions that arise concern (1) the defenses banks may assert and (2) the types of damages that are recoverable.

2. Defenses Banks May Assert

Most courts have held that to prove loss, a customer must do more than merely assert that an item was paid contrary to a stop payment order. Instead, the customer must prove that the payee had no enforceable right against the customer for the amount paid.

PROBLEM 13.6

Gert Gullible writes a check for $10,000 to "Honest Abe" Linkman as a down payment on what Abe has described as "a heavenly piece of property in Arizona." When Gert finds out that such land does not exist on the planet Earth, she immediately issues a stop payment order to her bank, Careless State Bank. Despite receiving the stop order in sufficient time to act and despite the fact that the stop payment order properly identified the check, Careless nevertheless paid the check when it was presented by Abe. Gert sues the bank to have her account recredited for the amount of the check and for consequential damages as well. What result?

Obviously, if the customer was not obligated on the instrument or on an underlying obligation, the customer can recover the amount wrongfully debited to its account. In addition, the customer may recover damages for any subsequent wrongfully dishonored items. Such losses may include emotional distress and injury to reputation. *See, e.g., Kunkel v. First National Bank*, 393 N.W.2d 265, 24 U.C.C.Rep.Serv.2d (Callaghan) 574 (N.D. 1986) (customer sued for $50,000 for mental anguish and $30,000 for injury to credit rating). For further discussion of damages available for wrongful dishonor, *see* Chapter 14.

Section 4-407 provides that a payor bank that pays an item contrary to a valid stop payment order, is subrogated, to the extent necessary to prevent loss to the bank, to the rights of (1) any holder in due course on the item against the drawer or maker, (2) the payee or any other holder of the item either on the item or under the underlying obligation, and (3) the drawer or maker against the payee or any other holder with respect to the underlying transaction. When a customer sues a bank for noncompliance with a stop payment or close account order, the bank's subrogation rights give it essentially the same defense against the customer as is provided by the § 4-403 requirement that the customer prove that it suffered a loss. *Cf.* UCC Comment 1 to § 4-407.

PROBLEM 13.7

Assume in the example above that Abe, the fraudulent land seller, had indorsed the check given to him by Gert over to Supplies-R-Us in exchange for $10,000 worth of office furnishings. Assume also that Supplies-R-Us took the check in good faith and without notice of Abe's shady dealings. Supplies-R-Us takes the check to Careless State Bank, demands payment and is paid despite Gert's timely and effective stop payment order. Gert sues the bank to have her *account recredited from the amount of the check paid contrary to her stop pay-ment order and for consequential damages as well. What result?*

Incidentally, a commonly cited, but incorrect, rule is that payment cannot be stopped against a holder in due course. This is not true. Payment may be stopped, but the bank is subrogated to the rights of the holder in due course against the customer. *See* UCC Comment 1 to § 4-407. The difference between the incorrect and correct rules can be illustrated by way of an example. Assume a bank wrongfully pays an item to a holder in due course contrary to a stop pay-ment order. After debiting the customer's account, the bank then wrongfully dis-honors subsequent checks for insufficient funds. If the stop payment order were as a matter of law ineffective as to a holder in due course, then the bank would not be liable for wrongful dishonor of the subsequent checks. In fact, however, § 4-403(c) makes it clear that the bank may be liable for such wrongful dishonor of the subsequent checks even though the drawer would not be able to recover for the check wrongfully paid to the holder in due course.

Banks may have other defenses to actions under § 4-403. As discussed above, it may be possible for banks to limit their liability pursuant to a separate agree-ment allowed under § 4-103. Banks may also have common law defenses, includ-ing ratification by the customer. *See* UCC Comment 7 to § 4-403. Furthermore, carefully re-read § 4-407 and answer the following problem.

PROBLEM 13.8

From whom, and under what theory, might the bank recover its loss after it has recredited Gert's account under the facts of Problem 13.6?

Chapter 14

WRONGFUL DISHONOR

Because the bank is its customer's agent, it is generally obligated to obey its customer's orders. If a customer issues orders to its bank to honor checks or other items, and the bank wrongfully fails to do so, the bank is liable for wrongful dishonor. *See* § 4-402. There are three principal issues to consider with respect to wrongful dishonor:

1. When is a bank's dishonor of an item "wrongful;"

2. To whom is a bank liable when it has wrongfully dishonored an item; and

3. For what sorts of damages is a bank liable when it has wrongfully dishonored an item?

1. When is Dishonor of an Item "Wrongful"?

The general rule under § 4-402 is that a bank is liable if it (a) dishonors (b) a "properly payable" item (c) when there are sufficient funds in the customer's account to cover the item. *See* §§ 4-402(a).

Dishonor of an Item

Section 4-104(a)(9) defines an item as "an instrument or a promise or order to pay money handled by a bank for collection or payment," but excludes from this definition a payment order governed by Article 4A or a credit or debit card slip. Thus, for instance, a savings account withdrawal order or a certificate of deposit are "items." *See, e.g., Shaw v. Union Bank & Trust Co.*, 640 P.2d 953 (Okla. 1981)(withdrawal order).

What constitutes dishonor of an item depends, in part, on the type of item. Most cases under § 4-402 involve the allegedly wrongful dishonor of a check. Before a bank can dishonor a check, the check must be presented to it. *See* §§ 3-502(b),(c). Presentment, in turn, involves a demand — by, or on behalf of, a person entitled to enforce the check — that the check be paid or accepted. See § 3-501. In addition, the person making presentment must first comply with the bank's demand (a) to exhibit the instrument, (b) to give reasonable identification, (c) if presentment is made on behalf of someone else, to provide reasonable evidence of the presenter's authority, and (d) to sign a receipt on the instrument for any payment made or, if full payment is made, to surrender the check. See § 3-501(b)(2).

In order to reduce their risks, many banks require a person who initiates a transaction at the teller's window, especially a transaction involving the presentment of a check, to provide a thumbprint. In a 2003 case, a person refused to provide his thumbprint, and the bank refused to honor the check. He sued and the court considered, among other issues, whether requiring a thumbprint was a demand for "reasonable identification" for purposes of § 3-501(b)(2). The plaintiff argued that the thumbprint was not a request for reasonable identification, because the bank did not intend to use the thumbprint to identify him prior to honoring the check. Instead, the bank only wanted to be able to use the thumbprint if a dispute subsequently arose as to whether the check was properly payable. Citing public policy considerations in favor of the use of thumbprint identification, the court ruled that a bank's right to require "reasonable identification" was not limited to identification that the bank would authenticate at the time of presentment. *See Messing v. Bank of America, N.A.*, 373 Md. 672, 821 A.2d 22 (Ct.App.Md. 2003).

PROBLEM 14.1

Dan Drawer writes a check out to Paul Payee on Dan's account at First National Bank ("FNB") in payment for merchandise bought by Dan from Paul. Paul goes to Currency Exchange ("CE") and tries to cash the check. CE says that it won't cash the check unless Paul shows him a valid United States passport. Paul says that he's never traveled abroad and doesn't even have a passport. Instead, Paul produces various forms of valid photo-id, including his driver's license and his workplace ID. In addition, Paul produces a certified copy of his birth certificate. Finally, Paul even offers to provide CE with his thumbprint. The CE refuses to cash the check. Assuming that the check is properly payable and there are adequate funds in Dan's account at FNB, is CE guilty of wrongful dishonor? CE not a bank

PROBLEM 14.2

Same facts as in Problem 14.1, but Paul presents the check to FNB in person. Paul offers the same forms of identification as in Problem 14.1, but FNB demands that Paul produce a valid United States passport, and Paul cannot. Consequently, FNB refuses to take or pay the check. Is FNB guilty of wrongful dishonor? unreasonable

If a check is property presented to a bank over the counter for immediate payment, dishonor occurs if the bank fails to pay the check on the day of presentment. *See* § 3-502(2). If presentment is made in a different way, such as through the bank collection system, then the bank dishonors the check if it makes timely return of the check, sends timely notice of dishonor, or becomes liable for returning the check late. *See* § 3-502(1).

A Properly Payable Item

An item is properly payable against an account if it is "authorized by the customer and is in accordance with any agreement between the customer and bank." *See* § 4-401(a). Unless different terms are specifically agreed on by the bank and its customer, a check is properly payable if (a) the drawer's authorized signature appears on the check, (b) it has not been altered, (c) it is payable on demand or, if on a specified date, on a date on or before the date of presentment, and (d) it is not subject to a stop payment order. For more details, see Chapter 13.

Sufficient Funds in the Customer's Account

Unless a customer and a bank otherwise agree, a bank is only obligated to honor the customer's item if doing so would not cause an overdraft. § 4-402(a). For various reasons, the balance in a customer's account may be inadequate to cover a particular item even if the customer's accurately kept records would tend to show the contrary. For example, if the customer is overdue on a loan owed to the bank, the bank may have exercised a right of setoff against the account, deducting from the account the amount of the overdue loan. Similarly, one of the customer's creditors may have garnished the customer's account so that amounts from the account are paid directly to the creditor.

Once a bank correctly determines that there are insufficient funds in the customer's account, the bank is justified in dishonoring the item. Even if the customer thereafter adds funds to the account, the bank is not obligated to make a new determination as to whether payment of the particular item would cause an overdraft. If, however, the payor bank does decide to reevaluate its decision whether to honor the item and, at the time it does so there are sufficient funds, the bank may not dishonor the item based on an insufficiency of funds. To do so under these circumstances would constitute a "wrongful dishonor" of the item.

Justified Dishonors

Sometimes, however, there are valid reasons for refusing to honor an item that is presented to an account. Thus, § 4-404 specifically provides that a bank is not obligated to honor a check, other than a certified check, that is presented more than six months after its date. Such a dishonor would not render the bank liable under § 4-402. Similarly, there are circumstances involving a customers death or incompetence, implicitly described to § 4-405, in which a bank will lack authority to honor an item. Similarly, a bank may be the subject of a valid court order enjoining it from honoring an item or from honoring any items. A bank that dishonors items in compliance with such an order would not be liable under § 4-402. In fact, some cases contend that a bank has an inherent right to freeze an account temporarily if it has legitimate reasons for suspecting that fraudulent items are about to be presented to it. Nevertheless, even these courts rule that this right is only temporary and that if the bank does not reverse such a freeze within a reasonable time, it will be liable under § 4-402 if it subsequently dishonors properly payable items. *See, e.g., Beshara v. Southern National Bank*, 928 P.2d 280 (Okla. 1996).

2. To Whom is a Bank Liable for Wrongful Dishonor?

Pursuant to § 4-402(b), a payor bank that wrongfully dishonors an item is liable to its "customer." Section 4-104(a)(5) defines "customer" as "a person having an account with a bank or for whom a bank has agreed to collect items, . . . including a bank maintaining an account at another bank." The party in whose name the account is at the time of the dishonor seems clearly qualified to sue as a "customer."

PROBLEM 14.3

Dan Drawer writes a check out to Paul Payee on Dan's account at First National Bank ("FNB") in payment for merchandise bought by Dan from Paul. Paul presents the check in person to FNB, but FNB inexplicably dishonors it. There are sufficient funds in Dan's account to cover the check, and Dan has not issued a stop payment order. Can Paul successfully sue FNB for wrongful dishonor? Would it matter if Paul happens also to have a checking account at the FNB?

Sometimes an account is opened in the name of a business entity, such as a partnership or corporation. In such cases, the question arises as to whether individuals — such as partners, shareholders or corporate officers — have standing as "customers" to sue under § 4-402. Under Former § 4-402, there was a split of authority, and UCC Comment 5 to the current version of § 4-402 suggests that the new provision is not designed to resolve this dispute.

Some cases have held simply that only the named entity is the "customer" for purposes of Former § 4-402. *See, e.g, Loucks v. Albuquerque National Bank*, 76 N.M. 735, 418 P.2d 191 (1966) (individual partner is not customer with respect to partnership account); *Koger v. East First National Bank*, 443 So.2d 141 (Fla.App. 1983) (principal shareholder not customer on corporate account); *Annot.*, 88 A.L.R.4th 613 (1991). Other courts have held that an individual partner or corporate officer may qualify as a "customer" under certain circumstances, such as when there is a "close intertwinement" between the individual and the business or when the bank has treated the individual and the business as one entity. *See, e.g., Murdaugh Volkswagen, Inc. v. First National Bank*, 801 F.2d 719, 725 (4th Cir. 1986); *Annot.*, 88 A.L.R.4th 568 (1991); *Annot.*, 88 A.L.R.4th 613 (1991); *Schoenfelder v. Arizona Bank*, 165 Ariz. 79, 796 P.2d 881, 65 Ariz.Adv.Rep. 12 (1990) (mandatory signer of corporate account); *Parrett v.*

Platte Valley State Bank & Trust Co., 236 Neb. 139, 459 N.W.2d 371 (1990) (principal shareholder of corporation who was guarantor of corporate bank debt; corporation really "shell"); *First National Bank v. Hobbs*, 248 Ark. 76, 450 S.W.2d 298 (1970) (president of corporation who was mandatory signer and who had told bank's president that account was opened for special purpose); *Kendall Yacht Corp. v. United California Bank*, 50 Cal.App. 3d 949, 123 Cal.Rptr. 848 (1975).

In addition, some courts that have applied a limited definition of "customer" have nonetheless found that an individual corporate officer may have a cause of action, although not under § 4-402, based on a payor bank's negligent dishonor. *See, e.g., Agostino v. Monticello Greenhouses, Inc.*, 166 A.D.2d 471, 560 N.Y.S.2d 690 (1990) (citing earlier cases) (bank owed corporate president duty of care because he could be held criminally liable for issuing bad check on corporate account); *Annot.*, 7 A.L.R.4th 655 (1981); *Annot.*, 7 A.L.R.4th 1111 (1981). UCC Comment 5 to § 4-402 points out that when such an individual is personally harmed by the dishonor, an issue arises as to whether, under the language of § 1-103, § 4-402 "displaces" such a cause of action. By implication, the Agostino court held that Former § 4-402 did not.

> **NOTE:** Sometimes the name on an account is apparently inexact and is neither that of an individual nor of a legal entity. In such a case, various factors must be evaluated to determine who precisely is the customer, including the name on the account, the circumstances surrounding the opening of the account, the persons who are authorized to control the account and the persons who have beneficial interests in the account. *See, e.g., Lietzman v. Ruidoso State Bank*, 113 N.M. 480, 827 P.2d 1294 (1992) (addressing the issue as to who was the "customer" in order to determine whether bank paid check drawn on account too long after customer's death). *See also First National Bank of Springdale v. Hobbs*, 248 Ark. 76, 450 S.W.2d 298 (1970).

3. For What Sorts of Damages is a Bank Liable?

Section 4-402(b) provides that a payor bank that wrongfully dishonors an item is liable "for damages proximately caused by the wrongful dishonor." There is no presumption that the customer suffered any damages. Instead, the payor bank's liability is limited to "actual damages proved."

> **NOTE:** Under common law, before enactment of Former Article 3, businesses or persons in business were often allowed to recover substantial amounts without any actual proof of loss. Some courts construed Former § 4-402 as continuing this "trader's rule," at least when the wrongful dishonor was intentional. The language of § 4-402 and that of Official Comment 1 to § 4-402 make it clear that the "trader's rule" is abolished.

If proved, however, such damages "may include damages for an arrest or prosecution of the customer or other consequential damages." Whether such arrest or prosecution was proximately caused by the wrongful dishonor is a matter for the trier of fact. *See* UCC Comment 3 to § 4-402.

It is unclear whether damages for emotional distress will be included as "actual damages." Cases basically split along two lines, with some generally allowing emotional distress damages (*see Twin City Bank v. Isaacs*, 283 Ark. 127, 672 S.W.2d 651 (1984) and some allowing emotional distress damages only when the payor bank's conduct was "outrageous" and when the distress was either severe or manifested itself physically (see *Buckley v. Trenton Savings Fund Society*, 111 N.J. 355, 544 A.2d 857 (1988) (applying same standard used to determine whether alleged tortfeasor is liable for infliction of emotional distress)). *See also Harrison v. Federal Deposit Insurance Corp.*, 1993 WL 124699 (W.D.N.Y.) (citing *Isaacs*, court held that there was a material issue of fact as to whether the dishonor was "so wrongful" as to justify damages for mental suffering).

The language of § 4-402 does not expressly provide for punitive damages even if the dishonor was willful or malicious. Nevertheless, although Former § 4-402 was silent as to punitive damages, its language was more ambiguous than § 4-402 and gave rise to a variety of holdings. *Compare Loucks v. Albuquerque National Bank*, *supra* (not available unless bank acted maliciously, intentionally, fraudulently, oppressively, or with reckless disregard as to customer) *with Buckley v. Trenton Savings*, *supra* (no punitive damages even if bank's conduct was intentional). UCC Comment 1 to § 4-402 suggests that the language of § 4-402 does not resolve this issue and that the availability of noncompensatory damages must be resolved by reference to §§ 1-103 and 1-106.

PROBLEM 14.4

When Monica tried to issue a stop payment order on a check she had issued to Joey, the bank teller at her bank, Perk National, with whom she spoke got the date and amount of the check right, but transposed the digits in the check number, so that a stop order was issued on the wrong check. As it worked out, the check on which the stop order was imposed was issued the same day and for the same amount as that made payable to Joey, but was made payable to Janet's Closet, a dress shop, where Monica had purchased an expensive evening gown that needed some minor alterations. When she went in to the store to pick it up the following week, she was publicly berated by Janet, the storeowner, in front of several people, including other shopowners where Monica regularly does business, for giving Janet a check that "bounced" (was not paid by the bank). She was also called several unflattering names. Monica left the store in tears without saying a word, spent several days locked in her room severely upset, and was visited by her doctor who diagnosed her condition as "emotional distress." When she felt a little better, she went out and bought the same exact gown in another store, for

$3,200. When she sues her bank, she and her witnesses testify only as to facts stated above. She then rests her case and submits a claim for $5,000 damages on the grounds of emotional distress, $5,000 for damage to her creditworthiness and the $200 difference in the price of the gown. On which grounds, if any, is she likely to recover?

Chapter 15

BANK COLLECTION

Various types of financial items, but mostly checks, are collected through banks. This process is governed by the following laws and regulations:

1. State statutory law, principally the applicable state's versions of UCC Articles 3 and 4. Where there is a conflict, the provisions of Article 4 supercede those of Article 3. UCC § 4-102.

2. State contract law, as it applies (a) to agreements between banks and their customers and (b) to agreements pertaining to private "clearinghouses," which are groups of banks or other institutions formed to streamline the collection of checks and other items. Such agreements can substantially alter the rules of UCC Article 4. UCC § 4-103.

3. Regulation J, promulgated by the Federal Reserve Board pursuant to the Federal Reserve Act. Regulation J applies to any items that are collected via the federal reserve system. To the extent that Regulation J is inconsistent with state law, Regulation J governs.

4. Regulation CC, promulgated by the Federal Reserve Board pursuant to the Expedited Funds Availability Act (EFAA). Regulation CC applies to the bank collection of any checks, whether or not the Federal Reserve System is used.

Type of item	Applicable law when sent through the Federal Reserve System	Applicable law when not sent through the Federal Reserve System
Check	State statutory and contract law; Regulation J; Regulation CC.	State statutory and contract law; Regulation CC.
Non-Check	State statutory and contract law; Regulation J.	State statutory and contract law.

Let's introduce some basic terminology by considering an example as to how the Federal Reserve System might be used in the collection of a check:

Collection through the Federal Reserve System: An Example

Alan Adler, who resides in New York City, sees a used set of books offered on the internet for $250 by Second Hand Books, Inc. ("SHB"), which is located in Palo Alto, California.

Alan, who is still a little leery about using his credit card over the internet, sends SHB an e-mail asking it to hold the book for him and telling SHB that he will be mailing it a check for the $250. Alan then mails SHB the check, which is drawn on Alan's account at BigBank, Inc. ("BigBank"), located in New York City. When SHB receives the check, it deposits it into its checking account at WestCoast Bank, Inc. ("WCB"), in Palo Alto.

WCB gives its depositor, SHB, a "provisional credit" for the $250 amount of the check. The fact that a credit is "provisional" allows a bank the right to "charge back" (i.e., to undo the credit) under certain circumstances. WCB then starts the "forward collection" process by magnetically coding the check with various data and sending it to the federal reserve bank in San Francisco (FRB-SF), where WCB has an account.

Terminology:

* "Forward collection means the process by which a bank sends a check on a cash basis to the paying bank for payment. Regulation CC § 229.2(q).

FRB-SF gives WCB a provisional credit and sends the check to the federal reserve bank in New York (FRB-NY), where FRB-SF has an account. FRB-NY gives FRB-SF a credit and makes presentment of the check to BigBank.

> **NOTE:** Under Regulation CC, all settlements made during forward collection of an item through the Federal Reserve System are "final" when made, rather than "provisional." Regulation CC § 229.36(d). The collecting banks in whose favor such settlements are made are immediately able to use the credited funds. Nonetheless, this does not prevent banks from making prompt revocation of such settlements when an item is dishonored in a timely manner. See Commentary to Regulation CC. Consequently, it seems correct to refer to these as "provisional" settlements.

More Terminology:

* WCB handled the check for the purposes of collection. Consequently, in addition to being the depositary bank, it is also a "collecting bank." UCC § 4-105(5). As a collecting bank, WCB is an "agent" for SHB, the owner of the check. UCC § 4-201(a).

* FRB-SF, because it handled the check for collection, is a "collecting bank." UCC § 4-105(5). Because it is neither the depositary bank nor the payor bank, FRB-SF is also an "intermediary bank." UCC § 4-105(4). As such, FRB-SF is also an agent for SHB. UCC § 4-201(a).

* FRB-NY, because it handled the check for collection, is a "collecting bank." UCC § 4-105(5). Because it is neither the depositary bank nor the payor bank, FRB-NY is also an "intermediary bank." UCC § 4-105(4). As such, FRB-NY is also an agent for SHB. UCC 4-201(a). In addition, because it made presentment of the check to BigBank, FRB-NY is also the presenting bank. UCC § 4-105(6). BigBank will either honor the check or it will dishonor it. If it dishonors the check, it will have to send the check back on its way to the depositary bank.

The following principal questions arise in connection with this Example:

1. When, and under what circumstances, will any of the banks become irrevocably liable as to the check?

2. How soon, and under what circumstances, will SHB be able to get any or all of the $250?

3. Assume that a payor bank dishonors a check and returns it to the despositary bank. Under what situations can the depositary bank obtain reimbursement from its customer?

QUESTION ONE: When, and under what circumstances, will any of the banks become irrevocably liable as to a deposited check?

A. Collecting Banks: Forward Collection

The forward collection process is primarily regulated by UCC Article 4. UCC § 4-202(a) requires a collecting bank to use ordinary care in:

(1) presenting an item or sending it for presentment;

(2) sending notice of dishonor or nonpayment or returning an item other than a documentary draft to the bank's transferor after learning that the item has not been paid or accepted . . . ;

(3) settling for an item when the bank receives final settlement; and

(4) notifying its transferor of any loss or delay in transit within a reasonable time after discovery thereof.

A collecting bank is deemed to have exercised ordinary care if it so acts before its "midnight deadline," i.e., before midnight on the first banking day after the banking day on which it receives the relevant item or notice. UCC § 4-202(b).

Still more Terminology

* A "banking day" is that part of the day when the bank is "open to the public for carrying on substantially all of its banking functions." UCC § 4-104(a)(3). A bank may set a cutoff hour at 2:00 p.m. or later and treat any item received after this time as having been received on the next banking day. UCC § 4-108. Consequently, if BigBank's cutoff hour is 2:30 p.m., and FRB-NY presented the check at 3:00 p.m. on Monday, the presentment would *not* be treated as having taken place during BigBank's Monday banking day. Instead, it would have taken place on BigBank's Tuesday banking day, and BigBank's midnight deadline as to the check would be midnight on Wednesday, assuming that Wednesday is a banking day for BigBank.

A collecting bank that acts after its midnight deadline may still exercise ordinary care, but the bank has the burden of proving that it acted within a reasonable period of time. Ibid. The collecting bank must send items by a "reasonably prompt method, taking into consideration relevant instructions, the nature of the item, the number of those items on hand, the cost of collection involved, and the method generally used by it or others to present those items." UCC § 4-204(a). Delay by a collecting bank may be excused if (1) the bank "exercises such diligence as the circumstances require," and (2) "the delay is caused by interruption of communication or computer facilities, suspension of payments by another bank, war, emergency conditions, failure of equipment, or other circumstances beyond the control of the bank." UCC § 4-109(b).

B. The Payor Bank: Accountability upon "Final Payment"

As a general rule, the payor bank becomes accountable for an item, whether it intends to or not, upon "final payment" of the item. Pursuant to UCC § 4-215, final payment occurs as soon as the payor bank has:

(1) paid the item in cash;

(2) settled for the item without having a right to revoke the settlement under statute, clearing-house rule, or agreement; or

(3) made a provisional settlement for the item and failed to revoke the settlement in the time and manner permitted by statute, clearing-house rule, or agreement.

A payor bank "settles" for an item when it pays it in cash or when it arranges for the amount of the item to be credited to an account or to be debited from its account. *See* UCC § 4-104(a)(11). Settlement may be either provisional or final, and a settlement may begin as provisional but later become final. Comment 1 to UCC § 4-215; UCC § 4-104(a)(11).

If a payor bank asserts that, while it is settling an item by crediting an account, it is "reserving" a right to revoke the settlement, the assertion is ineffective. Either the bank has the right to revoke based on statute, clearing-house rule or agreement or it does not. Its unilateral assertion is irrelevant. On the other hand, if the bank does have the right to revoke based on statute, clearing-house rule or agreement, then it may exercise that right even if it never asserted any "reservation." Comment 4 to UCC § 4-215.

When does a payor bank have the right to revoke a settlement? UCC § 4-301 is an important statutory basis for such a revocation. It states that a payor bank that settles a demand item before midnight of the banking day the item is received ordinarily has the right to revoke and recover the settlement if, before its "midnight deadline," it dishonors the item by either (1) returning it or (2) if the item is not available for return, sending written notice of dishonor or nonpayment. Comment 4 to UCC § 4-215.

In order to understand UCC § 4-301, we need to know two things: how an item is "returned" and what a bank's "midnight deadline" is. An item presented through a clearing-house is returned when it is either (1) delivered to the presenting bank, the last collecting bank or the clearing-house or (2) when it is sent or delivered to the payor bank's customer or transferor. UCC § 4-301(d). A bank has a "midnight deadline" as to each item that is presented to it. It is midnight on the next banking day following the *later* of (1) the banking day on which it received, or (2) the banking day "from which the time for taking action commences to run . . . ." UCC § 4-104(a)(10). In our Example, above, if FRB-NY makes presentment of the check to BigBank during BigBank's banking day on Monday, then, assuming Tuesday is also a banking day, BigBank's midnight deadline will be at midnight on Tuesday.

Clearing-house rules may also provide a payor bank a right to revoke a settlement. Such rules often provide that items that are settled in the morning may be returned, and the settlements revoked, until some specified time in the afternoon of the same day — or in some cases even the next day. Where such rules apply, the morning settlement is provisional and is not a final payment. Comment 4 to UCC § 4-215.

One scenario in which a payor bank may have a right to revoke a settlement as a matter of agreement is where one bank is both the payor and depositary bank. Suppose the bank has signed a receipt — or made an entry in the depositor's passbook evidencing receipt of the item — for credit into the customer's account. If the receipt, passbook, or other agreement (such as the account agreement) between the customer and the bank provides that any credit is provisional, then it is provisional and is not final payment. Comment 4 to § UCC 4-215.

Unless a payor bank has some statutory, clearing-house or contractual right to revoke a settlement, then once its midnight deadline lapses without its having dishonored an item, the payor bank is accountable for the item under UCC § 4-301. The EFAA and Regulation CC, however, provide several additional exceptions. First, a payor bank is permitted to dishonor a check, and avoid accountability on it, even after its midnight deadline if it returns the check to the presenting bank before the close of the presenting bank's next banking day. Regulation CC § 229.30(c). Why? The purpose of the EFAA was to expedite the availability of funds to bank customers. To accomplish this, the EFAA encourages payor banks to give prompt notice of dishonor. In order to meet their midnight deadlines, however, payor banks were often *mailing* notices of dishonor because such notices were deemed to have been given as soon as they were mailed. Yet mailed notices might not reach the presenting banks for two or more days. Regulation CC § 229.30(c) encourages payor banks to return the check earlier, by having it reach the presenting bank by the first banking day after the payor bank's midnight deadline.

Second, Regulation CC § 229.30(c)(1) permits a payor bank to dishonor a check, and avoid accountability on it, even after its midnight deadline if the payor bank uses a highly expeditious means of transportation to return the check. The Commentary to this provision states, for instance, that "a west coast bank may use this further extension to ship a returned check by air courier directly to an east coast depositary bank even if the check arrives after the close of the depositary bank's banking day."

Regulation J provides that a payor bank using the Federal Reserve System to pay an item must, before the end of the banking day of presentment, make actual payment — and not merely provisional settlement — to the Federal Reserve Bank that made presentment. 12 C.F.R. §§ 210.9, 210.12. Nevertheless, the payor bank may still revoke this payment and recover it, if it acts to do so prior to the midnight deadline.

C. The Payor Bank: Obligations under the EFAA

The EFAA requires depositary banks to give its customers relatively quick access to deposited funds. Of course, by doing so, such banks run a risk if the item that was deposited is ultimately dishonored. To reduce this risk, the EFAA imposes various duties on the payor bank.

The larger the check, the greater the depositary bank's risk. Consequently, if a payor bank decides to dishonor a check in the amount of $2,500 or more, it must send a direct notice to the depositary bank. Regulation CC § 229.33. The name and routing number of the payor bank, the name of the payee, the amount, the reason for return, the date of the indorsement of the depositary bank, the account number of the depositor, the branch at which the item was first deposited, and the trace number on the item of the depositary bank must all be included in the notice, provided that this information can be reasonably determined by examining the item. Notice may be provided by any reasonable means, such as returning the check, sending a writing (including return of the check), Fedwire, telex or telegraph, or making a phone call. Notice must be given so that it is "received by the depositary bank by 4:00 p.m. (local time) on the second business day following the banking day on which the check was presented to the paying bank . . . ." Regulation CC § 229.33(a). Failure to provide such notice renders the payor bank liable for actual damages up to the amount of the item and, if the payor bank failed to act in good faith, for consequential damages as well.

Terminology, again:

* A "business day" is "a calendar day other than a Saturday or a Sunday, January 1, the third Monday in January, the third Monday in February, the last Monday in May, July 4, the first Monday in September, the second Monday in October, November 11, the fourth Thursday in November, or December 25. If January 1, July 4, November 11, or December 25 fall on a Sunday, the next Monday is not a business day." Regulation CC § 229.2(g).

* "Good faith" means "means honesty in fact and observance of reasonable commercial standards of fair dealing." Regulation CC § 229.2(nn).

Regulation CC also requires a payor bank to meet one of two alternative tests as to how quickly it returns a check, even a check of less than $2,500. Suppose the payor bank is bank A and the depositary bank is bank B. The first test asks what if the roles were switched, and bank A were the depositary bank and bank B were the payor bank. How would bank A forward the check for payment from bank B? The first test requires bank A to use just as fast a process to return a check it dishonors to bank B. The second test (the "two day/four day test") depends on whether the payor bank and depositary are located in the same geographical region served by a Federal Reserve processing center. If they are, then the second test requires that the payor bank return the check in such a manner that it would usually be received by the depositary bank not later than 4:00 p.m. on the second business day following the original presentment to the payor bank. If the banks are not located in the same Federal Reserve region, then it is sufficient if the check is returned in such a manner that it would usually be received by the depositary bank not later than 4:00 p.m. on the fourth business day following the original presentment to the payor bank. Pursuant to Regulation CC, the check may be returned directly to the depositary bank, in a different route from the one through which the check reached the payor bank, or through the Federal Reserve System. The reason why the check is returned must be stamped on it.

A payor bank that returns a check must indorse the check and is liable as an indorser. Regulation CC § 229.35. Moreover, by returning the check, the payor bank makes warranties to their transferees that: (1) the payor bank returned the check within the times required by all applicable law; (2) the warrantor is authorized to return the check; and (3) the returned check has not been materially altered. Regulation CC § 229.34.

D. *Returning Banks: Obligations under the EFAA*

If a check is dishonored and is sent to one of the collecting banks for return to the depositary bank, the collecting bank is a "returning bank." A collecting bank must satisfy one of three alternative tests. The first is that it must act as expeditiously in returning a check to the depositary bank as it would in forwarding a check for payment. Regulation CC § 229.31. The second test provides it with one additional day if it creates a "qualified return check," which is encoded in magnetic ink so that it can be automatically processed. The encoding can be done either by placing a magnetic strip on the bottom of the check or by placing the check in a carrier envelope on which the information is magnetically coded. Regulation CC § 229.31. The third test is the same as the two-day/four-day test for payor banks.

A returning bank is authorized to impose a charge for handling the returned check. A returning bank must indorse the check and is liable as an indorser. Regulation CC § 229.35. In addition, by returning the check, the returning bank warranties to its transferees that: (1) the payor bank returned the check within the times required by all applicable law; (2) the warrantor is authorized to return the check; and (3) the returned check has not been materially altered. Regulation CC § 229.34. Moreover, under Regulation CC § 229.38, a bank that fails to use ordinary care or to act in good faith with respect to its obligations in the collection process can be liable to "the depositary bank, the depositary bank's customer, the owner of a check, or another party to the check." For failing to exercise ordinary care, a bank can be liable up to the amount of the check for the loss incurred, minus the loss of any amount that would have been incurred even if ordinary care had been exercised. If the bank failed to act in good faith, it may be liable for other proximately caused damages." *Id.*

QUESTION TWO: *How Soon are Deposited Funds Available to the Depositor?*

When a customer deposits a check or another item into his account, a bank can elect to make these funds available to the depositor, its customer, immediately. Nevertheless, if it does so, it exposes itself to possible loss should the item be dishonored. As a result, the relevant legal question is usually how soon the depositor has the legal right to demand such funds.

Although the applicable provisions of Regulation CC can be organized in various ways, we believe it is useful to think of them as three basic rules, subject to various exceptions. Of course, it is important to recognize that our discussion of Regulation CC will *not* be comprehensive. A comprehensive treatment of its provisions would require far more than a single chapter.

Rule #1: The first business day after the banking day of deposit

There are a number of scenarios in which part or all of deposited funds must be made available on the first banking day after the banking day on which the deposit is made.

Scenario #1: The depositary bank and the payor bank are the same bank

When the depositary bank and the payor bank are the same, Regulation CC requires the depositary bank make the funds available to the customer on the first business day after the banking day of the deposit so long as the item has not been dishonored. EFAA § 603(a)(2)(E); Regulation CC § 229.10(c)(1)(vi).

> **NOTE:** The old rule, pursuant to UCC § 4-215(e)(2), only required that the funds be made available on the *second* banking day after the banking day of deposit. Regulation CC, of course, supercedes UCC § 4-215(e)(2).

PROBLEM 15.1

Doug received a $1,200 check from his employer (E), drawn on MasterBank (MB). Doug deposits this check into his checking account, also at MasterBank on Monday at 1:30 p.m. Assume that Monday, Tuesday and Wednesday are banking days and that MasterBank's cutoff time is 2:30 p.m.

a. *By when must MasterBank make the $1,200 available to Doug?*

b. *Explain whether your answer would change (i) if Doug had deposited the check on Monday at 3:30 p.m., or (ii) if Tuesday were a banking holiday.*

Whenever funds must be made available on a particular business day, the funds must be available for withdrawal by the later of "(1) 9:00 a.m. (local time of the depositary bank); or (2) the time the depositary bank's teller facilities (including ATMs) are available for customer account withdrawals." Regulation CC § 229.19(b).

Scenario #2: The check is a certain type of check

A depositary bank must make deposited funds available on the first business day after the banking day of the deposit when a customer deposits certain types of checks, such as a government check, a cashier's check, a certified check or a teller's check that are made payable to him. EFAA § 603(a); Regulation CC § 229.10(c). The presumption is that such checks are generally reliable.

Cash deposits made in person to an employee of the depositary bank must also be made available on the first business day after the banking day on which they are deposited. Regulation CC § 229.10(a)(1). Regulation CC essentially requires that depositary banks make funds available regarding the specified, presumably reliable checks as if they were cash deposits.

> **NOTE:** Cash deposits that are not made in person to an employee of the bank need not be made available until the second business day after the banking day on which they are deposited. Regulation CC § 229.10(a)(2). Under UCC § 4-215(f), which applied before promulgation of Regulation CC, the rule for cash deposits — without reference as to whether or not made in person — required that the funds be available at the opening of the first banking day after the banking day of deposit.

Scenario #3: The first $100 of any check

Even if the check is neither a government, cashier's, certified or teller check and even if the depositary bank and the payor bank are not the same, the depositary bank must make the first $100 of the check deposits made by a customer in a particular banking day available on the next business day.

Rule #2: The second and third banking days after deposit

The second rule pertains primarily to cases in which the depositary bank and the payor bank, while not the same bank, are both located in the same federal reserve check-processing region.

Terminology (still more):

* When a payor bank is a "local payor bank" when it "is located in the same check processing region as the physical location of the branch, contractual branch, or proprietary ATM of the depositary bank in which that check was deposited." Regulation CC § 229.2(s).

Rule #2, however, also applies to deposits of government checks when they are not deposited into the accounts of the payees.

Under Rule #1, the first $100 of the deposited check must be made available to the customer on the first banking day following the banking day of deposit. Rule #2 deals with the availability of the rest of the deposited funds.

Rule #2 has two parts depending on whether the funds are to be available to pay the customer's checks or whether the customer wants to withdraw the funds as cash. The funds must be available to pay for the customer's checks by the second banking day after the banking day of deposit. If the customer wants to withdraw the funds as cash, however, only an additional $400 of such funds must be made available on that day. To the extent the deposited check exceeds $500 (the $100 made available under Rule #1 plus the $400), that excess must be made available on the third banking day after the banking day of deposit.

PROBLEM 15.2

Doug received a $1,200 check from his employer (E), drawn on MasterBank (MB). Doug deposits this check into his checking account at NationalBank (NB) on Monday at 1:30 p.m. Assume that MB and NB are both in the same federal reserve check-processing region. Assume also that Monday, Tuesday and Wednesday are banking days and that NB's cutoff time is 2:30 p.m.

   a. *Does Doug have the right to demand that NB allow him to withdraw $75 in cash on Tuesday?* yes, up to $100

   b. *Assuming that Doug did not withdraw any money on Tuesday, does he have the right to demand that NB allow him to withdraw $600 on Wednesday?* Only $500 (2d day)

Rule #3: The fifth and sixth banking days after deposit *Diff. Fed. region*

checks or 500 balance

The third rule pertains to cases in which the depositary bank and the payor bank are located in different federal reserve check-processing regions. Under Rule #1, the first $100 of the deposited check must be made available to the customer on the first banking day following the banking day of deposit. Rule #3 deals with the availability of the rest of the deposited funds.

Just like Rule #2, Rule #3 has two parts depending on whether the funds are to be available to pay the customer's checks or whether the customer wants to withdraw the funds as cash. The funds must be available to pay for the customer's checks by the fifth banking day after the banking day of deposit. If the customer wants to withdraw the funds as cash, however, only an additional $400 of such funds must be made available on that day. To the extent the deposited check exceeds $500 (the $100 made available under Rule #1 plus the $400), that excess must be made available on the sixth banking day after the banking day of deposit.

PROBLEM 15.3

Doug received a $1,200 check from his employer (E), drawn on MasterBank (MB). Doug deposits this check into his checking account at NationalBank (NB) on Monday at 1:30 p.m. Assume that MB and NB are not in the same federal reserve check-processing region. Assume also that Monday, Tuesday and Wednesday, Thursday, and Friday are banking days and that NB's cutoff time is 2:30 p.m.

a. *Does Doug have the right to demand that NB allow him to withdraw $75 in cash on Friday?* Y

b. *Does he have the right to demand that NB allow him to withdraw $400 on Friday?* N, 4Khday 100 max

Important Exceptions

There are a number of important exceptions to the three basic rules described above. For example, some of the rules do not fully apply to deposits made to a "new account" during the first 30 calendar days after it is established. An account is a "new account" if, within 30 calendar days before the account was established, at least one of the customers did not have another account at the same bank that had been open for at least 30 calendar days. Regulation CC § 229.13(a)(2). Thus, although Rule #1 generally requires a depositary bank to make the first $100 of a deposit available on the first business day after the banking day of deposit, this rule does not apply to deposits in new accounts. Similarly, although Rule #1 generally requires a depositary bank to make available funds from certain types of checks on the first business day after the banking day of deposit, this only applies to the first $5,000 of such checks deposited on any one banking day into a new account. The rest of such deposits need only be made on the ninth business day following the banking day of deposit.

Other exceptions apply to certain large deposits, to redeposited checks, to depositary accounts that have been repeatedly overdrawn, to cases in which the depositary bank has reasonable cause to believe that specific deposited items are uncollectible, and to situations involving certain specified emergency conditions. Regulation CC § 229.13 (b)-(f). When it relies on any of these other exceptions, the depositary bank must provide the depository with written notice. Regulation CC § 229.13(g).

Civil Liability for Violations

Regulation CC § 229.21 provides that a bank that violates the rules regarding the expedited availability of funds is liable to the aggrieved person for actual damages, additional damages — within a specified range — as the court may allow, plus attorneys fees and costs in any successful action taken to require compliance by the bank. The regulation identifies particular factors to be considered in determining the amount of any class action award. A bank can avoid liability if it proves by a preponderance of the evidence that its violation was not intentional and was the result of a good faith error which occurred despite the fact that the bank maintained procedures reasonably designed to avoid such an error. Nevertheless, a bank cannot avoid liability based on an error of legal judgment.

QUESTION THREE: Assume that a payor bank dishonors a check and returns it to the despositary bank. Under what situations can the depositary bank obtain reimbursement from its customer?

The "final payment rule" and its exceptions determine when a payor bank is liable for a check. If a check is dishonored and returned to the depositary bank, that bank will seek reimbursement from its customer on one of three theories: (1) the account agreement with its customer; (2) the customer's indorser's obligation; or (3) the statutory right of charge back set forth in UCC § 4-214. Let's focus on UCC § 4-214.

Assume that a depositary bank has made a provisional settlement for a check, but fails to obtain final settlement on the item because of "dishonor, suspension of payments by a bank or otherwise." UCC § 4-214(a). The depositary bank can revoke that settlement and charge back the amount of any credit, if, by midnight of the first banking day after the banking day on which it learned it would not obtain final settlement for the item, it either returns the item to the customer or it gives notice of these facts to the customer. If the bank is late in returning the check or giving notice, then it is liable for any loss caused by the delay.

It is important to note that if any settlement received by the depositary bank did become final, then the bank loses any right to charge back against any settlement it gave its customer for the item. In other words, if the payor bank made "final payment" and wants to make a late dishonor, the depositary bank cannot "cooperate" by charging back against the customer's account.

Chapter 16

SPECIAL PROBLEMS: FORGERIES
AND MISSING SIGNATURES

Now that we have covered each of the three basic forms of liability with respect to an instrument — party liability on an instrument, warranty liability arising from a transfer or presentment of an instrument, and conversion liability — it is useful to explore the consequences of missing or forged signatures. Much of this chapter will seem like a review to you because you will be asked to apply much of what you have already learned.

A. *Missing & Unauthorized Makers' and Drawers' Signatures*

If a writing lacks a maker's signature, then, even if it otherwise looks like a promissory note, it is not a note. Why? Because to be a "note," a writing must contain a "promise," see § 3-104(e), and a "promise" is "a written undertaking to pay money *signed* by the person undertaking to pay," § 3-103(a)(12)(emphasis added). Consequently, a person in possession of such a writing has no rights to enforce it under UCC Article 3. Similarly, if a writing lacks a drawer's signature, it is not a draft. To be a "draft," a writing must contain an "order," see § 3-104(e), and an "order" is "a written instruction to pay money *signed* by the person giving the instruction. § 3-103(a)(8)(emphasis added). A person in possession of such a writing has no right to enforce it under UCC Article 3, and a drawee bank that pays such a draft is not authorized under § 4-401 to debit its customer's account.

Most of the time, however, such a writing contains at least the signature of a *purported* maker or drawer. If the maker's or drawer's signature is fraudulent or unauthorized, the writing will be treated as a note or draft in favor of any person who (1) paid it in good faith or (2) either took it in good faith and for value or who, through the shelter doctrine, has the rights of someone who took it in good faith and for value. *See* § 3-403. The general rule is that a person entitled to enforce the instrument ("PETE") cannot enforce this note or draft against the purported maker or drawer. Nor would the drawee bank that pays such a note be authorized under § 4-401 to debit the purported drawer's account. Exceptions to these rules will be discussed in Chapter 17. A PETE could however, enforce the instrument either against the person (1) who signed the purported maker's or drawer's signature or (2) any other party, such as an indorser or guarantor, to the instrument. Alternatively, a PETE could sue prior transferors for breach of warranty.

[handwritten margin note, top left: "Pay to order Paul 1000 /s/ Marty (Carl)"]

PROBLEM 16.1

Carl Crook, fraudulently represents himself as Marty Maker, a famous patron of the arts and issues a note for $1,000 payable to the order of Paul Payee, signing it "Marty Maker," in exchange for a painting done by Paul, a struggling, but talented young artist. Paul presents the instrument to Marty Maker, who denies that the signature is his. Does Paul have any right to payment from Marty? If he does not, does he have a cause of action against anyone on the instrument? If so, who is that party and how does that person's liability arise? See § 3-403 and § 3-413.

PROBLEM 16.2

[handwritten margin note, left: "Paul → landlord = holder contractor = holder"]

Assume that instead of presenting the note to Marty Maker, Paul Payee from Problem 16.1, indorses the note in blank and gives it to his landlord for rent due on Paul's studio. The landlord in turn transfers the note, without indorsing it, to a contractor doing some work on the landlord's property. When the contractor presents the note to Marty for payment, Marty denies that the signature is his and refuses to pay. What causes of action does the contractor have, if any, against Marty, Paul or the landlord? See §§ 3-415 and 3-416. Is there anyone else the contractor could sue on this instrument?

[handwritten margin note, left: "Against Paul & landlord for breach warranty (defenses, auth sign)"]

[handwritten note, center: "Maker's liability → Carl   Indorser's liability → Paul"]

PROBLEM 16.3

Fred D. Frauder finds the checkbook of Dan Drawer and issues a check in Dan's name payable to Cara Seller in exchange for an automobile that Cara advertised for sale in a local newspaper. Cara indorsed the check over to Meg A. Byte as payment for a computer. Meg indorsed it over to Ryan Retailer when she purchased an Oriental rug from him. Ryan indorsed the check and gave it to Harry as payment for a camcorder, but signed it "without recourse." The front of the check then looks like this:

> Pay to the order of Cara Seller $1,000.
>
> First National Bank
>
>   s/ Dan Drawer *(really Fred)*

The back of the check looks like this:

> /s/ Cara Seller
> /s/ Meg A. Byte
> /s/ Ryan Retailer, Without Recourse

Harry can sue.
- Fred (Drawer's)
* - Cara/Meg*
*   (indorsers)*
↑ - Cara/Meg
*   (transfer*
*   #2+4)*
- Ryan
* (transfer)*

Harry then presents the check to First National Bank, which dishonors the check because it had been ordered to do so by Dan, who discovered his checkbook was missing. Whom can Harry successfully sue to recover the $1,000? On what theory or theories can he sue? Assume Harry presents the dishonored check to Meg for payment and Meg pays. What recourse does Meg have against other parties? Which parties can she recover from and on what theory(ies)?

Assume Meg did successfully present the check to Cara and Cara paid on her indorser's obligation. Cara then learned that at the time of the presentment, Meg knew that Dan's signature was forged. Can Cara successfully sue Meg on a breach of presentment warranty? See § 3-417(d).

Typically if the person who signed the draft lacked authority to do so, the drawee could not debit its customer's account. The drawee would have three principal ways of trying to recover the money it paid out. It could:

1. under § 3-418, sue for restitution from the person it paid;

2. under § 4-208 or § 3-417, sue for breach of presentment warrany against either the presenter or prior transferors; or

3. sue the person who made the unauthorized drawer's signature.

1. Drawee's Rights Under Section 3-418

If a drawee pays a check on the mistaken belief that drawer's signature was genuine or authorized, § 3-418 allows the drawee to recover the amount paid from the person to whom, or for whose benefit, payment was made. (In the case of a mistaken acceptance, § 3-418 allows the drawee to revoke the acceptance.) This right, however, is subject to a very important limitation: it may not be asserted against a person (1) who took the instrument in good faith and for value or (2) who in good faith changed position in reliance on the payment (or acceptance).

PROBLEM 16.4

a. On May 14, Frank Forger steals the checkbook of Dan Drawer and writes a check for $100 in Dan's name payable to Sam's Warehouse Outlet ("Sam's") for goods which are to be delivered to a specified location on May 28, 2 weeks after payment. On May 15, Sam's presents the check to the Drawee Bank, which pays it. Later that day, Dan alerts the bank that his checkbook has been stolen and confirms that he has not written any check to Sam's. Drawee Bank contacts Sam's on May 18th and demands that it give the $100 back. Sam's refuses and Drawee Bank sues. Who should win?

b. Assume, instead, that Sam's had in fact given the goods to Frank on May 14 when Frank transferred to it the check. Would this affect your answer to "a," above? See § 3-418(c). Would your answer to this question "b" be different if the check Frank forged was dated February 1, given that he purchased and received the goods on May 14 using that check? See § 3-304.

c. Assume, instead, that because of the payment it received from Drawee Bank on May 15, Sam's goes ahead and puts together Frank's order and delivers the goods on May 17th. Drawee Bank contacts Sam's on May 18th and demands that it give the $100 back. Sam's refuses and Drawee Bank sues. Who should win?

d. Under which, if any, of the scenarios described in "a," "b," or "c," does Drawee Bank have the right to debit Dan's account for the $100 it paid to Sam's?

To the extent that § 3-418 protects the rights of a good-faith presenter to retain the benefits of a drawee's acceptance or payment, § 3-418 memorializes the rule of the well-known common law decision, *Price v. Neal*, 3 Burr.1354, 97 Eng.Rep. 871 (1762), the details of which need not be recited.

2. *Drawee's Right to Pursue Violations of Presentment Warranties*

A party who presents an unaccepted draft to the drawee for payment warrants to the drawee who pays in good faith that (1) he is a person entitled to enforce the instrument, (2) there are no alterations, and (2) he has no knowledge that the signature of the purported drawer was unauthorized. *See* §§ 4-208 and 3-417. Prior transferors of the draft make the same warranties. *Id.* The right to sue to enforce these warranties is preserved by § 3-418(c).

Nevertheless, an unauthorized drawer's signature does not prevent someone in possession of the draft from being a PETE. Only an unauthorized "necessary indorsement" can do that. Nor is an unauthorized drawer's signature an "alteration." Consequently, if the only problem with a draft is an unauthorized drawer's signature, the only warranty that can be potentially breached is that the warrantor had no knowledge that the drawer's signature was unauthorized.

PROBLEM 16.5

Frank Forger steals Ivan Innocent's checkbook and writes a check payable to the Deuce Hardware store for $250 signing Ivan's name to the check in exchange for three power tools. Duece takes the check from Frank after seeing a false ID that Frank had prepared with Ivan's name on it and Frank's picture. Deuce indorses the check over to John Maddening, along with several other checks, in exchange for some promotional work John has done. That evening when John got home, he notices the check from Ivan and calls Deuce to remark on the coincidence that he knew Ivan, who had been John's teacher when John was in elementary school some 40 years ago. When the Deuce manager states that the man who presented the check could not possibly be that old, John looks up Ivan *in the phone book, calls him and finds out that Ivan's checkbook had been stolen. John nevertheless deposits the check into his account at the MNF Bank the next morning. Later that afternoon John tells the manager of Deuce about his phone call to Ivan and that the check had been forged. The following day MNF presents the check to the Drawee Bank and the check is paid. After Ivan objects to his account being debited, Drawee Bank seeks to recover the $250 on a breach of presentment warranty theory. Would such a suit be successful against MNF? Against John? Against Deuce Hardware Store? Against Frank? Could Drawee Bank instead bring a transfer warranty action against John or Deuce based on a breach of the warranty that all signtures are genuine and authorized? See § 3-417(a)(2).*

3. Drawee's Rights Against the Party Who Forged the Drawer's Signature

Pursuant to § 3-403(a), the unauthorized signature operates as that of the unauthorized signer in favor of a party who pays the instrument in good faith. Thus, when Frank Forger signs Dan Drawee's name to a check, it is ineffective as Dan's signature but, instead, serves to bind Frank. UCC Comment 2 to § 3-403(a) states that "[t]he signor's liability [under § 3-403(a)] is not in damages for breach of warranty of authority, but is full liability on the instrument in the capacity in which the signor signed." Thus, when a forger signs a check as the drawer, he is treated as if he himself were the drawer.

It is not obvious how this helps the drawee. A drawer is liable *on the instrument* only to a person entitled to enforce the instrument or a subsequent indorser who paid the instrument. *See* § 3-414. A drawee is neither. Furthermore, a drawer is liable only when an "unaccepted draft has been dishonored," and that is not the case when the drawee has, in fact, paid the check.

It is also not clear how the drawee could collect from the forger pursuant to § 4-401. Although § 4-401 allows a drawee bank to charge an account when it makes payment to a holder in good faith, § 4-401 pertains only to an account of the bank's "customer." Section 4-104(a)(5) defines a "customer as "a person having an account with a bank or for whom a bank has agreed to collect items, including a bank that maintains an account at another bank." If the forger has no account with the drawee bank, he is not a "customer," and nothing in § 3-403 or in Article 4 expressly changes this fact. Furthermore, when the drawee is not a "bank," § 4-401 is inapplicable.

Perhaps one can argue that when the forger signs the check with an unauthorized signature that becomes his own, the forger enters into an implied contract with the drawee named on the instrument that if it pays in accordance with his order, the drawee is entitled to charge him for any money paid out.

Alternatively, a drawee may be able to recover its payment from the forger pursuant to § 3-418(a). That section states, among other things, that if a drawee pays a draft on the mistaken belief that the signature of the drawer was author-ized, the drawee can recover the amount of the draft "from the person to whom or for whose benefit payment was made." It is true that § 3-418(c) states that no recovery may be had from persons who took the instrument in good faith and for value or from persons who in good faith changed their position based on the pay-ment. Nevertheless, a drawee may argue that the payment was made "for the benefit" of the forger, because, had the payment not been made, the forger would have been liable on the instrument to the person who was so paid.

The other likely theory is that the drawee is entitled to recover from the forger on a common law theory of fraud or the like. This would seem to be the only theory on which to sue when a wrongdoer purportedly issued the check *without* making any signature, i.e., by leaving the drawer's signature line blank, since such a check would not be a negotiable instrument.

B. Missing or Forged Necessary Indorsements

When a note or draft is payable to the order of an identified person (or a check is payable to an identified person), the indorsement of that person is commonly referred to as a "necessary indorsement" because the indorsement is required in order to negotiate the instrument and make another person its "holder." In fact, in most instances, the lack of a necessary indorsement prevents the person in possession of the instrument from being a PETE. One exception, discussed in chapter 4, above, involves the "shelter doctrine." To review, when an instrument is payable to an identified person, e.g., Tom, and Tom has possession of the instrument, Tom is the holder of the instrument. Tom can make George a PETE simply by giving the instrument to George because, under the shelter doctrine, George gets all of the rights Tom had to enforce the instrument. Therefore, George would have possession of the instrument and would be a nonholder with the rights of a holder, satisfying the § 3-301(ii) definition of a PETE. But, in the more typical situation — or at least the more typically litigated situation — if the person in possession of the instrument is not a holder because of a miss-ing or unauthorized necessary indorsement, he is not a PETE either. Why? Because, in most instances, the instrument has not been voluntarily trans-ferred by the person whose necessary indorsement is missing.

1. The Rights of Makers and Drawers

If the maker pays a note with a forged or missing necessary indorsement, the maker may be able to recover the amount paid in a presentment warranty action against the presenter or prior transferors. Similarly, if a draft with a forged or missing necessary indorsement is presented to the drawer, and the drawer pays, the drawer, too, can sue for breach of presentment warranty. See § 3-417(d) and do the following problem.

PROBLEM 16.6

Marty Maker issues a demand note payable to the order of Paula Payee. The note is stolen from Paula's desk by Lucy Larcenous, Paula's cleaning lady. On the back of the note, Lucy expertly forges Paula's name in a special indorsement making the note payable to Lucy. Lucy then takes the note and indorses it over to her landlord in payment for a month's rent. The landlord was at first hesitant to take the note but is convinced by Lucy that it was legitimately transferred to her by Paula, her employer. The note is presented to Marty and paid. Marty subsequently finds out from Paula that the note was stolen and seeks to recover from landlord. Can he successfully sue landlord? Can he successfully sue anyone else?

A check with a forged or missing necessary indorsement is not really properly payable. Consequently, if the drawee pays such a check, it may not debit the drawer's account. If the drawee bank does charge the drawer's account, the *sole* remedy for the drawer is the implicit cause of action based on § 4-401 to force the drawee to recredit the account.

[handwritten margin notes: Lucy (forge indors. necess.) → indorses to landlord → presented to Marty ("paid")]

[handwritten note on image: I, Marty Maker promise to pay Paula Payee /s/ Marty]

PROBLEM 16.7

George Costanza writes a personal check payable to Cosmo Kramer for $150 for some cigars Kramer had gotten for George's father. Kramer had the check in his pocket when he was pickpocketed at Times Square. The thief, Roger Dodger, forged Kramer's name on the back of the check, and cashed it at CD City, a retail store on 42nd Street. CD then indorsed the check and deposited it in its bank, Depositary National Bank. The check was presented to Steinbrenner State Bank, where George has his account, and paid. When Kramer informed him that the check had been stolen, George contacted the bank, who told George the check had already been paid and that his account had been debited $150. What action does George have against Steinbrenner State Bank? Can George sue CD City or Depositary National Bank on an indorser's obligation, warranty or conversion theory? Can he sue Roger on any theory, if he finds him?

[handwritten margin notes: Roger (indorse Kramer) → CD City (indorse) → Depository Bank → Steinbrenner bank (George's bank)]

[handwritten note on image: Pay to order of CD Kramer $150 /s/ George]

2. The Drawee's Rights

If the lack of a necessary indorsement prevents the person presenting a draft to a bank from being a PETE, the draft is not properly payable and the bank should not honor it. If the bank does honor it, it may not debit its customer's account. Assuming that a bank drawee that has paid the instrument is unable to charge the customer's account, the drawee may still be able to recover (1) in a warranty action against the presenter or prior transferors or (2) in an action against the person who made the unauthorized indorsement based along the lines of common law fraud. Refer to the facts of **PROBLEM 16.7** to answer the following questions.

PROBLEM 16.8

What rights, if any, does Steinbrenner State Bank have against Depositary National Bank? Against CD City? Against the thief, Roger Dodger? Can Steinbrenner sue CD City or Roger on a transfer warranty theory? On an indorser's obligation?

3. The Rights of the Party in Possession of the Instrument

If the lack of a necessary indorsement prevents the party in possession of the instrument from being a PETE, that party cannot enforce the instrument against anyone. Nevertheless, he may be able to successfully sue someone for breach of transfer warranty.

PROBLEM 16.9

Go back to the facts of PROBLEM 16.6 but assume that Landlord indorses the note over to Stevie Shoveler, who removes snow from Landlords property, as payment for services rendered. Stevie presents the note to Marty, but Marty, who has heard from Paula about the theft refuses to pay. What rights does Stevie have against Landlord? Would it make a difference if Landlord gave Stevie the note as a Christmas gift? Can Stevie sue Lucy on her indorser's liability? Can he sue her on any other theory?

PROBLEM 16.10

Refer to the facts of PROBLEM 16.7 , but just to make it more interesting, let's add one more party. Assume that Roger indorsed the check in blank by <u>forging</u> Kramer's signature and gave it to Nancy Naive in exchange for cash. Nancy used it for purchases at CD City and gave them the check without indorsing it (Remember she didn't have to because it was indorsed to her in blank). CD City then deposited the check at Depositary National Bank (DNB) which presented it to Steinbrenner State Bank. Assume now that Steinbrenner State Bank has recovered against Depositary National Bank on its breach of presentment warranty. Can DNB recover from CD City? On what theory? Can DNB recover directly from Nancy? Theory? From Roger? Theory? If DNB recovers from CD City, can CD City recover from Nancy? From Roger? And if CD City does recover from Nancy, can she recover from anyone? Can George, the drawer, be sued by any of these parties?

Handwritten marginalia:

Marty maker
↓
Lucy (steals)
↓
indorses to landlord
↓
indorses to Stevie
↓
presents to Marty

Roger
↓
indorsed in blank to Nancy
↓
CD City
↓
depository Bank
↓
presented to Steinbrenner

Nancy only made xfer warranty to immediate xferee

4.   *The Rights of the Payee Whose Purported Indorsement Is Unauthorized*

If the payee never received the instrument either directly or through delivery to an agent or co-payee, the payee never obtained any rights therein. Consequently, the payee would be entitled to no rights on the instrument and no right to sue for conversion or breach of warranty. However, the payee would have a cause of action on the underlying obligation, if any, for which the instrument was issued.

If the payee received the instrument but lost it or had the instrument illegally taken from him, the payee whose indorsement was unauthorized would have rights on the instrument or in conversion. In this situation, the payee *could not* sue on the underlying obligation. Section 3-310 provides that if the obligee is the person entitled to enforce the instrument but he "no longer has possession of it because it was lost, stolen, or destroyed, the obligation may not be enforced to the extent of the amount payable on the instrument. The obligee's rights *against the obligor are limited to* enforcement of the instrument"(Emphasis added.) The obligee would also, of course, have the right under § 3-420 to sue any other party who converted the instrument.

PROBLEM 16.11

Looking again at the facts of PROBLEM 16.9, what causes of action are available to Paula? On what theories could she recover from Marty, Lucy, Landlord and Stevie? See §§ 3-309, 3-310, 3-414, 3-420.

Chapter 17

UNAUTHORIZED SIGNATURES AND ALTERATIONS TREATED AS IF THEY WERE AUTHORIZED

Throughout the previous chapter, and elsewhere, we have referred to "exceptions" when unauthorized actions may be treated as if they were authorized. Treating an unauthorized signature as authorized may have many consequences. For example, a person who did not sign an instrument may be held liable as a party on it, a person not otherwise a PETE may be treated as such (which could give him standing to enforce an instrument and relieve him of possible warranty liability) and a bank that pays an item drawn on its customer's account may be entitled to debit that account even though the customer did not sign it. Treating an alteration as if it were authorized can have similarly significant results. These exceptions fall under 3 categories:

A. when an otherwise unauthorized signature is approved by a prior agreement or is subsequently ratified;

B. when a party is precluded from asserting that a signature is unauthorized; and

C. when the Code makes an unauthorized indorsement effective.

A. *Prior Agreement or Subsequent Ratification*

Sometimes parties may agree in advance that signatures that are actually unauthorized will be treated as authorized. *Case #4*, UCC Comment 2 to § 3-404, for instance, states that the drawer and the drawee may have a separate agreement that will allow the drawee to charge the drawer's account even if the drawer's signature is unauthorized. Why would the customer agree to this? For its own convenience, a customer might want to use an automated process for "signing" its checks. The drawee bank, however, may be concerned that someone who is unauthorized may gain access to the customer's check-writing machine and fraudulently issue checks that would be indistinguishable from the authorized checks. If after the bank paid those checks, the customer could prevent its account from being debited by pointing out the drawer's signatures were unauthorized, the bank could suffer a substantial loss. Consequently, to induce the bank to agree to honor checks "signed" by the check-writing machine, the customer might agree to have any and all checks "signed" by the machine treated as if they were authorized.

On the other hand, § 3-403(a) states that an "unauthorized signature may [subsequently] be ratified." UCC Comment 3 to that section emphasizes that ratification may be accomplished not only by "express statements" to that effect but through "conduct" as well. Ratification by conduct occurs, for example, when the purported signer fails to object to an unauthorized signature once he learns about it or when the purported signer keeps the benefits received in exchange for the instrument with knowledge of the unauthorized signature. A frequent effect of ratification is to hold a party liable as maker of a note even though the party's purported signature was unauthorized. Similarly, a bank customer's ratification of unauthorized signatures on items drawn on his account will allow his bank to debit the account for payments made on those items.

Although no statutory provisions says so specifically, it seems reasonable to believe that alterations could also be ratified. Thus, if a drawer examines his checkbook and sees that a check he issued for $100 was altered to $150, but purposely fails to notify the bank because he does not want the payee to get into any serious trouble, the drawer may be found to have ratified the change from $100 to $150.

B. Preclusions

The Code provides, in §§ 3-406 and 4-406, that under certain circumstances, a party may be precluded from asserting an unauthorized signature (or alteration). Each of these sections will be discussed separately.

1. Section 3-406

Section 3-406 provides that under certain circumstances a person is precluded from asserting (1) that a signature to an instrument (whether a signature purporting to be his own or a signature purporting to be someone else's) is unauthorized, or (2) that an instrument was altered. Section § 3-406 applies *against* any person whose failure to exercise ordinary care "substantially contributes to an alteration of an instrument or to the making of a forged signature on an instrument" and applies *in favor* of a person who in good faith either pays the instrument or takes it for value or collection. The party asserting the preclusion bears the burden of proving the other party's negligence. *See* § 3-406(c).

If, however, the person asserting the preclusion failed to exercise ordinary care in paying or taking the instrument, § 3-406(b) provides that the loss arising from the forgery or alteration is allocated between the two negligent parties according to the extent to which their respective negligence caused the loss. The party seeking such allocation bears the burden of proving the payor's or taker's negligence. *See* § 3-406(c).

PROBLEM 17.1

Suppose Bob and Carol Johnson are the holders of a joint checking account at First National Bank ("FNB"). Bob's failure to exercise ordinary care substantially contributes to the making of a forged drawer's signature on a check drawn on the account and honored by FNB. FNB debits the account, and Carol sues to force FNB to recredit the account, arguing that she was not negligent and should not suffer any loss because of John's negligence. Who do you think should win? See, e.g., Susen v. Citizens Bank & Trust Co., 111 Ill.App.3d 909, 444 N.E.2d 701, 67 Ill.Dec.465 (1st Dist.1982).

lose chose acct. partner

a. What Constitutes Negligence That Substantially Contributes to a False Signature or Alteration?

Section 3-406 raises two issues: (1) what constitutes "a failure to exercise ordinary care," and (2) when does such a failure substantially contribute to a false signature or alteration. The language of the Code provides little guidance as to either of these issues. 2002 Revised Section 3-103(a)(9), in part, defines "ordinary care" as, "in the case of a person engaged in business means observance of reasonable commercial standards, prevailing in the area in which the person is located, with respect to the business in which the person is engaged."

The Comments offer some additional assistance. UCC Comment 1 to § 3-406 states that

> [n]o attempt is made to define particular conduct that will constitute "failure to exercise ordinary care [that] substantially contributes to an alteration." Rather, "ordinary care" is defined in Section 3-103(a)(7) [2002 Revised § 3-103(a)(9)] in general terms. The question is left to the court or the jury for decision in the light of the circumstances in the particular case including reasonable commercial standards that may apply.

UCC Comment 2 to states that the "substantially contributes" test in §§ 3-404, 3-405, and 3-406 is intended to be "less stringent than a 'direct and proximate cause' test" that was used under the predecessor to § 3-406. That Comment also specifically endorses the analysis of "substantially contributes" set forth in *Thompson Maple Products, Inc. v. Citizens National Bank*, 211 Pa.Super. 42, 234 A.2d 32 (1967). Under *Thompson Maple Products*, the "substantially contributes" test can be satisfied by simple negligence that facilitates the making of the forgery or alteration, even though the conduct does not more directly affect the taker's or payor's decision to *take* or *pay* the instrument.

Even UCC Comment 2, however, does not state whether § 3-406 applies where a person's negligence does *not* contribute to the *making* of an alteration or a forged signature, but *does* contribute to another person's ability to succeed in his wrongful effort to convince someone to take or pay an instrument that already has been altered or that already bears an altered signature.

PROBLEM 17.2

In answering the following questions, explain whether and, if so, how § 3-406 may apply:

a. *Dan Drawer loves erasable pens because he can correct mistakes without messy cross-outs. Dan uses his erasable pen to draw a check payable to Sup-plyCo for $1,000. SupplyCo erases the words and figures written by Dan and fills in new words and figures so that the check appears to be made out for $10,000. SupplyCo presents the check to Drawee Bank, and, after Drawee Bank honors it, SupplyCo disappears. May Drawee Bank debit Dan's account for the $10,000? See Seibel v. Vaughan, 69 Ill. 257 (1873) and Harvey v. Smith, 55 Ill. 224 (1870).* Y, neg.

b. *Mary Maker issues a note for $100, with the amount written in words as "Hundred Dollars," but left a space in front of the word "Hundred." The payee filled in the space with the word "Thirteen," and transferred the note to a holder in due course, who sues Mary to force her to pay $1,300 on the note. Who should win? See Merritt v. Boyden, 191 Ill. 136, 60 N.E. 907 (1901); Yocum v. Smith, 63 Ill. 321 (1872). See also UCC Comment 3 to § 3-406, case #3.* P, neg.

c. *Bullwrinkle Billionaire hires Natasha Badenuf, whom he met at the coun-try club, as his new executive assistant without doing any background check on her. Unknown to Bullwrinkle, Badenuf had a criminal record including convictions for fraud, breaking and entering, and robbery. One night Badenuf, who has no authority to deal with Bullwrinkle's checks but who knew where he kept them, breaks into Bullwrinkle's office, steals a blank check from his locked desk, makes it payable to herself for $15,000, and deposits it into her account at First National Bank ("FNB"). FNB allows Badenuf to withdraw the money, which she does and promptly dis-appears. FNB presents the check to the drawee bank which pays it. Is the drawee bank entitled to debit Bullwrinkle's account for the $15,000? What would your answer be the same if a background check would not have dis-covered Badenuf's criminal background? See, e.g., Fireman's Fund Ins. Co. v. Bank of New Jersey, 146 A.D.2d 95, 539 N.Y.S.2d 339 (1989); G.F.D. Enterprises, Inc. v. Nye, 37 Ohio St. 3d 205, 525 N.E.2d 10 (1988).*

d. *Same facts as "c," above, except that (1) Badenuf had no past criminal record, (2) the blank checks were kept in Bullwrinkle's unlocked desk drawer, and (3) Badenuf stole them from the desk drawer during business hours. Compare UCC Comment 3 to § 3-406, case #1 to Fred Meyer, Inc. v. Temco Metal Products Co., 267 Or. 230, 516 P.2d 80 (1973).*

e. *Base Metals, Inc. ("BMI"), received a confidential message from an anony-mous source stating that one of BMI's corporate officers, who was named in the message, was altering his weekly paychecks by increasing the amounts payable. BMI ignored the message as preposterous. Nevertheless, when it received its next account statement, BMI found that the amounts on four checks, including 3 that were paid after BMI received the confidential message, had been increased. May BMI's drawee bank debit BMI's account for the full amounts that it paid on the last 3 of the checks? See, e.g., Zambia National Commercial Bank Limited v. Fidelity International Bank, 855 F.Supp. 1377 (S.D. N.Y. 1994), and West Penn Admin., Inc. v. Union National Bank of Pittsburgh, 233 Pa.Super. 311, 335 A.2d 725 (1975) (failure to inquire after learning of irregularity regarding first check)* is negligent.

f. *A corporation has its full corporate name printed at the bottom right of its checks with the intent, however, that this printed name will not serve as its signature. Instead, it intends to have two corporate officers sign each check. Nevertheless, the corporate checks contain no blank lines on which the corporate officers are supposed to sign. A thief breaks into the corporate offices, takes five of the blank checks, fills them out to cash and cashes them at Currency Exchange, which takes them for value and good faith and presents them to the drawee bank, which pays the checks. May the drawee bank debit corporation's account? See, e.g., Jacoby Transport Systems, Inc. v. Continental Bank, 277 Pa.Super. 440, 419 A.2d 1227 (1980).*

b. *What Constitutes Negligence in the Taking or Paying of Instruments?*

To the extent that the taker or payor who acted in good faith failed to exercise ordinary care in taking or paying the instrument, § 3-406 calls for principles of comparative negligence to be employed in allocating the loss.

Two statutory provisions are especially important to note in connection with the actions of taker's or payors who are banks. First, § 3-103(a)(9) states, in part:

> In the case of a bank that takes an instrument for processing for collection or payment by automated means, reasonable commercial standards do not require the bank to examine the instrument if the failure to examine does not violate the bank's prescribed procedures and the bank's procedures do not vary unreasonably from general banking usage not disapproved by this Article or Article 4.

Second, § 4-103(c) provides that:

> Action or non-action approved by this Article or pursuant to Federal Reserve regulations or operating circulars is the exercise of ordinary care, and, in the absence of special instructions, actions or non-action consistent with clearing-house rules and the like or with a general banking usage not disapproved by this Article, is *prima facie* the exercise of ordinary care.

PROBLEM 17.3

As to each of the following cases, explain whether the taker or payor exercised ordinary care in taking or paying the instrument:

a. *Customer has 15-year relationship with Drawee Bank during which time the amount of any single check drawn on the account never exceeded $10,000. One day, a check drawn on Customer's account for $100,000 is presented to Drawee Bank by Depositary Bank. The signature on the check is written in blue ink. The amount of the check is written in words and numbers in black ink in a handwriting that is distinctly different from that of the drawer's signature. See, e.g., Mortimer Agency, Inc. v. Underwriters Trust Co., 73 Misc.2d 970, 341 N.Y.S.2d 75 (1973).*

b. *Drawee Bank fails to notice or inquire into the fact that customer's husband has drawn checks on his wife's account with the brokerage firm, and Drawee Bank communicates directly with husband about the status of wife's account without any authorization from wife. Cf. Lichtenstein v. Kidder, Peabody & Co., Inc., 840 F.Supp. 374 (W.D. Pa. 1993).*

c. *Bank fails to follow its own voluntarily adopted security procedures with respect to checks drawn on customer's account. See, e.g., New Jersey Steel Corporation v. Warburton, 139 N.J. 537, 655 A.2d 1382 (1995).*

If the taker or payor does not take or pay the instrument in "good faith," then it cannot use § 3-406 against a negligent party, irrespective of any comparative negligence analysis. The expanded definition of "good faith," includes not only "honesty in fact" but also "the observance of reasonable commercial standards of fair dealing." Revised 2001 § 1-201(20).

2. *Section 4-406*

Section 4-406 deals with the relationship between a customer and his bank. As we learned in Chapter 12, when a customer opens a checking account at a bank, the customer becomes a principal and the bank becomes the customer's agent. As a consequence, the bank is typically only entitled to debit the account for payments it makes in accordance with its customer's orders. If the bank debits the account for payments it makes on items that are not properly payable from the account, then, subject to certain exceptions, the customer is entitled to have the account recredited. One of the most important exceptions to the general rule arises under § 4-406 and is known as the "bank statement rule."

a. Duty to Inspect Statements and Report Certain Irregularities

When a bank makes reasonably available to the customer a statement of account that includes or reasonably identifies items paid in support of the debit entries in the account, the customer must promptly examine that statement to determine whether any payments were improper because of (1) an alteration or (2) an unauthorized drawer's signature. Section 4-406 does not apply to payments that were improper because of the absence of a necessary indorsement.

Under § 4-406(a), a statement of account contains sufficient information if the items are described by item number, amount, and date of payment. The statement need not supply the payee's name or any date written on the item. If, based on the statement provided, the customer "should reasonably have discovered the unauthorized payment, the customer must promptly notify the bank of the relevant facts."

If a drawee bank fails to send or make available a statement of account to its customer, no part of § 4-406 precludes a customer from asserting an unauthorized signature or alteration. Nevertheless, note that the preclusive rules of § 4-406 may apply as long as the drawee makes the statement of account available even if it does not actually send the statement to the customer. It is not clear what types of restrictions a bank could impose on access to such information while still satisfying this "make available" criterion. An interesting question would arise if the bank solely made bank statements available via the internet.

PROBLEM 17.4

Marty steals two blank checks from Alex's checkbook. He makes both checks payable to cash, the first one for $750 and the second one for $800. He forges Alex's signature as drawer on the first check but forgets to do so on the second check. He then deposits the checks into his account at Second National Bank, withdraws the money and vanishes. Second National Bank presents the checks to Alex's bank, which pays them. Alex's bank sends him a statement showing that the two checks were paid and enclosing copies of the two checks.

a. *Does § 4-406 impose a duty on Alex to report that payment of the $750 check was improper because of an unauthorized drawer's signature?*

b. *Does § 4-406 impose a duty on Alex to report that payment of the $800 check was improper because of a missing drawer's signature?*

PROBLEM 17.5

Dan issues a check for $150 to the order of Paul. Benedict steals the check from Paul's desk, forges his indorsement and cashes the check at Currency Exchange. Currency Exchange presents the check to the drawee bank, which pays the check. When the drawee sends Dan a statement stating that the check was paid, and enclosing a copy of the check, does § 4-406 impose a duty on Dan to report that the bank's payment of the check was unauthorized?   *no, not aware of sig.*

Frequently, an account in the name of an "organization" requires the signature of two or more authorized persons, especially if the check exceeds some specific amount. Under § 3-403(b), the signature of an organization is unauthorized if any required signature is missing. Consequently, if the organization's drawee bank paid such a check when it bore the signature of only one authorized person, the organization's signature would be "unauthorized." Section 4-406 would therefore apply to limit the organization's ability to force its bank to recredit the account. *See* Comment 4 to § 3-403.

b. Failing to Fulfill this Duty

Suppose a drawee bank proves that, as to a particular item, the customer failed to fulfill its duty to promptly examine its bank statement and to report alterations or unauthorized drawer's signatures. If the drawee can also show that it suffered a loss because of such failure, the customer is precluded from asserting the alteration or unauthorized signature. *See* § 4-406(d)(1).

PROBLEM 17.6

a. In April of 2005, Pauly Walnuts, while working odd jobs at the home of Donna Drawer, came upon her checkbook and stole one of her blank checks. Later that day, when he got home he wrote a check payable to himself for $500 and expertly forged Donna's signature as the drawer. The next day he cashed the check at Donna's bank and set sail for Tahiti never to be seen again. The check that Pauly wrote appeared on Donna's bank statement for May, but as she does with all her statements, she filed it away without looking at it until the end of the year. On December 21, Donna informed the bank that the check written by Pauly and paid by the bank in April of that year was a forgery. She requested that the amount be recredited. Must the bank comply with her request or may it successfully raise the preclusion provided in § 4-406?

b. Tom Thief stole a blank check from Dan Drawer's checkbook and wrote a check payable to himself, expertly forging Dan's signature as the drawer. He then deposited the check in his account at Drawee State Bank, which, coincidentally, was the same bank as the one on which Dan's check was drawn. The check was paid, and Dan's account was debited, on April 7. The check was returned to Dan along with his statement on May 1, but Dan, as was his regular custom, filed the statement away without looking at it. Tom withdrew the proceeds of the check — along with the rest of the balance in his account — on July 6 and disappeared. On July 15, Dan was searching through his statements, came across the check forged by Tom and called the bank asking that his account be recredited because the check was improperly paid. The bank refused his request, citing § 4-406. If Dan sues the bank, should he win?

c. Repeated Wrongdoing by the Same Perpetrator

If a forgery or alteration was committed by the same perpetrator as to *additional* items, however, the bank may be able to prevail against its customer with respect to such additional items without proving that its loss as to such items was caused by the customer's failure to fulfill its duty to give prompt notice. Section 4-406(d)(2) applies when a bank makes a payment in good faith on any such additional other item before (a) receiving notice from the customer of the *first* unauthorized signature or alteration, and (b) after the customer had a reasonable period of time, not to exceed 30 days, in which to examine her bank statement and notify the bank as to the first item. In such cases, the customer is precluded from asserting against the bank that any such additional item contains an unauthorized drawer's signature or alteration. The bank is, in effect, irrebuttably presumed to have suffered a loss on the subsequent items because of the customer's failure to notify it promptly as to the first item. With such notification the bank could theoretically have taken measures to ensure that further unauthorized payments were not made.

The times that are critical in determining who prevails in § 4-406 problems involving repeated wrongdoing are: (1) the time the statement containing the first forged item is made available to the customer; (2) the times on which the various items are paid by the drawee bank; and (3) the time the customer notifies the drawee bank of the first or any subsequent wrongdoing by the perpetrator.

PROBLEM 17.7

Unbeknownst to him, a booklet of blank checks was stolen from Dan Drawer on March 14 by Larcenous Lenny. Forging Dan's signature, Lenny wrote a check for $100 cash, which was paid by Dan's bank on March 19. This check was returned to Dan with his statement on <u>April 1</u>, but Dan filed it away without looking at it. On April 27, Lenny wrote a second check for $200 to cash, which was paid by Dan's bank on May 2. A third check was written for $300 on May 11 and paid by Dan's bank on May 19. A fourth check for $400 was written on May 28 and paid by Dan's bank on June 4.

On June 15, Dan sat down with his April, May, and June statements to do his quarterly check-balancing exercise. He then noticed for the first time the three checks written by Louie for $ 100, $200 and $300. He then promptly called his bank and asked that the amounts be recredited.

The facts then look like this

March 14— checkbook stolen and Check # 1 written by Lenny

March 19— Check #1 for $100 paid by Drawee Bank

April 1— Statement with Check # 1 made available to Dan

April 27 — Check #2 for $200 written by Lenny

May 1 — Statement made available to Dan (no forged checks)

May 2 — Check #2 for $200 paid by Drawee Bank

May 11 — Check #3 for $300 written by Lenny

May 19 — Check #3 for $300 paid by Drawee Bank

May 28 — Check #4 for $400 written by Lenny

June 1 — Statement with Check #2 & Check #3 made available to Dan

June 4 — Check #4 for $400 paid by Drawee Bank

June 15 — Dan discovers and reports forgeries on Check #1, Check #2, & Check #3 and asks for recredit

As to each of Checks #1, #2, #3 and #4, explain whether Dan should be able to force Drawee Bank to recredit his account.

Section 4-406(d) provides very substantial protection to drawee banks. Assume that a customer does not complain to the bank within 30 days about an unauthorized drawer's signature on a small check, say for $10. If the bank thereafter in good faith pays a check drawn for $10,000 by the same wrongdoer, the customer is precluded from asserting the unauthorized signature. Based on § 4-401(a), the drawee bank could charge the customer's account, even if doing so caused an overdraft, and hold the customer liable for the overdraft. For a bank to assert the preclusion pursuant to § 4-406(d)(2), however, it seems that the bank must prove that the unauthorized signature or alteration on the subsequent item(s) were made by the same wrongdoer who signed or altered the first item.

d. Exceptions to the General Rules

There are three exceptions to the general rules. Two favor the customer so that, even if the customer fails to promptly examine her account statement and/or to notify the bank of any unauthorized drawer's signature or alteration and the bank thereby suffers a loss, she may be able to force the bank to recredit her account, at least in part. First, if the customer proves the bank did not pay the item in good faith, the customer is not precluded from asserting the forged drawer's signature or the alteration, and the bank would have to recredit the account. *See* Section 4-406(e). The bank would have to try to recoup its loss from the wrongdoer, if it can find him. The UCC defines "good faith" as "honesty in fact and the observance of reasonable commercial standards of fair dealing." *See* § 1-201(20).

The second exception, also set forth in § 4-406(e), applies if the customer proves that the bank failed to exercise ordinary care in paying the item and that this failure substantially contributed to the loss. In such a case the loss is allocated between the customer and the bank, respectively, according to the extent to which the customer's failure to fulfill her duty and the bank's negligence caused the loss. Section 3-103(a)(9) defines "ordinary care." One issue that increasingly arose prior to Revised Article 3 involved banks that adopted procedures not to verify signatures of items payable for less than certain stipulated amounts of money. Courts addressing this issue took different approaches. *See, e.g., Wilder Binding Co. v. Oak Park Trust & Savings Bank*, 135 Ill.2d 121, 552 N.E.2d 783, 142 Ill.Dec. 192 (1990) (whether practice of not verifying signatures on checks for under $1,000 was a lack of ordinary care under Former § 4-406 was a fact question that should not be resolved in connection with a motion for summary judgment); *Eason Publications, Inc. v. NationsBank of Georgia*, 217 Ga.App. 726, 458 S.E.2d 899 (1995) (fact issue existed as to whether bank's policy of not verifying commercial checks for less than $25,000). Revised 2002 § 3-103(a)(9) substantially resolves this issue by stating that such a prescribed procedure is not a lack of ordinary care if it does not "vary unreasonably from general banking usage not disapproved by this Article [3] or Article 4." *See* UCC Comment 5 to § 3-103 and UCC Comment 4 to § 4-406.

The third "exception," however, favors the bank. Section 4-406(f) provides that irrespective of whether the customer fulfills her § 4-406 duties or whether the bank was negligent, if a customer does not discover *and* report either an unauthorized drawer's signature or an unauthorized alteration within one year after the statement of account or items are made available to her, the customer is precluded from asserting such unauthorized signature or alteration against the bank.

It is not clear whether this one-year notice period applies even if the bank paid the item in bad faith. On the one hand, § 4-406(f), which establishes the one-year period, says it applies even if the bank was negligent; it does not say that it applies if the bank acted in bad faith. On the other hand, the only part of § 4-406 that refers to a bank's bad faith is § 4-406(e), and that provision merely states that if a customer proves a bank's lack of good faith, the preclusion rules of *§ 4-406(d)* do not apply. It does not state that a bank's lack of good faith affects the one-year limit of § 4-406(f)

PROBLEM 17.8

Suppose Dan, who has an account at First State Bank ("FSB"), receives a statement on April 2, 2003, showing that an altered check was paid from his account on March 20, 2003. Dan reports this to the FSB that very day (i.e., on April 2, 2003). Nevertheless, FSB refuses to recredit the account. Dan files suit against FSB on May 22, 2004. FSB argues that it should win because of § 4-406(f). Is FSB right?

When a customer is precluded from asserting an unauthorized signature or alteration because of a failure to notify within the one-year period, the payor bank is not allowed to recredit its customer's account and pursue the presenter for a breach of the presentment warranty based on that unauthorized signature or alteration. In addition, pursuant to § 4-208(c), if a drawee asserts a claim of breach of presentment warranty bused on an unauthorized signature or alteration, the warrantor may defend by proving that the drawer was precluded under § 4-406 from asserting against the drawee the unauthorized signature or alteration. Similarly, § 4-208(c) allows the warrantor to assert the preclusion afforded by § 3-406 (negligence substantially contributing) or that an indorsement is effective pursuant to § 3-404 (impostor rule; fictitious payee) or § 3-405 (employer's responsibility).

PROBLEM 17.9

Tony Tenor, the head of a "family business" in Northern New Jersey, has an unfortunate practice of writing out checks in his office in a fairly open area and leaving them on his desk. The area is often frequented by associates with criminal records, including "Michaelangelo" Vino, who has done time in prison for forgery. On many occasions Michaelangelo has plied his art and altered the amounts on checks payable to him and some of his associates. The first time Michaelangelo altered one of Tony's checks was on June 15, 2003, and he continued to do so at least once a week until Tony discovered what Michaelangelo was doing on April 7, 2005. All during that period, Tony had been receiving statements from his bank, Badabing National Bank ("BNB") that included copies of the altered checks, but Tony never bothered to look at the statements. Now Tony is requesting that his bank recredit the amount of all of the alterations and because of Tony's reputation, the bank is inclined to do so. Needless to say, Michaelangelo is not "available" to reimburse the amount due, but BNB figures that it can sue all the presenting banks for breach of the presentment warranty that the instruments were not altered. Is BNB correct? What if all the alterations were done in the past year only?

C. Code Provisions That Make Unauthorized Indorsements Effective

1. Section 3-404

When one issues an instrument to an impostor, a fictitious payee, or a payee not intended to have an interest in the instrument, § 3-404 provides generally that an indorsement in the name of the payee made by *anyone* is treated as the payee's indorsement, at least when such treatment benefits a person who in good faith paid the instrument or took it for value or for collection. The theory is that in such cases, either (a) the drawer dealt with the wrongful party (i.e., the impostor or a person who misled the drawer as to a fictitious payee) and was in the best position to avoid the loss or (b) the drawer committed the wrong herself by purposely drawing the check to a fictitious person or to one whom she did not intend to have an interest in the check. As such, the item is said to be properly payable, and the drawer rather than the drawee will have to bear the loss.

The first situation, covered by § 3-404(a), exists when an impostor has induced the drawer to issue the check to the impostor or her confederate "by impersonating the payee of the instrument or a person authorized to act for the payee." It is irrelevant whether the impostor induced the drawer in person, through the mail, or otherwise. A signature in the name of the payee, no matter who signs it, is effective as the payee's valid indorsement in favor of a person who either pays it or takes it or value or collection in good faith. Consequently, if there is no other irregularity, the check is properly payable under § 4-401, and the person who possesses the check is (1) a "holder for purposes of § 4-401(d) and (2) a person "entitled to enforce the instrument." Read § 3-404(a) and do the following problem.

PROBLEM 17.10

Fraudulent Fran solicits money from Naive Ned, representing that she is Sensitive Sally, the head of "Kindly Orphanage, Inc." Ned draws a check on First National Bank (FNB) payable to the order of Sensitive Sally and gives it to Fran. Fran fraudulently indorses the check "Sensitive Sally." After indorsing the check, Fran gives the check to Grocer, who in good faith takes it in payment for groceries. Grocer deposits the check in his account in Second State Bank (SSB). The check is then presented to FNB, which pays the check and debits Ned's account. A week later, Ned reads in the paper that a woman has been arrested for defrauding local residents. He recognizes her as the woman who claimed she was Sensitive Sally and calls the bank demanding that it recredit his account since the check was paid with a forged necessary indorsement. What result in an action by Ned against FNB based on § 4-401? Discuss also whether Fran, Grocer or SSB were parties entitled to enforce the instrument against Ned, if FNB had dishonored the check Would your answer have been any different for any of the questions above if the check was stolen from Fran before she indorsed it and the thief indorsed it in the name of Sensitive Sally?

PROBLEM 17.11

Does the case above come out differently if Ned had made the check payable to the order of Kindly Orphanage, Inc.," and Fran so indorsed it? What if instead of representing herself as Sensitive Sally, Fran truthfully identified herself as Fran, but fraudulently represented herself as an agent of Kindly Orphanage, Inc., and Ned made the check payable to "Kindly Orphanage, Inc.?"

Section 3-110(a) provides rules for determining the person to whom an instrument is initially payable. It states that this is determined "by the intent of the person, whether or not authorized, signing as, or in the name or behalf of, the issuer of the instrument." If more than one person signs in the name of the issuer and the signers have in mind different people as payees, then the instrument "is payable to any person intended by one or more of the signers." Where the issuer's signature "is made by automated means, such as a check-writing machine," the instrument is payable to the payee intended by the person "who supplied the name or identification of the payee, whether or not authorized to do so." § 3-110(b). A payee on an instrument can be identified "in any way, including by name, identifying number, office or account number." § 3-110(c).

PROBLEM 17.12

In each of the following cases, identify the person(s) to whom the instrument is payable:

a. *Dan Drawer issues a check payable to "First Insatiable Bank Account 671235." This account is held by Paula Payee. What if it had been made payable to "First Insatiable Bank Account 671235 belonging to Peter Paul," but the account really belonged to Paula Payee? See § 3-110(c)(1).*

b. *Both Arthur A. Gent and Randy Rep issue a check on behalf of PrincipalCo. made payable to "Mary." Arthur has in mind "Mary Martin" and Randy has in mind "Mary Wells."* either

Section 3-404(b) deals with cases in which an instrument is payable to a fictitious person or in which the person whose intent determines to whom the instrument is payable does not actually intend the non-fictitious payee to have any interest in the instrument. *See* § 3-404(b). In either of these cases: (1) any person in possession of the instrument is its holder, and (2) an indorsement by any person in the name of the stated payee operates as the indorsement of the payee in favor of anyone who in good faith either pays the instrument or takes it for value. *Id.*

PROBLEM 17.13

a. Agnes Accountant writes checks on behalf of her employer, Harry Attorney. Suppose Agnes makes up a phoney invoice for $850 for investigative services by Benita Baldwin (a name she invents). Agnes takes the check, indorses it in the name of "Benita Baldwin" and cashes it at a Currency Exchange. Currency Exchange presents it to Harry's drawee bank, which pays it. If Harry promptly discovers this debit and complains to the bank that the check was not properly payable from his account, can Harry force the drawee bank to recredit his account?

b. Same facts as in "a," except that Agnes indorses the check in the name "Bonita Baldwen." Can Harry Force the drawee bank to recredit his account? See § 3-404(c).

c. Same facts as in "a," except that Harry actually owed $850 to a person named Benita Baldwin, but Agnes, at the time she drew the check, had no intention that Benita ever obtain an interest in the check. Can Harry force the drawee bank to recredit his account?

d. Same facts as in "c," except that Agnes drew the check without any improper motives but, thereafter, decided she needed some extra money and took the check, indorsed it in the name of "Benita Baldwin," etc. Can Harry force the drawee bank to recredit his account?

Even if a person paid or took the instrument in good faith, he may be unable to assert § 3-404(a) or § 3-404(b) if he failed to exercise ordinary care. Specifically, if his failure to exercise ordinary care in paying or taking the instrument substantially contributed to someone's bearing a loss from payment of the instrument, the person bearing the loss (ordinarily the drawer of a check) may recover from the negligent party "to the extent the failure to exercise ordinary care contributed to the loss." § 3-404(d).

PROBLEM 17.14

Phoney Felice writes a letter to Nancy Naive, stating that she is Elizabeth Dole, former president of the American Red Cross, asking for donations. Nancy writes a check to the American Red Cross and sends it to the address stated in the letter. Felice takes Nancy's check and a few others she has received to Careless State Bank where she deposits them in an account she opens in the name of the American Red Cross. Careless does not demand any identification from her or any documentation that would authorize an account being opened in the name of that organization. Careless presents Nancy's check to Nancy's drawee bank, which pays it. When Nancy reads about Felice's scam in the newspaper several days later, she immediately demands that her drawee bank recredit her account.

Must her bank do so? If not, does Nancy have a remedy against any other party besides Phony Felice?

2. § 3-405

Section § 3-405 generally imposes responsibility on an employer for unauthorized indorsements made by those of its employees whom it has charged with responsibility regarding the instruments so indorsed. It also makes employers responsible for indorsements made by the accomplices of such employees. As to instruments payable to the employer, § 3-405 applies to indorsements in the name of the employer. As to instruments issued by the employer, § 3-405 applies to indorsements in the name of the designated payee.

Although § 3-405 does not apply to indorsements made by all employees or even by those employees who merely have access to instruments or to blank or incomplete instruments that are being stored, transported, or sent or received in the mail. § 3-405(a)(3). Nonetheless, it does apply to employees with many different types and levels of authority regarding the instruments, including those who prepare or process documents for issue in the name of the employee, those who process instruments for bookkeeping purposes, deposit into an account or other disposition, and those who supply information determining the names of payees in instruments the employer issues. *Id.*

The basic theory underlying § 3-405 is that, as a general rule, the employer should bear the loss from the employee's forgery, because the employer facilitated the forgery by entrusting the employee regarding the instrument. Section 3-405 operates to encourage employers to exercise care in selecting and supervising employees and in implementing measures to minimize the likelihood of employee forgeries. *See* UCC Comment 1 to § 3-405. Even if the employer was not negligent in these matters, however, § 3-405 places the risk of loss on the employer.

Nevertheless, the employer's liability may be reduced or eliminated if a person paid or took the instrument negligently and such negligence substantially contributed to the loss. In such a case the person suffering the loss (i.e., the employer) may recover from the negligent party to the extent that the negligence caused the loss.

PROBLEM 17.15

Sheryl Jones is an assistant to the Treasurer of the Big Business Company ("BBC"). As part of her job she prepares outgoing checks to the company's suppliers for signing by her boss, Armand Addison, and processes incoming checks from the company's customers.

a. Suppose Sheryl steals a check that was issued by BBC to one of its suppliers, forges the supplier's signature on the back, successfully presents the check for payment at First Insatiable Bank ("FIB"), BBC's drawee, and disappears. BBC promptly discovers what she has done and notifies FIB. Can FIB debit BBC's account for the amount it paid Sheryl? If Sheryl had cashed the check at a Currency Exchange and the Currency Exchange had successfully presented the check to FIB, could FIB sue Currency Exchange for breach of warranty? *responsible*

b. Suppose instead, Sheryl takes a check drawn by Notsobig Business Company ("NBC"), one of BBC's customers, to BBC as payee and indorses the check in BBC's name. (Sheryl is not authorized to do this.) Sheryl then takes the check and cashes it at a Currency Exchange. The check is presented to the bank at which NSB has an account and paid. When informed of Sheryl's actions by BBC, NBC demands that its account be recredited. Must NBC's bank recredit NBC's account? May NBC's bank sue the Currency Exchange for breach of presentment warranty? May BBC sue either the Currency Exchange or NBC's Bank for conversion? *no*

c. Assume this time, Sheryl, who has the authority to write checks for the company, writes a company check payable to one of BBC's regular suppliers, Reliable Stationery Company, to whom no money is presently owed. Sheryl leaves with the check in her purse at the end of the day intending to cash it herself, but her purse is stolen by Lightfingers Lenny who finds the check, indorses it "Reliable Stationery Company" and cashes it at a local currency exchange. The check is subsequently presented to FIB, BBC's drawee and paid. Can FIB debit BBC's account for the amount it paid out? On what theory will the bank rely? *3-404*

Just as § 3-404(c), § 3-405(c) provides that an indorsement is deemed to have been made in the name of the payee if (1) it is substantially similar to the name of the payee or (2) the instrument is deposited into a bank account in a name substantially similar to that of the payee. Similarly, just as § 3-404(d), § 3-405(b) provides that a person who did not exercise ordinary care when he paid or took an instrument, may not be able to successfully use § 3-405. If the failure to exercise ordinary care substantially contributed to someone's bearing a loss, the person bearing the loss (ordinarily the drawer of a check) may recover from the negligent party "to the extent the failure to exercise ordinary care contributed to the loss."

Chapter 18

CONSUMER ELECTRONIC FUND TRANSFERS

Technological advances have made it increasingly possible, and profitable, to transfer funds without the expenses and time delays inherent to a paper-based payment system. Many such mechanisms are additionally efficient because they do not need to be initiated by any person-to-person interaction, thus providing a substantial savings in labor costs. Yet the nature of these new procedures raises questions regarding the applicability of existing consumer protection laws. Moreover, the facts that transfers could be accomplished without any person-to-person interaction between a consumer and his financial institution and the limited technological and commercial sophistication of many consumers give rise to the need for new types of protections. To address these issues, Congress enacted the Electronic Fund Transfer Act (EFTA) in 1978 as Title IX to the Consumer Credit Protection Act, 15 U.S.C. § 1601 et seq. Pursuant to the EFTA, the Federal Reserve issued Regulation E, published at 12 Code of Federal Regulations (C.F.R.), Part 205, to explain the EFTA. The purpose of the EFTA is "to provide a basic framework establishing the rights, liabilities, and responsibilities of participants in electronic fund transfer systems." 15 U.S.C. § 1693(b) (EFTA § 902(b)). The principal objective of the EFTA "is the provision of individual consumer rights." *Id.*

EFTA's emphasis on consumer transactions is apparent from several of its statutory definitions. A "consumer" is defined as "a natural person." 15 U.S.C. § 1693a(5) (EFTA § 903(5)). An "electronic fund transfer" is defined as:

> any transfer of funds, other than a transfer originated by a check, draft, or similar paper instrument, which is initiated through an electronic terminal, telephonic instrument, or computer or magnetic tape so as to order, instruct, or authorize a financial institution to debit or credit an account (emphasis added). Such term includes, but is not limited to, point-of-sale transfers, automated teller machine transactions, direct deposits or withdrawals of funds, and transfers initiated by telephone. Such term does not include . . . .
>
> (D) any automatic transfer from a savings account to a demand deposit account pursuant to an agreement between a consumer and a financial institution for the purpose of covering an overdraft or maintaining an agreed upon minimum balance in the consumer's demand deposit account; or
>
> (E) any transfer of funds which is initiated by a telephone conversation between a consumer and an officer or employee of a financial institution which is not pursuant to a prearranged plan and under which periodic or recurring transfers are not contemplated . . .

15 U.S.C. § 1693a(6) (EFTA § 903(6)). In turn, an "account" is defined as "a demand deposit, savings deposit, or other asset account . . . established primarily for personal, family or household purposes." 15 U.S.C. § 1693a(2) (EFTA § 903(2)).

PROBLEM 18.1

Charles Customer comes into First Insatiable Bank ("FIB") with $5,000 in cash, and instructs the teller to make a wire transfer of this money to the account of Charles' nephew at a different bank in a different city. The teller takes the money and processes the transfer. Explain whether the EFTA applies to this transfer. See Wachter v. Denver National Bank, 751 F.Supp. 906 (D.Colo.1990).

not initiated by Elec. terminal

PROBLEM 18.2

Charles Customer has a savings account and a checking account account at FIB. Charles calls up FIB and speaks with Tom Teller. Charles instructs Tom to transfer $5,000 from his savings account to his checking account, and Tom does so electronically by entering the appropriate information in his computer. Explain whether the EFTA applies to this transfer. See Kashanchi v. Texas Commerce Medical Bank, N.A., 703 F.2d 936 (5th Cir.1983); Abyaneh v. Merchants Bank North, 670 F.Supp. 1298 (M.D.Pa. 1987).

What if Fraudulent Fred, posing as Charles Customer, had called up FIB and given the instruction to Tom and Tom had electronically made the transfer. Explain whether the EFTA applies to this transfer. What additional legal issue arises when it was Fred, and not Charles, who made the call? Kashanchi, supra; Abyaneh, supra.

PROBLEM 18.3

automatic

Suppose Charles has an agreement with FIB that, should he overdraw his checking account, FIB will transfer funds from Charles' savings account into the checking account to eliminate any deficit in the account. FIB honors one of Charles' checks in the amount of $7,500, thereby creating a deficit in the account of $5,000. To eliminate this deficit, FIB transfers into the checking account $5,000 from Charles' savings account. Explain whether the EFTA applies to this transfer.

PROBLEM 18.4

Suppose Charles receives his paycheck and wants to deposit it into his savings account at FIB. He walks to FIB and goes over to a teller. The teller asks Charles to swipe his bank identification card into the bank's card reading machine and, after Charles does so, the teller asks Charles to enter his PIN. Charles hands the teller the check and instructs the teller to deposit the check into his savings account. The teller takes the check and places it in one of FIB's check reading machines. The machine reads the check, adds the sum to Charles' account and prints out a receipt of the transaction. The teller hands Charles the receipt. Explain whether the EFTA applies to this transaction.

PROBLEM 18.5

Suppose that when Charles arrives at FIB to deposit his paycheck, the lobby is closed. The account agreement between Charles and FIB, however, permits him to make deposits via FIB's automated teller machine (ATM). Charles indorses the check, writes the number of his savings account on the check, places the check in an envelope, and, pursuant to the instructions provided by the ATM, he enters all of the applicable information and, at the appropriate time, inserts the envelope containing the check into the ATM. Explain whether the EFTA applies to this transaction. See Curde v. Tri-City Bank, 826 S.W.2d 911 (S.Ct. Tenn. 1992). See also Federal Reserve Official Staff Interpretation Q2-11, reprinted in 12 C.F.R. Pt. 205, Supp. II, at 130 (1991).

PROBLEM 18.6

Suppose Charles Customer is the president of Entertainment Theatrics, Inc. (ET), and ET has two corporate accounts, one a savings account and one a checking account, at FIB. Suppose Charles uses FIB's ATM to transfer $5,000 from ET's savings account to ET's checking account. Explain whether the EFTA applies to this transfer. not person ; not personal account

Now let's consider, one-by-one, the principal examples of electronic fund transfers (EFTs) to which the EFTA *does* apply.

A. *Point-of-sale Transfers/Debit Cards*

Point-of-sale transfers are transfers made by using a "debit card." A debit card is physically the same as credit card, and they both contain magnetically encoded information that is electronically read by the merchant's machine. In fact, an issuer may issue a customer a single card that can be used as a credit card or as a debit card. Its use as a credit card is governed by the Truth in Lending Act (TILA) and Regulation Z, as discussed in Chapter20; its use as a debit card is governed by the EFTA and Regulation E.

Just as with credit cards, the major actors in the debit card payment system are the consumer to whom the card is issued (cardholder), the merchant from whom a purchase is made (merchant), the financial institution that issues the card (issuer) and, usually, a network that processes debit card transactions.

The functions of credit and debit cards are different. A credit card serves as a mechanism for obtaining an extension of credit unrelated to any specific "account" that the cardholder may have in any financial institution. Each time a cardholder uses his credit card to make a purchase, he incurs debt which he must repay to the issuer at some future date. In contrast, a debit card is always related to some specific account that the cardholder has with the issuer, usually a bank. When a cardholder uses a debit card to make a purchase, he is typically drawing on the balance in his account rather than incurring any new debt. As will be explained below, the amount of the purchase is either instantaneously taken from his account or frozen in the account to be taken shortly thereafter.

> **NOTE:** It is possible for a debit card transaction to involve an extension of credit. Assume that the balance in a cardholder's account is inadequate to cover a particular purchase. Under this circumstance, an attempted debit card purchase might not be authorized. Suppose, however, that the debit cardholder has overdraft privileges in connection with his bank account. In this case, it is possible that the purchase will be approved, the account will be debited, and the negative balance treated as set forth in the overdraft agreement between the customer and the financial institution at which he has the account.

The volume of debit card transactions is growing. According to Merrill Lynch, debit card transactions increased by a 37% compounded rate from 1998 through 2001, while credit card transactions grew at a rate of under 7%.[1] And the likelihood is that such debit cards will become rapidly more popular over time.

The Mechanics of Point-of-Purchase/Debit Card Transaction

In order to make a purchase with his debit card, a cardholder must swipe his card through the merchant's card-reading machine and verify the transaction amount. In some systems, as explained below, the cardholder must then enter his personal identification number (PIN). The merchant electronically transmits this information to the issuing bank, either directly or through a network. The issuer or network ascertains whether there are sufficient funds in the cardholder's account. If there is, the issuer or network authorizes the transaction.

---

[1] Eric J. Savitz, "Profits from Debits: Concord-EFS is Reaping Rapid Growth from Debit-Card Transactions; And its Shares are Cheap," 8/19/02 *Barron's* 26, 2002 WL-BARRONS 22179017.

How does the merchant get paid? If the merchant has a contractual relationship directly with the issuer, then this contract governs how it is paid. More likely, though, a merchant will deal with either a PIN-based or PIN-less network. Many PIN-based debit cards (often referred to as "online debit cards") are associated with a network of financial institutions formed to facilitate debt card transactions. The networks provide information as to the technology the merchant must use to read the cards and to communicate electronically with the various banks in connection with the transaction. The merchant's terminal telephonically sends a message, including the cardholder's PIN, to the issuer bank, which determines whether the PIN matches the account and whether there are adequate funds in the account to cover the transaction. If so, then, absent some special circumstance, the issuer bank authorizes the transaction. It will telephonically communicate this decision to the merchant. When the issuer does so, it becomes liable to pay the merchant. The amount of the transaction is immediately withdrawn from the cardholder's account. Payment to the merchant typically occurs at the end of the day for all of the debit transactions involving the same issuer.

In addition to eliminating many of the transaction costs of a paper payment system — and some of the costs involved in the credit card collection process — this procedure, by making the issuer's liability final at the time of the sale, virtually eliminates the merchant's risk of nonpayment. Moreover, merchants get paid much more quickly than when checks or credit cards are used.

An alternative process involves a PIN-less debit card system introduced by Visa and MasterCard in the 1990's. This process involves much the same electronic authorization procedure as PIN-based systems, but the amount of the transaction is not immediately deducted from the cardholder's account. Instead, the authorization process results in a hold being place on the cardholder's account. The merchant receives funds in the same way as in a credit card transaction, and the money is then actually removed from the cardholder's account. This process generally takes a few days. Because the money is immediately frozen in the cardholder's account, this system does minimize a merchant's risks. Nevertheless, the collection process — because it involves as many steps as the credit card collection process — is much more costly than when a PIN-based network is used. Debit cards used in PIN-less systems are often referred to as "offline debit cards."

As of 2002, Visa and MasterCard controlled two-thirds of the debit card market, which, in 2001, totaled $414 billion in retail sales (compared to $1.4 trillion for all credit cards). One of the ways in which Visa and MasterCard had obtained such a dominant position was to require merchants who honored their credit cards to honor their debit cards as well.

The PIN-based and PIN-less approaches have one important thing in common. Once a transaction is authorized and payment is made, the cardholder cannot "undo" the payment by asserting against the issuer claims or defenses that the cardholder may have against the merchant. Instead, the cardholder must seek any applicable relief in an action against the merchant.

Creation of the Cardholder/Issuer Relationship

The EFTA restricts a person's ability to issue a card — or any code or "means of access to the customer's account for the purpose of initiating an electronic fund transfer" — to a consumer. As a general rule, no one may issue a new card, code or other means of access — as opposed to a renewal or substitution of an already accepted card, code or means — except in response to a request or application by the customer. 15 U.S.C. § 1693i(a) (EFTA § 911(a)). This is similar to TILA's rule regarding the issue of unsolicited credit cards. Unlike TILA, however, the EFTA expressly allows the issue of a debit card, code or other means of access even absent a request if:

(1) the card, code or other means of access is not validated;

(2) accompanying the card, code or other means of access is a complete disclosure of the customer's rights and liabilities upon validation;

(3) accompanying the card, code or other means of access is a clear explanation, complying with standards set forth in the EFTA, that (a) the card, code or means of access is not validated and (b) how the consumer may dispose of the card, code or means of access if validation is not desired; and •

(4) the card, code or other means of access is only validated on the consumer's request or application and after the consumer's identity is verified. *Id.*

Issuer's Liability for Failing to Make a Funds Transfer

Suppose a consumer properly instructs a financial institution in which it has an account to make an electronic funds transfer pursuant to the terms and conditions of the account. The general rule is that the financial institution is liable to the consumer for all proximately caused damages if the institution fails to make the transfer in the correct amount or in a timely manner. 15 U.S.C. § 1693h(a) (EFTA 910(a)). No such liability applies, however, if:

(1) the consumer's account has insufficient funds to cover the transfer, unless the reason for the insufficiency was the financial institution's failure to properly credit a deposit to the account, *id.*;

(2) the funds are subject to legal process or other encumbrance which prevents the transfer;

(3) the transfer would exceed the consumer's credit limit, *id.*;

(4) the relevant electronic terminal has insufficient cash to effectuate the transaction; or

(5) the Federal Reserve Board's regulations otherwise immunize the financial institution from liability under the circumstances, *id.*;

(6) the financial institution proves by a preponderance of the evidence that:

(a) its failure resulted from an act of God or circumstances beyond its control, and that it "exercised such diligence as the circumstances required"; or

(b) its failure resulted from a technical malfunction known to the consumer at the time he attempted to make the transfer.[2] 15 U.S.C.§ 1693h(b) (EFTA 910(b)).

If the financial institution's failure to make the transfer was unintentional and resulted from a bona fide error despite its maintenance of procedures reasonably adapted to avoid such error, the institution is only liable for actual damages proved. 15 U.S.C. § 1693h(c) (EFTA 910(c)).

Cardholder's Liability for Unauthorized Transfers

As we will see in chapter 20, TILA and Regulation Z substantially limit the liability of a cardholder for the unauthorized use of his credit card. The liability of a consumer for an unauthorized electronic transfer is *less* limited. In addition, not all consumers are aware that wrongdoers may be able to use many debit cards — the "offline debit cards" used in PIN-less systems — without any need to know the consumer's PIN. Consequently, they may not realize the importance of promptly alerting the issuer of any lost or stolen card.

An "unauthorized electronic transfer" means a transfer from a consumer's account that is initiated by a person other than the consumer without actual authority, unless the transfer inures to the consumer's benefit. The term does not, however, apply to:

(1) a transfer initiated by a person to whom the consumer furnished the consumer's card, code or other means of access to the consumer's account, unless the consumer has notified the financial institution that the said person is no longer authorized to use the account;

(2) a transfer initiated with fraudulent intent either by the consumer or by anyone acting with the consumer; and

---

[2] As discussed later in this chapter, some electronic fund transfers do not involve point-of-sale transactions but, rather, are preauthorized. A financial institution is not liable for the failure to make such a preauthorized transfer if the reason for its failure was a technical malfunction which was known to the consumer at the time the transfer was supposed to have occurred.

(3) a transfer which constitutes an error by a financial institution. 15 U.S.C. § 1693(11) (EFTA § 903(11)).

A cardholder is only liable for an unauthorized transfer if he had previously accepted the debit card, code or other means of access to the account. In addition, a consumer is only liable for an unauthorized transfer if the issuer provided him with a means by which he could be identified as the person authorized to use the account. Such means would include, for instance, a "signature, photograph, fingerprint, or electronic or mechanical identification." 15 U.S.C. § 1693(g)(a) (EFTA § 909(a)).

If the consumer reports a lost or stolen debit card within 2 business days from the time he learns of it, the cardholder's liability is limited to the lesser of $50 or the amount of the unauthorized transfers. If the consumer reports a lost or stolen debit card more than 2 days from the time he learns of it, the consumer's liability can be greater. Specifically, it is the lesser of $500 or the sum of (1) the amount of unauthorized transfers that could have been prevented had notice been given within the 2 business days, plus (2) the lesser of $50 or the aggregate amount of unauthorized transfers that took place within the 2 business days. 12 C.F.R. § 205.6.

Suppose a cardholder does not realize his card has been lost or stolen. If the issuer provides a cardholder with a periodic statement and an unauthorized transfer appears thereon, the cardholder must report the unauthorized transaction within 60 days of the issuer's transmittal of the statement. If he does not, then the cardholder becomes responsible for all unauthorized transfers after such 60 days that could have been avoided had the customer notified the issuer within the 60 days. *Id.* Since notification would probably have resulted in changing the PIN number or closing the account, it is likely that all such subsequent transfers could have been avoided.

A few miscellaneous rules provide some solace to cardholders. First, a cardholder is deemed to give notice as soon as he takes the reasonably necessary steps to provide the issuer with the necessary information. Thus, notice may be given in person, by telephone or in writing. If the cardholder mails the issuer a letter, notice is deemed to be given as soon as the letter is mailed. 12 C.F.R. § 205.6(b)(5). Second, notice is deemed to be constructively given if the issuer becomes aware of circumstances that lead to the reasonable belief that an unauthorized transfer — to or from — the cardholder's account has been — or may be — made. Third, if state law or an agreement between the cardholder and the issuer provide a lower limit as to the cardholder's liability, then the cardholder's liability is limited to such lesser amount. Fourth and finally, if the cardholder's delay in notifying the issuer was due to extenuating circumstances, both the 2-day and 60-day time limits are extended to "a reasonable period." 12 C.F.R. § 205.6(b)(4).

PROBLEM 18.7

Bob and Janet Williams each have a debit card for their checking account at First Insatiable Bank ("FIB"). On July 1, 2003, Bob realizes that his card has been lost, and he notifies FIB on July 2, 2003. Within 2 business days of July 1, 2003, one unauthorized transfer of $60 had taken place. What is the Williams' liability with respect to this $60? $50 if before notice

PROBLEM 18.8

‹ Would the answer to the previous question be any different, if Bob had sent FIB notice by mailing it a letter on the morning of July 2, 2003 (which arrived on July 4th) and the unauthorized transfer had taken place on July 3, 2003, at 10:00 a.m.?

PROBLEM 18.9

Same facts as in Problem 18.7, except that Bob does not notify FIB about his lost card on July 2, 2003. Instead, Bob notifies FIB on July 8th. By the time, Bob notified FIB, an additional $2,000 of unauthorized transfers had been made after the 2nd business day after July 1st. What is the Williams' liability with respect to the total of $2,060 of unauthorized transfers? $550

The same rules that apply to unauthorized debit card transfers apply to unauthorized transfers through the use of automatic teller machines (ATMs). The following case illustrates important aspects of the liability rules.

KRUSER v. BANK OF AMERICA NT&SA
230 Cal.App.3d 741 (Cal. App. 5. Dist., 1991)

Stone (W. A.), J.

In this appeal we interpret the language of a federal banking regulation establishing the respective liabilities of a bank and a consumer for unauthorized electronic transfers of funds from the consumer's account.

The Case

Appellants, Lawrence Kruser and Georgene Kruser, filed a complaint against Bank of America NT&SA (Bank) claiming damages for unauthorized electronic withdrawals from their account by someone using Mr. Kruser's "Versatel" card. The trial court entered summary judgment in favor of the Bank because it determined appellants had failed to comply with the notice and reporting requirements of the Electronic Fund Transfer Act (EFTA). (15 U.S.C. § 1693-1693r; 12 C.F.R. § 205.6(b)(2).)

The Facts

The facts are undisputed:

The Krusers maintained a joint checking account with the Bank, and the Bank issued each of them a "Versatel" card and separate personal identification numbers which would allow access to funds in their account from automatic teller machines. The Krusers also received with their cards a "Disclosure Booklet" which provided to the Krusers a summary of consumer liability, the Bank's business hours, and the address and telephone number by which they could notify the Bank in the event they believed an unauthorized transfer had been made.

The Krusers believed Mr. Kruser's card had been destroyed in September 1986. The December 1986 account statement mailed to the Krusers by the bank reflected a $20 unauthorized withdrawal of funds by someone using Mr. Kruser's card at an automatic teller machine. The Krusers reported this unauthorized transaction to the Bank when they discovered it in August or September 1987.

Mrs. Kruser underwent surgery in late December 1986 or early January 1987. She remained hospitalized for 11 days. She then spent a period of six or seven months recuperating at home. During this time she reviewed the statements she and Mr. Kruser received from the bank.

In September 1987, the Krusers received bank statements for July and August 1987 which reflected 47 unauthorized withdrawals, totaling $9,020, made from an automatic teller machine, again by someone using Mr. Kruser's card. They notified the bank of these withdrawals within a few days of receiving the statements. The Bank refused to credit the Krusers' account with the amount of the unauthorized withdrawals.

Discussion

. . . .

The ultimate issue we address is whether, as a matter of law, the failure to report the unauthorized $20 withdrawal which appeared on the December 1986 statement barred appellants from recovery for the losses incurred in July and August 1987. Resolution of the issue requires the interpretation of section 909 of the EFTA (15 U.S.C. § 1693g) and section 205.6 of regulation E (12 C.F.R. § 205.6), one of the regulations prescribed by the Board of Governors of the Federal Reserve System in order to carry out the purposes of the EFTA. (15 U.S.C. § 1693a(3); 15 U.S.C. 1693b(a).)

In order to show the framework of responsibility for unauthorized transactions, we set out extensive portions of 15 United States Code Annotated section 1693g, with the provisions directly applicable to this case emphasized:

> "(a) A consumer shall be liable for any unauthorized electronic fund transfer involving the account of such consumer only if the card or other means of access utilized for such transfer was an accepted card or other

mean[s] . . . of access and if the issuer of such card, code, or other means of access has provided a means whereby the user of such card, code, or other means of access can be identified as the person authorized to use it, such as by signature, photograph, or fingerprint or by electronic or mechanical confirmation. In no event, however, shall a consumer's liability for an unauthorized transfer exceed the lesser of-

"(1) $50; or

"(2) the amount of money or value of property or services obtained in such unauthorized electronic fund transfer prior to the time the financial institution is notified of, or otherwise becomes aware of, circumstances which lead to the reasonable belief that an unauthorized electronic fund transfer involving the consumer's account has been or may be effected. Notice under this paragraph is sufficient when such steps have been taken as may be reasonably required in the ordinary course of business to provide the financial institution with the pertinent information, whether or not any particular officer, employee, or agent of the financial institution does in fact receive such information.

"Notwithstanding the foregoing, reimbursement need not be made to the consumer for losses the financial institution establishes would not have occurred but for the failure of the consumer to report within sixty days of transmittal of the statement (or in extenuating circumstances such as extended travel or hospitalization, within a reasonable time under the circumstances) any unauthorized electronic fund transfer or account error which appears on the periodic statement provided to the consumer under section 1693d of this title. In addition, reimbursement need not be made to the consumer for losses which the financial institution establishes would not have occurred but for the failure of the consumer to report any loss or theft of a card or other means of access within two business days after the consumer learns of the loss or theft (or in extenuating circumstances such as extended travel or hospitalization, within a longer period which is reasonable under the circumstances), but the consumer's liability under this subsection in any such case may not exceed a total of $500, or the amount of unauthorized electronic fund transfers which occur following the close of two business days (or such longer period) after the consumer learns of the loss or theft but prior to notice to the financial institution under this subsection, whichever is less.

"(b) In any action which involves a consumer's liability for an unauthorized electronic fund transfer, the burden of proof is upon the financial institution to show that the electronic fund transfer was authorized or, if the electronic fund transfer was unauthorized, then the burden of proof is upon the financial institution to establish that the conditions of liability set forthin subsection (a) of this section have been met, and, if the transfer was initiated after the effective date of section 1693c of this title, that the disclosures required to be made to the consumer under section 1693c(a)(1) and (2) of this title were in fact made in accordance with such section.

"
 . . . .

"(d) Nothing in this section imposes liability upon a consumer for an unauthorized electronic fund transfer in excess of his liability for such a transfer under other applicable law or under any agreement with the consumer's financial institution.

"(e) Except as provided in this section, a consumer incurs no liability from an unauthorized electronic fund transfer." (Italics added.)

Section 205.6 of regulation E essentially mirrors 15 United States Code section 1693g, and in particular provides:

"(b) *Limitations on amount of liability.* The amount of a consumer's liability for an unauthorized electronic fund transfer or a series of related unauthorized transfers shall not exceed $50 or the amount of unauthorized transfers that occur before notice to the financial institution under paragraph (c) of this section, whichever is less, unless one or both of the following exceptions apply:

"
 . . . .

"(2) *If the consumer fails to report within 60 days of transmittal of the periodic statement any unauthorized electronic fund transfer that appears on the statement, the consumer's liability shall not exceed the sum of*

"(i) *The lesser of $50 or the amount of unauthorized electronic fund transfers that appear on the periodic statement or that occur during the 60-day period, and*

"(ii) *The amount of unauthorized electronic fund transfers that occur after the close of the 60 days and before notice to the financial institution and that the financial institution establishes would not have occurred but for the failure of the consumer to notify the financial institution within that time.*

"(3) Paragraphs (b)(1) and (2) of this section may both apply in some circumstances. Paragraph (b)(1) shall determine the consumer's liability for any unauthorized transfers that appear on the periodic statement and occur before the close of the 60-day period, and *paragraph (b)(2)(ii) shall determine liability for transfers that occur after the close of the 60-day period.*

"(4) If a delay in notifying the financial institution was due to extenuating circumstances, such as extended travel or hospitalization, the time periods specified above shall be extended to a reasonable time." (Italics added.)

The trial court concluded the Bank was entitled to judgment as a matter of law because the unauthorized withdrawals of July and August 1987 occurred more than 60 days after appellants received a statement which reflected an unauthorized transfer in December 1986. The court relied upon section 205.6(b)(2) of regulation E.

(2) Appellants contend the December withdrawal of $20 was so isolated in time and minimal in amount that it cannot be considered in connection with the July and August withdrawals. They assert the court's interpretation of section

205.6(b)(2) of regulation E would have absurd results which would be inconsistent with the primary objective of the EFTA-to protect the consumer. (See 15 U.S.C. § 1693.) They argue that if a consumer receives a bank statement which reflects an unauthorized minimal electronic transfer and fails to report the transaction to the bank within 60 days of transmission of the bank statement, unauthorized transfers many years later, perhaps totaling thousands of dollars, would remain the responsibility of the consumer.

The result appellants fear is avoided by the requirement that the bank establish the subsequent unauthorized transfers could have been prevented had the consumer notified the bank of the first unauthorized transfer. (12 C.F.R. § 205.6(b)(2)(ii).) Here, although the unauthorized transfer of $20 occurred approximately seven months before the unauthorized transfers totaling $9,020, it is undisputed that all transfers were made by someone using Mr. Kruser's card which the Krusers believed had been destroyed prior to December 1986. According to the declaration of Yvonne Maloon, the Bank's Versatel risk manager, the Bank could have and would have canceled Mr. Kruser's card had it been timely notified of the December unauthorized transfer. In that event Mr. Kruser's card could not have been used to accomplish the unauthorized transactions in July and August. Although appellants characterize this assertion as speculation, they offer no evidence to the contrary.

(3) In the alternative, appellants contend the facts establish that Mrs. Kruser, who was solely responsible for reconciling the bank statements, was severely ill and was also caring for a terminally ill relative when the December withdrawal occurred. Therefore, they claim they were entitled to an extension of time within which to notify the Bank. They argue these extenuating circumstances as recognized in both EFTA, 15 United States Code section 1693g(a)(2) and regulation E, section 205.6(b)(4) present a question of fact about the reasonableness of the time in which they gave notice.

The evidence appellants rely upon indicates in late 1986 or early 1987 Mrs. Kruser underwent surgery and remained in the hospital for 11 days. She left her house infrequently during the first six or seven months of 1987 while she was recuperating. Mrs. Kruser admits, however, she received and reviewed bank statements during her recuperation. Therefore, we need not consider whether Mrs. Kruser's illness created circumstances which might have excused her failure to notice the unauthorized withdrawal pursuant to the applicable sections. She in fact did review the statements in question.

Appellants cite no evidence in support of their contention Mrs. Kruser was also caring for her ill relative during the relevant time period. We need not determine whether that fact might have excused her failure to notice the unauthorized withdrawal.

Moreover, nothing in the record reflects any extenuating circumstances which would have prevented Mr. Kruser from reviewing the bank statements. The understanding he had with Mrs. Kruser that she would review the bank statements did not excuse him from his obligation to notify the bank of any unauthorized electronic transfers.

In *Sun 'n Sand, Inc. v. United California Bank* (1978) 21 Cal.3d 671 [148 Cal.Rptr. 329, 582 P.2d 920], the Supreme Court held in the case of a dishonest employee who altered her employer's checks to her benefit:

"We made clear in *Basch v. Bank of America* (1943) *supra*, 22 Cal.2d 316, 327-328, that an employer is charged with the knowledge that an honest agent would have gained in the course of a reasonably diligent examination; we explained that 'this rule reasonably imposes upon the depositor the further duty of properly supervising the conduct of his trusted employee . . . .' Sun 'n Sand's failure to discover its mistake within three years of the issuance of the first three checks thus derived from its failure to discharge with reasonable care its duty to supervise its employees." (*Id.* at p. 702.)

Although the record is clear Mrs. Kruser did nothing dishonest which led to the failure to report the unauthorized transaction, we see no distinction between the employer's inability to avoid liability by claiming it delegated that duty and Mr. Kruser's inability to avoid liability by claiming he delegated to his wife his duty to discover unauthorized withdrawals on his Versatel card.

(4) Finally, appellants contend evidence of mailing the December bank statement was insufficient to establish "transmittal" as that word is used in section 205.6(b)(2) of regulation E. They contend actual knowledge is required and rely on the Federal Reserve Board's official staff interpretation of regulation E relating to the loss or theft provision of section 205.6(b)(1). (See official staff interpretation, 12 C.F.R. pt. 205, supp. II (Jan. 1, 1987 ed.) p. 125.)

Section 205.6(b)(1) requires the consumer to notify the bank "within 2 business days after learning of the *loss or theft* of the access device . . . ." (Italics added.) The question addressed by the staff comment is whether the consumer's receipt of a periodic statement that reflects unauthorized transfers is sufficient to establish knowledge of loss or theft of an access device. The comment provides:

"Receipt of the periodic statement reflecting unauthorized transfers may be considered a factor in determining whether the consumer had knowledge of the loss or theft, but cannot be deemed to represent conclusive evidence that the consumer had such knowledge." (Official staff interpretation, 12 C.F.R. pt. 205, supp. II, (Jan. 1, 1987 ed.) § 205.6(b), p. 125.)

Here we are not concerned with the loss or theft of an access device. Rather, our question is whether the Bank has established the loss of $9,020 in July and August 1987 would not have occurred but for the failure of appellants to report timely the $20 unauthorized transfer which appeared on the December 1986 statement. (15 U.S.C § 1693g(a)(2).)

Appellants cite no authority which supports their claim the consumer must not only receive the statement provided by the bank, but must acquire actual knowledge of an unauthorized transfer from the statement. Such a construction of the law would reward consumers who choose to remain ignorant of the nature of transactions on their account by purposely failing to review periodic statements. Consumers must play an active and responsible role in protecting against losses which might result from unauthorized transfers. A banking institution cannot know of an unauthorized electronic transfer unless the consumer reports it.

The Bank has established that the losses incurred in July and August 1987 as a result of the unauthorized electronic transfers by someone using Mr. Kruser's Versatel card could have been prevented had appellants reported the unauthorized use of Mr. Kruser's card as reflected on the December 1986 statement. The Bank is entitled to judgment as a matter of law.

Disposition

We affirm the judgment and award costs on appeal to respondent.

Error Resolution

Regulation E establishes procedures that an issuer must follow to resolve any "errors." An "error" may include: (1) an unauthorized electronic fund transfer (EFT) that is initiated by the financial institution, 12 C.F.R. § 205.2(m)(3); (2) an incorrect EFT to or from an account, 12 C.F.R. § 205.11(a)(1)(ii); (3) a periodic statement that does not indicate an EFT that is supposed to be indicated, 12 C.F.R. § 205.11(a)(1)(iii); (4) a computational or bookkeeping error by the financial institution, 12 C.F.R. § 205.11(a)(1)(iv); (5) an incorrect amount of money received by a customer at an ATM, 12 C.F.R. § 205.11(a)(1)(v); (6) an EFT that is not property identified, 12 C.F.R. § 205.11(a)(1)(vi); and (7) a request by a consumer for clarification or documentation regarding an EFT, 12 C.F.R. § 205.11(a)(1)(vii).

If the financial institution receives notice of any of the above within 60 days of its transmittal of the periodic statement that first reflects it, then that circumstance is an "error." 12 C.F.R. § 205.11(b)(1)(i). The customer may provide such notice orally or in writing, but if notice is given orally, the financial institution may require the customer to give written notice within 10 days of the date on which oral notice was received. 12 C.F.R. § 205.11(b)(2).

The financial institution is not obligated to credit an account just because it receives timely notice of an alleged error. 12 C.F.R. § 205.11(c)(1). Instead, the institution has the right to conduct a good faith investigation. If the investigation is not complete within ten business days, the financial institution must issue a provisional credit. 12 C.F.R. § 205.11(c)(2)(i). After issuing a provisional credit, the financial institution has up to 90 calendar days to finish its investigation if an alleged unauthorized transfer resulted from a point-of-sale debit card transaction. 12 C.F.R. § 205.11(c)(3). As to other alleged errors, the financial institution only has up to 45 calendar days after issuing a provisional credit to finish its investigation. 12 C.F.R. § 205.11(c)(2).

If a financial institution finds that the error did occur, it must correct it within one business day of such finding. Whether the financial institution finds that an error occurred or did not occur, it must notify the consumer of its finding within three business days. A finding that no error occurred must be accompanied by a written explanation and a statement advising the consumer of his right to request the documentation the institution relied upon to make its finding. 12 C.F.R. § 205.11(d)(1). The institution can then debit the account in an amount up to the provisional credit. 12 C.F.R. § 205.11(d)(2), but the institution must notify the consumer of the date and amount of the debit and must advise the consumer that the institution "will honor checks, drafts, or similar paper instruments payable to third parties and preauthorized transfers from the consumer's account (without charge to the consumer as a result of an overdraft) for five business days after the notification." *Id.*

If the consumer reasserts the same error after the preceding requirements have been satisfied, the financial institution generally has no further responsibility. If the consumer believes that the financial institution has not complied with the requirement of the EFTA, the consumer can file suit. 15 U.S.C. § 1693m(a) (EFTA § 915(a)). The suit must be filed within 1 year of the date of the alleged EFTA violation. 15 U.S.C. § 1693m(g) (EFTA § 915(g)). If, in such litigation, it turns out that the financial institution did not engage in a good faith investigation, the consumer is entitled to treble damages. 15 U.S.C. § (EFTA § 908(e)(1)).

2. *Automated Teller Machines*

Automated teller machines provide a convenient way for customers to initiate electronic transfers. An ATM card is basically a debit card that can only be used in connection with ATMs rather than to effectuate direct purchases of goods and services from merchants. Consequently, essentially the same rules apply to the creation of the cardholder/issuer relationship, the issuer's liability for failing to make a funds transfer, the cardholder's liability for unauthorized use and the resolution of errors as apply with respect to other debit cards.

3. *Direct Deposits or Withdrawals of Funds*

EFTA also applies to prearranged and preauthorized deposits into, or withdrawals from, a consumer's account. For example, a person may arrange to have his salary or other benefits directly deposited into an account at a financial institution. Nevertheless, EFTA forbids any employer from requiring that its employees establish an account for the receipt of electronic funds transfers at any particular financial institution. 15 U.S.C. § 1693k(2) (EFTA § 913(2)).

Similarly, the establishment of an account for the receipt of electronic fund transfers at a particular financial institution cannot be made a condition of the receipt of a government benefit. Nevertheless, an employer can require that an employee open up such an account at a financial institution of the employee's choice, and a government benefit can be conditioned on a person's opening up such an account at a financial institution of that person's choice.

Preauthorized transfers out of a persons account must be authorized in writing, and the customer must be given a copy of the writing at the time it is executed. 15 U.S.C. § 1693e(a) (EFTA § 907(a)). The consumer has the right to stop payment of a preauthorized transfer orally or in writing at any time up to three business days before the scheduled date of the transfer.

If the consumer orally instructs the institution to stop payment, the institution can require written confirmation within 14 days, but it must notify the consumer of this requirement and of the address to which the confirmation must be sent at the time it receives the oral instruction.

Where preauthorized transfers from a consumer's account go to the same person and may vary in amount, the institution or the payee must provide reasonable advance notice to the consumer of the date and amount of each such transfer. It is illegal to condition the extension of credit on a consumer's repayment by preauthorized EFTs. 15 U.S.C. § 1693k(1) (EFTA § 913(1)).

The rules regarding a financial institution's liability for failing to make a funds transfer is the same as that of the issuer of a debit card. A consumer's liability for unauthorized transfers is the same as that of a cardholder for the unauthorized use of his debit card. Similarly, the rules regarding resolution of errors is the same as those that apply with respect to debit cards.

Chapter 19

COMMERCIAL ELECTRONIC
FUND TRANSFERS

Vast sums of money are electronically transferred each day in non-consumer transactions, referred to as "wholesale" transfers, that are not regulated by the Electronic Funds Transfer Act (EFTA). These transfers, which amount to more than $3 trillion *per day,* occur between and among businesses and governments. *See* Carlyle Ring, "Remarks on the Background and Development of UCITA," 8 RICH. J.L. & TECH. 2 (Spring 2001). Until the UCC Article 4A (Funds Transfers) was promulgated in 1989, the Federal Reserve's Regulation J, 12 C.F.R. § 210, was the only body of law designed to deal with these large transfers, and Regulation J applied only to disputes regarding transfers accomplished through the Federal Reserve System. By the time this casebook went to print, every state, the District of Columbia and the Virgin Islands had all enacted Article 4A. Morever, in 1991, the Federal Reserve Board amended Regulation J to incorporate most of Article 4A, and some major private fund-transfer networks have adopted those rules as well. *See* Alvin C. Harrell, "UCC Article 4A," 25 Okla. City U. L. Rev. 293 (2000).

Article 4A applies only to transfers through the banking system, not to transfers accomplished through other means such as Western Union. § 4A-103(a)(1) and Comment 2 to § 4A-104. It also applies only to transfers of funds *from* one account *to* another account. Such transfers are sometimes referred to as "push" transactions, because the order comes from the person from whose account the money originates, and the order pushes the funds from that account into another account. They are also referred to as "credit" transfers because they involve orders to credit someone else's account. Article 4A does not apply to transfers that "debit transfers" which involve orders to "pull" funds from someone else's account into the account of the person who gives the order. Comment 4 to § 4A-104. Even as to credit or push transfers, Article 4A does not apply if the customer's order states a "condition to payment other than time of payment." § 4A-103(a)(1) and Comment 2 to § 4A-104.

The National Conference of Commissioners on Uniform Laws and the American Law Institute promulgated Article 4A. In their Prefatory Note to that Article, they explain that the wholesale wire transfers covered by Article 4A are usually very different from consumer electronic funds transfers. The former typically involve truly large amounts of money, and the parties involved are ordinarily quite commercially sophisticated. The transfers, even those that involve several intermediary banks, are accomplished at great speed, often on the same day they are initiated. The transfers are designed to be effectuated at a very low cost that is largely unrelated to the value being transferred. Consequently, it is especially important that the law governing these transfers and allocating the inherent risks of loss be uniform and clear.

PROBLEM 19.1

a. *Dan Deeppockets, who lives in California, arranges for his employees to be paid by instructing the local branch of his California bank, World's Wealthiest Bank ("WWB"), to transfer, on a monthly basis, the appropriate amount of money to the accounts that each of his employees have at World's Less Wealthy Bank ("WLWB"). Does Article 4A apply to these transfers?*

b. *Dan also orders WWB to transfer $250,000 to SupplyCo's account at Acid State Bank in New York on the condition that SupplyCo submits to WWB signed receipts showing that it made certain deliveries to Dan's factory in New York. Does Article 4A apply to this prospective transfer of $250,000?*

c. *Does your answer to "a" or "b" depend on whether Dan issued his order or instruction to his bank in person, by phone, by mail, or by e-mail? See § 4A-103(a)(1).*

How Wire Transfers Are Accomplished

Suppose PayCo, Inc. (PC) wants to transfer $1,000,000 from its account at First Insatiable Bank ("FIB") to ReceiveCo, Inc. ("RC"), which has an account at All Your Money Bank ("AYM").[1] The transfer will be accomplished by a series of transactions centering on "payment orders." Article 4A calls this series of transactions a "funds transfer." § 4A-104(a).

A Simple Case

Step One

The first step is for PC to instruct FIB to pay, or to cause some other bank to pay, $1,000,000 to a specific account that RC has at AYM. Although PC may communicate this instruction to FIB electronically, Article 4A applies even if the instruction is conveyed orally or by writing. § 4A-103(a)(1) and Comment 6 to § 4A-104.

According to Article 4A:

1. PC's instruction to FIB is a "payment order," § 4A-103(a)(1);

---

[1] The funds transfer would be even simpler if RC had an account at FIB and PC were to instruct FIB to transfer money to that account. *See* Comment 1, Case #1 to § 4A-104.

2. PC is the "sender" of the payment order to FIB, § 4A-103(a)(5), and, since this is the first payment order used in this funds transfer, PC is also the "originator" of the funds transfer, § 4A-204(c);

3. Because FIB received PC's payment order, it is the "receiving bank," § 4A-103(a)(4), and because PC is the originator of the funds transfer, FIB is the "originator's bank," § 4A-104(d);

4. RC is the "beneficiary" of the payment order, § 4A-103(2); and

5. AYM is the "beneficiary's bank," § 4A-103(3).

Step Two

The next step is for the receiving bank, FIB, to decide whether to "accept" the payment order. FIB cannot accept a payment order until it receives it. § 4A-209(c). Unless the order specifies an execution date, FIB accepts a received order when it executes it. § 4A-209(a). If the payment order does specify an execution date, then FIB cannot "accept" the order until that date.

> **NOTE:** Suppose the payment order specifies an execution date, FIB executes the order before the execution date, and PC properly cancels the payment order, pursuant to § 4A-211(b), before the execution date. FIB is not entitled to payment from PC and it cannot recover any money it may have paid or may have become liable to pay to AYM. Nevertheless, FIB may be able to recover such money from the beneficiary, RC, to the extent that applicable non-UCC law regarding mistake and restitution so allows. § 4A-209(d).

Article 4A does not specifically require that a bank accept a payment order. Of course, if a bank has contractually agreed to accept a person's payment order and then fails to do so, the bank can be sued for breach of contract. § 4A-212. Section 4A-305(d) provides that, in such a case, the receiving bank is liable to the sender for its expenses in the transaction, for incidental expenses, and for interest losses from its failure to execute the order. Additional damages, including consequential damages, may be recovered from the receiving bank only to the extent so provided in the receiving bank's express written agreement. If, however, the sender makes demand for statutory damages recoverable under § 4A-305(d), the receiving bank refuses to pay, the sender can subsequently sue to recover those statutory damage and reasonable attorney's fees. § 4A-305(e). Official Comment 4 makes it clear, however, that attorney's fees are not recoverable in a suit seeking non-statutory damages.

The payment order is accepted when FIB executes it. But how does FIB execute the order? It does so by issuing a new payment order intended to carry out the payment order that it received. § 4A-301(a). In our case, FIB executes PC's payment order by sending out its own payment order to AYM, instructing AYM to credit $1,000,000 to RC's account. As to FIB's payment order:

1. FIB is the sender;

2. AYM is the receiving bank and the beneficiary's bank; and

3. RC is the beneficiary.

NOTE: When FIB executes PC's payment order, FIB becomes entitled to payment from PC, unless the beneficiary of PC's payment order is not ultimately paid or certain bank errors or other circumstances limit or eliminate the originator's liability. § 4A-402. Usually, FIB will collect payment from PC by debiting an account that PC has at FIB.

Step Three

The third step is for AYM to decide whether to accept the payment order it received from FIB and, if so, to actually accept it. If AYM, as the beneficiary's bank, accepts this payment order, the funds transfer is completed and AYM becomes liable to pay the beneficiary. Until acceptance, any credit to the beneficiary's account is only provisional. Comment 2 to § 4A-502.

AYM's acceptance of FIB's payment order does not make it liable to FIB, the sender of the payment order, or to PC, the originator of the funds transfer.

Subject to several conditions explained below, AYM, as the beneficiary's bank, accepts the payment order at the earliest of the following times:

1. AYM either (i) pays RC, as set forth in § 4A-405(a) or (b), or (ii) notifies RC of receipt of the payment order or that its account has been credited regarding the order.

However, if such notice indicates that AYM is rejecting the order or that the funds may not be withdrawn until AYM receives payment of the order from FIB, AYM has not accepted the payment order. § 4A-209(b)(1);

2. AYM receives full payment of the order from FIB, § 4A-209(b)(2); or

3. Lapse of a statutorily specified time. § 4A-209(b)(3).

NOTE: To protect itself, AYM may want to delay acceptance until it has received payment from the sender of the payment order. If it fails to receive payment before the lapse of the statutorily specified time, the only way AYM can avoid liability to the beneficiary is by rejecting the payment order.

What is the statutorily specified time? If AYM has already received payment from FIB or if FIB has an account at AYM with a balance of withdrawable funds in an amount at least equal to the amount of payment (i.e., in our case, $1,000,000), then, subject to one exception, the statutory period is the opening of AYM's next funds-transfer business day following the payment date of the order. § 4A-105(4). What is the exception? This statutory period is ineffective if the payment order was rejected before that time, or if it is rejected within (1) one hour after that time; or (2) one hour after the opening of the next business day, if that time is later.

> **EXAMPLE:** Suppose FIB sends AYM a payment order on Monday, and it is received during AYM's Monday business day and Monday funds transfer day. Assume that Monday and Tuesday are both business days and funds-transfer business days for AYM.
>
> a. If, on Monday, AYM notifies RC that its account has been redited and that notice does not indicate that the payment order has been rejected, then AYM has accepted the order on Monday.
>
> b. If AYM receives payment from FIB on Monday, but does not give notice to RC until Tuesday, AYM has accepted on Monday.
>
> c. If AYM neither notifies RC nor receives payment from FIB, and AYM has not rejected the order within one hour after the opening of its funds transfer day or business day on Tuesday, then AYM has accepted the order at the later of one hour after the opening of its Tuesday funds transfer day or Tuesday business day.

What are the conditions that can prevent operation of these rules regarding acceptance by the beneficiary's bank? First, no bank, including the beneficiary's bank, can accept a payment order until it receives it. § 4A-209(c). Second, acceptance by the beneficiary's bank is not effectuated either by its receipt of payment from the sender or by lapse of the statutory period of time if (1) the beneficiary does not have an account with the beneficiary's bank, (2) the account has been closed, or (3) the beneficiary's bank is precluded by law from receiving credits for the beneficiary's account. § 4A-209(c).

PROBLEM 19.2

Suppose the owner of a failed business contributes his building to the local municipality, Smalltown. Smalltown seeks bids from prospective buyers and begins negotiations with InterCorp, a Japanese corporation. Although Smalltown and InterCorp have a number of issues to work out before signing a contract, Smalltown demands that InterCorp, as a sign of good faith, transfer the agreed upon purchase price, $185,000, to the escrow account of a Smalltown title insurance company, TitleCo, which is held in Unpredictable Bank ("UB"). InterCorp orders its Japanese bank, Asian International ("AI"), to transfer the funds to TitleCo's escrow account at UB. AI orders UB to transfer the funds to TitleCo's escrow account at UB.

> a. *Who is the originator of the funds transfer?*
>
> b. *Who is the originator's bank?*
>
> c. *Identify each and every "payment order" that has been made with respect to this funds transfer and, as to each, identify*

   i.   *the sender;*

   ii.   *the receiving bank;*

   iii.   *the beneficiary; and*

   iv.   *the beneficiary's bank.*

PROBLEM 19.3

Same facts as in Problem 19.2. Suppose UB receives AI's order on Monday, January 2nd, during UB's business day and funds-transfer business day. UB receives payment from AI during its business and funds transfer day on Tuesday. UB neither communicates to AI that is is rejecting AI's order nor notifies TitleCo that it has credited TitleCo's account. In fact, UB has not taken any steps to credit TitleCo's account. Has UB accepted AI's order and, if so, when?

PROBLEM 19.4

Same facts as in Problem 19.3, except that UB credited TitleCo's account on Monday, January 2nd, the same day it received AI's order, but, as of Friday, had still not notified TitleCo that the order had even been received. Has UB made payment pursuant to AI's order and, if so, when? See §§ 4A-404(b), 4A-405; First Security Bank of New Mexico, N.A. v. Pan American Bank, 215 F.3d 1147 (10th Cir. 2000).

PROBLEM 19.5

Suppose BigCo, Inc., orders First Insatiable Bank to transfer $200,000 to a new account to be opened at First State Bank ("FSB") in the name of Maximum, Ltd. ("Maximum"). FSB receives payment of the funds during its business and funds transfer day on Monday and, on that same day, opens up an account in Maximum's name and credits the account in the amount of $200,000. It is now later on that same Monday. Has FSB made payment of the funds to Maximum? See First Security Bank of New Mexico, N.A. v. Pan American Bank, 215 F.3d 1147 (10th Cir. 2000).

    The simple case discussed above involved a bilateral transaction involving a direct communication from the originator's bank to the beneficiary's bank. Such communications could be sent in many different ways, such as by phone. Of course, it is extremely important that such communications be secure and reliable. Most international transactions involve use of a system known by the acronym "SWIFT," which stands for Society for Worldwide Interbank Financial

Telecommunications. On the average, the SWIFT system is used for over 2 million transmissions totaling about $2 trillion each day.

A Slightly More Complicated Case

Practical considerations make it difficult for each bank to be able to deal bilaterally with each other bank. Consequently, in a slightly more complicated case, FIB does not deal directly with AYM but, instead, accomplishes the funds transfer through one or more intermediary banks.

> **NOTE:** Why might it be necessary to use an intermediary bank? A bank will not usually carry out a funds transfer for another bank unless there is some preexisting agreement between the banks regarding the transmittal of payment orders. This agreement might, for instance, include reference to certain security systems that may be used to authenticate orders transmitted between the two banks. If there is no such preexisting arrangement between FIB and AYM, FIB might want to route the funds transfer through an intermediary which has preexisting arrangements with both FIB and AYM. See Comment 1, Case #3 to § 4A-104.

Step One still involves a payment order from PC to FIB, and Step Two involves FIB's acceptance of the payment order by its issue of a payment order to an intermediary bank (IB). According to Article 4A, FIB is the sender of this second payment order, and IB is the receiving bank.

Step Three in this more complicated case involves IB's decision whether to accept the FIB's payment order and, if so, its actual acceptance of the order. IB accepts FIB's payment order by issuing its own payment order — the third one so far in this funds transfer — with the intention of thereby fulfilling FIB's order. If IB is the only intermediary bank involved in this transaction, then IB's payment order would be made to AYM. IB would be the sender of this third payment order, and AYM would be its receiving bank as well as being the beneficiary's bank.

Variations and Permutations

In many cases, as in the examples above, a person originates a funds transfer to transfer funds to an account of another party. Sometimes, however, a person originates a funds transfer to transfer funds to the person's own account at another bank. In such a case, the originator of the funds transfer is also its beneficiary. In many cases, as in the examples above, a person originates a funds transfer by issuing an order to its bank. Sometimes, however, a bank is the originator of the funds transfer and the issuer of the first payment order. In such a case, this bank is both the originator and the originator's bank.

Transfers Via FedWire

Many multilateral commercial wire transfers are accomplished through one of two networks: (1) Fedwire or (2) Clearing House Interbank Payment System (CHIPS). Fedwire is a network used by domestic banks; it coordinates wire transfers that are effectuated via Federal Reserve banks. CHIPS is an automated clearing facility run privately by the New York Clearing House for transfers arising out of international transactions.

Let's consider how PC might accomplish its transfer to RC through FedWire.

Step One: PC issues a payment order to FIB to pay $1,000,000 to RC's account at AYM. Suppose FIB has an account (FIB's "Reserve Account") in Federal Reserve Bank X and AYM has an account (AYM's "Reserve Account") at Federal Reserve Bank Y. Reserve Bank Y has an account at Reserve Bank X and vice versa.

> **REMEMBER:** It may be useful to review a few points about the federal reserve system. The only "customers" that Federal Reserve Banks have are other banks. In addition, each Federal Reserve Bank has an account at each other Federal Reserve Bank.

Step Two: FIB accepts PC's payment order by issuing its own payment order to Reserve Bank X, instructing it to debit FIB's Reserve Account $1,000,000 and to credit AYM's Reserve Account $1,000,000.

Step Three: Reserve Bank X: (1) debits FIB's Reserve Account $1,000,000, and credits Reserve Bank Y's account $1,000,000; and (2) issues a payment order to Reserve Bank Y to credit $1,000,000 to AYM's Reserve Account.

Step Four: Reserve Bank Y: (1) executes Reserve Bank X's payment order by crediting the $1,000,000 to AYM's Reserve Account; (2) notifies AYM of the credit; and (3) issues a payment order to AYM instructing it to credit the $1,000,000 to RC's account.

Step Five: AYM accepts Reserve Bank Y's payment order and credits $1,000,000 to RC's account.

Errors and Other Mishaps in Funds Transfers:

A Receiving Bank's Liability for Improper Execution of a Payment Order

By accepting a payment order, a receiving bank, other than the beneficiary's bank, becomes liable to the originator of the funds transfer. It does not become liable to the sender of the particular payment order unless that sender happens also to be the originator. Thus, in the preceding discussion, if IB accepts FIB's payment order, IB becomes liable to PC, the originator of the funds transfer, and not to FIB. Section 4A-302 establishes standards as to how and when payment orders must be executed. Should the receiving bank fail to meet these standards, the measure of its liability is governed by § 4A-305.

If the receiving bank's breach of § 4A-302 delays payment to the beneficiary, the bank must pay interest to either the originator or the beneficiary for the period of the delay. § 4A-305(a). Additional damages are only recoverable to the extent provided in a written agreement of the bank. §§ 4A-305(a), (c). If the originator or beneficiary demands interest for the period of delay — and not for any additional damages pursuant to the bank's written agreement — and such demand is refused, then, if the originator or beneficiary subsequently sues to recover such interest, reasonable attorney's fees are also recoverable. § 4A-305(e). Official Comment 4 makes it clear that attorney's fees are not recoverable in a suit seeking additional damages.

If the receiving bank's breach of § 4A-302 results in:

> (i) non-completion of the funds transfer; (ii) failure to use an intermediary bank designated by the originator, or (iii) issuance of a payment order that does not comply with the terms of the payment order of the originator, the bank is liable to the originator for its expenses in the funds transfer and for incidental expenses and interest losses, to the extent not covered by subsection (a), resulting from the improper execution. § 4A-305(b).

Additional damages are only recoverable to the extent provided in a written agreement of the bank. § 4A-305(b), (c). If the originator demands damages to which it is entitled under these Sections 4A-305(a) or (b) and the bank refuses this demand, and the originator sues to recover these damages, reasonable attorney's fees are also recoverable. § 4A-305(e). Official Comment 4 makes it clear, however, that attorney's fees are not recoverable in a suit seeking additional damages pursuant to the bank's written agreement.

May a receiving bank be liable under common law or statutory theories that go beyond § 4A-305? While courts are in agreement that Article 4A preempts some such theories, it does not preempt all of them. Thus, at least one court has held that a receiving bank which accepts a payment order — and payment of that order — with knowledge that the funds constituting the payment were stolen (or with bad faith that is tantamount to such knowledge) may be liable for common law conversion. *See Regions Bank v. Provident Bank, Inc.*, 345 F.3d 1267, 2003 WL 22158774 (11th Cir. 2003)(finding, however, that no such knowledge or bad faith was proven). On the other hand, consider the next case, which discusses whether a negligent receiving bank may be liable for consequential damages even though such damages are unavailable under § 4A-305.

MOODY NAT. BANK v. TEXAS CITY
DEVELOPMENT LTD., CO.
Court of Appeals of Texas, Houston (1st Dist.)
46 S.W.3d 373 (2001)

JENNINGS, J.

Appellant, Moody National Bank, challenges a damages award based on the jury's finding that the bank was negligent when it erroneously informed the parties it had not received a wire transfer of funds. We are asked to determine whether this funds transfer gone awry fell within the scope of Article 4A of the Texas Business and Commerce Code . . . thus preempting a common law negligence claim. We conclude that it does, and we reverse.

. . . .

The parties do not disagree about the essential facts underlying this dispute. The owners of an out-of-business Holiday Inn donated the property to Texas City. A city agency sought proposals from various sources to develop the property. Xenos Yuen formed TCD to acquire title to the property, intending to open an amusement park on the premises. Yuen knew the city agency's representative, Douglas Hoover, from previous business dealings, and submitted his proposal to Hoover. Of the various proposals it received, the city found Yuen's the most appealing; in the summer of 1995, it passed a resolution authorizing Hoover to negotiate with TCD regarding the sale of the property. Although they negotiated for several months, TCD and Hoover never developed a contract for sale.

Originally, the city had intended to give away the property, not sell it. However, after it spent $156,108.10 to remove asbestos from the building, it decided to sell it for that amount. TCD sought investors to help it acquire title and develop the property. Sinotrans, a Hong Kong company owned by Yuen and his brother, agreed to provide the money to buy the property in exchange for a 25% ownership share of TCD. Hopu, a Taiwanese company experienced in building amusement parks, agreed to invest $2.3 million in the project in exchange for a 75% ownership share of TCD.

In November 1995, Hoover asked TCD to demonstrate its seriousness and good faith by depositing the purchase price in a Stewart Title Co. escrow account at Moody Bank. Yuen arranged for the Bank of East Asia to wire transfer $156,108.10 to Stewart Title's account at the bank. The transfer order was received, and the money credited to Stewart Title's account on December 4, 1995. Both Stewart Title and Yuen, however, were erroneously informed that the wire transfer had not been received.

Over the next couple of days, Yuen and Don Lera, a Stewart Title representative, made numerous calls to the bank about whether the funds had been transferred. Sandra Messinger, the bank's wire transfer clerk, repeatedly told Lera that the bank did not have the funds and did not know where they were.

Each time he called, Lera asked Messinger to look for a transfer amount of $150,000 or $151,000. When Yuen was on the line, he told Messinger the money was important and that a land deal would fall through if it were not located. Messinger testified she did not mention the wire transfer to Stewart Title for $156,108.10 when Yuen was also on the phone, because that information was confidential. Yuen, however, contends he mentioned that precise amount. Messinger did not pull up Stewart Title's account history, or look for all wire transfers the bank received on December 4. Had she done so, she would have seen that only one wire transfer came in, it was for $156,108.10, and it was deposited into Stewart Title's account. Lera did not ask to speak to Messinger's supervisor. Although Messinger suggested that Yuen initiate a trace of the transfer, he never did so.

When Yuen attempted to buy the property on December 6, Hoover refused to close the deal because Stewart Title told Hoover it had not received the money. The minutes of the council meeting that followed on the heels of Hoover's meeting with Yuen shows that Hoover thought this turn of events might be best for the city. Hoover noted Yuen was continuing to press points Hoover thought had been finally settled. Yuen discovered a month later that the money had been in Stewart Title's account all along, and tried again to buy the property; by then, the city had made other arrangements and it was too late.

TCD sued Moody Bank and Stewart Title for negligence, gross negligence, breach of contract, DTPA violations, and breach of fiduciary duty. Before trying the case to a jury, the trial court directed a verdict in favor of the bank and the title company on all causes of action except negligence against both, and breach of fiduciary duty against Stewart Title. The court denied Moody's motion for directed verdict based on Article 4A preemption. The jury found that both the bank and the title company were negligent, apportioned fault at 45% and 55% respectively, and found that the title company breached its fiduciary duty to TCD. The trial court denied the bank's motions for judgment notwithstanding the verdict and new trial.

TCD and Stewart Title settled before appeal. Moody now appeals the award of $302,981.44 in damages against it based on negligence. On appeal, it argues the negligence claim was preempted by Article 4A of the Texas Business and Commerce Code, it owed no duty to TCD, and 'capital investments lost' is not a proper measure of damages.

The Scope of Article 4A

In its first issue presented for review, Moody contends TCD's negligence claim was preempted by Article 4A. Funds transfers are governed by Article 4A, which Texas adopted from the Uniform Commercial Code in 1993. Section 4A.104 defines a 'funds transfer' as

> [T]he series of transactions, beginning with the originator's payment order, made for the purpose of making payment to the beneficiary of the order. The term includes any payment order issued by the originator's

bank or an intermediary bank intended to carry out the originator's payment order. A funds transfer is completed by acceptance by the beneficiary's bank of a payment order for the benefit of the beneficiary of the originator's payment order.

Tex. Bus. & Com.Code Ann. § 4A.104(1) [UCC § 4A-104(a)] (Vernon 1994). The funds transfer here was completed when Moody Bank received payment of the entire amount of the order. See id. at § 4A.209(b) (Vernon 1994) . . . .

No Texas case addresses the scope of Article 4A. Relying on virtually the same federal cases, both parties note that Article 4A has never been interpreted to preempt all common law claims; it is intended only to bar those claims that would be inconsistent with any of the article's provisions. Tex. Bus. & Com.Code Ann. § 4A.102, UCC cmt. (Vernon 1994); see also *Sheerbonnet, Ltd. v. American Express Bank, Ltd.,* 905 F.Supp. 127, 131 [28 UCC Rep Serv 2d 330] (S.D.N.Y.1995); *Impulse Trading, Inc. v. Norwest Bank Minnesota, N.A.,* 907 F.Supp. 1284, 1289 [29 UCC Rep Serv 2d 1283] (D.Minn.1995); *Grain Traders, Inc. v. Citibank, N.A.,* 160 F.3d 97, 100 [36 UCC Rep Serv 2d 1141] (2nd Cir.1998).

The bank argues that TCD's complaint falls squarely within the parameters of Article 4A, thus its claim for negligence is preempted. TCD contends article 4A does not apply and therefore the claim is not preempted because (1) the bank's negligence occurred after the funds transfer was complete; (2) TCD had no relationship to the funds transfer-i.e., it was neither an originator nor a beneficiary of the funds transfer; and (3) Article 4A does not specifically address the subject matter of TCD's complaint.

Timing

We cannot agree that the acts complained of were not preempted merely because they occurred after acceptance of the funds. Section 4A.404(b) requires a bank to follow instructions to notify the beneficiary [FN3] when it accepts a payment order, and provides a remedy if the bank does not do so. Tex. Bus. & Com.Code Ann. § 4A.404(b) (Vernon 1994). A beneficiary may also recover consequential damages if the bank had notice of such damages and wrongfully refused to pay after demand. Id. at § 4A.404(a) (Vernon 1994). These provisions necessarily contemplate that a bank may be liable for acts that occur after funds are received, specifically, for failing to notify the beneficiary, as occurred here. Moreover, the authority TCD cites for the proposition that its common law remedy for the bank's conduct is not preempted because it happened after acceptance of the funds does not so hold. It was not the timing of the conduct that was at issue in either case; rather, it was whether the complained-of conduct bore any relationship to the funds transfer. See Centre Point, 913 F.Supp. at 207-08 (holding advice regarding rollover account unrelated to funds transfer); Impulse Trading, 907 F.Supp. at 1289 (holding advice regarding rupee/dollar exchange unrelated to funds transfer); Sheerbonnet, 905 F.Supp. at 136 (concluding bank engaged in self-dealing to appropriate funds to pay debt owed by insolvent transferee bank). Here, the conduct complained of was clearly related to the funds transfer.

TCD's Relationship to the Funds Transfer

After listing the parties to the transaction and their respective roles, TCD argues it was outside the scope of Article 4A as a matter of law because it had no relationship to the funds transfer. It bases this argument on what it contends the bank argued on appeal, that Yuen was the 'sender' or 'originator' of the wire transfer. What the bank actually argued was that 'Xenos Yuen or one of the corporations he was associated with' was the sender or originator. Moreover, although TCD again relies on Centre Point and Impulse Trading to support its argument that it was not a party to the transaction, neither case addresses this issue. By exercising jurisdiction over this case, it is evident the trial court made an implied finding of fact that Yuen was acting on behalf of TCD when he originated the funds transfer. Thus, TCD was a sender whose rights and remedies are governed by Article 4A.

Subject Matter of TCD's Complaint

Finally, we must decide whether the subject matter of TCD's complaint is addressed with sufficient specificity in Article 4A to preclude a negligence claim. The facts in this case do not readily identify it as one in which the complaint is clearly outside the scope of Article 4A, as is true in Centre Point, 913 F.Supp. at 207-8 (holding advice regarding rollover account unrelated to funds transfer) and in Impulse Trading, 907 F.Supp. at 1289 (holding advice regarding rupee/dollar exchange unrelated to funds transfer). Nor do the facts readily identify the case as one unquestionably addressed by a particular provision of Article 4A. *See Aleo Int'l, Ltd. v. Citibank, N.A.,* 612 N.Y.S.2d 540, 541 (N.Y.Sup.Ct.1994) (showing provision of statute was directly on point); *Corfan Banco Asuncion Paraguay v. Ocean Bank,* 715 So.2d 967, 970 (Fla.Ct.App.1998) (applying 'clear and unambiguous terms' of statute to complaint); *cf.* Sheerbonnet, 905 F.Supp. at 136 (concluding that because none of Article 4 A's provisions directly addressed claim for conversion, claim not preempted).

Common law claims are precluded when a claim would impose liability inconsistent with any of the Article's provisions. Grain Traders, Inc., 160 F.3d at 103. The official commentary provides in regard to the drafting of Article 4A:

> Funds transfers involve competing interests-those of the banks that provide funds transfer services and the commercial and financial organizations that use the services, as well as the public interest. These competing interests were represented in the drafting process and they were thoroughly considered. The rules that emerged represent a careful and delicate balancing of those interests and are intended to be the exclusive means of determining the rights, duties and liabilities of the affected parties in any situation covered by particular provisions of the Article. Consequently, resort to principles of law or equity outside of Article 4A

is not appropriate to create rights, duties and liabilities inconsistent with those stated in the Article.

Tex. Bus. & Com.Code Ann. § 4A.102, UCC cmt . . . . The bank characterizes the mistake as a notification issue, and we agree.

When we apply the rules of statutory construction, and consider the purposes for which Article 4A was drafted, we conclude it applies here even though the precise nature of the mistake the bank made here is not specifically set out in the statute. Whatever the reason for the mistake — funds not received at all, funds lost, funds credited to the wrong account, or, as here, funds erroneously reported as not received — the outcome would have been the same: Stewart Title would have told Hoover the funds were not received, and the deal would have fallen through. We conclude that this is the sort of circumstance the notification portion of the statute was intended to address; as such, it is governed by Article 4A. See Tex. Bus. & Com.Code Ann. § 4A.404(b).

Misinforming the parties was tantamount to failing to send proper notice. A bank's duty to notify a beneficiary when it deposits a funds transfer is set out as follows:

> If a payment order accepted by the beneficiary's bank instructs payment to an account of the beneficiary, the bank is obliged to notify the beneficiary of receipt of the order before midnight of the next funds transfer business day following the payment date. *Id* . . . . In addition, the remedy is set out in this section. If the bank does not properly notify a beneficiary of a payment order it has accepted, it must pay interest to the beneficiary on the amount of the payment order from the day notice should have been given until the day the beneficiary learned of receipt of the payment order by the bank. *Id.*

We hold that TCD was limited to the remedies in Article 4A, and was not entitled to recover under a common law negligence claim . . . .

Payment Order Discrepancies Between the Account Number and the Beneficiary's Name

Suppose a payment order states both the account number into which the money is to be transferred and the name of the person into whose account the money is to be transferred — and there is a discrepancy; the account belongs to someone else. Is the receiving bank liable if it transfers the money into the specified account? Section 4A-207 implicitly acknowledges that receiving banks typically ignore the name of the beneficiary and pay attention only to the account number, and it implicitly approves this practice. Section 4A-207 provides that, as a general rule, if the beneficiary's bank does not know of the discrepancy and credits the given account number, it is entitled to payment on the payment order, and the loss is borne by the party who made the error. Nonetheless, if there is a material dispute as to the whether the receiving bank knew of the discrepancy, the receiving bank will not prevail on a motion for summary judgment but, instead, the matter must be resolved at trial. *See First Security Bank of New Mexico, N.A. v. Pan American Bank*, 215 F.3d 1147 (10th Cir. 2000).

If the receiving bank is not liable and the originating bank erroneously executed the payment order, e.g., by mistyping the account number when it sent its own payment order to the receiving bank, then the originating bank will be liable. § 4A-207(b)(1). On the other hand, the discrepancy might not be the originating bank's fault. An originator may be duped into thinking that a particular account was in a different person's name and, therefore, may have mistakenly provided the discrepant information to the originating bank. Or the originator may have simply been careless in providing the account number, If so, the customer — and not either of the banks — will bear the loss. Of course, a receiving bank, an originating bank or an originator that would bear the loss from payment to the wrong party may try to recover the money from the person's whose account was erroneously credited under the law of mistake and restitution.

Other Originating Bank Errors

Various types of errors can and do arise in funds transfers for which the originator is not liable. For example, suppose an originator issues a payment order instructing its bank to pay $1,000,000, but the originator's bank erroneously issues a payment order for $10,000,000. The bank cannot recover the extra $9,000,000 from the originator. Similarly, if the originator's bank issues a payment order and then erroneously issues a duplicate payment order, it is only entitled to one payment from the originator. In both cases, the bank can only seek recovery of the excess payment from the beneficiary of the erroneous order to the extent allowed by the law of mistake and restitution. § 4A-303(a).

Suppose an originator orders payment to one person, but the originator's bank or an intermediary bank orders payment to the wrong person and that wrong person is paid. The bank that issued the erroneous payment order is not entitled to payment on the order it received (because it did not accurately execute the order it received) and none of the senders of prior orders in this funds transfer are liable to pay on their orders. § 4A-303(c). The bank that issued the erroneous order, however, is liable to the bank that received and executed its erroneous order and can only seek to recover its money from the beneficiary of its erroneous order.

Nevertheless, suppose an originator specifies a particular intermediary bank through which the funds transfer is to be routed. The originator's bank is obligated to comply with this instruction. § 4A-302. Suppose the specified intermediary bank issues a payment order to the wrong beneficiary. Although the originator's bank is not obligated to make payment to the intermediary bank in such a case, suppose it has already done so and the intermediary bank has suspended payments or is prohibited by law from refunding payments. In such a case, the originator must pay the originator's bank and is subrogated to that bank's rights against the specified intermediary bank. § 4A-402(e). Any bank that issues a payment order and specifies for the first time that the funds transfer be routed through a particular intermediary bank is treated the same way as an originator who specifies such a bank.

Unauthorized Payment Orders

Suppose a person designated in a payment order as its sender did not in fact authorize the payment order. The person may nonetheless be legally bound by the payment order if (1) the person who did authorize the payment order had actual, implied or apparent authority to do so on behalf of the designated sender, (2) the designated sender ratified the act, or (3) the designated sender is estopped from asserting that the order was unauthorized. § 4A-202(a) and Comment 1 to § 4A-203.

Agency law and equity, however, provide only limited protection. Typically, the originator's payment order is electronically communicated to the originator's bank, and it is often impossible to ascertain the identity of the person who sent the order. The customary practice, to ensure that the communication is authorized, is to employ security procedures, agreed to by the customer and bank, using codes or identifying numbers or words, encryption, callback procedures, or other devices. § 4A-201. If the originator's bank accepts the payment order in good faith and verifies its authenticity by using the designated security procedure and the procedure is a commercially reasonable method of protecting against unauthorized payment orders, the order is effective as that of the customer, § 4A-202(b), unless § 4A-203, see below, applies. The commercial reasonableness of a security system is a question of law to be determined by considering a variety of factors identified by § 4A-202(c).

In order to defeat a commercially reasonable security system, a person might well require inside information regarding the applicable technology. Section 4A-203 basically provides that the customer is not liable for such an unauthorized transfer if it can prove that it was not responsible for allowing the wrongdoer to get that information. Specifically, it states that the customer is not liable if it proves that the unauthorized order was not directly or indirectly caused

> by a person (i) entrusted at any time with duties to act for the customer with respect to payment orders or the security procedure, or (ii) who obtained access to transmitting facilities of the customer or who obtained, from a source controlled by the customer and without authority of the receiving bank, information facilitating breach of the security procedure, regardless of how the information was obtained or whether the customer was at fault. § 4A-203.

Because an unauthorized payment order is likely to involve a considerable sum, the receiving bank is likely to engage in an internal investigation, and bank examiners and police or FBI authorities may thoroughly investigate the incident. Evidence developed by such investigations may be available to enable the designated sender to carry its burden of proof.

If a bank's customer is not responsible for an unauthorized payment order issued by the bank, the bank must refund any payment received from the customer in connection with the payment order and must pay interest from the time the bank received payment until the time of the refund. § 4A-204(a). Nevertheless, the customer loses the right to interest if it fails to exercise ordinary care to determine that the payment order was unauthorized and to so notify the bank within a reasonable time not to exceed 90 days after the customer was notified that the bank accepted the order or that the customer's account was debited based on the order.

Chapter 20
CREDIT CARDS

This Chapter addresses: (1) the evolution of credit cards; (2) the basic laws governing consumer credit cards; and (3) the principal issues that arise between a bank that issues a card and a consumer to whom the card is issued.

I. *Evolution of Credit Cards*

Sometimes a merchant is unwilling to rely on a customer's personal check, especially if the check is drawn on a distant bank, for fear that the customer's account lacks sufficient funds. Similarly, sometimes a customer wants to purchase an item even though he knows that his account currently lacks sufficient funds; he wants to buy "on credit."

Of course, it would be *theoretically* possible for a store to evaluate a customer's creditworthiness each time he wants to make a purchase. But this would require the customer to complete detailed forms and the store to verify the customer's information expeditiously and make a credit decision at the time of each purchase. Such a procedure would be too cumbersome and inconvenient to be practical. Instead, in the early twentieth century, some retail stores began offering "charge cards" (originally known as "charge plates," possibly because the cards were made of metal), which customers could apply for in advance and with which customers could make purchases at the particular retail store — or at any of that store's outlets. This permitted the store to evaluate the customer's application in advance and to come to a deliberate decision as to whether it would extend credit to particular customers. Because this type of retailer-issued card is to be used only at the issuer's stores, the cards are called "proprietary cards."

Because a separate card was needed for each store, a person might have to apply for and carry many different charge cards. To address this problem, a new kind of card, the "universal card," was introduced. Universal cards could be used at stores other than those of the issuer. In fact, the issuer might not own any stores. Instead, the issuer would convince stores to honor its cards and would enter into separate contracts with each store that agreed to do so. When "universal cards" were initially issued in the 1950s, they were universal in name only, because there were many businesses that did not accept them. The first universal cards were intended for travel and entertainment expenses (and are sometimes referred to as "travel and entertainment" or "T & E" cards), because such expenses were frequently incurred by people from "out-of-town" with whom merchants therefore had no past dealings. Rather than take the personal checks of such "strangers," merchants preferred to rely on the more established creditworthiness of the card's issuer. Among the most famous of the early

T & E cards were the Diner's Club Card, first issued in 1949, and the American Express Card, which came out in 1958.

By the 1960s, banks began to realize that they could profitably parlay their own creditworthiness, and promote their traditional business of money-lending, by issuing universal cards. Although cardholders of proprietary cards and of early universal cards were expected to make full payment at the end of each month, issuers, and especially bank issuers, began to offer different terms, allowing cardholders to pay over time, but with interest. This functional change in the way cards were used is reflected by the fact that "charge cards" became known as "credit cards." The first major bank issued card was issued by Bank of America under the name BankAmericard in 1966. A year later, in 1967, a consortium of banks, the Interbank Card Association, issued MasterCard. Bank of America reorganized its credit card business in 1970 and replaced BankAmericard with VISA. Today, although there are many universal credit card issuers, MasterCard and VISA continue to dominate the field.

This chapter will describe the basic elements of a consumer credit card transaction, survey the statutes and regulations that apply thereto, and focus on specific legal issues pertaining to the cardholder-issuer relationship.

Elements of a Consumer Credit Card Transaction

Use of proprietary credit cards is a bilateral transaction between the customer using the card (the "cardholder") and the store that issued the card (the "issuer"). Use of universal cards is more complicated and involves a trilateral transaction, at least, among the cardholder, the issuer and the merchant whose goods or services the cardholder uses the card to obtain. By explaining the universal card paradigm, we will also cover all of the interesting aspects of a proprietary card deal.

The Simple Case

We will start by discussing a simple, streamlined scenario involving three parties: the issuer, the cardholder and the merchant. *See* Figure 20-1. Afterwards, we will discuss the few extra issues that arise in the more common, and complicated, scenario.

FIGURE 20-1

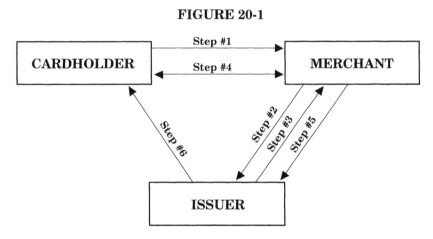

The Steps

One:

The transaction begins with the cardholder's attempt to use his credit card account to purchase goods or services from the merchant. The cardholder must provide the merchant with information regarding his account. In a face-to-face transaction — such as when he checks out at the grocery store — the cardholder will swipe his card in one of the merchant's machines which will read the magnetically embedded information in the card. If the transaction is not face-to-face — e.g., it takes place over the phone or through the internet — the cardholder will give the merchant information in a different way — e.g., orally or by e-mail.

Two:

The merchant seeks the issuer's authorization of the transaction by communicating with the issuer and providing it with encrypted information, including the card number, its expiration date, the transaction amount, and the merchant's location and Standard Industry Classification code. In typical face-to-face transactions, the same machine that reads the cardholder's card communicates this information to the issuer via modem. If the transaction is authorized, a specific authorization number is attached to it.

Three:

The issuer will evaluate this information, usually by using a computer program, to determine whether to authorize the transaction. For example, the issuer will ascertain whether the account is still open and valid, whether cardholder has exceeded his credit limit, and whether the nature of the purchase is consistent with the cardholder's prior purchases.

Four:

If the transaction is authorized, the merchant consummates the sale and generates a sales slip containing the relevant information, especially regarding the cardholder's account, the amount of the sale, and the authorization number of the transaction. In a face-to-face transaction, the merchant typically obtains the customer's signature on this slip.[1]

Five and Six:

The final two steps may take place in any particular order.

In step five, the merchant uses the sales slip to demand payment from the issuer. In step six, the issuer bills the cardholder for the amount of the purchase.

Benefits to Participants

Cardholders who do not have enough money currently in their checking accounts for a particular purchase (or cash advance) benefit from credit cards because they enable them to borrow money from the issuer efficiently and — if they pay back on time — on an interest-free basis. Even cardholders who do have money enjoy the fact that their credit cards are accepted by merchants who might be unwilling to take their personal checks. Sometimes there is an additional sweetener for cardholders, because issuers may rebate to them a small fraction of the total amount that they charge on the card.

Merchants benefit from credit cards because they increase reliably collectible sales. As already noted, cards essentially provide cardholders with a line of credit from their issuers, enabling cardholders to make extra purchases and merchants to make more sales. Also, as noted, by allowing the merchant to collect from the issuer, the cards make collection more reliable. In addition, the fact that cardholders have credit cards makes it much easier for them to make spontaneous purchases.

---

[1] Sometimes the slip will contain an express promise by the cardholder to be responsible to pay the amount set forth on the slip.

The issuer benefits in several ways. Some issuers charge cardholders a fixed annual fee, while others charge interest on unpaid balances, late fees and fees for exceeding one's credit limit. Similarly, issuers customarily do not pay merchants the full face value of the cost of the goods or services that were charged. Instead, these issuers retain a small, agreed-upon percentage as compensation for the risk they take in connection with the amount charged. The agreement may provide for this percentage to vary based on factors relevant to the issuer's risk and convenience. For example, because certain types of long-distance transactions (such as via the phone or internet) may entail greater risk of fraud than face-to-face transactions, the agreement between the issuer and the merchant may include larger discounts for long-distance transactions.

The More Complicated Case

In practice, credit card transactions usually include a few more participants than those named in the simplified case discussed above. See Figure 20-2. There is usually a separate entity — a network of banks — that is responsible for the issue of a major universal credit card. Visa and MasterCard are the largest networks. These networks are not-for-profit organizations whose primary functions are: (1) to serve as a clearance network for their respective credit cards; and (2) to promote advertising, research and other common interests in a coordinated manner. To obtain the card, the cardholder must enter into an agreement with one of the banks that belongs to the network. This is the "issuing bank." In order to collect payments for purchases made with the cards, a merchant must also have an agreement with one of the banks (called the "merchant bank"), which is a member of that card's network. This agreement will cover a number of issues, including the discounts to which the merchant bank is entitled for its risk and inconvenience in connection with processing the credit card transactions. (These are the same discounts to which the "issuer" was entitled in the Simple Case discussed above.)

FIGURE 20-2

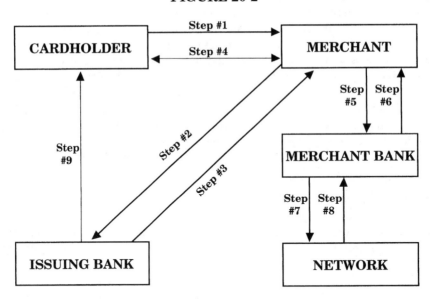

The Steps

One Through Four

Just as in the simple case: (1) the transaction begins with the cardholder's attempt to use the card to purchase goods or services; (2) the merchant attempts to obtain authorization, in this case from the issuing bank; (3) the issuing bank decides whether to provide authorization; (4) if the authorization is given, the merchant permits the transaction to proceed and generates a sales slip.

Five

The merchant attempts to collect payment by submitting the sales slips — usually via a single electronic message describing all of the relevant transactions — to the merchant bank. Typically, this is done on a daily basis.

Six

The merchant bank pays the merchant an amount equal to the gross amount of the sales slips minus the discounts as set forth in the agreement between the merchant and the merchant bank.

Seven

In order to receive payment to it, the merchant bank then submits the slips — usually via a single electronic message describing all of the relevant transactions — to the network for the relevant credit card.

Eight

The network assesses a service fee (an "interchange fee") to the merchant bank, but credits to the merchant bank's account the difference between the gross amount of the sales slips minus this interchange fee. The network then sorts the transactions according to issuing banks and debits each such issuing bank the amount that was credited for such transactions to the merchant banks.

Nine

The issuing banks sort the transactions and bill each cardholder on a monthly basis.

Benefits to Participants

The benefits to the cardholder and merchant are essentially the same as described in the Simple Case, with the issuing bank and the merchant bank "sharing" the difference between the face amount of the charges and the amount paid to the merchant. The issuing bank, of course, also enjoys the other benefits of the issuer in the Simple Case, namely, any annual fees, interest, or other charges imposed on the cardholder.

II. Basic Applicable Law: the Truth in Lending Act

Initially, the rights and responsibilities of the various participants in credit card transactions were governed almost exclusively by state contract law. There were some statutory protections, such as state usury laws that restricted the rate of interest that could be imposed on unpaid balances. Nevertheless, consumer cardholders were vulnerable to overreaching because many of the costs were less than obvious. Congress responded in 1968 by enacting the Federal Truth in Lending Act ("TILA"), which is Title I of the Consumer Credit Protection Act, 15 U.S.C. §§ 1601-1693r. TILA authorizes the Board of Governors of the Federal Reserve System (the "Board") to prescribe regulations to carry out its purposes. 15 U.S.C. § 1603 (TILA § 105). Pursuant to this authority, the Board promulgated Regulation Z, published in Part 226 of Title 12 of the Code of Federal Regulations (C.F.R.). These are "legislative regulations," and they have the force of law. *See General Elec. Credit Corp. v. Smail*, 584 S.W.2d 690, 694

(Tex. 1979). The Board annually issues a staff commentary which interprets TILA, *12 C.F.R. § 226.2, Supp. I*, and this commentary is generally regarded as authoritative. *See Johnson v. Fleet Finance, Inc.,* 4 F.3d 946, 949 (11th Cir. 1993). TILA was substantially amended in 1980 by the Truth in Lending Simplification and Reform Act.

TILA almost exclusively applies to relatively small consumer credit transactions. It only applies to credit extensions to natural persons. 15 U.S.C. § 1603(1) (TILA § 104(1)); Regulation Z, § 226.3(a)(2). It does not apply to credit granted primarily for business, commercial or agricultural purposes. 15 U.S.C. § 1603(1) (TILA § 104(1)); Regulations Z § 226.3(1)(1). Morever, it does not apply to a credit extension of over $25,000, even when the extension is to a natural person for a consumer purpose, unless the credit is secured by an interest in either real property or in personal property used by the consumer as his principal dwelling. 15 U.S.C. § 1603(3) (TILA § 104(3)); Regulation Z, § 226.3(b). There are several additional explicit exemptions.

Although many states have also enacted "truth in lending" laws, we will focus on the much more developed body of law relating to TILA.

III. *Principal Issues*

One of TILA's most important goals is to ensure that consumers are provided enough information in a clear and understandable way so that they can make informed decisions regarding credit transactions. A considerable amount of litigation arises — as to credit cards and other extensions of credit — regarding the adequacy of the disclosures that were made. Beyond disclosure matters, the principal legal issues that arise between a cardholder and issuer concern: (1) formation of the cardholder-issuer relationship; (2) the cardholder's ability to assert against the issuer claims or defenses that he might have had against the merchant; and (3) the cardholder's liability for unauthorized charges.

A. *Formation of the Cardholder-Issuer Relationship*

In the early days of the credit card revolution, banks issued and mailed millions of credit cards to people who had never asked for them. For instance, in one month in 1969, the New England Bankcard Association mailed out two million unsolicited cards. *See* 26 Am.Jur. Proof of Facts, Liability for Unauthorized Use of Credit Card, § 1 at p. 497 (citing the Congressional Record). Entire neighborhoods were saturated with such mailings, and, at least where mailboxes were accessible, thieves could steal many, many cards which they could sell for $50 or $100 apiece. *Id.* Such practices could cause troublesome practical problems for those who might be billed for — and might inadvertently pay — unauthorized charges made with such cards.

TILA proscribes the issuance of a new credit card, as opposed to renewal or replacement cards, except in response to a request or an application for one. *See* 15 U.S.C.A. § 1642 (TILA § 132); Regulation Z, 12 C.F.R. § 226.12(a)(1). This proscription applies not only to the issuance of cards to individuals but also to businesses. 15 U.S.C. § 1645 (TILA § 135). Although the request may be oral, see Regulation Z, 12 C.F.R. § 226.12(a)(1), it must be for a credit card. A request for overdraft privileges, for instance, is not enough to authorize a bank to issue a credit card. *See* F.R.B., Official Staff Commentary on Regulation Z, Comment 12(a)(1)-1. If there is a request for a new credit card, however, a bank, without violating TILA, may issue one that has a different name from the one requested or that has certain additional features than the one requested. *Id.,* at Comment 12(a)(1)-3. Moreover, TILA does not forbid banks from contacting consumers and suggesting that they apply for a credit card. Id., at Comment 12(a)(1)-4.

Any action for a violation of 15 U.S.C. § 1642 (TILA § 132) must be brought within one year of the violation. *See* 15 U.S.C. § 1640(e) (TILA § 130(e)).

PROBLEM 20.1

Luke Jackson answers the phone and it's Mike Morgan, a representative of Credit Card, Inc. ("CC"), who asks to speak to Edith Jackson, Luke's wife. Luke says Edith's not home and asks what the call is about. Mike says that Edith has been pre-approved for a CC credit card and needs to ask her a few question. Luke says, "Great. She just told me yesterday that she wanted to get a card. I'll answer your questions." At the end of the conversation, Mike asks, "Now, you're sure your wife wants the card?" Luke says "Absolutely. You can count on it," the conversation ends politely, and CC mails Edith a card. Has CC violated TILA?

PROBLEM 20.2

Nancy Niles has a credit card issued by All Your Money Bank ("AYM"). It is due to expire on December 7th of this year. On November 21st of this year, Nancy receives a new card from AYM which is to be effective as of December 1st. Nancy is told that various additional technological safeguards have been built into the new card. Has AYM violated TILA? See F.R.B., Official Staff Commentary on Regulation Z, Comment 12(a)(2)-1.

PROBLEM 20.3

Emile Zola has an "Insatia-Card," a credit card issued by First Insatiable Bank ("FIB"). He calls up FIB and says he would like an extra card for his account so that his wife, Catherine Zola, can use it. May FIB issue the card without receiving a request for the card from Catherine? If it does issue the card, and Emile gives it to Catherine, who uses it, is Catherine a "cardholder," as defined by TILA? See 15 U.S.C. § 1602(m), which defines "cardholder" as "any person to whom a credit card is issued or any person who has agreed with the card issuer to pay obligations arising from the issuance of a credit card to another person."

Would it make a difference whether FIB issues the card with Emile's name printed on it or with Catherine's name printed on it? See F.R.B., Official Staff Commentary on Regulation Z, Comment 12(a)(1)-6; 15 U.S.C. § 1602(m) (1994).

PROBLEM 20.4

Binge Buying, Inc. ("BBI") sends out a card to Sally Druthers with a letter saying, "You are pre-approved for the enclosed card. You may activate by dialing "1-800-BBUYING" and following the directions you will hear. The terms of the credit card plan are explained in the enclosed brochure. Has BBI violated TILA?

2. *The Cardholder's Right to Assert Against the Issuer Underlying Claims and Defenses*

Sometimes a cardholder may dispute all or part of a charge based on circumstances relating to the underlying transaction with the merchant. For example, the cardholder may assert that the merchant engaged in fraud or that the item or services purchased were defective. Nonetheless, for various reasons it may be impractical for the cardholder to pay the issuer's monthly bill (which includes the disputed charge) and then try to litigate with the merchant. For example, the amount in issue may be less than the transaction costs involved in bringing suit or the merchant may simply no longer be solvent.

TILA addresses this problem by allowing a cardholder, under certain conditions, to assert against the issuer claims (other than tort claims) or defenses that the cardholder has vis-a-vis the merchant. See 15 U.S.C. § 1666i)(TILA § 170); Regulation Z, 12 C.F.R. § 226.12(c). Specifically, a cardholder can so assert such defenses subject to the following conditions:

1. The cardholder may not assert a claim or defense for an amount greater than the unpaid amount of credit with respect to the transaction as of the time the cardholder first notifies the issuer or the person honoring the credit card (whom we will continue to call the "merchant") of the claim or defense. Consequently, the cardholder should notify the merchant or issuer *before* paying the disputed charge. TILA provides a specific formula for allocating payments on an account to the various charges and fees entered to the account. Payments are credited: (a) first to late charges, (b) then to finance charges, in the order in which they were entered to the account,

and (c) finally to other debits, in the order in which they were respectively entered to the account. *Id.*

2. Before being able to assert a claim or defense against the issuer, the cardholder must have first made a good faith attempt to satisfactorily resolve the matter with the merchant.

3. If the merchant is not the same person as the issuer, is not controlled by the issuer, is not under direct or indirect common control with the issuer, is not a franchised dealer in the issuer's products or services, and has not obtained the order for the transaction through a mail solicitation made by or participated in by the issuer which solicits the cardholder to enter the transaction using the credit card, then:

   a. The amount of the initial transaction must have exceeded $50; and

   b. The transaction must have taken place either (1) in the same state as the mailing address that the cardholder previously provided to the issuer or (2) within 100 miles from such address. Courts use applicable state law to determine where a particular transaction is said to have occurred. 12 C.F.R. § 226.12. *See, e.g., Plutchok v. European American Bank*, 540 N.Y.S.2d 135 (N.Y.Dist.Ct. 1989). In appropriate circumstances, an issuer may be found to have waived its right to assert this geographical limit as a defense. *See, e.g., Hyland v. First USA Bank*, 1995 WL 595861 (E.D. Pa. Sept. 28, 1995).

PROBLEM 20.5

Carol Cardholder's residence, which was the address she had provided her credit card issuer, was in Buffalo, New York. When visiting Manhattan, approximately 300 miles away, she used her card to purchase a computer software program for $29 from a merchant who guaranteed to her that the program would be compatible with her computer. When visiting Toronto, she used her card to purchase a coat for $175. When she returned to her home in Buffalo, she discovered that the software program was not compatible with the computer and that the coat was made of defective material. Assume that Carol has not yet paid this month's credit card bill, which includes both of these charges. As to each such charge, explain whether Carol may assert her claims or defenses directly against the issuer. As to either of these charges, would Carol have to do anything before she would be able to assert her claims or defenses against the issuer?

PROBLEM 20.6

Same facts as in the preceding problem, except that Carol also used her credit card to purchase a supposedly new book over the internet for $80. She did this by sending an e-mail from her home computer, through the internet, to the mer-

chant's computer in Chicago, Illinois. When the book arrived, it was obviously used, as the previous owner's name was written on the cover and passages on several pages were underlined. Assuming that this charge, too, was on this month's bill that had not yet been paid, explain whether Carol could assert directly against the issuer her claim or defense on this book. Assuming that she could so assert her claim or defense, would she have to do anything first in order to be able to assert the claim or defense?

PROBLEM 20.7

What do you think might explain the geographical limit for allowing a cardholder to assert claims or defenses against an issuer? See Roland E. Brandel and Carol A. Leonard, "Bank Charge Cards: New Cash or New Credit," 69 Mich. L. Rev. 1033, 1068-9 (1971). protect merchant

3. *The cardholder's liability for unauthorized charges*

Suppose a cardholder's card — or its number — is lost or stolen and is used by the finder or thief to make purchases. Such use is "unauthorized." To what extent, if any, is the cardholder liable for unauthorized use of its card? TILA limits such liability in the following ways:

1. If the unauthorized use occurs after the issuer has been notified that an unauthorized use may occur because of loss, theft or otherwise, the cardholder is not liable for any part of the unauthorized use;

2. If the unauthorized use occurs before any such notice, and the issuer has given the cardholder adequate notice that he may be liable for unauthorized use, has provided a method whereby the user of the card can be identified as an authorized user, and has provided the cardholder a description of a way to notify the issuer of loss or theft, then the cardholder is liable, but only for up to $50 of the unauthorized use. *See* 15 U.S.C. § 1643 (TILA § 133).

These rules protect not only consumer cardholders but also businesses or other organizations that are cardholders. *See* 15 U.S.C. § 1645 (TILA § 135). Nevertheless, a business and issuer may, under certain circumstances, contractually agree to alter these rules.

What, exactly, is an "unauthorized use"? TILA provides that an "unauthorized use," for purposes of the above provision, "means a use of a credit card by a person other than the cardholder who does not have actual, implied, or apparent authority for such use and from which the cardholder receives no benefit." 15 U.S.C. § 1602(o) (TILA § 103(o)). But it is not intuitively clear when a person is deemed to have "implied or apparent authority." Suppose a cardholder, Naive Ned, gives one of the cards on his account (Ned's wife has the other) to a friend,

Untrustworthy Uriah, and tells him he can use it to make a purchase for no more than $75, and the "friend" goes off and uses it to make a $2,500 purchase. One might intuitively think that this $2,500 purchase was clearly an "unauthorized use," but the cases go the other way. Although the cases regard Uriah's purchase as a "misuse" of the card, they distinguish between such a misuse and an "unauthorized use," the latter being restricted to cases in which the user had not been given any authority to use the card. The courts find that Uriah, in this case, had at least "apparent authority" to make the purchase. *See, e.g., Martin v. American Express, Inc.*, 361 So. 2d 597, 559 (Ala. Civ. App. 1978).

But suppose that Ned had previously allowed Uriah to use his card to make purchases from TestBuy, Inc., and Uriah had done so without misusing it. Now, a few months later, Uriah, without permission, uses Ned's card number to order goods from TestBuy over the phone. Would the purchase of the new goods be deemed an "authorized use"? Consider the following case:

DRAIMAN v. AMERICAN EXPRESS TRAVEL RELATED SERVICES COMPANY
892 F.Supp. 1096 (N.D. Il. 1995)

MEMORANDUM OPINION AND ORDER

SHADUR, Senior District Judge.

Nachson Draiman ("Draiman") brings this three-count action, both on his own behalf and for a purported class of similarly situated individuals, against American Express Travel Related Services Company ("American Express"). Draiman contends that by reinstating his cancelled [sic] credit card ("Platinum Card") without his express permission and by then seeking to collect a debt for charges incurred on that resuscitated account, American Express violated the federal Truth-in-Lending Act ("TILA," 15 U.S.C. §§ 1642 and 1643) (Count I), the Illinois Consumer Fraud Act (the "Illinois Act," 815 ILCS 505/2) (Count II) and New York General Business Law § 349 (Count III).

. . . .

[T]his Court has entertained American Express' promptly-filed motion for summary judgment under Rule 56 as to all three counts of the Amended Complaint ("AC") [footnote omitted] . . . For the reasons stated in this memorandum opinion and order, American Express' motion is granted in its entirety.

Facts[2]

On several occasions between 1988 and 1992 Draiman used his American Express Platinum Card to purchase airline tickets through the Travel Dimen-

---

[2] In its opinion, the [lower] court emphasized that the statement of "facts" did not reflect any actual factual findings but, rather, the facts as they had to be characterized in favor of the plaintiff for purposes of deciding defendant's motion for summary judgment.

sions travel agency. Draiman provided Travel Dimensions with his Platinum Card number, and when he needed tickets he would call and place an order. Travel Dimensions would send the tickets to Draiman and the bill to American Express. American Express would then secure payment from Draiman by including the cost of the tickets plus applicable financing charges in its periodic billing statement.

On January 21, 1992 Draiman cancelled [sic] his Platinum Card. Sometime thereafter Draiman deposited an undisclosed sum of money with Travel Dimensions. On July 20, 1992 Draiman purchased four El Al tickets to Israel at $2,077 each, for a total cost of $8,308. Draiman instructed Travel Dimensions to pay for the El Al tickets by drawing upon his deposited funds. Travel Dimensions did not honor that request — instead it charged the amount against the number that it had for Draiman's Platinum Card.

American Express of course knew nothing of Draiman's deposit with, or his instructions to, Travel Dimensions. When American Express received the $8,308 charge from Travel Dimensions, that triggered its reinstatement policy, as set out in these terms in the cardholder agreement:

> If you ask us to cancel your account, but you continue to use the Card, we will consider such use as your request for reinstatement of your account. If we agree to reinstate your account, this Agreement or any amended or new Agreement we send you will govern your reinstated account.

American Express does not communicate with cardholders to confirm that it is in fact their desire to revive their accounts. In accordance with its written policy, American Express reinstated Draiman's Platinum Card on August 26, 1992 and billed him $8,308. Draiman later actually used the El Al tickets (each of which had his Platinum Card number printed on its face) to travel to Israel.

On October 15, 1993 Draiman paid American Express $3,399.98 of the $8,308 total and threatened suit if it tried to collect the $4,908.02 balance, citing purported violations of the Fair Credit Billing Act, TILA and other applicable laws. When American Express attempted to collect the debt, the threatened legal action ensued on January 11, 1995 with one twist: Draiman filed not only on his own behalf but also on behalf of a purported class of similarly aggrieved persons.

Section 1642

Draiman first contends that by resuscitating his cancelled [sic] Platinum Card without express permission American Express issued an unsolicited credit card in violation of Section 1642:

> No credit card shall be issued except in response to a request or application therefor. This prohibition does not apply to the issuance of a credit card in renewal of, or in substitution for, an accepted credit card.

It is unnecessary to decide whether Draiman might at one time have had a valid Section 1642 claim against American Express, for if so he lost it when he failed to bring suit within the applicable statute of limitations.

Section 1643

Draiman's other TILA-based claim centers on his contention that Travel Dimensions used his credit card without permission. From that he argues that he is entitled to the protection afforded by Section 1643. Under that provision, if certain conditions are met (see Section 1602(*o*)), there is a $50 limit on the liability of cardholders for charges that are made by third parties without actual, implied or apparent authority *and* from which the cardholder receives no benefit. That Section 1643 argument fails not only on limitations grounds (for Section 1640(c) applies to an alleged Section 1643 claim as well, and any alleged violation of the latter statute also took place when Draiman's account was charged for the El Al tickets) but also (1) because Draiman benefited [sic] by flying to Israel with the use of the tickets and (2) because Travel Dimensions possessed apparent authority to have charged Draiman's Platinum Card. Although the limitations bar would alone suffice to defeat this claim as well, it is worth reviewing those added deficiencies too.

Draiman's assertion that he derived no benefit from the use of his credit card to buy airline tickets *that he then used* is patently frivolous and merits no further discussion. For the answer to the second question (the existence or nonexistence of Travel Dimension's authority), the Federal Reserve Board's Regulation Z (12 C.F.R. Part 226) and Section 226.12(b)(1) of its accompanying Official Staff Interpretations (Supplement I to the Regulations) point to state agency law.

Universal agency law divides the concept of an agent's authority into the same three familiar subcategories (actual, implied or apparent) that are listed in Section 1643. Here Draiman says that he told Travel Dimensions to take the tickets' cost out of his previously-deposited funds. Because no reasonable travel agent would have interpreted that instruction as authorization to charge the customer's credit card . . . , Travel Dimensions plainly lacked both actual and implied authority. That leaves for consideration only the concept of apparent authority.

Apparent authority binds Draiman to the credit card transaction if it was reasonable for American Express to conclude from Draiman's words and actions that he had authorized Travel Dimensions to charge his Platinum Card for the four El Al tickets, even if (as it must be assumed here) Travel Dimensions had in fact been forbidden from doing so (*Gilbert v. Sycamore Mun. Hosp.,* 156 Ill.2d 511, 522-24, 190 Ill.Dec. 758, 764-65, 622 N.E.2d 788, 794-95 (1993); Restatement (Second) of Agency §§ 8, 27 and 49 (1957)). What follows in this opinion therefore focuses on the elements of that reasonableness concept.

What (if anything) had Draiman done to make it appear to American Express that he had authorized Travel Dimensions to charge his account? For starters, he had given Travel Dimensions his Platinum Card number. And perhaps most importantly, he had then over an extended period of time honored various charges to his account that Travel Dimensions had relayed to American Express.

Several state courts treat the voluntary relinquishment of a credit card or voluntary disclosure of a credit card number, in either event for purposes of making an expressly authorized charge, as by itself rendering the cardholder liable for all later charges (*Mastercard v. Town of Newport,* 133 Wis.2d 328, 396 N.W.2d 345, 348 (App.1986); *Standard Oil Co. v. Steele,* 22 Ohio Misc.2d 27, 489 N.E.2d 842, 844 (1985); *Cities Serv. Co. v. Pailet,* 452 So.2d 319, 322 (La.Ct.App.1984); *Martin v. American Express, Inc.,* 361 So.2d 597, 600-01 (Ala.Civ.App.1978)). Those courts place a heavy burden on cardholders to safekeep their accounts and to trust no one, because under that concept about the only way to escape liability for unanticipated charges by a third person is to argue that the card or its number was stolen or was obtained surreptitiously (*Elder-Beerman v. Nagucki,* 55 Ohio App.3d 10, 561 N.E.2d 553 (1988) (per curiam)).

Another view, which would seem to strike a more sensible balance among the several competing interests involved, is that such voluntary relinquishment or disclosure is an important factor to be considered in the context of other conduct and circumstances, especially industry custom, prior course of dealing and the presence or absence of characteristics that tend to distinguish authorized from unauthorized uses (*Towers World Airways, Inc. v. PHH Aviation Sys. Inc.,* 933 F.2d 174, 177-78 (2d Cir.1991); *Blaisdell Lumber Co. v. Horton,* 242 N.J.Super. 98, 575 A.2d 1386, 1389-91 (App.Div.1990); *Vaughn v. United States Nat'l Bank,* 79 Or.App. 172, 718 P.2d 769, 770-71 (1986)). For example, in finding an airplane owner liable for a pilot's fuel purchases made in connection with chartered flights where the owner had granted the pilot permission to use the card only for non-chartered flights, *Towers World Airways,* 933 F.2d at 178 emphasized (1) that it was industry custom to entrust pilots with credit cards to make airplane-related purchases and (2) that because the only thing that distinguished authorized from unauthorized uses was the identity of the passengers, the credit card agency had no effective way to tell one from the other.

Although Illinois courts appear not to have taken sides in that debate, this Court need not agonize here over a choice in those terms. Under either of those perspectives, Travel Dimensions possessed apparent authority as a matter of law to charge Draiman's Platinum Card account for the four El Al tickets. Draiman had not only given Travel Dimensions his credit card number voluntarily, but an abundance of background circumstances also confirmed to American Express that the travel agency had been authorized to charge his account. First, the extended course of prior dealings among the parties had created the appearance that Travel Dimensions was a competent and responsible ticketing outfit that faithfully executed its customer's orders. Travel Dimensions had charged Draiman's account several times in the past, and Draiman had reimbursed American Express without objection. Second, from what American

Express could see there was nothing to distinguish the final transaction from its predecessors: Travel Dimensions was not submitting charges for mink coats and diamond rings, but was simply ordering yet another set of airplane tickets. Third, travel agencies use customer credit cards all the time, and nothing in that settled practice could reasonably be expected to have raised American Express's corporate eyebrow.

PROBLEM 20.8

What are the differences between the Draiman case and the hypothetical about Ned and Uriah that immediately preceded it? Explain whether any of these differences would matter according to the two approaches identified in Draiman.

PROBLEM 20.9

• *Suppose that after Draiman found out that Travel Dimensions had made the charges, he contacted American Express and told it that Travel Dimensions was not authorized to use his card to make any further purchases. Nevertheless, Travel Dimensions used the card number to make another purchase from El Al a week later. According to the Draiman decision, would Draiman be liable for that purchase as well? Explain whether Draiman's argument to avoid liability would be greater or lesser if he had notified El Al itself rather than American Express. Contrast Cities Service Co. v Pailet, 452 So. 2d 319 (1984, La App 4th Cir) and Standard Oil Co. v . Steele , 22 Ohio Misc. 2d 27 (1985, Mun Ct), 489 N.E.2d 842 to Towers World Airways, Inc. v PHH Aviation Systems, Inc. , 933 F.2d 174 (2nd Cir. 1991), cert. den. 502 US 823.*

PROBLEM 20.10

Who has the burden of proving whether a particular use was or was not authorized? See 15 U.S.C. § 1643(b) (TILA 133(b)).

4. *Resolution of Billing Errors*

Regulation Z provides that any of the following may constitute a "billing error":

(1) an indication on a periodic statement or sent with a periodic statement that an extension of credit was made when, in fact, no such extension of credit was made either to the cardholder or to a person who has actual, implied or apparent authority to use the cardholder's card;

(2) an indication on or with a periodic statement of an extension of credit that is not properly identified;

(3) an indication on or with a periodic statement of an extension of credit for property or services that were either not accepted by the cardholder or his designee or that were not delivered to the cardholder or his designee as agreed;

(4) an indication on the period statement of the issuer's failure to promptly credit the cardholder's account;

(5) an indication on the periodic statement of a computational or similar accounting error by the issuer;

(6) an indication on a periodic statement of an extension of credit as to which the cardholder requests additional clarification, including documentation; or

(7) the issuer's failure to mail or deliver a periodic statement to the cardholder's last known address if notice of the address was received by the issuer at least 20 days before the end of the billing cycle for which the statement was required. 12 C.F.R. § 226.13(a).

The issuer is said to have received a "billing error notice" if it receives written notice from the cardholder of any of the above circumstances within 60 days after the issuer transmitted the first periodic statement reflecting that circumstance, provided that such notice enables the issuer to identify the cardholder's name and account number and indicates (a) the cardholder's belief that the error exists; (b) the reasons for such belief; and (c) the type, date and amount of the error. 12 C.F.R. § 226.13(b).

If an issuer receives a billing error notice, it must investigate the alleged error. The cardholder need not pay, and the issuer may not try to collect, any portion (including related finance or other charges) of any required payment that the cardholder believes is related to the alleged error. 12 C.F.R. § 226.13(d). Similarly, suppose the cardholder has a deposit account with the issuer and has agreed to pay his credit card bill by periodic deductions from that account. If at any time up to 3 business days before a scheduled payment date the issuer receives a billing error notice, it may not deduct from the cardholder's account any part of the disputed amount (including related finance or other charges). Id. Nor may the issuer, directly or indirectly, make or threaten to make an adverse credit report based on the cardholder's failure to pay any part of the dispute amount (including related finance or other charges). 12 C.F.R. § 226.13(d)(2).

If the issuer concludes that the asserted error has occurred, it must — by the earlier of the end of 2 complete billing cycles or 90 days after receiving the billing error notice — correct the error, credit the cardholder's account appropriately, and mail or deliver a correction notice to the consumer. If the issuer concludes that no error occurred, it must — by the earlier of the end of 2 complete billing cycles or 90 days after receiving the billing error notice — mail or deliver to the cardholder an explanation of the reasons for its conclusion and, if the cardholder requests, furnish copies of documentary evidence of the cardholder's indebtedness. If the issuer concludes that the asserted error did not occur, but that a different error occurred, it must — by the earlier of the end of 2 complete billing cycles or 90 days after receiving the billing error notice — correct the error and credit the cardholder's account as appropriate given the actual error.

Sometimes an issuer can resolve billing error notices in the way described in the preceding paragraph long before the applicable time limits expire. On other occasions, the entire time periods may need to be used. Unless the issuer has already resolved a particular billing error notice, the issuer must mail or deliver to the cardholder a written acknowledgment of receipt of the notice within 30 days after receiving it. 12 C.F.R. § 226.13(c)(1).

If, after following the above procedures, the issuer concludes that the cardholder is responsible for all or part of the disputed amount (and any finance or other charges), the issuer:

(1) must promptly notify the cardholder in writing of the amount due and of the time on which payment is due;

(2) must give the cardholder some time, as specified in Regulation Z, within which to make such payment without incurring additional finance or other charges; and

(3) if such time elapses without payment from the cardholder, may report the account or amount as delinquent; but it may not report the account or amount as delinquent if the issuer receives additional written notice from the cardholder that the amount is still disputed, unless the issuer also: (a) promptly reports that the account or amount is still disputed; (b) at the same time it reports the delinquency, mails or delivers to the cardholder written notice of the name and address of each person to whom the delinquency report is made; and (c) promptly reports to each such persons any subsequent resolution of the reported delinquency.

If a cardholder reasserts a dispute after the issuer has complied with all of the requirements we have discussed, the issuer has no further statutory responsibilities. At such a juncture, the cardholder's recourse is to file suit against the issuer. 123 C.F.R. § 226.1(e).

If a cardholder asserts that a particular use of its card was unauthorized, but the issuer does not receive a timely "billing error notice," the error resolution procedures described above do not apply. Nevertheless, the issuer must still conduct a reasonable investigation to determine whether the disputed use of the card was authorized. *See* Official Staff Commentary to Reg. Z, 12 C.F.R. § 226.12(b)-3.

Appendix 1
GLOSSARY

This glossary provides guidance as to how terms are either deemed by or apparently used in the Uniform Commercial Code (UCC) or this text . Sections 4-104 and 4-105, which are the authority for some of the explanations provided, state that those explanations are limited to Article 4.

Acceptance: An acceptance is a drawee's signed agreement, written on the draft, to pay a draft when presented. Section 3-409(a). The acceptance "may consist of the drawee's signature alone." Unless a drawee accepts a draft, the drawee has no liability *on the draft*. By accepting the draft, the drawee becomes primarily liable thereon. Section 3-413. If the drawee is also the drawer of a cashier's check, its obligation is governed by Section 3-412. The "acceptance" of a draft should be contrasted with the "taking" of a draft. *See also* Cashier's check; Draft; Drawee; Drawer; Primarily liable; Taking of an instrument.

Acceptor: An acceptor is a drawee of a draft who, by signing the instrument, has agreed to pay the draft when presented. Sections 3-103(a)(1); 3-409(a). *See also* Draft; Drawee; Instrument.

Accommodated party: An accommodated party is one for whose benefit an accommodation party signs an instrument. Section 3-419(a) and UCC Comment 1 thereto. By signing the instrument, however, the accommodation party does not undertake any liability to the accommodated party. In fact, the accommodation party has a right of reimbursement against the accommodated party. Section 3-419(e). *See also* Accommodation party; Instrument.

Accommodation party: An accommodation party is one who "signs [an] instrument for the purpose of incurring liability on the instrument without being a direct beneficiary of the value given for the instrument." Section 3-419(a). *See also* Accommodated party; Instrument; Value.

Account: An account is "any deposit or credit account with a bank, including a demand, time, savings, passbook, share draft, or like account, other than an account evidenced by a certificate of deposit." Section 4-104(a)(1).

Agreement: An agreement is "the bargain of the parties in fact, as found in their language or by implication from other circumstances . . . ." Such a bargain need not be enforceable to constitute an "agreement" as that term is used in the UCC. Section 1-201(3).

Alteration: An alteration is either (a) an unauthorized change of terms in an instrument, such as of the payee or amount due, that purports to modify the obligation of a party to the instrument or (b) an unauthorized addition of words or numbers to an incomplete instrument that relates to the obligation of a party. Section 3-407(a). *See also* Instrument.

Anomalous indorsement: An anomalous indorsement is an indorsement made by a person who is not the holder of the instrument. An anomalous indorsement is usually that of an accommodation party. An anomalous indorsement does not affect the manner in which the instrument may be negotiated. Section 3-205(d). *See also* Accommodation party; Holder; Indorsement; Instrument; Negotiation.

Bank: A bank is "any person engaged in the business of banking, including a savings bank, savings and loan association, credit union, or trust company." Section 4-105(1).

Banking day: A banking day is "the part of a day on which a bank is open to the public for carrying on substantially all of its banking functions." Section 4-104(a)(3).

Bearer: A bearer is a "person in possession of a negotiable instrument . . . payable to bearer or indorsed in blank." Section 1-201(5). Instruments payable to bearer include those using the words "bearer" or "cash" or that fail to state a payee. Sections 3-109, 3-205(b). *See also* Blank indorsement: Indorsement; Instrument.

Blank indorsement: A blank indorsement is an indorsement that is made by the holder of an instrument that does not specify a person to whom it makes the instrument payable (i.e., is not a "special indorsement"). When indorsed in blank, an instrument becomes payable to bearer and may be negotiated by transfer of possession alone until specially indorsed. Section 3-205(b). *See also* Bearer; Holder; Person; Special indorsement.

Branch: A branch of a bank "includes a separately incorporated foreign branch of a bank." Section 1-201(7). *See also* Bank.

Burden of establishing a fact: The burden of establishing a fact means "the burden of persuading the trier of fact that the existence of the fact is more probable than its non-existence." Section 1-201(8).

Cashier's check: A cashier's check is a check as to which the drawer and drawee are either the same bank or branches of the same bank. A cashier's check is often purchased by a customer to satisfy an obligation of a creditor who wants assurance that funds will be available when he seeks payment. Sections 3-104(g), 3-412. *See also* Bank; Branch; Check; Customer; Drawee; Drawer.

Certificate of deposit: A certificate of deposit is "an instrument containing an acknowledgment by a bank that a sum of money has been received by the bank and a promise by the bank to repay it (usually after a specified period of time and at a specified interest rate). A certificate of deposit is a note of the bank." Section 3-104(j). *See also* Bank; Instrument; Money; Note.

Certified check: A certified check is a check that has been accepted by the bank on which it is drawn. The acceptance may be made by the drawee's signature on the check or by a writing on the check that indicates the check is certified. The drawee of a check has no obligation to certify the check, and refusal to certify is not dishonor of the check. Section 3-409. Upon certification of the check, the drawee bank becomes primarily liable (Section 3-413), and the drawer, and any indorser prior to certification, is discharged. Sections 3-414(c), 3-415(d). *See also* Acceptance; Bank; Check; Drawee; Drawer; Dishonor; Indorser; Primarily liable.

Check: A check is a draft, other than a documentary draft, that is payable on demand and in which the drawee is a bank. The term "check" includes a cashier's check or teller's check. An instrument may be a check even though it is described on its face by another term such as a "money order." Section 3-104(f). *See also* Bank; Cashier's check; Draft; Drawee; Instrument; Teller's check.

Claim in recoupment: Although not precisely defined by the UCC, a claim in recoupment is a claim that arises out of a transaction between a particular obligor on an instrument and the obligee with whom he dealt. The claim arises because, although the original obligee initially performed its part of the transaction, a subsequent breakdown gave the obligor a right to a separate monetary claim against that obligee. *See* UCC Comment 3 to Section 3-305. See also Instrument.

Claim to an instrument: A claim to an instrument is a "claim of a property or possessory right in the instrument or its proceeds, including a claim to rescind a negotiation and to recover the instrument or its proceeds." Section 3-306. *See also* Instrument; Negotiation.

Clearing house: A clearing house is "an association of banks or other payors regularly clearing items." Section 4-104(a)(4). *See also* Bank; Item.

Collecting bank: A collecting bank is any bank, except the payor bank, that handles an item for collection. Section 4-105(5). *See also* Bank; Item; Payor bank.

Consideration: Consideration is somewhat circuitously defined as "any consideration sufficient to support a simple contract." Section 3-303(b). Thus, the term "consideration" seems to mean any bargained for exchange sufficient to support a simple contract. In addition, if an instrument is issued for "value" as that term is defined in Section 3-303(a), then it is also issued for consideration. Section 3-303(b). The drawer or maker of an instrument has a defense if the instrument is issued without consideration. If an instrument is issued for a promise of performance, the issuer has a defense to the extent performance of the promise is due and the promise has not been performed. Section 3-303(b). *See also* Defense; Drawer; Issuer; Maker; Instrument; Value.

Conspicuous: "A term or clause is conspicuous when it is so written that a reasonable person against whom it is to operate ought to have noticed it." Section 1-201(10). Whether a term is conspicuous is for decision by the court. *Id.*

Customer: A customer is a person either having an account with a bank or for whom a bank has agreed to collect items. The definition of "customer" includes a bank maintaining an account at another bank. Section 4-104(a)(5). See Chapter 14 for a discussion as to who is considered a bank's customer when a bank has wrongfully dishonored an item. *See also* Account; Bank; Item; Person.

Consumer Account: A consumer account is "an account established by an individual primarily for personal, family, or household purposes." 2002 Revised Section 3-103(a)(2).

Consumer Transaction: A consumer transaction is one in which "an individual incurs an obligation primarily for personal, family or household purposes." 2002 Revised Section 3-103(a)(3).

Defense: Although the term "defense" is not precisely defined by the UCC, the term seems to refer to three categories of contentions that an obligor may assert to avoid making payment. These three categories are (i) "real defenses" listed in Section 3-305; (ii) defenses explicitly created by particular provisions of Article 3; and (iii) defenses that would be available if the person entitled to enforce the instrument were attempting to enforce a right to payment under a simple contract. *See also* Personal defenses; Real defenses.

Delivery: A delivery of an instrument is a "voluntary transfer of possession" thereof. 2001 Revised Section 1-201(15). *See also* Instrument.

Depositary bank: A depositary bank is the first bank to take an item from a customer unless the item is presented to the payor bank for immediate payment over the counter. The payor bank itself can be a depositary bank if the item is not presented for payment, such as when the customer deposits it in an account at the same bank as that of the maker or drawer. Section 4-105(2). *See also* Bank; Customer; Item; Payor bank; Presentment.

Discharge: Although the term "discharge" is not precisely defined by the UCC, the term seems to refer to the termination of a person's obligations on an instrument based on specific grounds established by various Article 3 provisions. A defendant being sued by a person entitled to enforce an instrument may assert the fact that her obligation has been discharged *in the nature of* a defense. [But note UCC Comment 3 to Section 3-302, which states that "[e]xcept for discharge in an insolvency proceeding . . . discharge is not expressed in Article 3 as a defense."] Nonetheless, a discharge is not effective against a holder in due course who took the instrument without notice of the discharge. Section 3-601. Regarding discharges generally, see Chapter 8. *See also* Holder in due course; Instrument; Person entitled to enforce.

Dishonor: Dishonor is a refusal or failure to pay an instrument when due. Under some circumstances it is also a dishonor to refuse to accept an instrument upon presentment. Section 3-502(b)(3),(4). Dishonor of an instrument is governed by detailed rules. Section 3-502. In some instances, an instrument may be dishonored even if no presentment is made. Sections 3-502(a)(3), 3-504. Dishonor of an instrument and notice of dishonor, unless excused (Section 3-504) are preconditions for the liability of parties who are secondarily liable. *See also* Acceptance; Instrument; Notice of dishonor; Presentment; Secondarily liable.

Documentary draft: A documentary draft is "a draft to be presented for acceptance or payment if specified documents, certificated securities (Section 8-102) or instructions for uncertificated securities (Section 8-308), or other certificates, statements, or the like are to be received by the drawee or other payor before acceptance or payment of the draft." Section 4-104(a)(6). *See also* Acceptance; Draft; Drawee; Payment of an instrument.

Draft: A draft is an instrument that is in the form of an order. Section 3-104(e). In a draft, the "drawer" orders the "drawee" to make payment to a specified "payee" or to bearer. Sometimes, as in the case of a cashier's check, the same person may be both the drawer and drawee. *See also* Bearer; Drawee; Drawer; Order; Payee; Person.

Drawee: A drawee is the person ordered in a draft to make payment. Section 3-103(a)(2). The drawee's name usually appears in the lower left-hand corner of the draft. On a check, the drawee is always a bank. *See also* Bank; Check; Draft; Person.

Drawer: A drawer is "a person who signs or is identified [presumably by an authorized agent] in a draft as a person ordering payment." Section 3-103(a)(3). A drawer normally signs in the lower right-hand corner of the draft or check. *See also* Check; Draft; Drawee; Person; Signed.

Fiduciary: A fiduciary is "an agent, trustee, partner, corporate officer or director, or other representative owing a fiduciary duty with respect to an instrument." Section 3-307(a)(1). The rules for when one who has taken an instrument from a fiduciary has notice of a breach of a fiduciary duty resulting from that transaction are found in Section 3-307. *See also* Notice; Instrument.

Good faith: Good faith is "honesty in fact and the observance of reasonable commercial standards of fair dealing." 2001 Revised Section 1-201(20); Pre-2002 Revision Section 3-103(a)(4). The phrase "reasonable commercial standards of fair dealing" is not itself defined.

Holder: A holder is a person in possession of an instrument that is payable either to herself or bearer. Revised 2002 Section 1-201(21). A holder has the right to transfer, negotiate, enforce, or discharge an instrument. *See also* Bearer; Discharge; Instrument; Negotiation; Person: Transfer.

Holder in due course: Subject to Sections 3-302(c) and 3-106(d), a "holder in due course" is the holder of an instrument if

(1) **the instrument when issued or negotiated to the holder does not bear such apparent evidence of forgery or alteration or is not otherwise so irregular or incomplete as to call into question its authenticity, and**

(2) **the holder took the instrument (i) for value, (ii) in good faith, (iii) without notice that the instrument is overdue or has been dishonored or that there is an uncured default with respect to payment of another instrument issued as part of the same series, (iv) without notice that the instrument contains an unauthorized signature or has been altered, (v) without notice of any claim to the instrument stated in Section 3-306, and (vi) without notice that any party has a defense or claim in recoupment stated in Section 3-305(a).** Section 3-302(a).

When a holder in due course seeks to enforce an instrument, she is subject to only a few defenses of the obligor and is free from all third-party claims to the instrument. *See* Chapter 9.

See also Alteration; Claim to an instrument; Claim in recoupment; Defense; Dishonor; Good faith; Holder; Instrument; Issue; Notice; Signed; Value.

Incomplete instrument: An incomplete instrument is one that is signed but that lacks some element of an instrument, such as the amount or the party to be paid. The contents must show, however, that at the time of signing the signer intended it to be completed by the addition of words or numbers. The incomplete instrument need not have been issued. An incomplete instrument completed in an unauthorized manner is said to be "altered." Section 3-115(a). *See also* Instrument; Signed; Written.

Indorsement: An indorsement is "a signature, other than that of a signer as maker, drawer, or acceptor, that alone or accompanied by other words is made on an instrument for the purpose of (i) negotiating the instrument, (ii) restricting payment of the instrument, or (iii) incurring indorser's liability on the instrument." Usually an indorsement is found on the reverse side of an instrument. Regardless of the intent of the signer, a signature and its accompanying words is an indorsement unless it is unambiguously clear that the signature was not intended as an indorsement. Section 3-204(a). *See also* Acceptor; Drawer; Instrument; Maker; Negotiation; Signed.

Indorser: An indorser is a person who makes an indorsement. Section 3-204(b). An indorser is generally obligated to pay the amount due on an instrument only if it has been dishonored and he has been given timely notice of the dishonor. Section 3-415. *See also* Dishonor; Notice of dishonor.

Insolvency proceedings: The term "insolvency proceedings" "includes any assignment for the benefit of creditors or other proceedings intended to liquidate or rehabilitate the estate of the person involved." Section 1-201(22). A discharge pursuant to insolvency proceedings is effective even against a holder in due course. Section 3-305(a)(1)(iv). *See also* Holder in due course; Person.

Insolvent: Insolvent means (i) "having generally ceased to pay debts in the ordinary course of business" other than debts subject to a good faith dispute; (ii) "being unable to pay debts as they become due"; or (iii) being insolvent as that term is defined in the federal bankruptcy law. 2001 Revised Section 1-201(23). *See also* Insolvency proceedings; Person.

Instrument: An "instrument" is a "negotiable instrument." Section 3-104(b). The term "negotiable instrument," defined by Section 3-104(a), appears below.

Intermediary bank: An intermediary bank is a bank, other than the depositary or payor bank, to which an item is transferred in the course of collection. Section 4-105(4). *See also* Bank; Depositary bank; Payor bank.

Issue: An issue is "the first delivery of an instrument by the maker or drawer . . . for the purpose of giving rights on the instrument to any person." The delivery need not be to a holder, but it must be a voluntary transfer of possession. Section 3-105(a). *See also* Delivery; Drawer; Holder; Instrument; Maker; Transfer of an instrument.

Issuer: An issuer is any person that signs an instrument as maker or drawer, regardless of whether the instrument is issued. Section 3-105(c). *See also* Drawer; Instrument; Issue; Maker; Signed.

Item: An item is "an instrument or a promise or order to pay money handled by a bank for collection or payment. The term does not include a payment order governed by Article 4A or a credit or debit card slip" (Section 4-104(a)(9)) but is more inclusive than the word "instrument." *See also* Bank; Instrument; Order: Promise.

Knowledge: Knowledge means "actual knowledge" and knows means having actual knowledge. 2001 Revised Section 1-202(b).

Maker: A maker is "a person who signs or is identified [presumably by an authorized party] in a note as a person undertaking to pay." Section 3-103(a)(5). The maker is primarily liable on the instrument as set forth generally in Section 3-419. *See also* Instrument; Note; Person; Primarily liable; Signed.

Money: Money is "a medium of exchange authorized or adopted by a domestic or foreign government and includes a monetary unit of account established by an intergovernmental organization or by agreement between 2 or more nations." Section 1-201(24).

Negotiable instrument: A negotiable instrument is an unconditional promise or order to pay a fixed amount of money, with or without interest or other charges described in the promise or order, if it

> **(1) is payable to bearer or to order at the time it is issued or first comes into possession of a holder**

(2) is payable on demand or at a definite time: and

(3) does not state any other undertaking or instruction by the person promising or ordering payment to do any act in addition to the payment of money, except that the promise or order may contain (i) an undertaking or power to give, maintain, or protect collateral to secure payment, (ii) an authorization or power to the holder to confess judgment or realize on or dispose of collateral, or (iii) a waiver of the benefit of any law intended for the advantage or protection of any obligor. Section 3-104(a).

See also Bearer; Holder; Issue; Money; Order; Person; Promise.

Negotiation: A negotiation is "a transfer of possession, whether voluntary or involuntary, of an instrument by a person other than its issuer to a person who thereby becomes its holder." Section 3-201 (a). If an instrument is payable to an identified person, negotiation requires transfer of possession of the instrument and its indorsement by the identified person. If an instrument is payable to bearer, it may be negotiated by transfer of possession alone. Section 3-201(b). *See also* Bearer: Holder; Instrument; Indorsement; Issuer; Person.

Note: A note is an instrument containing a promise to pay. Section 3-104(e). In a note, a "maker" promises to make payment to a "payee." *See also* Instrument; Maker; Payee; Promise.

Notice: A person generally has "notice" of a fact when

(a) he has actual knowledge of it; or

(b) he has received a notice or notification of it; or

(c) from all the facts and circumstances known to him at the time in question he has reason to know that it exists. 2001 Revised Section 1-202(a).

The rules for when one who has taken an instrument from a fiduciary has notice of a breach of a fiduciary duty resulting from that transaction are found in Section 3-307. *See also* Fiduciary; Instrument; Person.

Notice, time when effective: "[K]nowledge or a notice or notification received by an organization is effective for a particular transaction from the time when it is brought to the attention of the individual conducting that transaction, and in any event from the time when it would have been brought to his attention if the organization had exercised due diligence. An organization exercises due diligence if it maintains reasonable routines for communicating significant information to the person conducting the transaction and there is reasonable compliance with the routines. Due diligence does not require an individual acting for the organization to communicate information unless such communication is part of his regular duties or unless he has reason to know of the transaction and that the transaction would be materially affected by the information." 2001 Revised Section 1-202(f). *See also* Organization.

Notice of dishonor: The obligation of an indorser and, in some situations, the obligation of a drawer may not be enforced unless the indorser or drawer is given notice of dishonor as required by Section 3-503(a). Notice of dishonor may in some cases be excused. Section 3-504. *See also* Dishonor; Drawer; Indorser.

Notifies: "A person 'notifies' or 'gives' a notice or notification to another by taking such steps as may be reasonably required to inform the other in ordinary course whether or not such other actually comes to know of it" 2001 Revised Section 1-202(d). A person "receives a notice or notification when

    (1) it comes to that person's attention; or

      (b) it is duly delivered in a form reasonable under the circumstances at the place of business through which the contract was made or at another location held out by that person as the place of receipt of such communications."
      2001 Revised Section 1-202(e).

See also Notice; Person.

Order: An order is "a written instruction [to a party] to pay money signed by the person giving the instruction." The person giving the instruction is called the "drawer." The instruction may be directed to any person (called the "drawee"), including the person giving the instruction, or to one or more persons jointly or in the alternative but not in succession. " An authorization to pay is not an order unless the person authorized to pay is also instructed to pay." 2002 Revised Section 3-103(a)(8). *See also* Drawee; Drawer; Person; Written.

Ordinary care: "[I]n the case of a person engaged in business, [ordinary care] means observance of reasonable commercial standards, prevailing in the area in which that person is located with respect to the business in which that person is engaged. In the case of a bank that takes an instrument for processing for collection or payment by automated means, reasonable commercial standards do not require the bank to examine the instrument if the failure to examine does not violate the bank's prescribed procedures and the bank's procedures do not vary unreasonably from general banking usage not disapproved by [Article 3] or Article 4." 2002 Revised Section 3-103(a)(9). *See also* Bank; Instrument.

Organization: An organization means "a person other than an individual." See 2001 Revised Section 1-201(25). *See also* Person.

Paid: An instrument is generally paid to the extent payment is made by or on behalf of a party obliged to pay the instrument to a person entitled to enforce the instrument. Section 3-602(a). Nevertheless, 2002 Revised Section 2-602 introduces specific changes to its predecessor that are too complex to explain in this Glossary. *See also* Instrument; Person entitled to enforce.

Party: A party is a person who has engaged in a transaction or made an agreement and is distinguished from a "third party." 2001 Revised Section 1-201(26). *See also* Agreement; Person.

Payable at a definite time: "A promise or order is 'payable at a definite time' if it is payable on elapse of a definite period of time after sight or acceptance or at a fixed date or dates or at a time or times readily ascertainable at the time the promise or order is issued, subject to rights of (i) prepayment, (ii) acceleration, (iii) extension at the option of the holder, or (iv) extension to a further definite time at the option of the maker or acceptor or automatically upon or after a specified act or event." Section 3-108(b). *See also* Acceptance; Acceptor; Holder; Maker; Order; Promise.

Payable on demand: "A promise or order is 'payable on demand' if it (i) states that it is payable on demand or at sight, or otherwise indicates that it is payable at the will of the holder, or (ii) does not state any time of payment." Section 3-108(a). *See also* Holder; Order; Promise.

Payable to bearer: A promise or order is payable to bearer if it

(1) **states that it is payable to bearer or to the order of bearer or otherwise indicates that the person in possession of the promise or order is entitled to payment;**

(2) **does not state a payee; or**

(3) **states that it is payable to or to the order of cash or otherwise indicates that it is not payable to an identified person.** Section 3-109(a) .

See also Bearer; Order; Payee; Promise.

Payable to order: "A promise or order that is not payable to bearer is payable to order if it is payable (i) to the order of an identified person or (ii) to an identified person or order. A promise or order that is payable to order is payable to the identified person." Section 3-109(b). *See also* Order; Payable to bearer; Person; Promise.

Payee: The payee of an instrument is the person, if any, to whose order payment is to be made. *See also* Instrument; Order; Person.

Payment of an instrument: An instrument is paid when a drawee or a person obligated to make payment on the instrument makes such payment. The payment of an instrument is often referred to in contrast to the taking of an instrument for value. *See also* Drawee; Instrument; Paid; Taking of an instrument.

Payor bank: A payor bank is the drawee of a draft. Section 4-105(3). *See also* Bank; Draft; Drawee.

Person: The term "person" means "an individual, corporation, business trust, estate, trust, partnership, limited liability company, association, joint venture, government, governmental subdivision, agency, or instrumentality, public corporation, or any other legal or commercial entity." 2001 Revised Section 1-201(27).

Personal defenses: The term personal defenses is often used to contrast certain defenses from those that are "real defenses." In the context of the UCC, it seems that two categories of defenses could be characterized as "personal defenses": (i) those explicitly created by particular provisions of Article 3 and (ii) those that would be available if the person entitled to enforce the instrument were attempting to enforce a right to payment under a simple contract. *See also* Defense; Instrument; Person entitled to enforce: Real Defenses.

Person entitled to enforce (PETE): A person entitled to enforce an instrument is either

> **(i) the holder of the instrument, (ii) a nonholder in possession of the instrument who has the rights of a holder, or (iii) a person not in possession of the instrument who is entitled to enforce the instrument pursuant to Section 3-309 or 3-418(d). A person may be a person entitled to enforce the instrument even though the person is not the owner of the instrument or is in wrongful possession of the instrument.** Section 3-301.

See Chapter 3. *See also* Holder; Instrument; Person.

PETE: See **Person Entitled to Enforce**

Presentment: "[A] demand made by or on behalf of a person entitled to enforce an instrument (i) to pay the instrument made to the drawee or a party obliged to pay the instrument or, in the case of a note or accepted draft payable at a bank, to the bank or (ii) to accept a draft made to the drawee." Section 3-501(a). *See also* Draft; Drawee; Instrument; Note; Person entitled to enforce.

> **NOTE:** Notwithstanding this definition of presentment, the warranty provisions of the UCC seem to assume that when one who is not entitled to enforce an instrument nonetheless demands such payment or acceptance from a drawee or other party obliged to pay the instrument, the party so demanding payment has presented the instrument.

Presentment Warranties: Presentment warranties are made if some party has presented an instrument for acceptance or payment and the party to whom to it was so presented in fact accepted it or paid it in good faith. Presentment warranties are made only to the person who accepts or pays the instrument and are made by the person who presents the instrument as well as all prior transferors of the instrument. When an unaccepted draft is presented to the drawee for payment or acceptance and the drawee, in good faith, pays or accepts the draft, the presentment warranties are that (1) the warrantor is either a person entitled to enforce the draft or is authorized to obtain payment or acceptance of the draft on behalf of a person entitled to enforce it; (2) the draft has not been altered; and (3) the warrantor has no knowledge that the drawer's signature is unauthorized. Sections 3-417(a) and 4-208(a). In all other cases the warranty is simply that the warrantor is either a person entitled to enforce the draft or is authorized to obtain payment or acceptance of the draft on behalf of a person entitled to enforce it. Sections 3-417(d) and 4-208(d). *See, generally,* Chapter 10. *See also* Acceptance; Alteration; Draft; Drawee; Good faith; Instrument; Payment of an instrument; Person entitled to enforce; Presentment; Unauthorized signature.

Primarily liable: Parties, such as makers and acceptors, are primarily liable because their liability is not dependent on presentment, dishonor, or the provision of notice of dishonor. Comment 1 to Section 3-414 states that the obligation of a drawer of an unaccepted draft is also primary. *See* Acceptor; Dishonor; Draft; Drawer; Maker; Notice of dishonor; Presentment.

Principal obligor: As to a negotiable instrument, a "principal obligor" is "the accommodated party or any other party to the instrument against whom a secondary obligor has recourse under this article." 2002 Revised Section 3-103(a)(11).

Promise: A promise is "a written undertaking to pay money signed by the person undertaking to pay. An acknowledgment of an obligation by the obligor is not a promise unless the obligor also undertakes to pay the obligation." 2002 Revised Section 3-103(a)(12). *See also* Money; Person; Promise; Written.

Prove: The obligation to 'prove" a fact means the obligation to meet the burden of establishing the fact. 2002 Revised Section 3-103(a)(13). *See also* Burden of establishing a fact.

Purchase: The term purchase "includes taking by sale, discount, negotiation, mortgage, pledge, lien, issue or reissue, gift or any other transaction creating an interest in property." 2001 Revised Section 1-201(29). *See also* Issue; Negotiation.

Purchaser: A "purchaser" is "a person that takes by purchase." 2001 Revised Section 1-201(30). *See also* Person; Purchase.

Qualified Indorsement: An indorsement, which by its terms, disclaims the contractual liability usually undertaken by the indorser on the instrument. See Section 3-415. The way this is almost always done is to include the words "without recourse" before (most commonly) or after the signature. Other words to that effect may be used, but the disclaimer must appear on the instrument itself. *See also* Indorsement; Indorser; Instrument; Without recourse.

Ratification: Ratification, when used in the context of a signature on an instrument, is the retroactive adoption of an unauthorized signature by the person whose name has been signed. See Section 3-403 and comment 3 thereto. Ratification can be found not only by an express statement by that person, but also from conduct, such as knowingly retaining benefits received from the transaction in which the unauthorized signature was used or deliberately deciding not to object to it. *See also* Instrument; Signed; Unauthorized signature.

Reacquisition: "Reacquisition of an instrument occurs if it is transferred to a former holder, by negotiation or otherwise. A former holder who reacquires the instrument may cancel indorsements made after the reacquirer first became a holder of the instrument. If the cancellation causes the instrument to be payable to the reacquirer or to bearer, the reacquirer may negotiate the instrument. An indorser whose indorsement is canceled is discharged, and the discharge is effective against any subsequent holder." Section 3-207. *See also* Bearer; Discharge; Holder; Indorsement; Instrument; Negotiation.

Real defenses: Real defenses are those that may be successfully asserted against any person entitled to enforce the instrument, including a holder in due course. They are set forth in Section 3-305(a)(1) and include, under specified circumstances, infancy, duress, lack of legal capacity, illegality of the transaction, fraud in the factum, and discharge in insolvency proceedings. *See* Chapter 8. *See also* Defense; Holder in due course; Insolvency proceedings; Person entitled to enforce.

Record: This term "means information that is inscribed on a tangible medium or that is stored in an electronic or other medium and is retrievable in perceivable form." 2001 Revised Section 1-201(31) and 2002 Revised Section 3-103(a)(14).

Remedy: A remedy is "any remedial right to which an aggrieved party is entitled with or without resort to a tribunal." 2001 Revised Section 1-201(32). *See also* Party.

Remitter: A remitter is "a person that purchases an instrument from its issuer if the instrument is payable to an identified person other than the purchaser." 2002 Revised Section 3-103(a)(15). *See also* Instrument; Issuer; Person; Purchaser.

Representative: The term representative "means a person empowered to act for another, including an agent, an officer of a corporation or association, and a trustee, executor or administrator of an estate." 2001 Revised Section 1-201(33). *See also* Person.

Represented person: A represented party means "the principal, beneficiary, partnership, corporation, or other person to whom [a] fiduciary duty . . . is owed." Section 3-307(a)(2). *See also* Fiduciary; Person.

Restrictive Indorsement: A restrictive indorsement purports to limit the rights and powers transferred in the instrument by placing restrictions on the way the proceeds of the instrument are to be applied or paid. Pursuant to Section 3-205, an instrument purports to be restrictive if it:

a. **purports to limit payment to a particular person or prohibit further transfer of the instrument;**

b. **is conditional;**

c. includes the words "for collection," "for deposit," or like terms indicating a purpose of having the item collected for the indorser or a particular account; or

d. otherwise states that it is for the benefit or use of the indorser or of another person.

See also Account; Indorsement; Instrument; Item; Person.

Rights: The term "right" includes remedy. 2001 Revised Section 1-201(34). *See also* Remedy.

Secondarily liable: Parties such as indorsers are secondarily liable because their liability may be dependent on presentment, dishonor, and/or the provision of notice of dishonor. *See also* Dishonor; Indorsers; Notice of dishonor; Presentment.

Security interest: A security interest is "an interest in personal property or fixtures which secures payment or performance of an obligation. The retention or reservation of title by a seller of goods notwithstanding shipment or delivery to the buyer (Section 2-401) is limited in effect to a reservation of a 'security interest'. The term also includes any interest of a buyer of accounts or chattel paper which is subject to Article 9." 2001 Revised Section 1-201(35).

Send: As to any writing or notice, send means (1) "to deposit in the mail or deliver for transmission by any other usual means of communication with postage or cost of transmission provided for and properly addressed and, in the case of an instrument, to an address specified thereon or otherwise agreed, or if there be none to any address reasonable under the circumstances;" or (2) "in any other way to cause to be received any record or notice within the time it would have arrived if properly sent." 2001 Revised Section 1-201(36). *See also* Instrument; Notice; Written.

Signed: The term "signed" "includes any symbol executed or adopted by a party with present intention to authenticate a writing." 2001 Revised Section 1-201(37). "A signature may be made (i) manually or by means of a device or machine, and (ii) by the use of any name, including a trade or assumed name, or by a word, mark, or symbol executed or adopted by a person with present intention to authenticate a writing." Section 3-401. A party may be liable on an instrument if its agent or representative signed the instrument and the signature would be binding on such party if the signature were on a simple contract. Sections 3-401(a), 3-402(a). A party may ratify an unauthorized signature. Section 3-403(a). In addition, a party may be precluded from asserting that its signature was unauthorized. *See, e.g.,* Sections 3-406, 4-406. *See* Chapter 17. *See also* Instrument; Party, Ratification.

Special indorsement: A special indorsement is one that is made by a holder and identifies a person to whom it makes the instrument payable. An instrument that is specially indorsed is "payable to the identified person and may be negotiated only by the indorsement of that person." Section 3-205(a). *See also* Holder; Indorsement; Instrument; Negotiation; Person.

Suspends payments: With respect to a bank, the term "suspends payments" means "that it has been closed by order of the supervisory authorities, that a public officer has been appointed to take it over, or that it ceases or refuses to make payments in the ordinary course of business." Section 4-104(a)(12). *See also* Bank.

Taking of an instrument: An instrument is taken when it is acquired by someone other than the drawee or a party obligated to make payment thereon. The taking of an instrument for value is often referred to in contrast to the payment of an instrument. *See also* Drawee; Instrument; Payment of an instrument.

Teller's check: A teller's check is "a draft drawn by a bank (i) on another bank, or (ii) payable at or through a bank." Section 3-104(h). *See also* Bank; Check; Draft.

Transfer of an instrument: "An instrument is transferred when it is delivered by a person other than its issuer for the purpose of giving to the person receiving delivery the right to enforce the instrument." Section 3-203(a). Because this definition incorporates the term "delivery," it refers only to a voluntary transfer. Do not confuse this transfer of an instrument with the phrase "transfer of possession" used in the explanation of negotiation. *See also* Delivery; Instrument; Issuer; Person; Person entitled to enforce.

Transfer warranties: Ordinarily, when a person transfers a negotiable instrument for consideration to someone who takes it in good faith, that transfer carries with it certain implied warranties about the transferor and the instrument itself. These warranties include that (1) the transferor is a person entitled to enforce the instrument; (2) all signatures appearing on the instrument are authentic and authorized; (3) the instrument has not been altered; (4) the instrument is not subject to any defense or claim in recoupment that can be asserted against the transferor; and (5) the transferor has no knowledge of an insolvency proceeding begun regarding the maker or acceptor or, as to an unaccepted draft, the drawer. Sections 3-416 and 4-207. *See also* Acceptor; Alteration; Claim in recoupment; Consideration; Defense; Draft; Drawer; Good faith; Instrument; Maker; Person; Person entitled to enforce; Signed; Transfer of an instrument.

Traveler's check: A traveler's check is an instrument that "(i) is payable on demand, (ii) is drawn on or payable at or through a bank, (iii) is designated by the term 'traveler's check' or by a substantially similar term, and (iv) requires, as a condition to payment, a countersignature by a person whose specimen signature appears on the instrument." Section 3-104(i). *See also* Check; Signed.

Unauthorized signature: An unauthorized signature is "one made without actual, implied, or apparent authority and includes a forgery." 2001 Revised Section 1-201(41). *See also* Signed.

Value: An instrument is issued or transferred for value if

(1) **the instrument is issued or transferred for a promise of performance, to the extent the promise has been performed;**

(2) **the transferee acquires a security interest or other lien in the instrument other than a lien obtained by judicial proceeding;**

(3) **the instrument is issued or transferred as payment of, or as security for, an antecedent claim against any person, whether or not the claim is due;**

(4) **the instrument is issued or transferred in exchange for a negotiable instrument; or**

(5) **the instrument is issued or transferred in exchange for the incurring of an irrevocable obligation to a third party by the person taking the instrument.** Section 3-303(a).

See also Instrument; Issue; Security interest; Transfer of an instrument.

Without Recourse: The term used, in connection with a signature on an instrument, to disclaim the contractual liability otherwise undertaken by the signer. Most commonly, the term is used in connection with an indorsement to create a "qualified indorsement." *See also* Indorsement; Indorser; Instrument; Qualified Indorsement.

Writing: This term includes "printing, typewriting or any other intentional reduction to tangible form" and "written" has a "corresponding meaning." 2001 Revised Section 1-201(43).

Appendix 2

TAKING AN INSTRUMENT AS ACCORD AND SATISFACTION

As discussed in Chapter 5, unless otherwise agreed, the taking of a note or uncertified check (except for a bank or teller's check) suspends the obligor's underlying obligation, but only *to the extent* that the obligation would have been discharged if, instead of giving the instrument, the obligor had given an amount of money equal to the amount of the instrument. In practice, however, parties frequently attempt to settle their disputes in full by giving their creditors checks payable for amounts less than the creditors' claims.

In a typical case, one party issues a check with a legend, below which the payee is expected to indorse. The legend declares that, by indorsing the check, the payee agrees to take payment as full settlement of any and all claims against the drawer. Often, the legend also states that the payee, in exchange for payment, waives any and all claims against the drawer. Nevertheless, the payee frequently sues the drawer for the balance of its original claim. The drawer alleges, as an affirmative defense, that the payee's claim was settled when the payee obtained payment of the check. The drawer contends that such payment concluded an "accord and satisfaction." Section 3-311 was designed to deal with this "informal method of dispute resolution carried out by use of a negotiable instrument." UCC Comment 1 to § 3-311.

For a defendant to assert successfully that, pursuant to § 3-311, an accord and satisfaction was reached through the tender of an instrument, he must first prove that:

a. he made tender to the claimant in good faith;

b. he made the tender for the purpose of fully satisfying the claim;

c. the amount of the claim had either been unliquidated or subject to a bona fide dispute (i.e., there is legitimate question either as to a party's duty to pay or as to the amount the party is obligated to pay); and

NOTE: For examples of what might not be a "good faith" tender in payment of a "bona fide dispute," see, e.g., *Alpine Haven Property Owners Association, Inc.*, 830 A.2d 78, 51 UCC Rep.Serv.2d 195 (Vt. 2003) (homeowner who had lost multiple lawsuits regarding fees due to property owners association had not tendered check either in good faith or in connection with a bona fide dispute); *Walden v. Vaughn*, 157 N.C.App. 507, 579 S.E.2d 475, 50 UCC Rep.Serv.2d 507 (2003) (§ 3-311 does not apply where there is no good faith dispute as to the amount of the claim). *See also, generally,* Comment 4 to § 3-311.

d. the claimant obtained payment of the instrument.

If these requirements are all satisfied, the claim will generally be discharged under § 3-311(b) if the defendant also proves that the instrument or an accompanying writing contained "a conspicuous statement to the effect" that tender was made as full satisfaction of the claim.

However, to protect against an inadvertent accord and satisfaction, § 3-311(c) provides that a claimant can nevertheless prevail if it proves that it and any agent with direct responsibility for the claim had *no actual prior knowledge* of the intent of the defendant to settle the claim by tendering the instrument, *and*:

a. if the claimant is an organization, that (1) within a reasonable period of time before tender of the instrument to it the claimant sent a conspicuous statement, presumably in writing, to the defendant that any communications regarding disputed debts, including an instrument tendered in satisfaction of a debt, must be sent to a specific person, office, or place, and (2) the instrument or accompanying statement was not received by that designated person, office, or place; *or*, when not applicable,

b. that, within 90 days after the instrument was paid, the claimant tendered repayment to the defendant.

One important ambiguity is whether an accord and satisfaction can be established under § 3-311 even when neither the instrument tendered nor any accompanying writing contained a conspicuous statement to the effect that tender was made as full satisfaction of the claim. Section 3-311(d) suggests that such an accord and satisfaction could be so established as long as the claimant or its agent with direct responsibility for the claim had actual prior knowledge of the defendant's intent to settle the claim by tendering the instrument.

PROBLEM 1

Under the following circumstances, would the cashing of the tendered instrument constitute a valid accord and satisfaction?

a. *Franny's Fruit Market routinely prints "in full satisfaction" language on all of its checks used to pay suppliers. After submitting its invoice to Franny's for $1,000, Alvin's Apple Orchards receives a check bearing this language payable to Alvin's for $800. Will Alvin's relinquish its ability to sue for the $200 balance if it cashes this check? See Comment 4 to § 3-311.* No, lack good faith

b. *John, a struggling artist, is asked by the very wealthy Sidney Slime, to paint a portrait of his wife. The agreed upon price is $1,000. After several weeks, John completes the work and presents it to Slime who dishonestly asserts that he is unsatisfied with the end product and will only pay John*

$150. He presents John with a check conspicuously bearing the legend, "This check is tendered as payment in full satisfaction for the commissioned portrait of my wife given to me this day by John." John, whose rent on his studio is overdue, cashes the check. Has he relinquished his ability to sue for the $850 balance? No, must be good faith dispute

PROBLEM 2

Bob Buyer orders $5,000 worth of supplies from Sam Seller. Sam delivers the goods and bills Bob for the $5,000. Bob calls Sam and says that the goods are defective and only worth $2,000. Sam disagrees and demands the entire $5,000. Bob then sends Sam a letter, with a check enclosed for $2,000. In the letter, Bob writes:

> *As I told you on the phone, the goods were defective. The enclosed check for $2,000 is in full payment of any and all claims you have against me.*

Sam cashes the check on 2/1/2004, allegedly without realizing what Bob said in his letter. Nothing else happens until 8/1/2004, when S sues B for the $3,000 difference between the $5,000 originally billed and the $2,000 paid. What result?

S lost claim by cashing check

PROBLEM 3

Same as Problem 2, above, except that Sam operates a large company. When Bob calls Sam and tells Sam that the goods are defective and only worth $2,000, Bob tells Sam that he is going to send in a check for $2,000 in full payment. Sam tells Bob not to do so, that Sam will not take less than the full $5,000. Bob nonetheless sends the letter with the statement as above and a check for $200, and someone in Sam's office deposits it on 2/1/2004 and the check is paid by the drawee bank on 2/10/2004. When Sam sues Bob on 8/1/2004, what result?

PROBLEM 4

Assume that, in each of the problems above, that on 4/15/2004, Sam sent Bob a check for $200 as repayment of the monies Sam had collected from cashing Bob's check. Is the result the same in both cases?

PROBLEM 5

Sid and Nancy enter into an agreement whereby Nancy agrees to take care of Sid's dog for a month. At the end of the month when Nancy returns the dog, a dispute develops over how much Sid had agreed to pay for Nancy's services. Nancy claims that Sid had agreed to pay $300 and Sid says it was $200. They argue for *quite some time and finally Nancy agrees to take the $200 as payment in full. But when Sid sends the check, he does not send a letter with it and he does not write on the check that it is in full payment. Nancy cashes the check. Assuming Nancy makes no offer to repay the $200 Sid has already paid her, can Sid assert that an accord and satisfaction has been established, such that he is discharged from any further obligation when Nancy sues him for the remaining $100 she claims he owes her?*

One final note on Accord and Satisfaction

Sometimes a check contains language stating that it is in full satisfaction of a debt, and a claimant strikes the language out. Under the common law, the claimant's action was a nullity. A claimant was required either to accept the condition or to refuse the payment. Before § 3-311 was written, there was a split of judicial authority on whether § 1-207, (which allows a party who assents to a "performance" by the other party, e.g., obtains payment on the check offered, to nevertheless do so without prejudicing any rights reserved) was applicable to an accord and satisfaction. When Article 3 was revised, and § 3-311 was added, § 1-207 was also amended to specifically say that it does not apply to an accord and satisfaction. Instead, UCC Comment 3 to § 1-207 states that § 3-311 governs any attempt to create an accord and satisfaction by the tendering of a negotiable instrument. *See* UCC Comment 3 to § 3-311 which indicates that § 3-311 generally follows the common law rule. *See also Morgan v. Crawford*, 106 S.W.3d 480, 50 UCC Rep.Serv.2d 373 (S.Ct. Ky. 2003) (by crossing out "payment in full" and writing "under protest," payee did not prevent an accord and satisfaction under § 3-311)

In some jurisdictions, there were statutes that specifically overturned the common law approach and held that a person could avoid an accord and satisfaction by striking out the "full satisfaction" language. Where such jurisdictions have adopted § 3-311, § 3-311 overrules any such prior, inconsistent statute. *See, e.g., Woodridge V. J.F.L. Electric, Inc.*, 96 Cal.App.4th Supp. 52, 117 Cal.Rptr.2d 771 (2002).

Appendix 3

PLAINTIFF-DEFENDANT TABLE

Plaintiff	Defendant	Theory of Recovery	Code § §
Payee-holder	Maker	Maker's Obligation	§ 3-412
		Underlying Obligation	§ 3-110
	Drawer	Drawer's Obligation	§ 3-414
		Underlying Obligation	§ 3-110
	Acceptor	Acceptor's Obligation	§ 3-413

Payee

(If Instrument Is Stolen or Lost and Payees Signature Is Forged and Instrument Is Wrongfully Paid to Someone Other than the Payee)

	Maker	Maker's Obligation	§ 3-412, § 3-309
	Drawer	Drawer's Obligation	§ 3-414, § 3-309, § 3-312
		Underlying Obligation	§ 3-110
	Acceptor	Acceptor's Obligation	§ 3-413, § 3-309, § 3-312
	Drawee	Conversion	§ 3-420
	Depository Bank	Conversion	§ 3-420
	Transferor	Conversion	§ 3-420
	Presentor	Conversion	§ 3-420
Holder	Maker	Maker's Obligation	§ 3-412
	Drawer	Drawer's Obligation	§ 3-414
	Acceptor	Acceptor's Obligation	§ 3-413
	Indorser	Indorser's Obligation	§ 3-415
		Transfer Warranty	§ 3-416, § 4-207
	Transferor	Transfer Warranty	§ 3-416, § 4-207

Drawer	Drawee Bank	Wrongful Payment	§ 4-401
		Wrongful Dishonor	§ 4-402
Maker or Drawer (Who Paid the Instrument)	Comaker or Codrawer	Contribution	§ 3-116
	Presentor	Payment by Mistake	§ 3-418(b)
	Presentor and Prior Transferors	Presentment Warranty	§ 3-417, § 4-208
Drawee (Who Paid the Instrument)	Presentor	Payment by Mistake	§ 3-418(a)
	Presentor and Prior Transferors	Presentment Warranty	§ 3-417, § 4-208
Indorser (Who Paid the Instrument)	Maker	Maker's Obligation	§ 3-412
	Drawer	Drawer's Obligation	§ 3-414
	Acceptor	Acceptor's Obligation	§ 3-413
	Prior Indorser	Indorser's Obligation	§ 3-415
		Transfer Warranty	§ 3-416, § 4-207
	Anomalous Indorser	Contribution	§ 3-116
	Presentor	Payment by Mistake	§ 3-418
	Presentor and Prior Transferors	Presentment Warranty	§ 3-417, § 4-208
Acceptor	Presentor	Acceptance by Mistake	§ 3-418
		Payment by Mistake	§ 3-418
	Presentor and Prior Transferors	Presentment Warranty	§ 3-417, § 4-208
Transferee	Transferor	Transfer Warranty	§ 3-416, § 4-207
	Indorser	Transfer Warranty	§ 3-416, § 4-207
Accommodation Party	Accommodated Party	Reimbursement	§ 3-419(e)

Appendix 4

PRE-2002 REVISION §3-605

§ 3-605. Discharge of Indorsers and Accomodation Parties.

(a) In this section, the term "**indorser**" includes a drawer having the obligation described in Section 3-414(d).

(b) Discharge, under Section 3-604, of the obligation of a party to pay an instrument does not discharge the obligation of an indorser or accommodation party having a right of recourse against the discharged party.

(c) If a person entitled to enforce an instrument agrees, with or without consideration, to an extension of the due date of the obligation of a party to pay the instrument, the extension discharges an indorser or accommodation party having a right of recourse against the party whose obligation is extended to the extent the indorser or accommodation party proves that the extension caused loss to the indorser or accommodation party with respect to the right of recourse.

(d) If a person entitled to enforce an instrument agrees, with or without consideration, to a material modification of the obligation of a party other than an extension of the due date, the modification discharges the obligation of an indorser or accommodation party having a right of recourse against the person whose obligation is modified to the extent the modification causes loss to the indorser or accommodation party with respect to the right of recourse. The loss suffered by the indorser or accommodation party as a result of the modification is equal to the amount of the right of recourse unless the person enforcing the instrument proves that no loss was caused by the modification or that the loss caused by the modification was an amount less than the amount of the right of recourse.

(e) If the obligation of a party to pay an instrument is secured by an interest in collateral and a person entitled to enforce the instrument impairs the value of the interest in collateral, the obligation of an indorser or accommodation party having a right of recourse against the obligor is discharged to the extent of the impairment. The value of an interest in collateral is impaired to the extent (i) the value of the interest is reduced to an amount less than the amount of the right of recourse of the party asserting discharge, or (ii) the reduction in value of the interest causes an increase in the amount by which the amount of the right of recourse exceeds the value of the interest. The burden of proving impairment is on the party asserting discharge.

(f) If the obligation of a party is secured by an interest in collateral not provided by an accommodation party and a person entitled to enforce the instrument impairs the value of the interest in collateral, the obligation of any party who is jointly and severally liable with respect to the secured obligation is discharged to the extent the impairment causes the party asserting discharge to pay more than that party would have been obliged to pay, taking into account rights of contribution, if impairment had not occurred. If the party asserting discharge is an accommodation party not entitled to discharge under subsection (e), the party is deemed to have a right to contribution based on joint and several liability rather than a right to reimbursement. The burden of proving impairment is on the party asserting discharge.

(g) Under subsection (e) or (f), impairing value of an interest in collateral includes (i) failure to obtain or maintain perfection or recordation of the interest in collateral, (ii) release of collateral without substitution of collateral of equal value, (iii) failure to perform a duty to preserve the value of collateral owed, under Article 9 or other law, to a debtor or surety or other person secondarily liable, or (iv) failure to comply with applicable law in disposing of collateral.

(h) An accommodation party is not discharged under subsection (c), (d), or (e) unless the person entitled to enforce the instrument knows of the accommodation or has notice under Section 3-419(c) that the instrument was signed for accommodation.

(i) A party is not discharged under this section if (i) the party asserting discharge consents to the event or conduct that is the basis of the discharge, or (ii) the instrument or a separate agreement of the party provides for waiver of discharge under this section either specifically or by general language indicating that parties waive defenses based on suretyship or impairment of collateral.

COMMENT § 3-605

1. Section 3-605, which replaces former Section 3-606, can be illustrated by an example. Bank lends $10,000 to Borrower who signs a note under which Borrower is obliged to pay $10,000 to Bank on a due date stated in the note. Bank insists, however, that Accommodation Party also become liable to pay the note. Accommodation Party can incur this liability by signing the note as a co-maker or by indorsing the note. In either case the note is signed for accommodation and Borrower is the accommodated party. Rights and obligations of Accommodation Party in this case are stated in Section 3-419. Suppose that after the note is signed, Bank agrees to a modification of the rights and obligations between Bank and Borrower. For example, Bank agrees that Borrower may pay the note at some date after the due date, or that Borrower may discharge Borrower's $10,000 obligation to pay the note by paying Bank $3,000, or that Bank releases collateral given by Borrower to secure the note. Under the law of suretyship Borrower is usually referred to as the principal debtor and Accommodation Party is referred to as the surety. Under that law, the surety can be discharged under certain circumstances if changes of this kind are made by

Bank, the creditor, without the consent of Accommodation Party, the surety. Rights of the surety to discharge in such cases are commonly referred to as suretyship defenses. Section 3-605 is concerned with this kind of problem in the context of a negotiable instrument to which the principal debtor and the surety are parties. But Section 3-605 has a wider scope. It also applies to indorsers who are not accommodation parties. Unless an indorser signs without recourse, the indorser's liability under Section 3-415(a) is that of a guarantor of payment. If Bank in our hypothetical case indorsed the note and transferred it to Second Bank, Bank has rights given to an indorser under Section 3-605 if it is Second Bank that modifies rights and obligations of Borrower. Both accommodation parties and indorsers will be referred to in these Comments as sureties. The scope of Section 3-605 is also widened by subsection (e) which deals with rights of a non-accommodation party co-maker when collateral is impaired.

2. The importance of suretyship defenses is greatly diminished by the fact that they can be waived. The waiver is usually made by a provision in the note or other writing that represents the obligation of the principal debtor. It is standard practice to include a waiver of suretyship defenses in notes given to financial institutions or other commercial creditors. Section 3-605(i) allows waiver. Thus, Section 3-605 applies to the occasional case in which the creditor did not include a waiver clause in the instrument or in which the creditor did not obtain the permission of the surety to take the action that triggers the suretyship defense.

3. Subsection (b) addresses the effect of discharge under Section 3-604 of the principal debtor. In the hypothetical case stated in Comment 1, release of Borrower by Bank does not release Accommodation Party. As a practical matter, Bank will not gratuitously release Borrower. Discharge of Borrower normally would be part of a settlement with Borrower if Borrower is insolvent or in financial difficulty. If Borrower is unable to pay all creditors, it may be prudent for Bank to take partial payment, but Borrower will normally insist on a release of the obligation. If Bank takes $3,000 and releases Borrower from the $10,000 debt, Accommodation Party is not injured. To the extent of the payment Accommodation Party's obligation to Bank is reduced. The release of Borrower by Bank does not affect the right of Accommodation Party to obtain reimbursement from Borrower or to enforce the note against Borrower if Accommodation Party pays Bank. Section 3-419(e). Subsection (b) is designed to allow a creditor to settle with the principal debtor without risk of losing rights against sureties. Settlement is in the interest of sureties as well as the creditor. Subsection (b), however, is not intended to apply to a settlement of a disputed claim which discharges the obligation.

Subsection (b) changes the law stated in former Section 3-606 but the change relates largely to formalities rather than substance. Under former Section 3-606, Bank in the hypothetical case stated in Comment 1 could settle with and release Borrower without releasing Accommodation Party, but to accomplish that result Bank had to either obtain the consent of Accommodation Party or make an express reservation of rights against Accommodation Party at the time it released Borrower. The reservation of rights was made in the agreement between Bank and Borrower by which the release of Borrower was made. There was no requirement in former Section 3-606 that any notice be given to Accommodation Party. Section 3-605 eliminates the necessity that Bank formally reserve rights against Accommodation Party in order to retain rights of recourse against Accommodation Party. See PEB Commentary No. 11, dated December 15, 1993.

4. Subsection (c) relates to extensions of the due date of the instrument. In most cases an extension of time to pay a note is a benefit to both the principal debtor and sureties having recourse against the principal debtor. In relatively few cases the extension may cause loss if deterioration of the financial condition of the principal debtor reduces the amount that the surety will be able to recover on its right of recourse when default occurs. Former Section 3-606(1)(a) did not take into account the presence or absence of loss to the surety. For example, suppose the instrument is an installment note and the principal debtor is temporarily short of funds to pay a monthly installment. The payee agrees to extend the due date of the installment for a month or two to allow the debtor to pay when funds are available. Under former Section 3-606 surety was discharged if consent was not given unless the payee expressly reserved rights against the surety. It did not matter that the extension of time was a trivial change in the guaranteed obligation and that there was no evidence that the surety suffered any loss because of the extension. *Wilmington Trust Co. v. Gesullo*, 29 U.C.C. Rep. 144 (Del. Super. Ct. 1980). Under subsection (c) an extension of time results in discharge only to the extent the surety proves that the extension caused loss. For example, if the extension is for a long period the surety might be able to prove that during the period of extension the principal debtor became insolvent, thus reducing the value of the right of recourse of the surety. By putting the burden on the surety to prove loss, subsection (c) more accurately reflects what the parties would have done by agreement, and it facilitates workouts.

Under other provisions of Article 3, what is the effect of an extension agreement between the holder of a note and the maker who is an accommodated party? The question is illustrated by the following case:

> *Case #1.* A borrows money from Lender and issues a note payable on April 1, 1992. B signs the note for accommodation at the request of Lender. B signed the note either as co-maker or as an anomalous indorser. In either case Lender subsequently makes an agreement with A extending the due date of A's obligation to pay the note to July 1, 1992. In either case B did not agree to the extension.

What is the effect of the extension agreement on B? Could Lender enforce the note against B if the note is not paid on April 1, 1992? A's obligation to Lender to pay the note on April 1, 1992 may be modified by the agreement of Lender. If B is an anomalous indorser Lender cannot enforce the note against B unless the note has been dishonored. Section 3-415(a). Under Section 3-502(a)(3) dishonor occurs if it is not paid on the day it becomes payable. Since the agreement between A and Lender extended the due date of A's obligation to July 1, 1992 there is no dishonor because A was not obligated to pay Lender on April 1, 1992. If B is a co-maker the analysis is somewhat different. Lender has no power to amend the terms of the note without the consent of both A and B. By an agreement with A, Lender can extend the due date of A's obligation to Lender to pay the note but B's obligation is to pay the note according to the terms of the note at the time of issue. Section 3-412. However, B's obligation to pay the note is subject to a defense because B is an accommodation party. B is not obliged to pay Lender if A is not obliged to pay Lender. Under Section 3-305(d), B as an accommodation party can assert against Lender any defense of A. A has a defense based on the extension agreement. Thus, the result is that Lender could not enforce the note against B until July 1, 1992. This result is consistent with the right of B if B is an anomalous indorser.

As a practical matter an extension of the due date will normally occur when the accommodated party is unable to pay on the due date. The interest of the accommodation party normally is to defer payment to the holder rather than to pay right away and rely on an action against the accommodated party that may have little or no value. But in unusual cases the accommodation party may prefer to pay the holder on the original due date. In such cases, the accommodation party may do so. This is because the extension agreement between the accommodated party and the holder cannot bind the accommodation party to a change in its obligation without the accommodation party's consent. The effect on the recourse of the accommodation party against the accommodated party of performance by the accommodation party on the original due date is not addressed in § 3-419 and is left to the general law of suretyship.

Even though an accommodation party has the option of paying the instrument on the original due date, the accommodation party is not precluded from asserting its rights to discharge under Section 3-605(c) if it does not exercise that option. The critical issue is whether the extension caused the accommodation party a loss by increasing the difference between its cost of performing its obligation on the instrument and the amount recoverable from the accommodated party pursuant to Section 3-419(e). The decision by the accommodation party not to exercise its option to pay on the original due date may, under the circumstances, be a factor to be considered in the determination of that issue. See PEB Commentary No. 11, supra.

5. Former Section 3-606 applied to extensions of the due date of a note but not to other modifications of the obligation of the principal debtor. There was no apparent reason why former Section 3-606 did not follow general suretyship law in covering both. Under Section 3-605(d) a material modification of the obligation of the principal debtor, other than an extension of the due date, will result in discharge of the surety to the extent the modification caused loss to the surety with respect to the right of recourse. The loss caused by the modification is deemed to be the entire amount of the right of recourse unless the person

seeking enforcement of the instrument proves that no loss occurred or that the loss was less than the full amount of the right of recourse. In the absence of that proof, the surety is completely discharged. The rationale for having different rules with respect to loss for extensions of the due date and other modifications is that extensions are likely to be beneficial to the surety and they are often made. Other modifications are less common and they may very well be detrimental to the surety. Modification of the obligation of the principal debtor without permission of the surety is unreasonable unless the modification is benign. Subsection (d) puts the burden on the person seeking enforcement of the instrument to prove the extent to which loss was not caused by the modification.

The following is an illustration of the kind of case to which Section 3-605(d) would apply:

> *Case #2.* Corporation borrows money from Lender and issues a note payable to Lender. X signs the note as an accommodation party for Corporation. The loan agreement under which the note was issued states various events of default which allow Lender to accelerate the due date of the note. Among the events of default are breach of covenants not to incur debt beyond specified limits and not to engage in any line of business substantially different from that currently carried on by Corporation. Without consent of X, Lender agrees to modify the covenants to allow Corporation to enter into a new line of business that X considers to be risky, and to incur debt beyond the limits specified in the loan agreement to finance the new venture. This modification releases X unless Lender proves that the modification did not cause loss to X or that the loss caused by the modification was less than X's right of recourse.

Sometimes there is both an extension of the due date and some other modification. In that case both subsections (c) and (d) apply. The following is an example:

> *Case #3.* Corporation was indebted to Lender on a note payable on April 1, 1992 and X signed the note as an accommodation party for Corporation. The interest rate on the note was 12 percent. Lender and Corporation agreed to a six-month extension of the due date of the note to October 1, 1992 and an increase in the interest rate to 14 percent after April 1, 1992. Corporation defaulted on October 1, 1992. Corporation paid no interest during the six-month extension period. Corporation is insolvent and has no assets from which unsecured creditors can be paid. Lender demanded payment from X.

Assume X is an anomalous indorser. First consider Section 3-605(c) alone. If there had been no change in the interest rate, the fact that Lender gave an extension of six months to Corporation would not result in discharge unless X could prove loss with respect to the right of recourse because of the extension. If the financial condition of Corporation on April 1, 1992 would not have allowed any recovery on the right of recourse, X can't show any loss as a result of the extension with respect to the amount due on the note on April 1, 1992. Since the note accrued interest during the six-month extension, is there a loss equal to the accrued interest? Since the interest rate was not raised, only Section 3-605(c) would apply and X probably could not prove any loss. The obligation of X includes interest on the note until the note is paid. To the extent payment was delayed X had the use of the money that X otherwise would have had to pay to Lender. X could have prevented the running of interest by paying the debt. Since X did not do so, X suffered no loss as the result of the extension.

If the interest rate was raised, Section 3-605(d) also must be considered. If X is an anomalous indorser, X's liability is to pay the note according to its terms at the time of indorsement. Section 3-415(a). Thus, X's obligation to pay interest is measured by the terms of the note (12%) rather than by the increased amount of 14 percent. The same analysis applies if X had been a co-maker. Under Section 3-412 the liability of the issuer of a note is to pay the note according to its terms at the time it was issued. Either obligation could be changed by contract and that occurred with respect to Corporation when it agreed to the increase in the interest rate, but X did not join in that agreement and is not bound by it. Thus, the most that X can be required to pay is the amount due on the note plus interest at the rate of 12 percent.

Does the modification discharge X under Section 3-605(d)? Any modification that increases the monetary obligation of X is material. An increase of the interest rate from 12 percent to 14 percent is certainly a material modification. There is a presumption that X is discharged because Section 3-605(d) creates a presumption that the modification caused a loss to X equal to the amount of the right of recourse. Thus, Lender has the burden of proving absence of loss or a loss less than the amount of the right of recourse. Since Corporation paid no interest during the six-month period, the issue is like the issue presented under Section 3-605(c) which we have just discussed. The increase in the interest rate could not have affected the right of recourse because no interest was paid by Corporation. X is in the same position as X would have been in if there had been an extension without an increase in the interest rate.

The analysis with respect to Section 3-605(c) and (d) would have been different if we change the assumptions. Suppose Corporation was not insolvent on April 1, 1992, that Corporation paid interest at the higher rate during the six-month period, and that Corporation was insolvent at the end of the six-month period. In this case it is possible that the extension and the additional burden placed on Corporation by the increased interest rate may have been detrimental to X.

There are difficulties in properly allocating burden of proof when the agreement between Lender and Corporation involves both an extension under Section 3-605(c) and a modification under Section 3-605(d). The agreement may have caused loss to X but it may be difficult to identify the extent to which the loss was caused by the extension or the other modification. If neither Lender nor X introduces evidence on the issue, the result is full discharge because Section 3-605(d) applies. Thus, Lender has the burden of overcoming the presumption in Section 3-605(d). In doing so, Lender should be entitled to a presumption that the extension of time by itself caused no loss. Section 3-605(c) is based on such a presumption and X should be required to introduce evidence on the effect of the extension on the right of recourse. Lender would have to introduce evidence on the effect of the increased interest rate. Thus both sides will have to introduce evidence. On the basis of this evidence the court will have to make a determination of the overall effect of the agreement on X's right of recourse. See PEB Commentary No. 11, supra.

6. Subsection (e) deals with discharge of sureties by impairment of collateral. It generally conforms to former Section 3-606(1)(b). Subsection (g) states common examples of what is meant by impairment. By using the term "includes," it allows a court to find impairment in other cases as well. There is extensive case law on impairment of collateral. The surety is discharged to the extent the surety proves that impairment was caused by a person entitled to enforce the instrument. For example, suppose the payee of a secured note fails to perfect the security interest. The collateral is owned by the principal debtor who subsequently files in bankruptcy. As a result of the failure to perfect, the security interest is not enforceable in bankruptcy. If the payee obtains payment from the surety, the surety is subrogated to the payee's security interest in the collateral. In this case the value of the security interest is impaired completely because the security interest is unenforceable. If the value of the collateral is as much or more than the amount of the note there is a complete discharge.

In some states a real property grantee who assumes the obligation of the grantor as maker of a note secured by the real property becomes by operation of law a principal debtor and the grantor becomes a surety. The meager case authority was split on whether former Section 3-606 applied to release the grantor if the holder released or extended the obligation of the grantee. Revised Article 3 takes no position on the effect of the release of the grantee in this case. Section 3-605(b) does not apply because the holder has not discharged the obligation of a "party," a term defined in Section 3-103(a)(8) as "party to an instrument." The assuming grantee is not a party to the instrument. The resolution of this question is governed by general principles of law, including the law of suretyship. See PEB Commentary No. 11, supra.

7. Subsection (f) is illustrated by the following case. X and Y sign a note for $1,000 as co-makers. Neither is an accommodation party. X grants a security interest in X's property to secure the note. The collateral is worth more than $1,000. Payee fails to perfect the security interest in X's property before X files in bankruptcy. As a result the security interest is not enforceable in bankruptcy. Had Payee perfected the security interest, Y could have paid the note and gained rights to X's collateral by subrogation. If the security interest had been perfected, Y could have realized on the collateral to the extent of $500 to satisfy its right of contribution against X. Payee's failure to perfect deprived Y of the

benefit of the collateral. Subsection (f) discharges Y to the extent of its loss. If there are no assets in the bankruptcy for unsecured claims, the loss is $500, the amount of Y's contribution claim against X which now has a zero value. If some amount is payable on unsecured claims, the loss is reduced by the amount receivable by Y. The same result follows if Y is an accommodation party but Payee has no knowledge of the accommodation or notice under Section 3-419(c). In that event Y is not discharged under subsection (e), but subsection (f) applies because X and Y are jointly and severally liable on the note. Under subsection (f), Y is treated as a co-maker with a right of contribution rather than an accommodation party with a right of reimbursement. Y is discharged to the extent of $500. If Y is the principal debtor and X is the accommodation party subsection (f) doesn't apply. Y, as principal debtor, is not injured by the impairment of collateral because Y would have been obliged to reimburse X for the entire $1,000 even if Payee had obtained payment from sale of the collateral.

8. Subsection (i) is a continuation of former law which allowed suretyship defenses to be waived. As the subsection provides, a party is not discharged under this section if the instrument or a separate agreement of the party waives discharge either specifically or by general language indicating that defenses based on suretyship and impairment of collateral are waived. No particular language or form of agreement is required, and the standards for enforcing such a term are the same as the standards for enforcing any other term in an instrument or agreement.

Subsection (i), however, applies only to a "discharge under this section." The right of an accommodation party to be discharged under Section 3-605(e) because of an impairment of collateral can be waived. But with respect to a note secured by personal property collateral, Article 9 also applies. If an accommodation party is a "debtor" under Section 9-105(1)(d), the accommodation party has rights under Article 9. Under Section 9-501(3)(b) rights of an Article 9 debtor under Section 9-504(3) and Section 9-505(1), which deal with disposition of collateral, cannot be waived except as provided in Article 9. These Article 9 rights are independent of rights under Section 3-605. Since Section 3-605(i) is specifically limited to discharge under Section 3-605, a waiver of rights with respect to Section 3-605 has no effect on rights under Article 9. With respect to Article 9 rights, Section 9-501(3)(b) controls. See PEB Commentary No. 11, supra.

Appendix 5

JURISDICTIONS THAT HAVE ADOPTED THE 1990 REVISIONS TO ARTICLES 3 & 4

JURISDICTION	Effective Date	Statutory Citation
Alabama	1-1-1996	Ala.Code 1975, §§ 7-3-101 to 4-504
Alaska	1-1-1994	AS 45.03.101 to 45.04.504
Arizona	7-17-1993	A.R.S. §§ 47-3101 to 47-4504
Arkansas	7-15-1991	A.C.A. §§ 4-3-101 to 4-4-504
California	1-1-1993	CA COML §§ 3101 to 4504
Colorado	1-1-1995	C.R.S.A. §§ 4-3-101 to 4-4-504
Connecticut	6-1-1992	C.G.S.A. §§ 42a-3-101 to 42a-4-504
Delaware	7-1-1995	6 Del.C. §§ 3-101 to 4-504
Dist. of Columbia	3-23-1995	D.C.Code1981, §§ 28:3-101 to 28.4-504
Florida	1-1-1993	West's F.S.A. §§ 673.101 to 674.504
Georgia	7-1-1996	O.C.G.A. §§ 11-3-101 to 11-4-504
Hawaii	1-1-1992	HRS §§ 490:3-101 to 490:4-504
Idaho	7-1-1993	I.C. §§ 28-3-101 to 28-4-638
Illinois	1-1-1992	S.H.A. 810 ILCS 5/3-101 to 5/4-504
Indiana	7-1-1994	West's A.I.C. 26-1-3-101 to 26-1-4-504
Iowa	7-1-1995	I.C.A. §§ 554.3101 to 554.4504
Kansas	2-1-1992	K.S.A. 84-3-101 to 84-4-504
Kentucky	1-1-1997	K.R.S.A. §§ 355.3-101 to 355.4-504
Louisiana	1-1-1994	LSA-R.S. 10:3-101 to 10:4-504
Maine	10-13-1993	11 M.R.S.A. §§ 3-1101 to 4-504
Maryland	1-1-1997	Md.Code.Anno. §§ 3-101 to 4-504
Massachusetts	5-13-1998	Mass.Gen.Laws 106 §§ 3-101 to 4-504
Michigan	9-30-1993	M.C.L.A. §§ 440.1301 to 440.4504
Minnesota	8-1-1992	M.S.A. §§ 336.3-101 to 336.4-504
Mississippi	1-1-1993	Code 1972, §§ 75-3-101 to 75-4-504
Missouri	8-24-1992	V.A.M.S. §§ 400.3-101 to 400.4-504
Montana	10-1-1991	MCA 30-3-101 to 30-4-504

Nebraska	1-1-1992	Neb.Rev.St.U.C.C. §§ 3-101 to 4-504
Nevada	7-2-1993	N.R.S. 104.3101 to 104.4504
New Hampshire	1-1-1994	RSA 382-A:3-101 to 382-A:4-504
New Jersey	6-1-1995	N.J.S.A. 12A:3-101 to 12A:4-504
New Mexico	7-1-1992	NMSA 1978,§§ 55-3-101 to 55-4-504
New York	Not yet adopted	Introduced SB 2260 in 2003
North Carolina	10-1-1995	G.S. §§ 25-3-101 to 25-4-504
North Dakota	7-1-1993	NDCC 41-03-01 to 41-04-42
Ohio	8-19-1994	R.C. §§ 1303.01 to 1304.40
Oklahoma	1-1-1992	12A Okl.St.Ann. §§ 3-101 to 4-504
Oregon	7-1-1993	ORS 73.0101 to 74.5040
Pennsylvania	7-9-1993	13 Pa.C.S.A. §§ 3101 to 4504
Rhode Island	7-1-2001	RI ST §§ 3-101 to 4-504
South Carolina	Not yet adopted	No action
South Dakota	7-1-1995	SDCL 57A-3-101 to 57A-4-504
Tennessee	7-1-1996	West's Tenn.Code §§ 47-3-101 to 47-4-504
Texas	1-1-1996	V.T.C.A., Bus. & C. §§ 3.101 to 4.504
Utah	7-1-1993	U.C.A.1953, 70A-3-101 to 70A-4-504
Vermont	1-1-1995	9A V.S.A. §§ 3-101 to 4-504
Virgin Islands	2-1-2001	11A VIC §§ 3-101 to 4-504
Virginia	1-1-1993	Code 1950, §§ 8.3A-101 to 8.4-504
Washington	7-1-1994	West's RCWA 62A.3-101 to 62A.4-504
West Virginia	7-8-1993	W.Va.Code, 46-3-101 to 46-4-504
Wisconsin	8-1-1996	Wis.Stats §§ 403.101 to 404.504
Wyoming	7-1-1991	W.S.1977, §§ 34.1-3-101 to34.1-4-504

Table of Cases

(Principal cases are in all caps; references are to pages.)

INDEX

[References are to page numbers.]

A

ACCEPTOR
Obligations...62

ACCOMMODATION PARTIES
Generally...81
Defense to enforcement, assertion of third person's claim as...113
Guarantors...82
Reimbursement, right of...83
Status, proof of...86
Sureties, common law and equitable rights of...85

ACCOUNTS
Closing account (See STOP PAYMENT ORDERS, subhead: Close account, stop payment or)

AGENCY RELATIONSHIP
Bank-customer relationship...171

AGENTS, INSTRUMENTS SIGNED BY
Generally...73; 80
Authorized agent's signature...75
Extrinsic evidence...78
Personal liability...74
Principal's liability on...73
Representative capacity...77
Unauthorized agent's signature...74

ALTERATIONS
Authorized, treated as (See SIGNATURE, subhead: Alterations treated as authorized, unauthorized signatures and)
Fraudulent alteration
    Generally...111
    Exceptions...112
Properly payable items, effect on...174

ANTECEDENT DEBTS
Value...122

ARTICLE 1
Bank charges for items not properly payable under §1-103...179
Provisions...5

ARTICLE 3
Alterations and unauthorized signatures treated as authorized, preclusions under §3-406 as to (See SIGNATURE, subhead: Alterations treated as authorized, unauthorized signatures and)
Bank charges for items not properly payable under §3-407...176

ARTICLE 3—Cont.
Defenses to enforcement under
    Generally...90
    Discharge of liability...102; 105; 108
Discharge of liability
    §3-605 provisions...105; 108
    2002 revision approach...102
Holder in due course under revised §3-305(e)...141
Missing or unauthorized signatures, drawee's rights under §3-418 as to...221
Non-UCC law superceding...6
Notes and drafts (See NOTES AND DRAFTS, subhead: Article 3, authorization under)
Person not in possession of instrument entitled to enforcement pursuant to §3-309 or §3-418(d)...50
Presentment warranties under revised §3-417...154
Transfer warranties under §3-416...150; 151

ARTICLE 4
Alterations and unauthorized signatures treated as authorized, preclusions under §4-406 as to (See SIGNATURE, subhead: Alterations treated as authorized, unauthorized signatures and)
Banks charges for items not properly payable (See BANK-CUSTOMER RELATIONSHIP, subhead: Charges for items not properly payable)
Non-UCC law superceding...6
Presentment warranties under revised §4-208...154
Transfer warranties under §4-207...150; 151

AVOIDANCE
Indorser's liability...61

B

BANK COLLECTION
Generally...207
Availability of deposited funds
    Generally...214
    Rule 1 -first business day after banking day of deposit
        Check, certain type of...215
        Exceptions...218
        First $100 of any check...216
        Same bank, depository and payor bank are...215
    Rule 2 -second and third banking days after deposit
        Generally...216

[References are to page numbers.]

[References are to page numbers.]

[References are to page numbers.]

[References are to page numbers.]

[References are to page numbers.]

STOP PAYMENT ORDERS—Cont.

Checks—Cont.

    Cashier's check...183; 184

    Certified check...183; 184

    Teller's check...184

Close account, stop payment or

    Agreement, effect of...195

    Failure to comply with order

        Generally...196

        Defenses bank may assert...196

    Item, payment of...187

    Length of time provisions...196

    Right to...187

    Rovell v. American National Bank...188

    Time provisions, length of...196

Failure to comply with order

    Generally...196

    Defenses bank may assert...196

Item, payment of...187

Length of time provisions...196

Money orders...182

Non-bank drafts...182

Notes...181

Rovell v. American National Bank...188

Teller's check...184

Time provisions, length of...196

SURETIES

Common law and equitable rights of...85

T

TELLER'S CHECKS

Generally...25

Stop payment orders...184

THIRD PARTIES

Defense to enforcement, assertion of third person's claim as...113

Irrevocable commitment to...118

TIME

Payable at definite...20

Presentment, timeliness of (See PRESENTMENT)

TRANSFERS

Generally...31

Bearer paper, change of possession pertaining to...32

Consumer electronic fund transfers (See CONSUMER ELECTRONIC FUND TRANSFERS)

Conversion of transferred but not negotiated instruments taken from non-PETE...162

Indorsement (See INDORSEMENT)

Point of sale...CONSUMER ELECTRONIC FUND TRANSFERS, subhead: Point of sale transfers by debit card

TRANSFERS—Cont.

Warranties (See WARRANTIES)

TRAVELER'S CHECKS

Generally...26

U

UNDERLYING OBLIGATION

Taking of instrument for...53

UNIFORM COMMERCIAL CODE (UCC)

Analysis of provisions, problems associated with...6

Article 1 provisions...5

Article 3 (See ARTICLE 3)

Article 4, non-UCC law superceding...6

Historical evolution...3

Negotiable instruments law, treatment of...4

Structure...4

V

VALUE

Holder in due course (See HOLDER IN DUE COURSE)

W

WARRANTIES

Generally...145

Breach

    Remedies...156

    Transfer warranties...148

Dishonored drafts or instruments, presentment of...155

Made, to whom transfer warranty is...147

Maker of transfer warranty...146

Presentment warranties

    Generally...152

    Dishonored drafts or instruments...155

    §3-417...154

    §4-208...154

    Unaccepted draft to drawee...153

    Violations, drawee's rights to pursue...224

Proximate cause and recovery by transferee...150

Recovery by transferee, proximate cause and...150

Transfer warranties

    Generally...145

    Breach...148

    Defined...148

    Made, to whom warranty is...147

    Maker of warranty...146

    Proximate cause and recovery by transferee...150

    Recovery by transferee, proximate cause and...150